KU-061-050

CONTENTS

Preface   9
Mafia Structure   11
Introduction: *Rattus Norvegicus*   15

Part I: Birth of the Grim Reaper
Chapter 1: Mortal Sin Indeed   28
Chapter 2: Mean Streets   34
Chapter 3: Sticky Fingers   40
Chapter 4: First Blood   42
Chapter 5: Reborn   51
Chapter 6: The De Cavalcantes   57
Chapter 7: Here Today, Gone Tomorrow   62
Chapter 8: Long Walks, Short Piers   67
Chapter 9: A Triple Play   74
Chapter 10: Murder for Hire   78
Chapter 11: The Enforcer   83
Chapter 12: Mob Guys and Crooked Cops   94
Chapter 13: Independent Contractor   101
Chapter 14: Tough and Rough and Ready to Go   110

Part II: Barbara
Chapter 15: Bambi Meets the Ice Man   117
Chapter 16: Possession   122
Chapter 17: Aunt Sadie   128
Chapter 18: This Is for You, Richard   133

Chapter 19: Betrayal   143
Chapter 20: Love and Marriage and a Baby Carriage   150
Chapter 21: Enter the Lone Ranger   170

Part III: Very Bad Goodfellas

Chapter 22: Making Ends Meet   175
Chapter 23: Murder Runs in the Family   181
Chapter 24: Let's Do the Twist   185
Chapter 25: The Gambinos   193
Chapter 26: Partnership Born in Hell   200
Chapter 27: Forgive Me, Father, for I Have Sinned   205
Chapter 28: The Porn King of New York   207
Chapter 29: Family Man   212
Chapter 30: Hit Man   218
Chapter 31: 'Lady' and Pouilly-Fuissé   232
Chapter 32: Blood Money   239
Chapter 33: The Big Guy   257
Chapter 34: Rolling Over in his Grave   266
Chapter 35: Double Suck   276
Chapter 36: The Office   292
Chapter 37: Mister Softee   301
Chapter 38: Joe and Mary's   311
Chapter 39: Off the Record   329
Chapter 40: Sammy 'the Bull' Gravano   342

Part IV: The Manhattan Project

Chapter 41: The Gang that Couldn't Shoot Straight   348
Chapter 42: The Lone Ranger   352
Chapter 43: The Disassembling of Roy DeMeo   368
Chapter 44: The Elusive Muskie   385
Chapter 45: How the Fuck You Doin'?   391
Chapter 46: 'The Store'   396
Chapter 47: Sparks Steak House   408
Chapter 48: Would You Like Some Tea?   419
Chapter 49: I've Got Some Rats I Have to Get Rid Of   428
Chapter 50: Operation Ice Man   436
Chapter 51: Hit Kit   449

THE ICE MAN

CONFESSIONS OF A MAFIA CONTRACT KILLER

PHILIP CARLO

MAINSTREAM
PUBLISHING

EDINBURGH AND LONDON

18 20 19

Copyright © Philip Carlo, 2006
All rights reserved
The moral right of the author has been asserted

First published in the United States of America
in 2006 by St Martin's Press

First published in Great Britain in 2007 by
MAINSTREAM PUBLISHING COMPANY
(EDINBURGH) LTD
7 Albany Street
Edinburgh EH1 3UG

ISBN 9781845963392

No part of this book may be reproduced or transmitted
in any form or by any other means without permission
in writing from the publisher, except by a reviewer
who wishes to quote brief passages in connection with
a review written for insertion in a magazine,
newspaper or broadcast

This book is a work of non-fiction based on the investigations of the
author. In some cases, names of people, places, dates, sequences or the
detail of events have been changed to protect the privacy of others. The
author has stated to the publishers that except in such respects, the contents
of this book are true.

A catalogue record for this book is available
from the British Library

Typeset in Garmina and Helvetica Extended

The Random House Group Council® (FSC®), the le Our books carrying the FSC is the only fores environmental paper pr www.r

Forest Stewardship certification organisation. FSC®-certified paper. pported by the leading resource. Our curement policy can be found at ndomhouse.co.uk/environment

DUMFRIES &
GALLOWAY
LIBRARIES

Askews & Holts	Jan-2015
920 KUK	£7.99

Printed and boun

in Great Britain by Clays ld, St Ives plc

A 19

Part V: Homicide Superstar

Chapter 52: The Quiet Before the Storm   472
Chapter 53: With a Wiggle   476
Chapter 54: The Politics of Murder   486
Chapter 55: The State of New Jersey v. Richard Leonard
       Kuklinski   490
Chapter 56: It Was Due to Business   493
Chapter 57: It's Not TV, It's HBO   499
Chapter 58: Secrets of a Mafia Hit Man   507
Chapter 59: The Ice Man Versus Sammy the Bull   511
Chapter 60: No Sunset, No Sunrise   519
Chapter 61: A Flying Fuck   521

Epilogue: The Melting of the Ice Man   522
Postscript   527

PREFACE

This book is based on over 240 hours of one-on-one interviews with Richard Kuklinski at Trenton State Prison. When and where possible all the crimes and murders Richard and I discussed were verified with underground Mafia contacts, police sources, documents, crime-scene reports and photographs. When Richard and I discussed his life and the crimes he committed over a 43-year period, he never bragged or boasted. Indeed, much of what is contained in this book had to be prodded and encouraged out of him. In my estimation, Richard was always honest and truthful, sincere and forthright in the extreme.

The names of certain individuals connected with this story have been changed.

I first wish to thank my editor, Charlie Spicer, at St Martin's Press, for all his expert advice, his guidance and his belief in this book from the moment it arrived on his desk. Also his right-hand man, Joe Cleemann, was a huge help, on numerous levels. Many thanks also to John Murphy and Gregg Sulivan for their belief in and support of this book. Gaby Monet at HBO was an invaluable friend and assisted me greatly in understanding the enormous complexities of this story. Many thanks to my loyal friend and confidant Mike Kostrewa for all his guidance and expertise about Jersey City and the Polish people and culture. I also wish to thank Trenton State Prison for allowing me access to Richard Kuklinski at the facility. Also, thanks to

Anna Bierhouse for her suggestions, and to all the good people at Sanford Greenburger, the best literary agency in the world; they still treat writers like sensitive artists – a rare thing these days. I would be remiss if I didn't thank my parents, Dante and Nina Carlo, for their unwavering support. My gratitude to Crystal Proenza for her patience and good cheer in turning my voluminous handwritten drafts into flawless manuscripts. I also wish to thank Barbara, Merrick, Chris and Dwayne Kuklinski for their honest feelings and kind input.

Lieutenant Patrick Kane of the New Jersey State Police was an invaluable source of detail, facts, emotions, times and places. Also, Sergeant Rob Anzalotti and his partner, Detective Mark Bennul, were very helpful in shining light on the dark, violent phenomenon that was Richard Kuklinski's life.

This work is dedicated to my agent and dear friend, Matt Bialer, for always being there, for his constant help, guidance and unwavering support. This has been a long, bumpy road, Matt, a harrowing journey. I could not have made it without you.

MAFIA STRUCTURE

Capo crimini/capo di tutti capi: superboss/boss of bosses

Capo: boss/don

Consigliere: trusted adviser or family counsellor

Sotto capo/capo bastone: underboss, second-in-command

Contabile: financial adviser

Caporegime/capodecina: lieutenant, typically heads a 'crew' comprising ten or more soldiers

Sgarrista: a foot-soldier who carries out the day-to-day business of the family, a 'made' member of the Mafia

Picciotto: lower-ranking soldier, enforcer; also known in the streets as the 'button man'

Giovane d'honore: Mafia associate, typically a non-Sicilian or non-Italian member

'My husband is a good man, a kind man – a great father. All my children's friends are always saying they wish they had a dad like my husband – like Richard.'

Mrs Barbara Kuklinski on the day Richard was arrested

'Richard is both fascinating and as frightening as your worst nightmare. He represents the worst of who we are – yet he is absolutely fascinating to listen to.'

Sheila Nevins, HBO producer

'He's responsible for over 200 murders – I mean personally responsible. He's a monster; this guy lived to kill.'

Gaby Monet, HBO producer

'I'd never hurt a woman or a child. It's just not in me.'

Richard Kuklinski

'He killed with guns, poison, bats, knives, strangulation, his fists, ice picks, screwdrivers, hand grenades and even fire. We've never seen anything like him. Truth is, we've never even heard of anything like him.'

Bob Carroll, New Jersey deputy attorney general

'Even now, I mean so many years later, my stomach gets all tense and my hands tremble when I think about him. But I love my dad. I love him a lot! None of it was his fault . . . My father married the wrong woman.'

Merrick Kuklinski, Richard's oldest daughter

'When he told me he loved me, which he often did, I'd say "Me too". That's it . . . just "Me too".'

Barbara Kuklinski

'My father terrorised us. We never knew when or where he'd explode. We tried to hide it from my brother because he would have tried to do something, protect us, you know, protect my mother, and my father would've killed him, I'm sure. One time, this woman with kids in her car cut him up and he got out of the car at a light and tore the woman's door right off her car.'

Chris Kuklinski, Richard's daughter

'They thought I didn't know what he was doing, but I saw all the broken furniture and I knew my father did it. I saw my mother's black eyes. I kept an axe under my bed and a machete just next to the bed because of him.'

Dwayne Kuklinski, Richard's son

'He's very crafty and cunning, like some kind of jungle predator that nobody ever sees until it's too late. We knew about him – I knew about him, was tracking him for years, but could never pin anything on him.'

Detective Pat Kane, New Jersey State Police

'My mother was cancer. She slowly destroyed everything around her. She produced two killers: me and my brother Joe.'

Richard Kuklinski

'There are two Richards, and I never knew who would be walking in the door. He could be generous to a fault or the meanest man on earth.'

Barbara Kuklinski

'We called him "the Ice Man" because he froze some of his victims, kept them in a freezer he had for a while, then put them out so we could not tell when the murder actually took place, you see.'

Paul Smith, New Jersey Organized Crime and Racketeering Bureau investigator

'I became very promiscuous because of my father. The only thing I had control of was my body. I did what I wanted – I did what he didn't want me to do. I lost my virginity when I was 12 to an older man in a van. Just some guy who picked me up at a bus stop on the corner there.'

Chris Kuklinski

'I feel nothing inside for any of them. Nothing. They had it coming and I did it. The only people I ever had any kind of real feelings for were my family. Those others, nothing. Sometimes I wonder why I'm like this, feel nothing inside . . . I wish someone could tell me. I'm curious.'

Richard Kuklinski

'Richard is totally unique. There's not been anyone like him in modern times. He trusts me because I've never lied to him. He does have a nice side. Once he asked me if I was scared of him, and I told him I wasn't and asked him if I should be. He just stared at me. That was kind of scary – having him just stare with those chilling eyes of his.'

Gaby Monet, HBO producer

'What the feds did was outrageous. I mean, they knew Sammy Gravano ordered Richard to kill a cop and they still made a deal for Gravano to walk.'

Sergeant Robert Anzalotti, Bergen County prosecutor's office

'I beat them to death for exercise.'

Richard Kuklinski

* * *

'The Law, alone and aloof by its very nature, has no access to the emotions that might justify murder.'

The Marquis de Sade

INTRODUCTION

RATTUS NORVEGICUS

Richard Kuklinski was first drawn to the sprawling woods of Bucks County, Pennsylvania, because of their peace and tranquillity, solitude and fresh air. The woods reminded Richard of church, one of the few places in his life where he found solace and comfort and could think without distraction. Like a church, the woods were peaceful, quiet and serene.

The woods of Bucks County were also a good place to get rid of bodies. By profession, Richard was a contract killer, and the disposal of bodies was always a concern. Sometimes it was OK to leave the victims where they dropped, in alleys, parking lots and garages. Other times they had to disappear – that was specifically requested. One time Richard left a victim in an ice-cold well for nearly two years – preserving the corpse – purposely seeking to confuse the authorities as to the accurate time of death, thus earning his eventual moniker: 'the Ice Man'.

Richard was careful never to leave two bodies close to each other here in the woods, lest the authorities became suspicious and staked out a given area. His business was the business of murder, and he was particularly adept at it. He had honed killing to a kind of fine art form. No job was too difficult. He had successfully carried out every contract he'd ever been given. He prided himself on that. In the netherworld of murder, Richard Kuklinski was a much sought-after specialist – a homicide superstar.

THE ICE MAN

Richard was unique in that he filled murder contracts for all five New York crime families, as well as the two New Jersey mob families, the Pontis and the notorious De Cavalcantes.

It was mid-August of 1972, and the woods were thick with lush green vegetation. As Richard moved in the quiet shade of elm, maple, pine and tall, elegant poplar trees, he carried a double-barrelled Browning shotgun with fancy engraving on the stock. The weapon, in Richard's enormous hands, seemed like a child's toy.

Richard very much enjoyed this kind of cat-and-mouse game he had invented, sneaking up on unsuspecting animals and shooting them before they knew he was there. He was a very large man, 6 ft 5 in. in his stocking feet and 290 lb of solid muscle, yet he had an uncanny ability to move silently and with great stealth, suddenly just being there, and in this way Richard managed to shoot unsuspecting squirrels, woodchucks, skunks and deer, which was all practice for the thing that Richard excelled at, his one true passion in life: stalking, hunting and killing human beings.

I don't particularly enjoy the killing, you know; I enjoy the stalk, the planning and the hunt much more, Richard explained.

On one of these 'practice outings' in Bucks County, Richard spotted it: a large, rodent-like animal standing next to a thick oak tree. Thinking it was a woodchuck, he snuck up on the creature. All was quiet and still except for the rustling of leaves in a gentle breeze. Moving on just the balls of his size-14 feet, using trees and shrubbery to get close enough for a clean shot – it was important to Richard that he kill with the first round – he managed to outflank the animal by staying upwind. When in a good position, he took aim and fired.

He hit the animal, but it was still alive, its rear legs futilely kicking the warm August air. As Richard drew closer, he realised it was actually a huge brown rat – *Rattus norvegicus* – and it was snarling at him, baring its two large incisor teeth. *Tough guy*, Richard thought. He did not particularly want to cause the creature to suffer, and, admiring its moxie, he quickly killed it. As Richard began to walk away, he noticed a cave behind a thick mulberry bush at the foot of a steep granite slope dotted with green moss.

Always curious, Richard made his way to the cave and went inside. He immediately smelled them – rats – and saw their droppings but could not see any of them. The cave went deep into the rise of granite, and it became too dark to see. Richard had a small penlight and used it. No rats anywhere, but he sensed them; he could smell them. Besides being endowed with nearly superhuman strength, Richard had amazingly strong senses of smell and hearing. His senses were like those of a predatory animal, a creature that regularly hunts for meat to survive.

He left the cave and slowly made his way back to his car, thinking about the huge brown rat, a diabolical idea coming to him. He slid his shotgun into its fleece-lined leather case and put it into the boot of his car. He didn't want his wife or children to see it. Richard was always scrupulously careful about not letting his family know what he really did, taking care that they didn't see any of his extensive collection of killing tools, which included: razor-sharp knives; all sorts of pistols, some equipped with silencers; garrotes; different poisons (his favourite was cyanide); spiked clubs; hand grenades; a crossbow; ice picks; rope; wire; explosives; and plastic bags, to name but a few. He was particularly fond of .22 pistols, because he knew when the bullet entered the skull it had a tendency to bounce about, causing massive damage to the brain. He also very much liked .38 derringers: they were small, could be easily hidden and at close range, loaded with dumdums, they were quite lethal . . . could knock down a horse. Richard usually carried two .38 derringers, a knife and a large-calibre automatic when going to work.

Several days later, Richard returned to the Bucks County cave. It was drizzling. The deep August greens of the woods were shiny and more pronounced. Richard again had his shotgun with him. He also carried a brown paper bag containing 2 lb of minced chuck steak. As he reached the darkened cave mouth, he saw hundreds of rat tracks in the wet soil. He took 15 or so steps into the cave. The musky, fetid stink of the rats came to him. He put down the meat and left.

When Richard returned the next day, all the meat was gone; he smiled. Knowing rats were scavengers and would eat anything, Richard wondered if they would actually eat a human being. He wondered if he could make them unwitting accomplices in torture and murder.

Curious, Richard got back into his Lincoln and returned to New Jersey. He lived with his wife, Barbara, and their three children in a split level cedar house at 169 Sunset Street in the town of Dumont. It was a nice, upper-middle-class neighbourhood, a good place to bring up children. Here, everyone knew their neighbours. People said good morning and good evening and really meant it.

Barbara was a tall, attractive woman of Italian descent. She had a natural air of style and elegance about her. Even in old jeans and a baggy sweatshirt, Barbara appeared carefully put together, comfortable in her own skin. She had particularly long legs, was thin and had curves in all the right places. She did not look as if she had given birth to three children – two girls, Merrick and Chris, who were then eight and seven respectively, and a son, three-year-old Dwayne. Barbara had lost two children while pregnant because of physical abuse she had suffered at Richard's enormous hands. Barbara explained: *When Richard lost his temper, he was like a bull in a china shop: anything could break; nothing had value. He could be the sweetest, most considerate man one moment and the meanest son of a bitch on the face of the earth whose cruelty knew no bounds in the next.*

When Richard arrived home that day, Barbara was preparing dinner. She never knew what kind of mood he'd be in when he walked into the house, and she always greeted him with a kind of wary trepidation. She did not smile until he smiled. He smiled now and kissed her and the children hello. She immediately knew he was not in a bad mood.

Barbara was married to two different men, the good Richard and the bad Richard, as she had come to think of them. Thankfully, right now he was the good Richard. After washing up, Richard assembled a red fire engine for Dwayne, patiently sitting on the floor with his boy and the toy and a screwdriver.

Barbara tried her best to shelter Dwayne from the bad Richard. Just about every weekend she sent him off to her mother's house to keep him out of harm's way, and she was quick to ferret Dwayne out of the house if she saw Richard's mood changing, his lips tightening against his teeth, his face growing pale. Whenever he made a soft clicking sound out of the left side of his mouth, they all knew it was time to run. That sound was like an air-raid siren warning of attack.

Richard's daughter Merrick was his favourite. She had had a failing kidney since she was a very young child, often had to be hospitalised and had undergone several operations. Richard was always there for her, by the side of her bed, holding her hand, stroking her head. *He could not have been more caring and attentive*, Barbara said.

Merrick never held anything her father did against him. The beatings he gave Barbara, the furniture he broke, the toys he tore apart, the cups and keepsakes smashed – all was forgiven. None of it was his fault. He couldn't help himself. He just couldn't control his anger, he had explained to Merrick – only Merrick – and she believed him. He was her daddy. She would love him deeply and profoundly no matter what.

However, daughter Chris remembered all her father's outbursts and held them against him, particularly the way he abused her mother. Chris, too, loved her father; he was the only dad she had ever known, and when he was nice he was truly golden. But she hated the man her father became when he flew into one of his irrational rages. No matter how mad

Richard became, though, he never hit either of his daughters or Dwayne.

If, Barbara explained, *he ever laid a finger on any of my children, I would've found a way to kill him, and he knew it.*

Still, Barbara did not take into account, or perhaps just could not accept, the realities of the psychological damage Richard's outbursts were causing her girls deep inside. Both Chris and Merrick had golden blond hair and sweet heart-shaped faces – the best features of both their parents. Chris had light-blue eyes; Merrick's were honey coloured. They were both particularly attractive, with Richard's wide Slavic cheekbones, Barbara's long, perfectly straight nose and strong jaw line, and the fair skin of the Polish. They looked so much alike that people often mistook them for twins. Barbara enjoyed buying them twin outfits, always two of everything. In most of the family pictures, the girls are dressed alike, and there is a discernible sadness behind the smiles for the camera. The girls attended private Catholic school and were shy and polite, perfect little ladies. Warm and giving and quick to smile, they both made friends easily.

Chris and Merrick were now helping their mother set the table. The family soon sat down for dinner – roast chicken and potatoes, one of Richard's favourite meals. To an outsider, they would have seemed perfectly normal, a well-adjusted, happy family. In truth, however, the man sitting at the head of the table, patiently slicing the roast chicken, lovingly doling out preferred pieces, was America's most prolific contract killer.

The contract came down in the first week of September. The mark had to suffer. That was the order. If he did suffer, the price would be doubled, the client said, from ten to twenty thousand dollars, cash. The mark lived in Nutley, New Jersey, in a fancy house with a curved driveway and elegant white pillars on either side of a large mahogany door with a big brass knocker in the shape of a ram's head. Richard didn't know anything about the mark other than that he had to suffer before he died. Richard preferred it that way. The less he knew about the mark, the better.

Richard had access to the camera because he produced pornographic movies for distribution all over the East and West coasts and everywhere in between. Richard's partner, the man who fronted Richard the money to start the production company, was the infamous Roy DeMeo – a psychopathic soldier attached to the Gambino family. DeMeo was an excellent money-maker. He dealt in stolen cars, drugs, loan-sharking, pornography and murder. He ran the most brutal, feared crew of killers organised crime ever knew. They were responsible for literally hundreds of murders. His immediate boss, his captain, was Nino Gaggi, who reported directly to Paul Castellano, the recently appointed head of the Gambino crime family, the largest, most successful crime family in New York's rough-and-tumble history. Castellano had inherited the mantle from a genuine organised-crime legend: his brother-in-law, Carlo Gambino himself.

The camera, grey duct tape and handcuffs needed for what Richard had in mind were in the boot. Richard knew the mark left for work every day at 10 a.m. He had carefully plotted the mark's route to work and planned to snatch him at a desolate corner where there was a stop sign and he had to stop to make a turn. Richard preferred not to work in broad daylight, but he'd do whatever the job called for; and, he knew, people tended to be less defensive in the light of day, a natural instinct he repeatedly exploited.

When the mark came down the road towards the stop sign, Richard was there, innocently standing next to his car, its bonnet and boot open, emergency lights blinking, a pleasant smile on his handsome face. He had a .357 Magnum in his hand, which was hidden in his coat pocket. Richard flagged the man down. As the mark reached the corner, Richard made sure to approach him on the driver's side. Somewhat annoyed, the mark rolled down the window. 'Yeah?' he demanded.

'Thanks for stopping, pal,' Richard began, and in the next instant, really just the blink of an eye, Richard pressed the thick, blue-black .357 to the man's head while with his other hand he snatched the car keys from the ignition, done so quick it was like a magic trick.

'What the fuck?' the man exclaimed. He was a large, heavy-set individual with a huge round face, several double chins, a bald head. Richard opened the door, pulled him out and, keeping the gun in his side, quickly made him get in the open boot of Richard's car.

'I'll pay you – I'll give you – '

'Shut up.' Richard stopped him, cuffed his hands behind his back and taped his mouth shut.

'Make any noise and I'll kill you,' Richard said in a practised modulation that was a chilling thing to hear, like the growl of a nearby hungry lion. Richard closed the boot and bonnet of his car, got into it and slowly pulled away. In a matter of seconds, he had snatched the mark, without anyone seeing him. The first aspect of the job was done.

By now, the leaves of the trees in Bucks County had taken on colours – bright reds, hot oranges, bold yellows. Slowly falling leaves seemed like multicoloured butterflies in the first days of spring. Richard parked his car in a remote spot. He pulled the mark from the boot, led him to the cave he'd found and located the spot where he had laid out the meat. He made the mark lie down here and carefully wrapped duct tape around his ankles and legs and arms, bound him tightly as a diligent spider wraps silk around its prey. The man's panic-stricken eyes bulged out of his large round face. He desperately tried to talk, to offer Richard all the money he had, anything he wanted, but the grey duct tape held tight and only panicky, mumbled grunts came from him. What he wanted to say Richard had heard many times over. They were words he had become deaf to. Richard had no remorse, no conscience, no compassion. He was doing a job, and none of those feelings even remotely came into play. Richard calmly went back to his car. He retrieved the camera and tripod, as well as a light and a motion detector that would trigger both the light and the camera when the rats came out. Richard carefully set up the camera, the light and the motion detector just so. Satisfied, he cut the man's clothes off – he had dirtied himself – and left him there like that.

As Richard made his way back down the hill to his car, he was curious, even a bit amused, to see what would happen; would the rats in fact eat a man while he was still alive? Curious, also, to see his own reaction to such a thing. Richard often wondered how he could be so cold-blooded. Was he born that way or made that way? Was it nature or nurture that had made him the remorseless monster he'd become? It was a question he'd been asking himself for many years now, since he was a young boy.

That day, Richard had promised to take his daughters, Merrick and Chris, to Lobel's, a specialist shop that sold private-school uniforms. Barbara was feeling a bit under the weather and didn't go. Both the girls enjoyed shopping with their dad because he bought them whatever they wanted. All either of them had to do was look at something and it was suddenly theirs. Richard had been brought up in extreme poverty, had had to steal food to eat as a boy in Jersey City, and his own children would never want for anything.

Excited, the girls sat next to their dad in the front seat. They both knew that their father often got into arguments with people about how they drove, and the girls silently hoped that nothing like that would happen today. It was a kind of ritual they had – hoping their dad would not explode as he drove.

Barbara explained: *Richard was like the cop of the road. He couldn't see someone do something wrong, take a turn without signalling, without saying something. I mean something, you know, nasty.*

Each of the girls needed four blouses and two skirts for the school year. At the shop in Emerson, Richard bought them five grey pleated skirts, fifteen blouses, two dozen pairs of knee-high socks, two blue blazers, five vests and half a dozen sets of gym outfits. Going shopping with Dad was like Christmas morning.

Pleased his girls were happy, Richard paid in cash, and off they went. They were going to stop at Grand Union supermarket to pick up some groceries before returning home. Two blocks from the shop, a woman in a station wagon cut Richard up. Incensed, he stopped next to her at a light, rolled down his window and berated her. There were several children in the back seat of the wagon.

'Daddy – Daddy, don't get mad,' Merrick begged. 'Please, Daddy.' But the woman gave Richard a dirty, condescending look and ignored him as if he were crazy, a fool. In the next instant, Richard was out of the car. He quickly walked to the station wagon, opened the door and actually ripped it right off its hinges in two powerful pulls.

Terrified, the woman stared at Richard.

Satisfied, he got back in his car and pulled away.

'Please, Daddy, please calm down,' Chris now begged.

'Quiet!' he demanded, the word seeming more like a growl than any word in the English language.

Four days later, Richard returned to the cave. The rats had eaten the man alive. All his flesh was gone. In the pale yellow glow of Richard's flashlight, the mark was now only disjointed, haphazard bones – an unspeakable sight.

Curious, Richard stared at his work, this monster he had created. He made sure the camera had captured what had happened . . . how the huge rats first approached the hapless man with trepidation as he furiously squirmed to free himself; how the rats, more and more of them, bolder and bolder still, began taking bites out of him, first his ears, then his eyes. *Vicious little bastards*, Richard thought.

Richard retrieved his equipment and left. A gentle snowfall

had covered the forest with a pearly white blanket. Everything was white and clean and story-book lovely. A solemn white silence had descended upon the forest. He knew the fresh snow would cover any tracks he left.

Richard took the videotape of the mark being eaten alive to the man who had ordered the hit.

'Did he suffer?' the man asked, his voice gruff, his manner callous, his eyes dead, like two bullet holes.

'Oh yeah, he really suffered,' Richard said.

'Really?' the man asked.

'Really,' Richard said, and gave him the tape. They both watched it. Overjoyed, yet slightly appalled that Richard would even think of, let alone do, such a thing, the man gave him ten thousand dollars for the contract, and a second ten thousand dollars for the incredible suffering the mark had experienced.

'You did a good job,' he said. Richard liked to please his customers; that was how his business had grown over the years. Richard did not know what the mark had done to deserve such a fate. He didn't care. None of that was his business. The less he knew, the better.

After a job well done, Richard made his way home, again wondering why such things didn't bother him, how he had become so cold, so devoid of human feelings. He thought about his childhood, and his jaw muscles clenched into tight knots and he made that slight clicking sound out of the left side of his heart-shaped mouth. He took a long, deep breath, turned on the radio and tuned into a country-music station. Richard liked country music. The simple lyrics and meandering repetition soothed him.

Still thinking about his childhood, the barbaric cruelty he had suffered, Richard made his way home, where he would again wrap himself in the cloak of a loving husband, a doting father, a devoted family man.

He parked his car in front of his house and sat there for a while, wondering how he had become so unlike other people.

THE ICE MAN

With these thoughts filling his enormous head, Richard slowly stepped from his car and made his way inside, walking with his quiet, catlike gait, like a heavyweight prizefighter in his prime.

PART I

BIRTH OF THE GRIM REAPER

1

MORTAL SIN INDEED

At the turn of the twentieth century, Jersey City, New Jersey, the place where Richard Kuklinski was born and raised, was a bustling Polish enclave. Because of its many Polish Catholic churches and an abundance of blue-collar work, Polish immigrants flocked to Jersey City in large numbers.

The Lackawanna, Erie, Pennsylvania and Central railroad companies all had bases in Jersey City. Trains from across the United States brought all kinds of produce to the East Coast, and this was the final stop. Sprawling railroad yards filled the area. Rail tracks ran on just about every other street. Jersey City's main thoroughfare, Railroad Avenue, had an elevated track running right down the centre of the wide two-way street. Powerful black locomotives pulling long, rust-coloured trains to the waterfront were the norm; the heavy 'chug-chug' sound and high-pitched screams of steam locomotives came from all directions, both day and night, seven days a week.

Situated at the north-east end of the state of New Jersey, Jersey City was ideally located near the bustling metropolis of Manhattan, and from here all types of goods and produce were shipped up and down the Eastern Seaboard. At its closest point, at the southernmost end of the Hudson River, Jersey City was only three-quarters of a mile away from Lower Manhattan – the centre of the world – and ferries were constantly bringing goods to the piers that crowded the busy Manhattan waterfront. On a clear day, it seemed as if you could easily throw a stone to Manhattan from Jersey City it appeared so close – the proverbial stone's throw away.

In truth, Jersey City was as different from New York City as another planet. In Jersey City lived the working poor, those struggling to make ends meet, put food on the table. Yes, there was a lot of work in Jersey City, but it was backbreaking menial employment, and the wages were pitifully low. In the summertime, it was unbearably hot and humid. Because of underdeveloped swampland near by, undulating dark clouds of mosquitoes filled the night air. In the winter, Jersey City was brutally cold, constantly battered by powerful winds that came tearing down the Hudson River and off the nearby Atlantic Ocean. It seemed during those months like a place in the far northern reaches of Siberia.

Just next to Hoboken, Frank Sinatra's home town, Jersey City was a rough-and-tumble town filled with hard-boiled blue-collar workers and their hard-boiled blue-collar offspring. This was a place where a kid quickly learned to defend himself or was victimised and bullied. The strong were respected and prospered. The weak were marginalised and put upon.

Richard Kuklinski's mother, Anna McNally, grew up in the Sacred Heart Orphanage on Erie and Ninth streets. Her parents had emigrated from Dublin in 1904 and settled in Jersey City, which was then the tenth-largest city in America. Anna had two older brothers, Micky and Sean. Shortly after the family arrived in Jersey, Anna's father died of pneumonia and her mother was killed when a truck ran her down on Tenth Street. Anna and her brothers wound up in the orphanage. Though skinny and malnourished, Anna was a physically attractive child with dark, almond-shaped eyes and flawless cream-coloured skin.

In the Sacred Heart Orphanage, religion was forced upon the children, and Anna had the fear of God, hell and damnation beaten into her by sadistic nuns who treated their charges as though they were personal servants and whipping-posts. Before

Anna was ten years old, she was sexually abused by a priest, and she lost both her virginity and a part of her humanity; she grew into an austere, cold woman who rarely smiled and came to view life through hard, unfeeling dark eyes.

When, at 18, Anna was forced to leave the orphanage, she went into a Catholic convent, planning to become a nun herself. She had no skills as such and nowhere else to turn. But Anna was not cut out for a cloistered life. She soon met Stanley Kuklinski at a dance sponsored by the church, and her destiny was sealed.

Stanley Kuklinski had been born in Warsaw, Poland, and had immigrated to Jersey City with his mother, father and two brothers. At 26, when Stanley met Anna, he cut a handsome figure, resembling Rudolph Valentino. He wore his hair parted in the centre and slicked back tight against his scalp, as was the fashion of the day. Stanley was smitten by Anna and pursued her relentlessly, and she agreed to marry him some three months after they met. They wed in July of 1925, and their wedding picture shows a particularly good-looking couple who appear well matched, a union that holds much promise. Anna had grown into a truly beautiful woman. She looked like Olivia de Havilland in *Gone with the Wind*.

Stanley had a reasonably good job as a brakes-man for the Lackawanna Railroad. It was not hard work as such, though it was always outdoors and he regularly suffered in the summer heat and the frigid, brutal winters. At first, the hasty union between Stanley and Anna seemed a good one. They rented a cold-water flat in a two-storey clapboard house on Third Street, just down the block from St Mary's Church. But Stanley liked to drink, and when he drank he became short-tempered and mean, and Anna soon came to know that she had married a jealous, possessive tyrant who would beat her as if she were a man for the slightest provocation. Because Anna was not a virgin on their wedding night – she could never bring herself to tell her husband that she'd been raped by a priest over and over again – Stanley accused her of being a tramp, a whore. She hated this but stoically suffered through his verbal abuse, which all too often became physical. Stanley was not a large man, but he was strong as a bull. When drunk, he'd toss Anna about as if she was a rag doll. Anna was tempted to tell her brother Micky about the abuse, but she didn't want to make a bad situation worse, and divorce wasn't even an option back then. Anna was still hyper-religious, and good Irish Catholics did not divorce, end of story. Anna learned to accept her lot in life.

In the spring of 1929, she gave birth to a baby boy, one of four children she'd eventually have with Stanley before the marriage soured and finally ended. They named him Florian after Stanley's father. Anna had little memory of her own parents; the only memories she had of her childhood were bad ones – beatings and abuse.

Anna was hoping Stanley would mellow with a child in the house, but just the opposite happened. When he'd been drinking, he took to accusing Anna of infidelity, even said Florian was not his, that she had fucked another man while he was away working.

Sometimes Stanley was kind to young Florian, but for the most part he seemed indifferent to the child, and it didn't take long for Stanley to start beating Florian too. If Florian cried he got hit, if Florian dirtied his bed he got hit, and Anna could do nothing. Her answer was to go to St Mary's down the block and light candles and pray. There was nowhere else for Anna to turn, and she grew to loathe Stanley and often thought of leaving him, even killing him; but none of that ever came to pass.

Still, Stanley frequently had sex with Anna, whether she wanted to or not. He considered himself quite the ladies' man and was often on Anna without notice or warning or any kind of foreplay: wham, bam, it was over.

Anna became pregnant a second time and gave birth to another boy on 11 April 1935. They named this child Richard. He was a mere 5 lb and had a thick head of shiny hair so blond it seemed white.

With mounting bills and another mouth to feed, Stanley became even meaner and more remote. When he came home on Friday night, he was always drunk and often had the smell of other women about him and lipstick on his collar, but Anna could do little, for Stanley would beat her at the drop of a hat. He viewed her as his personal property to be used and abused any way he wished. Worse, he took to beating Florian and Richard for both real and imagined infractions, and both boys grew to fear and dread their father, becoming sullen and quiet, painfully shy. Stanley always wore a thick, black leather belt, and he'd quickly slide it off and lay into his sons with it, mercilessly whipping them. If Anna tried to intercede, she too was beaten. Violence seemed to fuel Stanley's sexual appetite: often after beating his wife and young sons he wanted to have sex, and before Anna knew it he was forcing himself inside her.

As far back as Richard could remember, his father was beating him. He related: *When my father – father, that's a joke – came home and I said hello, he'd say hello by slapping me across the face.*

Stanley drank whisky with beer chasers – 'boilermakers'. When he drank, he became even meaner and his violence grew more indiscriminate. He took to wrapping his belt around his hard-knuckled fist and punching his sons with it. It was like being struck with a brick. He was fond of hitting them in the head with his belted fist and often knocked both Florian and Richard out cold. Richard became so utterly terrified of his father that he wet his pants at the very sight of him or the sound of his voice, which caused Stanley to become angry and beat the boy for wetting himself. Little by little, Stanley was, in effect, beating the very necessary human elements of compassion and empathy out of his second-born, clearly delineating the path Richard's life would ultimately take.

Finally, Stanley Kuklinski did the unspeakable: he murdered his son Florian with one of his beatings. He hit the frail boy on the back of the head one too many times, knocking the hapless boy to the floor, and Florian never got back up. Stanley made Anna tell family, friends and the authorities that Florian died as a result of falling down the stairs and striking his head. No one questioned their story, and Florian was laid out in the Kuklinski living-room, just down the block from St Mary's Church, where the ill-matched couple had been wed.

Richard was just five when his brother was killed by Stanley. Anna told Richard that Florian was hit by a car 'and died'. Richard had no conception of what death really was. He just knew that Florian was lying in the living-room in a cheap wooden coffin that smelled of pine, as if he were asleep, but he would not wake up. His mother and other relatives were there, crying, praying, lighting candles, holding shiny black rosary beads, but, no matter what, Florian would not wake up. Five-year-old Richard stared at his ghostly-pale dead brother, the only friend he had ever known, wondering why he wouldn't get up. He had always gotten up before . . .

Wake up, Florian, wake up, he silently begged. *Don't . . . please don't leave me here alone. Florian . . . Florian, please wake up . . .*

Florian never woke up.

2

MEAN STREETS

After Florian's murder, Stanley let up on Richard for a while, but it didn't take long before he went back to his old ways. Now the beatings became even more brutal and frequent. Stanley seemed to blame Richard for everything unjust that ever happened to him, for all the curveballs that life threw him, and he regularly and indiscriminately beat his son. Anna's answer was still to go to church and silently ask God for help – even after Stanley had murdered Florian. She took to facing a wall and praying fervently as Stanley beat the young Richard. Richard often went to sleep with bruises, aches and pains; sometimes he was so bruised and covered with vivid purple welts that he couldn't go outside or to school.

Richard grew, not surprisingly, into a painfully shy, awkward child with little confidence in himself. He viewed the world as a brutal, violent place filled with pain and turmoil. He often wondered where his brother Florian was but could never find out. His mother told him 'in heaven', but he had no idea how to get to this place. Richard had been very close to Florian, held him tight when his father beat their mother and smashed the meagre possessions the family had, and now Florian was gone and Richard had to face his father alone. He was a thin, frail boy, and it didn't take long for neighbourhood toughs to start picking on him, which only compounded Richard's feelings of isolation and resentment; his anxieties mounted.

Two Irish brothers who lived on the block regularly accosted Richard. One Saturday morning, they gave him a particularly severe beating. Richard managed to get away from them by running. Stanley was home that day and saw what happened from the front window. When Richard arrived upstairs, Stanley took off his belt and beat the boy, demanding that he go back downstairs and fight the brothers. 'No kid a mine's gonna be a chicken shit!' he bellowed, and struck Richard across the face with his belt.

Confused, his face burning, a red welt forming, Richard hurried back downstairs. 'Go get 'em,' Stanley ordered from the window, and Richard did exactly what he was told. With new-found ferocity and pent-up hostility, he laid into the brothers, caught them off guard and gave them both a terrific beating. Their father, a tall, gangly Irishman named O'Brien, then came out of the house and roughly pushed Richard away.

Amazed, Richard watched Stanley actually leap out of the second-storey window, land squarely on his feet, storm across Third Street and slap O'Brien, saying, 'When your kids beat up my kid, you watched and did nothing. When my kid fought back, you stopped it.' Stanley then hit O'Brien so hard that he knocked him out right there on the sidewalk in front of everyone, just down the block from St Mary's Church.

Richard wanted to run to his father, hold him and thank him for sticking up for him, for making everything right, but he knew he could never do such a thing. Showing outward affection to his father was forbidden. Richard learned that Saturday afternoon that might was right.

He often wondered why his father and mother didn't like him, what he had done to deserve their indifference and violence. He drew further and still further into himself, was always alone, couldn't seem to make friends – and a seething, fiery rage slowly grew inside the small boy.

Because Stanley spent most of the money he earned on

weekend drinking binges and whoring around Jersey City and Hoboken bars, the family had little, and there was never enough food or warm clothes. All of Richard's clothes were tattered and dirty, and his schoolmates took to calling him names – dumb Polack, skinny, scarecrow – because of his gangly arms and legs. Richard quickly developed an inferiority complex he would carry with him for the rest of his life. There were running feuds among the Polish, Italian and Irish kids, and Richard became a target for the Irish and Italian kids' barbs, taunts and put-downs. They made fun of the holes in his clothes, the ripped and tattered shoes he wore. Anna didn't seem at all interested in Richard's appearance. Her only concern was the church: praying, lighting holy candles and saying the rosary – none of which helped her son.

Anna was soon pregnant for a third time and gave birth, prematurely, to a girl they named Roberta. She became pregnant yet again, and the Kuklinskis soon had a fourth child, a boy they named Joseph, who, like his older brother, Richard, would grow into a remorseless killer – a psychopath.

Having three small children to feed and clothe made Stanley meaner still. He took to bringing home loose women he found in bars and openly fornicating with them as he pleased. When Anna complained, he beat her with his belt, fists and feet. He was the king of the house and would do whatever the fuck he pleased. Once Richard tried to come to his mother's rescue, and Stanley hit him in the head so hard he knocked the boy out for half the night. When Richard came to, he had a lump on the side of his head the size of a lemon, and for hours he didn't even remember who he was. Richard grew to hate his father and often fantasised about killing him.

Finally, Stanley took up with a Polish woman and, thankfully, came around less and less. Anna was now working two jobs: one at the Armond Meatpacking Company, the other cleaning floors at St Mary's Church in the evenings.

Anna, who had become a flaming religious zealot, tried to force the fear of God on her children, particularly Richard

– she insisted he attend Catholic school – but he had come to loathe the Church and its restrictive, hypocritical teachings. Much of that had to do with how brutal the nuns and priests at St Mary's School were, how quick they were to use corporal punishment; they seemed, he came to believe, even more wicked and mean than his father – no easy task, Richard explained. Richard was severely dyslexic, had a lot of difficulty reading, and when he tried to use his fingers to keep his eyes in the right place, a nun would inevitably slap his hand with a metal ruler.

Richard took to fooling around in class. He enjoyed making others laugh, and this invariably earned him a slap. Sometimes the bitter-faced, austere nuns yanked his overly protrusive ears. Richard believed they actually enjoyed hitting and slapping their young charges.

At Anna's insistent urging, Richard became an altar boy. Every Sunday, he got up early, went to St Mary's and assisted the priest with mass. In the pulpit, the priests seemed nice enough, talked glowingly about giving and kindness and avoiding sin; they acted compassionate, as if they cared. But Richard believed that they were mean-spirited men who drank alcohol, were quick to condemn, and reprimanded, even slapped, boys who didn't do their assigned tasks around the altar to their liking. One priest made inappropriate overtures to Richard about sex, started talking about the virtues of masturbation, and Richard made sure he was never alone with this priest. He knew little about sex, but he knew that what was in the priest's eyes, behind his face, was wrong – a sin.

The nuns, too, were quick to use sudden, irrational violence against the children in their care. One nun liked to use the narrow edge of a metal ruler and would hit Richard so hard across his knuckles she caused him to bleed. After this happened several times, he became fed up and said, 'You hit me again, you cunt, I'll break your fucking head – bitch!'

The nun, stunned by Richard's words, the sudden fire in his eyes, hurried from the classroom and soon returned with an irate, red-faced priest who slapped Richard so hard his face stung and a huge strawberry-coloured welt quickly formed. Rubbery dots swirled before his eyes. The priest grabbed Richard by the ear and dragged him to his office, where he proceeded to beat the boy with a book – a Bible, Richard realised. Later that night, Richard received a second beating from his mother.

From that day on, Richard had even less interest in religion and came to believe that the nuns and priests were a bunch of sadistic creeps who used religion and the always ominous spectre of God to scare and manipulate people into doing what they wanted, when they wanted, how they wanted. Religion was one big con job, he thought, and he soon turned away from the Catholic Church, its teachings, mandates and disciplines. He did, however, find solace sitting in the church when it was empty. He'd stare at the pained face of Christ up on the cross and ask him questions: where Florian was, why people were so cruel, why his mother and father beat him. He never received an answer. If there really was a God, he came to believe, he would never allow the violence that parents, nuns and priests so readily dished out to children.

Not surprisingly, Richard soon turned his rage on animals.

Stray dogs and cats became the targets of his anger. Richard devised terrible tortures, sadistic beyond what a child should be capable of. He'd capture two cats, tie their tails together, then hang them over a clothes-line and gleefully watch them tear one another apart. He threw stray cats down the incinerator, then lit it and enjoyed their screams, the way they tried to claw their way up the chute, to no avail. He'd hunt down dogs, set them on fire with gasoline, and watch them run around in flames. He used clubs and pipes and hammers to beat the dogs to death.

He killed so many stray animals – all practice for the

indiscriminate killing of human beings – that he cleared the neighbourhood of them. Something was very wrong with the young Richard Kuklinski, but no one addressed his problems, the demons already inside him, and they grew to monumental proportions.

3

STICKY FINGERS

Richard first started stealing to eat. As religious as Anna Kuklinski was, she was not a good mother. She didn't seem to realise that her children had to eat, and eat on a regular basis. When Stanley finally abandoned the family, Anna became the lone, hard-pressed provider, working at the meatpacking company by day and cleaning St Mary's floors at night. However, with four to feed and rent and utilities to pay, there was never enough of anything, and Richard took to stealing food. He'd get up early and lift cakes and cookies from the Drake's bakery truck which made daily deliveries to shops and homes all around Jersey City. Although shy and awkward, Richard was particularly ballsy when it came to stealing.

Catlike, he'd stalk the Drake's truck, and when the delivery-man made a drop-off, Richard would sneak into the truck, quickly grab cakes and milk, and take off. He did this several times a week, and in this way his sister, Roberta, and brother, Joseph, had something more to eat than the cheap porridge Anna provided – somewhat reluctantly, it seemed.

Anna was also a firm believer in corporal punishment. She'd had a mean streak beaten into her at the Sacred Heart Orphanage, and Richard sometimes thought his mother was even meaner than his father – no small thing. Anna tried to stop Richard from stealing, hit him with anything she found in the house: shoes and broom handles, hairbrushes, wooden spoons, pots and pans. She often hit Richard on the head – this even after Florian had been killed that way – and knocked him out cold. She'd come up behind him and strike him when he didn't expect it. One time after Anna hit him with a broom handle, Richard ripped it out of her hands. Like his father, Richard had a very bad temper. Anna picked up a skillet, and he hurried from the house.

Why, Richard often wondered, did his mother hate him so? Why, he wondered, was she so cruel? What had he done to make her so hateful?

Another good source of food was the railway wagons that lined the huge railroad yards all over Jersey City. The boxcars were filled with all kinds of food from across the country, and Richard took to breaking into them and stealing pineapples, oranges and huge chunks of frozen meat from icy freezer cars. Anna learned to accept the bounty Richard brought home. She could never afford such things, and she soon stopped punishing Richard for his pilfering. He was, after all, the man of the house now, and he was inadvertently filling the role of his father. He had effectively taken the place of Stanley, and Anna, Roberta and Joseph looked on the young Richard as the breadwinner. Richard liked this role. It made him feel important, grown up, older than his years. His stealing got so bad that if it wasn't nailed down, Richard would bring it home.

4

FIRST BLOOD

Somehow, Anna managed to get a federally subsidised apartment in a new four-storey red-brick housing project complex at New Jersey Avenue and Fifteenth Street. This was a real step up for the family. The project was heated, well insulated, had all the modern conveniences. Everything was spanking new and clean. Richard loved this new home, the new hardwood floors, how the sun streamed in through the windows, how everything was clean and shiny and nice to look at.

The projects were filled with low-income blue-collar people, and there were many potential friends and playmates for Richard. He had grown into a tall, skinny, very shy boy with glistening blond hair, almond-shaped light-brown eyes and excessively protruding ears. The boys of the projects quickly took to teasing Richard; they made fun of his appearance – his clothes, his thinness, his shaggy blond hair, his ears. 'Hey, you dumb Polack,' was a frequent insult.

The 'project boys', a gang of five or six of them who were always in a group, not only teased Richard but took to physically abusing him: pushing him, slapping him, throwing his baseball cap to and fro, demanding that he give them money. Richard had little money, which caused him more and more abuse, slaps and kicks in the ass as he walked. Whatever fires of discontent were already burning inside of Richard, the abuse he suffered from the project boys was further fuelling them.

FIRST BLOOD

The leader of this group of punks was a big dark-haired kid named Charley Lane. He was a few years older than Richard, a foot taller and much more heavily built. He seemed to get the most joy out of making Richard's life miserable.

Richard had no friends. He was a loner. There was no one he could confide in, talk to, throw a ball with. He wanted friends, someone to be his ally, his buddy, to stick up for him; but all the boys in the projects wanted was to taunt and tease him, bring him down and call him names: 'Hey, dumb Polack; hey, locked brain!' Richard's brother, Joseph, was too young to be his friend, and his sister, Roberta, had her own interests and little in common with her older brother.

As it happened, Richard found solace in true-crime magazines. He discovered them in a neighbourhood candy store and, with his nimble sticky fingers, managed to steal new, exciting, eye-opening issues every few weeks. Richard had grown into a bold, particularly adept thief; he was, he would later confide, a born thief. He already knew his lot in life would be crime – on the outside of the law, the underbelly of society – and learned to accept that fact, indeed to embrace it.

For the most part, Richard did not enjoy reading, but he devoured these true-crime magazines. He'd read slowly, using his long, thin fingers to keep his place, often having to go over the same passage several times to comprehend the words, their hidden, secret meanings. Because he was so drawn to the subject of crime, he made it his business to understand the words, to turn them over in his young mind, to imagine the larcenies, robberies and murders they vividly described in short, simple sentences. When the weather was nice, Richard liked to go down to the Hudson River and read there by the silent, swift-moving water. There it was quiet and no one harassed or bothered him. Just opposite Jersey City, he could see Lower Manhattan, a teeming, lively place filled with tall, stately buildings and rich people who ate steak and fancy food every day, everything they wanted, as much as they wanted, Richard was sure.

What interested Richard the most was how crimes, especially murders, were solved. For hours on end, Richard buried his face in these magazines, and they gave him an insight into criminal behaviour he could find nowhere else, insight he would put to good use. The words in these simply written pulp magazines with colourful covers, brimming with violence, filled Richard's head like sinister clouds of poison gas with fantasies of violence, of murder, of striking back at those who abused him, taunted him, called him names. He began thinking about hurting people . . . killing people. Getting even. Having revenge.

Like all teenage boys, Richard wanted to do grown-up things. He pined for a car, to drive around and show the world that he had the wherewithal to own a car, to go where he pleased, even to go to Manhattan, 'the city', if he had a mind to. Just down Sixteenth Street, near his house, there was a parking lot, and Richard took to stealing cars, parking them in the lot and taking them on short, exciting jaunts around Jersey City. He was tall for his age now and quickly learned the nuances of the steering wheel, brake and gas pedal. Richard savoured these little excursions. Some day, he resolved, he'd own a fancy car – a Cadillac or maybe a Lincoln Continental. He wanted to drive through the Holland Tunnel, go visit the city, but he was afraid one of the tollbooth operators would stop him, question him. All this Richard did by himself, and this made him feel grown up and more independent. He was just 13 years old, proud that he had the balls to do such things.

That winter, the situation with the project boys became intolerable. They wouldn't leave him alone; the taunts and pointed barbs became more and more frequent, violent, vicious. He tried to fight back one day, and they gave him a terrible beating – four of them kicked him, punched him and spat on him when he was down. He was so beaten up that he couldn't leave the apartment for a solid week. Anna Kuklinski wanted to go to the police and have the boys arrested, but

Richard wouldn't do that. 'I'm no rat!' he kept saying. 'I'll settle this my own way.'

Already, Richard knew the strict rules of the street – and the cardinal rule was never go to the cops. Nearby Hoboken had a large Mafia contingent, indeed was a Mafia hub, the home base for the notorious De Cavalcante family (which in later years would become the inspiration for the hit series *The Sopranos*), and the young Richard already knew well that only rats went to the cops.

No, he would take care of this in his own way, in his own time. Charley Lane, the leader of the project boys, had hurt Richard the most, and Richard's wrath and need for revenge centred on this oversized bully who swaggered like an ape when he walked. Plans of destruction ran through Richard's head night and day, for days on end, throughout his convalescence. He thought about stabbing Charley, hitting him with a wrench, dropping a concrete block on his head as he made his way about the narrow walkways that crisscrossed the project grounds. He would, he decided, stalk and attack Charley late at night.

It happened on a biting cold Friday evening. Richard removed the rail, a two-foot-long, thick wooden pole, from the hall cupboard. It was perfect for what he had in mind: light and lethal. Just next to the cupboard there was a photograph of Florian, which Anna always kissed as she went out. Anna still had much guilt over what had happened to her first-born – that Stanley had got away with killing him, that she had conspired to cover up the murder – and it was a suffocating, colossal weight she would carry with her for the rest of her days. The weight would slowly drag her down, round her shoulders, actually make her appear smaller, shorter; the weight would eventually speed up her demise. There were also pictures of a pained Jesus and a virtuous Mary in a blue dress next to Florian's picture, which the hyper-religious Anna also kissed on her way out. The only other photograph in the house was of Anna's brother Micky. He lived in upstate New York with his wife, Julia. Micky was a kind, gregarious man and gave his sister what he could. He was the only person who had ever been kind to Richard; he gave him a watch when he graduated from grade school. One summer, Richard spent a few weeks at Uncle Micky's house, and it was a dream-like experience he would savour for his entire life.

My Uncle Micky, Richard explained, *was the only adult that was ever good to me. He was a real nice guy, and I'll never forget him.*

In Micky's house, everything was clean and shining and all the food was first class, and for the first time Richard saw that people lived another way, a better way, and he would never forget that either. It would always be something he coveted for himself.

The powerful winds on that frigid January night howled through the project grounds, bending trees and rattling windows. It had snowed that week and glistening sheets of ice covered the walkways. Richard had one warm coat – a pea-coat so threadbare that his elbows showed through. Richard donned a few tattered sweaters, slipped the wooden dolly up the worn sleeve of his coat and went out to find Charley Lane with a need for revenge burning inside him like a tropical fever. He positioned himself facing the New Jersey Avenue entrance to the project, his back up against the wall of the building in which the Kuklinski family lived. More than likely, he knew, Charley would come home via this entrance. He had seen him do so many times. The red-brick wall Richard stood against contained the flue for the building's incinerator, and the warmth gave Richard some comfort, but the fire burning inside him was what really kept him warm. He watched men who lived in the projects leave the bar across the street, a place his father, Stanley, sometimes went. Standing there in the Jersey City cold, Richard thought about his father; the hatred he had for him had grown inside him like a festering tumour, and Richard often thought about getting his hands on a gun, going and killing Stanley. He didn't think of him as his father any more. He thought of him as just Stanley and would for the rest of his life refer to him as 'Stanley', never 'my father' or 'Dad'.

Richard had no idea how long he'd been standing there, and he was just about to give up and go back upstairs when he saw Charley come off New Jersey Avenue and start onto the project grounds. He was by himself. Richard's stomach tightened. His heart began to race. At just the right moment, Richard left his hiding place. Charley sneered when he saw Richard suddenly in front of him. 'What the fuck do you want, Polack?' he demanded. Richard stayed mute, just stared at him with calm, cold hatred. 'Get the fuck outta my way or I'll give you another beating, fuckin' dumb Polack!'

'Yeah, try,' Richard said, and Charley quickly came at Richard, but Richard pulled out his secreted weapon and without a moment's hesitation swung with all his might and hit Charley square on the side of the head, just above the ear. Shocked, Charley held his head, backed up, his eyes filling with rage, surprise and indignation.

With a combination of fear and pent-up animosity filling him, Richard went after Charley, struck him on the head and knocked him down. And Richard kept hitting him, hitting him, hitting him. He didn't want to kill the boy; he just wanted to teach him a lesson he'd never forget, wanted only to be left alone. But all the rage Richard had stored up inside, a world of it, came to the surface, and he kept striking the prostrate boy with all his might. When he was finally finished, Charley didn't move. Richard kicked him, again and again, cursing him, crying with rage. Still Charley Lane didn't move. Richard demanded that he get up, fight. 'Come on, come on,' he hissed through clenched teeth. Charley stayed still as a log. Richard slapped him, moved him over and felt for a pulse in his neck – he knew about this because of the true-crime magazines. Nothing.

Stunned, horrified, the young Richard realised that Charley Lane was dead and he had killed him. His mind reeled with the dire implications of such a thing. He would be sent to prison, the dreaded 'big house', for the rest of his life. He stood and staggered. As much as he hated Charley, he had wanted only to hurt him, certainly not kill him. He had wanted to make Charley suffer the way Charley had made him suffer, cause him pain and anxiety. Not this. What to do, where to turn? There was no one he could tell about this – not his mother, not his Uncle Micky, no one. Richard forced himself to take long, deep breaths, to think, to form a plan, his mind racing furiously to and fro.

By instinct, Richard knew the only way out of this was to get rid of the body. But how? Where?

He had a stolen car in the lot down on Sixteenth Street, a dark-blue Pontiac he had found two days ago in front of a store on Hudson Boulevard with the keys inside. He hurried to get it, drove it to New Jersey Avenue and parked just by the project entrance. Charley was very heavy – a dead weight. Richard grabbed him by the coat, made sure the coast was clear, and boldly pulled the body towards the Pontiac, using the slippery ice to slide it across the frigid ground. He opened the boot and managed to pick up the dead boy and get him in. As he closed the boot, he noticed a battered tool. On one side it was a hatchet and on the other a hammer. Before getting into the car, he looked around and made certain that no one was watching him from one of the project windows. All seemed clear. He got into the car, drove onto the nearby Pulaski Skyway and headed south. He wasn't sure what he'd do or how he'd do it, but Richard was intent upon not getting caught. He put on the car's heater and calmed himself. He knew that if he was pulled over by the police, he'd be in deep shit, so he purposely drove at the speed limit, and, as he drove, a different feeling slowly swept over Richard: a feeling of power and omnipotence. A kind of invincibility. He remembered all the abuse he had suffered over the years because of Charley, the taunts and put-downs, the random punches and slaps and kicks, and he was suddenly glad he'd killed him. He'd been fantasising about killing people for the longest time, almost as far back as he could remember, and now he'd done it, and he liked the way it made him feel.

'I will never,' he said out loud in the quiet interior of the moving car, 'ever allow anybody to fucking abuse me again.' And he never did.

After two hours of driving, his mind playing over what he'd do, Richard reached an area of South Jersey, known as the Pine Barrens, filled with desolate marshland and pine forests. He pulled over on a small bridge above a frozen pond surrounded with tall blond-coloured reeds, which he could see in the car's headlights. There was no one about. The wind howled. He got out of the Pontiac and opened the boot. Charley Lane was much heavier than he'd been before, but rigor mortis had not set in yet, and he was still malleable. Struggling, Richard got him out of the car, laid him on the frozen ground and returned with the axe-hammer. Knowing Charley's teeth could be used to identify him and put the murder on his doorstep, Richard used the hammer to knock out all of Charley's teeth. He then laid out the lifeless hands and chopped the tips of the fingers off. He gathered up the fingertips and teeth, planning to get rid of them elsewhere. Last, he made sure Charley had no ID on him, found some paper money, took it, picked up the body and dumped it off the small bridge. It broke through the ice. He returned to the car and turned back towards Jersey City, stepping on the accelerator. As he went, he got rid of the pieces of Charley he'd kept, knowing birds and animals would eat them sooner or later. All this he had learned by avidly reading true-crime magazines. Thus Richard's path in life was set irrevocably and forever.

By the time Richard got back to Jersey City, a frigid pale dawn was rapidly coming on. He watched the sky in the east turn a tawny winter orange. He figured it would be best to get rid of the car now, so he left it in a parking area in Hoboken and walked back home, changed forever.

THE ICE MAN

Proud of himself, how cool he was under pressure, how clever his actions were, he lay in bed, but he couldn't sleep. He felt, for the first time in his entire life, like *a someone*, a person who merited respect. He could control who lived and who died, when and where and how. The last thought Richard had before he finally fell asleep was: *Fuck with me and I'll kill you . . . I will kill you!*

5

REBORN

In the ensuing days, Richard saw the project boys, but without Charley to lead them and egg them on, encourage and compel them, they left Richard alone. Richard, however, didn't leave them alone. They had tormented him for years, a thing he'd not forgotten. Using a length of wood he found, he went after them all, one by one, and beat them mercilessly, and from then on they did not trouble Richard again. Indeed, they moved out of his way when they saw him coming, wouldn't even look him in the eye.

It was then I learned it was better to give than to receive, Richard explained.

There were a lot of questions about what happened to Charley, but no one ever tied his sudden disappearance to Richard, the wooden rail, the stolen Pontiac. Richard believed he had committed the perfect crime, came to think of himself as a cunning, menacing criminal, a force to be reckoned with. He went from a cowering boy to a dangerous man in just a few days. He began carrying around a baseball bat and was quick to use it on anyone, man or boy, who bothered him. He had a lot of old scores to settle, and he methodically went about Jersey City seeking out and beating anyone who had ever bullied or abused him. He was very tall for his age and had a long-limbed, wiry strength beyond his years. In no time, he garnered a reputation as a tough guy, no one to fuck with, and he liked that — a lot.

The bat, however, was too large and conspicuous, so instead Richard started carrying an inexpensive hunting knife, and he had no qualms about using it with very bad intentions.

Richard never thought about Charley Lane. He was dead and gone and to hell with him. Whether it was Stanley's brutality, his mother's beatings, the many head traumas Richard had suffered or the way he'd been born – with some kind of bad gene – Richard had no concern, no guilt, no qualms about cutting someone across the face, even taking a life.

The thought of murder was the natural result of living in a jungle, and Richard had come to know the world as a brutal jungle. He resolved to be a predator, not prey. Richard was, it was apparent even back then, a natural born killer.

Richard had little use for school and barely went any more. He began hanging out in smoke-filled pool halls and bars with pool tables. He really liked the game, its neat precision, its rules, its timing and strategy. He practised constantly, for hours at a time, perfecting his skills, his hand-eye coordination, the correct stroke needed to make good, then very difficult shots. With his tall, thin body and unusually long arms, he was able to lean in to difficult shots and make them easily. He soon learned you could make money if you shot pool well, and he had visions of becoming a famous pool shark, a slick, soft-spoken hustler who could beat the pants off all challengers.

Richard had an uncanny ability to move quietly. He naturally walked on only the balls of his enormous feet, and he could readily move up on people without them noticing. One afternoon, he came home unexpectedly. Walking into the house, he heard a strange noise, heavy breathing, rhythmic grunting. He slowly moved forward and looked into the living-room, and there was his mother, having sex with a man on the couch – a married man with three children who lived next door. His mother's legs were high in the air, wide open, and the man was pumping into her, his fat, white, hairy ass exposed. Richard wanted to plunge his knife into the man's back, but instead he quietly turned and left, disgusted, hating his mother. She was always talking about how dirty sex was, don't do this, don't do that, and there she was in broad daylight fucking the married guy next door. What a hypocrite, what a tramp – *a whore*, he thought, and went back to Jake's Pool Hall in Hoboken and began to practise.

Richard became better and better at shooting pool and actually did start making money. With his shy ways and innocent baby face, most people he played were sure they could beat him, but they would inevitably lose to him. He got into arguments and fights with guys in pool halls and bars, and he was quick to smack with a cue anyone who got in his face or reneged on a bet. He quickly came to realise that if you struck first with a lot of force, you won; the fight was over, the dispute settled. End of story. Might really was always right.

His reputation quickly spread all over Jersey City and Hoboken, and few wanted to tangle with Richard Kuklinski. Several times, Richard got into run-ins with guys who were with friends, and even then he wouldn't back down. He was fearless to the point of being reckless. On one such occasion, he fought two brothers who, with a third guy, got the better of him. But Richard waited for these three guys to leave the bar, followed them home, found out where they lived, and went back a few nights later. He waited in the shadows for the right moment and stabbed, from behind, one of the brothers. He then went after the friend and stabbed him in the stomach as he went up the stairs to his home. He tried to find the second brother, but he had hightailed it out of Jersey City. Richard earned a reputation as a genuinely dangerous guy. Other toughs his age quickly gravitated to him. He was a natural leader, had a quick acerbic wit and would cut a throat as readily as spit on a soiled sidewalk.

Soon, Richard had his own gang of sorts. There were five of them: three Polish guys (including Richard), an Irish kid and an Italian. They called themselves 'the Coming Up

Roses', and each of them got a tattoo of a parchment scroll with those words, 'Coming Up Roses', on his left hand. For them, the words meant that there were bright things ahead, and that if anyone fucked with any of them, he'd end up plant fertiliser. They swore an oath of loyalty and soon began plotting robberies and stick-ups together.

Richard bought his first gun from a guy he played pool with. It was an old .38 revolver with a six-inch barrel. He and his gang went to the abandoned Jersey City waterfront and took target practice. They were all the children of two-fisted, heavy-drinking, blue-collar people; they were high-school dropouts, antisocial toughs, fearless and reckless – trouble waiting to happen.

The second individual Richard killed was a man named Doyle, a red-faced Irishman who talked out the side of a thin-lipped mouth. He hung around a pool hall/bar in Hoboken called Danny's. He drank a lot, and when he drank he became loud, mean and abusive. Richard was playing pool for money with Doyle, winning game after game, and Doyle began calling Richard names: 'dumb Polack', 'cheater'.

Everyone knew Doyle was a Jersey City cop, and even Richard, with his homicidal hair-trigger temper, would not assault him out in the open. But the more Doyle abused him, the madder Richard became. Doyle very much reminded him of his father – a fatal resemblance. Rather than tangle with Doyle in public, Richard quietly put down his cue, left the bar and waited for Doyle. After a time, Doyle also left the bar, got into his car parked down the block, lit up a cigarette and just sat there. Richard soon realised that Doyle had fallen asleep. As always, Richard had a knife on him. But Doyle was a cop, and if Richard stabbed him, he'd have to kill him, and he'd be first on the list of likely suspects, a thing Richard was intent on avoiding. He turned away, went to a nearby garage, bought a quart of petrol and quickly made his way back to the sleeping Doyle. The driver's window was open. Without a second thought, Richard quickly and silently poured the petrol into the car, over Doyle, struck a match and threw it into the car. A fireball exploded. Doyle was quickly consumed and killed by the ferocious flames and intense heat. Richard stayed near by and actually enjoyed hearing Doyle scream, the smell of his burned flesh coming to him on a strong breeze off the nearby Hudson River. Satisfied, smiling, Richard made his way home. He never said a word to anyone about what he had done, not even his Coming Up Roses cronies.

Richard had grown into a very tall, handsome young man. He had light-blond hair, honey-coloured almond-shaped eyes, wide Slavic cheekbones and heart-shaped lips. He looked like a young Jimmy Stewart and had a beguiling shy way about him that women were drawn to. In the bars and pool halls where Richard hung out, there were older women, as he had come to think of them, and they soon found their way to him and invited him home with them, and thus Richard lost his virginity. It didn't take him long to realise that women found him attractive, which he enjoyed, and he began dressing to please women; but he was still painfully shy, and unless a woman approached him he was hard-pressed to strike up a conversation.

Often, however, women did approach him. One such woman, a 25 year old named Linda, took Richard home with her when he was 16, and he began to live with her. She always wanted to have sex, and he was always happy to accommodate her. She was short with black hair, attractive in a simple way. But she was always 'in the mood', it seemed, and Richard gave her what she wanted, when she wanted it – and how and where she wanted it. He had a particularly large member, which she couldn't seem to get enough of.

By this time, Richard had come to hate his mother and visited her less and less. His sister, Roberta, had acquired a reputation as a loose girl, easy to have, and Richard didn't like that. He warned her several times to 'keep your drawers on', to no avail.

His younger brother, Joseph, like him, was tall and thin with a thick mop of blond hair. Joseph did not do well in school, was always in fights; he had punched out a teacher. At Anna's urging, Richard spoke to Joe, tried to get him to behave, but it was like talking to a wall.

Joseph, like his brother, had an antisocial personality and was clearly a budding psychopath . . . would think nothing of breaking a bottle and cutting someone's face wide open. Their father, Stanley, was a short man, 5 ft 7 in. or so, with black hair, yet both Richard and Joseph were blond and well over 6 ft and still growing. This sometimes caused Richard to wonder if Stanley was really his father. Richard had come to think of his mother as an unkempt, slovenly whore and had little use for her. However, when he found out that Stanley came round to the house, yelling at and slapping Anna, he went and found his father, put a .38 to his head, pulled the hammer back, and warned him through tight lips and clenched teeth that if he ever went near his family again, he'd kill him and dump him in the river. After that, Richard didn't speak to his father for many years, and Stanley never troubled Anna again. The truth was, Richard was sorry he hadn't killed Stanley and often thought about going back and finishing the job.

Even many years later, in middle age, Richard regretted not having blown Stanley away. He confided: *Stanley was a first-grade, sadistic prick. He shouldn't've never been allowed to have children. A thousand times if once I wondered why I didn't kill him. If I had to do it over, I would've done the job right for sure.*

6

THE DE CAVALCANTES

The Coming Up Roses gang, under Richard's leadership, committed more and more crimes: broke into warehouses, held up liquor stores and drugstores, burglarised rich people with nice homes in Jersey City Heights and Lincoln Park, the most exclusive areas in Jersey City. Because Richard was cautious and carefully planned all their jobs, thinking about them from numerous angles, they were successful. In his short life, Richard had excelled at three things: playing pool, sudden violence and crime.

Richard began making good money and usually walked around with a large roll of bills. He soon acquired a penchant for gambling, playing cards and going to the racetracks, and as quickly as he made money, he pissed it away. He said he was 'nigger rich' and had no comprehensive concept of money, how to manage it, save it and parlay it into more. For him, money was for spending, when and where and how he wished. Easy come, easy go.

Wanting to look good – 'sharp', as he said – he bought garish suits for himself, bright yellows and pinks. Thus attired, Richard and the Coming Up Roses made the rounds of all the Hoboken bars. There were literally two or three bars on every block, more bars per capita than anywhere in the country. They also went to dance halls. Once in a while, men made comments about the way Richard dressed, and he assaulted these individuals quickly and violently. He'd pull out his knife and use it at the drop of a hat, and it got so that no one commented on his outlandish outfits. Still, he was quite a sight in a pink, large-collared suit, tall and thin and gangly, particularly broad at the shoulders, with his light-blond hair combed straight back and his intense honey-coloured eyes. Even then, it must have been an unsettling experience having Richard Kuklinski stare directly at you with his pale, deadpan face.

Richard took to drinking more than he should, and when he drank he – like his father and more than likely his grandfather – became mean and belligerent. He and the Coming Up Roses often got into bar brawls, and they rarely, if ever, lost a fight, because all of them were vicious in the extreme and were always sending people to hospital with gaping knife wounds, cracked heads, broken bones. Richard and his friends became notorious, not an easy feat in the tough blue-collar cities of Hoboken and Jersey City, both filled with the notorious. It didn't take long for members of the De Cavalcante crime family to notice the Coming Up Roses gang.

His name was Carmine Genovese, no relation to the infamous boss Vito Genovese. Carmine was a made man, a cunning individual who had his sausage-thick fingers in many juicy pies. He was short and round like a meatball, with a large round head. Indeed, his nickname was 'Meatball'. Carmine had heard about the Coming Up Roses crew many times over the years, that they were very violent, stand-up and fearless, all neighbourhood kids who had come up the hard way, looking to earn. He invited them to his house one afternoon and sat them down in the kitchen as he prepared a meat sauce for pasta. With his heavy tough-guy accent, talking out of the left side of his mouth, he said, 'I'm hearing all the time about you, and I like what I hear. I got a piece a work for you. You do this good, I'll make sure you earn big.' He added some spicy sausages to the pot. 'There's this guy in Lincoln Park. Here's his address and his picture. He's a problem. He's got his head up his ass; he's gotta go. You do a good job, I make sure you earn, *capisce*? I did everything for you already – just finish the work. He's gotta go . . . understand?' With that, he handed Richard a black-and-white photograph of a man getting into his car, a black Lincoln. Richard passed it to the others. They all looked.

Richard knew this could be a golden opportunity for his crew, that the door was opening to a bona fide 'in' with organised crime – a thing they had always hoped for. Because four of them were not Italians, they could never be made, but they could become 'independent contractors'. The mob, they knew, controlled New Jersey commerce; it had an absolute stranglehold on the unions, the piers, all vices, hijackings, robberies, loan-sharking and murder.

Carmine then added a pile of neat, round meatballs to the sauce. 'You want the work?' he asked, looking at them out of the corners of his reptilian eyes.

'Yeah, absolutely,' Richard said.

'Good. This gotta happen quick, understand? Anything goes wrong, you call me. We own the cops here, OK?'

'OK,' Richard said, as the others nodded in solemn agreement.

'You guys stay. Eat lunch with me,' Carmine said, and soon they all sat down to a simple, hearty meal of spaghetti, meat sauce and a salad with big green Sicilian olives, which Carmine had cured – one of his hobbies, he explained.

When the Coming Up Roses left Carmine, they went to a Hoboken bar near the waterfront called the Final Round. There they sat down to discuss this sudden opportunity; all of them except Richard were nervous and unsure. Bar-room brawls were one thing, but cold-blooded murder was a horse of a different colour. The baddest of the group was a tall, bull-like guy named John Wheeler. He was an amateur heavyweight boxer, tough as nails. Despite his anxiety, he said, 'I'll do it. I'll pull the trigger. No problem.'

Good, OK, that was settled. Richard said, 'Let's do this

quick, and let's do it right. Guys, this is a great chance for us, OK? We don't wanna blow it.'

They all agreed and piled into John's car and drove over to Lincoln Park. Richard was behind the wheel. John had the gun, a mean little .32 revolver. This was a good neighbourhood. People who lived here were rich, and the Coming Up Roses had robbed numerous houses in the area. They found the address, a stately timber-frame house with fancy columns and porticoes and a beautiful, well-tended garden. It was early spring, and already the grounds were bursting with young flowers. This was a far cry from where these guys had grown up; this was the proverbial other side of the tracks. As they sat there discussing how to do the job, the mark walked right out the front door as if on cue, without a care in the world, it seemed. All of the Coming Up Roses were nervous, had butterflies in their stomachs.

'There he is, go do it, John,' Richard said.

But John didn't move. He froze, got pale. The mark slid into his fancy Lincoln and drove away.

'What happened?' Richard asked, annoyed.

'I don't know . . . I just, I just . . . I don't know,' big, tough-as-nails Wheeler said.

'OK, not to worry, we'll follow him, nail him in his car, OK, at a light,' Richard said.

'Yeah. Yeah, OK,' Wheeler said. Richard put the car in gear, and off they went, this inexperienced impromptu hit team.

They caught up with the Lincoln at a light on West Side Avenue. 'Get ready,' Richard said, easing up right next to the Lincoln. Wheeler's hands, however, were trembling so much he couldn't even take proper aim.

'What's wrong?' Richard asked, and the others asked the same thing.

'I don't fuckin' know. I can't.'

The light turned green. The mark drove off.

'We have to do this,' Richard said. 'We have no choice any more.' They trailed the mark to a Hoboken bar, watched him go in, have a drink and shoot the breeze with the bartender.

'I'll do it,' Richard solemnly said, and took the gun from Wheeler. Silently, contemplatively, they sat there. Night came on quickly. It began to rain. The mark left the bar and headed for his Lincoln. He seemed a little wobbly now. The coast was clear. Without a word, Richard stepped from the car and quickly made his way to the Lincoln, deadly purpose in each step. Making sure no one was looking, he put the gun up close to the mark's head and pulled the trigger, boom, one shot to the left side of his head, just above the ear. It was done.

Calm, cool, collected, Richard walked back to the car and got in, and they drove away. *Wow!* was the collective feeling of the others, but no one said anything, each of them looking at Richard with a new-found respect.

Finally, after several blocks, the big, bad Wheeler said, 'Man, Rich, you're cold like ice.'

'Cool as a fuckin' cucumber,' another said.

Richard enjoyed the adulation. He felt no pangs of conscience, no emotion, no guilt at all. Indeed, he felt nothing. He had killed the mark as easily as belching and never looked back.

Near noon the following day, the Coming Up Roses went back to Carmine's place. Richard knocked on the door. Carmine opened it.

'What's up?' he said. 'I told you not to come back till you did the thing.'

'You see the papers?' Richard asked.

'No . . . why?' Carmine asked.

Richard's answer was a slight, coy smile.

'Ah, you sons of bitches! You did it. Bravo! You sons of bitches,' Carmine exclaimed. He invited them in, graciously poured drinks for them, gave them each five hundred dollars, and thus the door to organised crime opened wide.

7

HERE TODAY,
GONE TOMORROW

True to his word, Carmine gave Richard and his crew a lot of work. Suddenly, they were making money hand over fist. They proved without question they could be trusted, were ruthless and got the job done, no matter what it was. Carmine knew the best way to test potential associates was to have them commit a murder. Once that was done, they could, theoretically, be trusted, for they had incriminated themselves in a serious crime. In those days, there were few people involved with La Cosa Nostra – 'Our Thing' – who became 'rats'. The best way to guarantee someone's loyalty was to have him commit a murder, which is exactly what Carmine had done with the Coming Up Roses. Indeed, the first step on the road to induction into any Mafia family was carrying out a killing, or 'making one's bones'. That created the lifetime bond that proved so successful for many years, first in Italy, then around the world. The Italian Mafia was, and still is, the most successful criminal enterprise of all time. And Richard Kuklinski would become one of its premiere killers – a homicide superstar.

Carmine Genovese had amazing sources of information all over New Jersey. He knew which trucks to hijack, when and where and what they were carrying, even had the trucks' licence-plate numbers, which he gave to Richard's crew. Carmine received half the proceeds from all their ill-gotten gains, and the gang split the other half five ways among themselves. They hijacked trucks that were filled with appliances, jewellery, clothing, albums, razor blades, furniture, tools and machinery, even fancy foods such as steak and tins of caviar – anything that could be turned into hard cash quickly.

No matter how much Richard's crew made, they spent it all, gambling and living large. Richard was not too fond of the horse tracks, but he loved Las Vegas, and he went there by himself and with Linda – the older woman with whom he was still living – and gambled up a storm. He also very much enjoyed watching the garish, extravagant Las Vegas shows. His favourite entertainer was Liberace, of all people. He loved the game of baccarat and won a lot but lost far more. He explained: *I had no idea what money was, and I spent it like water. I should've been investing it, buying property, but I threw it all away.*

Richard also enjoyed seeing all the gorgeous showgirls. Often, he was propositioned by Las Vegas prostitutes. He was hard to miss, with his huge size and decked out in a yellow suit, but he never went with any of the very lovely prostitutes who came on to him. He thought of prostitutes as whores and wasn't turned on by them. *A girl that screwed eight guys that day does nothing for me*, he later explained.

The largest score Richard and his crew made – thanks to Genovese – was taking off an armoured-truck company in North Bergen, New Jersey. Genovese had given them the combination to the alarm and locking system, and after pressing a few buttons they were inside the small red-brick warehouse, in which armoured trucks were neatly lined up. There was a huge safe filled with boxes of cash and gold bullion. Carmine told them it couldn't look like an inside job, so the first thing they did was break a hole in the wall. They then proceeded to blow open the safe and completely fill up one of the armoured trucks with bullion, cash and coins.

Unfortunately, they overloaded the truck, and as they were pulling out of the garage, they hit the outside kerb, and all four rear tyres blew out with loud explosions, startling them. They tried to drive to a prearranged warehouse they had rented not far way, but the armoured truck couldn't make it, and the gang was forced to go back and take two more trucks. Working at triple speed, they emptied the contents of the first into the other two there on the side of the road and finally took off. If a cop car had come along, they would certainly have been busted, but they were lucky and made it to their safe haven just as it was getting light.

All together, they stole two million dollars' worth of currency and gold. Carmine took half, and Richard and his group split one million: two hundred thousand each – a great score for these young toughs still wet behind the ears. The Coming Up Roses gang now really lived it up, squandering their share, and before any of them knew it the money was gone, mostly lost at the racetracks and poker tables or spent on women. Richard made several first-class flights to Vegas and managed to lose all his ill-gotten gains.

I was a dumb kid. I didn't know any better, he said; *but, boy, did I have a ball* – smiling as he thought about it even then.

With all their success, the gang became more and more bold and began to think they were invincible. Two of the Coming Up Roses, John Wheeler and Jack Dubrowski, got it into their heads that it would be OK to stick up a card game sponsored by a made man in the De Cavalcante family. They did this without consulting Richard, which proved to be a fatal error in judgement. One of the group they robbed recognised John, even though they both sported plaid bandannas over their faces. Word quickly reached a De Cavalcante soldier. Knowing that Richard led the Coming Up Roses and that they worked with Genovese, this soldier – his name was Albert Parenti – found Richard and solemnly sat him down in a quiet corner of a bar called Phil's. Parenti was a barrel-chested Italian American of Sicilian extraction, balding, weasel-faced, so bow-legged he walked like he'd just got off a horse. He said, 'I know two of your guys stuck up my game on Washington Street. I also know you had nothing to do with it or I wouldn't be talking nice. I'm coming to you here like this as a courtesy, see. We all know you are a stand-up guy; we hear only good things about you. That's why I'm talking to you nice like this, see. Those guys of yours gotta go. There ain't no other way.'

Angry but controlling himself, Richard knew better than to try and deny his guys' involvement or to become belligerent in any way. What he did was plead for mercy.

'First, let me say I appreciate you talking to me like this,' he said. 'I had no idea 'bout any of this. I'm real sorry. I'll make sure every fuckin' penny is paid back, all –'

'It's not the money I'm talking about here, it's the principle.'

'I know that, I'm just saying –'

'Look, let me cut to the chase: these guys gotta go. And you gotta do it, see. They're your responsibility, see.'

This hit Richard like a bare-knuckled punch in the face. In his own quiet way, he loved John and Jack; they were his first and only friends. How could he kill them? But Richard knew enough about the rhyme and reason of street justice to know that if he didn't do what Parenti was asking – demanding, in fact – he himself could very well be marked for removal.

He tried again: 'Let me talk to them, let me make sure they leave town and never, I mean never, come back.'

'They gotta go. That's it. You do it or we do it, capisce?'

'Capisce,' Richard said, seeing clearly the writing on the wall; it was written in John and Jack's blood, and if he was not careful, his blood.

'Good. I'm glad that's settled,' Parenti said, with solemn finality. He stood up and left, the two goons he travelled with close behind. A heavy life-and-death weight suddenly on his shoulders, Richard sat there as still as a tombstone, knowing he and his small crew could never fight with the De Cavalcantes. They were many, and notoriously violent, and defying or fighting with them would mean only sure death for all of them. Richard knew, too, that John and Jack had fucked up big-time, gone against the basic tenets of the street and his strict rule of never taking off any mob guys. They had, he knew, sealed their own fates. Richard got up slowly, left the bar, first found Jack, shot him in the head before he knew it and left him where he dropped. He then found John, leaving his girlfriend's apartment, and shot him down, killing him, leaving him on the street so the De Cavalcantes would know the deed was truly done. They both died without pain – before they knew what had hit them.

Still, Richard felt terrible. He had just killed two of the people he'd been closest to, whom he loved more than brothers. They had done much together. Now they were dead, dead by his hand.

It was them or me, he kept telling himself, but that didn't help much, he later confided.

The De Cavalcantes immediately heard, of course, about what Richard had done, and it didn't take long for them to realise that Richard Kuklinski could be a great asset to them: a made-to-order killer who knew what to do and how to do it, and kept his mouth shut . . . something all mob families everywhere are always scouting for. True, Richard could never be made, but he could surely work as an independent contractor if he proved that he could keep his mouth shut, that he understood that silence was golden. Before they approached him with anything more, they'd wait and see if he could be trusted.

The Jersey City police found no witnesses, no links to Richard; no one knew anything about the murders of John and Jack, and they were soon forgotten, two hoods who got their just deserts.

8

LONG WALKS, SHORT PIERS

It was the spring of 1954. Richard was just 19 years old but comported himself as if he were much older. He had a stoical seriousness about him beyond his years. Perhaps it was because of his parents' brutality; perhaps it was because he'd always been an outsider, put-upon, victimised; perhaps it was because he'd never had a real childhood. Perhaps it was because he had killed his two best friends. Whatever it was, Richard was no longer a boy. He was a man about to make his mark on the world.

Like many Poles, Richard had a penchant for walking, the outdoors and fresh air. He'd regularly walk miles at a time. He didn't believe in exercise – lifting weights, working out in a gym, jogging – but he loved to walk, and to think as he went. Though he didn't make an effort to exercise, Richard was endowed with unusual strength. He did menial work between his financial highs, loading and unloading trucks, always keeping an eye out for something he could rob and turn into hard cash. His strength, however, seemed to be something he was born with, something in his genes. The people of northern Poland, where his father had come from, were a hardy, powerful lot, and all the best physical traits of his bloodline seemed to manifest themselves in Richard. When asked if he exercised as a young man, went to a gym, lifted weights, he said: *The only exercise I ever got was carrying dead bodies.*

Curious to see more of New York, Richard took the ferry to Manhattan, marvelling as the boat crossed the river at the multicoloured, rich skyline – how different it was from Jersey City and Hoboken. He had been to the city several times already with the Coming Up Roses crew, but never by himself. Now the Coming Up Roses were a thing of the past, part of his youth. There were rumours on the street that Richard had killed John and Jack, and the other members steered clear of him. As it happened, they soon began using heroin, and Richard, in turn, stayed away from them. He did not like drugs or the people who used them. He viewed drug users as weak and unreliable – people you couldn't trust. Richard had become a kind of solemn, slow-moving, very dangerous lone wolf. His solitariness was an attribute that would serve him well for many years to come. He enjoyed being alone. He avoided friends.

When Richard stepped off the ferry near Fortieth Street, he took a right and began to walk downtown along the riverfront, under the West Side Highway. This was a dark, dank, desolate place. Most of the great piers that had once lined West Street, bustling with commerce, ships and affluent people, were now rusting and dying, mere skeletons of their former selves. Here there were few streetlamps, and the streets were rough cobblestones, slick when wet. Richard now always carried a knife or a gun. He didn't feel fully dressed unless he was armed, something that would stay with him all his professional life. He didn't, he said, have any designs on hurting anyone during this first lone foray into Manhattan, but a nasty bum with an attitude approached him, asking for money. Richard ignored him. He followed, demanding money, and still Richard walked on. The bum, a large, dirty, bearded bear of a man, grabbed Richard by the shoulder and swung him around.

'Hey, you deaf, motherfucker?' he said. Smiling, Richard quickly turned and, before the bum realised it, pulled out his knife and slammed it into the man's chest in two swift movements.

'Get the fuck away from me!' Richard growled, as the bum went to his knees and hit the ground hard. It was all over in a split second. Richard watched the light in his eyes go out, wiped his blade on him and walked on, knowing he had killed the man, glad he had killed him.

I enjoy seeing the lights go out. I enjoy killing up close and personal. I always wanted the last image they had to be my face, he explained.

Richard had come to enjoy having control over who lived and who died. It made him feel omnipotent. He viewed the man he had just killed as vermin, and he kept his eyes open for more. He walked all the way to the Battery Tunnel at the southern tip of Manhattan and solemnly stared at Jersey City across the water, remembering how he used to read crime magazines over there when he was a kid, remembering his brother Florian, remembering his father's brutality, remembering the friends he had killed. He could just about see the place where he had shot John Wheeler to death. Hell of a thing, he thought.

His handsome face a mask of unfeeling granite, Richard turned and made his way back uptown, passing the bum he had killed as he went, enjoying the sight of him there like that, dead at his hand, still lying where he had left him, though now a ghostly pale in the forlorn yellowish light of a streetlamp.

Richard felt sure this murder would not be tied to him, that the New York police would not communicate with the Jersey police.

He came back to Manhattan numerous times over the ensuing weeks and months and killed people, always men, *never a female*, he said, always someone who had rubbed him up the wrong way, for some imagined or real slight. He shot and stabbed and bludgeoned men to death. He left some where they dropped. He dumped some in the Hudson River.

Murder, for Richard, became sport.

The New York police came to believe that the bums were attacking and killing one another, never suspecting that a full-blown serial killer from Jersey City was coming over to Manhattan's West Side for the purpose of killing people, to practise and perfect murder.

Richard made the West Side of Manhattan a kind of lab for murder, *a school*, he said. He learned the finer points and intricacies of where to put a knife for maximum effect: in the back of the head and up into the brain; an inverted slice across the throat, cutting the carotid arteries and windpipe at the same time; directly into the heart was also very effective. But in the back of the head and into the brain, he realised, was the quickest way and much less bloody than others. That – blood – became a constant concern, for Richard did not want to get blood on himself or his clothes. With respect to a gun, a bullet to the head, just above the ear, under the jaw, proved to be the most efficient method. He hung a man one time, looped a piece of hemp across his neck, hoisted him off the ground, holding him with the rope over his shoulder. *I became the tree*, he explained. He also used an ice pick, which proved to be a good killing tool – easy to conceal – when stuck in the right place – directly into the ear, or directly into the eyeball – it was quite lethal.

Even back then, the darkened cobbled streets of Manhattan's far West Side were a gathering place for gay men. There were numerous dark bars that discreetly accommodated a homosexual clientele. One such place was Scottish Annie's, a safe haven for men who liked to wear skirts and dress as women. The bars on these dark, out-of-the-way streets were the perfect place for men to lead what often amounted to a second, hidden life.

Richard had nothing against homosexuals, he claimed, and didn't seek them out, though his steely-eyed Jimmy Stewart good looks invariably drew gay men to him, and if they were too pushy, he hurt them; indeed, he killed them. These murders had, he said, nothing to do with sex; they had to do only with someone being too pushy.

One evening, Richard was drinking in a bar near Grove Street, and a man kept coming on to him.

'Look,' Richard finally said, 'I ain't into that, OK; go somewhere else, OK?'

But the guy, a tall gentleman with a military crew cut, wouldn't take no for an answer. He was so insistent that Richard was forced to leave the bar. The guy followed him outside and propositioned him, saying, 'I know you want to. Come on, come on, big guy.' Finally, after two blocks of this, Richard saw a loose cobblestone, picked it up and struck the fellow in the head so hard that brain matter hit a shop window.

'I fuckin' told you to leave me alone,' Richard told the dead man, and walked on.

Richard came to realise that when he drank he became outright mean, and during most of these homicidal forays into Manhattan he was drinking – certainly not drunk, but definitely buzzed. He told himself that he should drink less, and beer instead of whisky. He also travelled to other places to kill people: Newark, Rhode Island and Hoboken, too. But those areas were less heavily populated, people seemed more on the lookout, nosy, so Richard kept going back to Manhattan, enjoying the hubbub of his own private killing field.

Because, for the most part, Richard was murdering 'throwaway people', bums and hobos (and occasional gay men), the New York police did little, if anything, to solve these many sudden, impromptu killings.

No one cared.

'Let 'em kill each other,' a police captain told his detectives in the Tenth Precinct. There were no stakeouts set up, no curious detectives asking questions with notebook in hand, and Richard quickly picked up on this, for he saw no extra police in the area.

THE ICE MAN

He didn't kill someone every time he went to New York. There were times he just walked around, had a drink, thought over different schemes he had in his head. With the Coming Up Roses finished and Carmine Genovese in jail on gambling charges, Richard was making far less money and was working at a menial job unloading trucks, a thing he didn't like; but he always had his eye out for a score – something he could steal and turn into cash. He had a friend in the Teamsters union, known as 'Tony Pro', who made sure he always had a job if he wanted to work. Richard still shot a lot of pool. The problem now was that just about everyone knew how good a pool shark he was, so he was hard-pressed to find anyone willing to play him for money.

Then Linda became pregnant. Richard had no feelings about the pending birth. He did not love Linda, didn't think she was a good homemaker. She was just a warm body in the bed on cold Jersey City nights, a convenient way to get his rocks off. He wanted her to get an abortion. She wouldn't. She didn't believe in abortion. He threatened her. She still wouldn't get one. Richard had no qualms about hitting Linda. He had been brought up in a household where the beating of women was the norm, and he struck Linda without a second thought if she annoyed him, which she did more and more often: she wanted to get married, he didn't; she wanted him to get a straight job and hold it, he didn't; she wanted him to stay home nights, he wanted to go out. Most of their disagreements were settled when Richard slapped her and said 'Shut up!' out of the side of his thin-lipped mouth. He even tried to make her lose the baby by punching her in the stomach; that didn't work. Her stomach became larger and larger still every week.

As cruel as Richard often was to Linda, he could be sweet and gentle, considerate to a fault. He brought her cute stuffed toys, freshly cut flowers, fancy chocolates and clothing. But the truth was that Linda never knew what he would be like when he walked in the door – kind or mean, with a present or a slap. In the end, Richard wound up marrying Linda at

City Hall. He didn't tell anyone he was getting married. He was doing it, he said, 'for the kid's sake'.

Richard had grown into a particularly moody young man who had extreme highs and lows. When he was in a bad mood – most of the time – he was outright dangerous to be around for man or beast. By now almost everyone in Jersey City and Hoboken knew about Richard Kuklinski, how dangerous he was, and they gladly gave him a wide berth; but he still got into altercations with other men, which most often ended with Richard killing them.

For Richard, murder had become an integral part of everyday life . . . just as night followed day and the tides moved in and out of the nearby Hudson River. Richard seemed to have the perfect disposition for killing people without reservation or remorse, indeed without a second thought. Richard was always careful: if he got it into his head to kill someone, *or hurt him*, as he put it, he tried to pick the time and place. Oddly enough, Richard was most dangerous when he was quiet. If someone did something to offend him and he stayed quiet, it was a good time to run for the hills. When he got angry, when murder filled his eyes, he always made that slight clicking sound out of the left side of his mouth, a trait that stayed with him throughout his life.

If I was going to hurt someone, I'd never tell him. Why let him know what your intention is? he asked later.

9

A TRIPLE PLAY

It was the middle of February 1956. Horrific cold winds came barrelling down the Hudson River from upstate New York and whipping off the Atlantic. The water in the river was choppy and rough, filled with large, sharp-edged pieces of ice the colour of nicotine-stained fingers. Richard was in a bar called Rosie's Place in Hoboken, playing eight-ball with a large, square-shouldered truck driver with a glistening bald head and hands as big as ham hocks. There were a few pool tables, a long slate bar, some wobbly tables and chairs. It was a Friday night. Considering the weather, the place was crowded, cigarette smoke hanging in the air like a thick, fallen cloud. There was a jukebox, and country music came from it. Richard kept winning. He seemed to make every shot. The bald-headed truck driver became more and more angry and started making nasty comments to his two friends at the bar, who were trying to pick up girls.

Staying quiet, Richard kept running all the balls, not missing a shot. Soon the truck driver started calling Richard 'Polack'. 'Hey, Polack, you got a rabbit's foot up your ass? Hey, Polack, how 'bout you give me a chance to shoot? Hey, Polack, where'd you get that fuckin' fag suit?'

Richard abruptly stopped playing, quietly walked over to the truck driver and without a single word smashed him on the side of the head with his pool cue, breaking the stick into pieces. The truck driver went right down. His friends at the bar stayed put. Richard started towards the door. 'Fuck you,' he said as he went. Before he knew it, however, the truck driver was up and throwing fast, furious punches at him, well-placed combinations, like a boxer. He was exceedingly strong and was beating Richard. The fight moved to a pool table. The truck driver managed to get Richard down on top of it and proceeded to pummel him. Richard grabbed an eight ball and, with all his strength, struck the guy on his bald head. Again, he went down.

Richard didn't want anything more to do with this situation – fighting for dear life in a bar over what amounted to nonsense. He left the Hoboken bar, got into a blue Chevy he had and drove towards Jersey City, licking his wounds as he went. The bald-headed truck driver was the toughest, strongest guy he'd ever gone up against, and it was all over nothing. Thinking he had to learn to control his drinking and homicidal impulses, Richard drove under a low railway bridge between Fifteenth and Sixteenth streets, where a car suddenly cut him up and forced him to a screeching stop. The truck driver jumped out of the car, red-faced with anger, followed by his friends; they were carrying pipes, storming towards Richard.

Under the seat of the car, Richard had a snub-nosed .38. He quickly grabbed it, and as the truck driver reached him, cursing, raising the length of pipe in his hand, Richard shot him square in the forehead. He went down and this time he stayed there, a finger of blood gushing in squirts from the sudden penny-sized hole in his head. Richard got out of the car and proceeded to shoot the other two dead, the report of the gunshots deafeningly loud under the cold metal bridge. Shaking his head in disbelief, Richard knew he had to move and move fast unless he wanted to go to jail. His mind raced. Quickly, he put the three bodies into the back of the bald-headed guy's car and drove it down to the frozen, bleak waterfront, only a few blocks away. He retrieved his own car, parked it near the car with the bodies, put the three of them in the boot and took off for Pennsylvania's Bucks County. He knew he had to get rid of the bodies, that they could never be found; if they were, it would be a foregone conclusion that he had killed them. He had thought about just driving the car into the river, but he was concerned it would be spotted there and the bodies would be found and, of course, linked with him.

The year before, Richard had been in Bucks County hunting deer and had come across some interesting caves in which there were apparently bottomless pits. He had made a mental note then of these endless holes in the ground as good places to get rid of a body, never imagining he'd have three corpses to dispose of. Richard had an uncanny sense of direction, and without much difficulty he managed to find the caves. One by one, he carried the bodies inside and tossed them down a gaping, ominous hole. He could hear them banging along the sides of the hole as they went down, but he didn't hear them hit the bottom. Huffing and puffing, his breath fogging in the February cold, he hurried back and forth, throwing each body in turn down the hole, amazed at how heavy a body became when life left it.

Dead weight. There really is such a thing as dead weight, he explained.

Finished, a job well done, Richard drove back to Jersey City listening to country music and resolved to stop getting into bar-room brawls, fights over nothing. But he never could. If someone, anyone, insulted him, spoke down to him or was disrespectful, Richard wanted to kill him, and often did. This would be a recurring theme that played out often and tragically in Richard's incredibly violent life.

Back in Jersey City, Richard carefully wiped his prints off the car, took off the licence plates, drove it to the edge of a pier along the Hudson where he knew the water was deep and eased it into the frigid, secret-holding, accommodating river. The car quickly disappeared. If it was found at some point without any bodies inside it, he'd have no problems. The sky was still dark, but a thick, leaden dawn was coming on quickly. The wind blew hard. Richard walked back to his car and drove home, proud of his quick thinking, proud of the fact that he had met the enemy head-on and prevailed.

He felt they had got what they deserved, and he was, in the end, glad he had killed them. The last thought before he went to sleep, the February winds whistling and rattling the windows, was: *They got what they deserved.*

Oddly enough, Richard wasn't even questioned about the disappearance of the three men. He had, it seemed, amazing luck. He'd killed them on a quiet, desolate street with few houses near by; a passing car could very well have come along, but none did. This luck would follow Richard for many years. It was almost as if he had some kind of dark, demonic archangel watching over him, keeping him safe . . . off the police radar.

There were rumours that Richard had done in the three guys, but no one ever asked him, no cops questioned him, and Richard certainly wasn't about to tell anyone what he'd done. He was tight-lipped in the extreme – another aspect of his personality that would serve him well for many years to come.

10

MURDER FOR HIRE

Carmine Genovese was out of jail and needed another man killed, though this time, he told Richard, the mark had to suffer before he died and the body had to 'disappear'.

'This guy,' Carmine said, 'did something to a friend of mine's wife. Something very disrespectful. You make sure he suffers, understand? Do it good and I'll pay you double . . . OK?'

'OK, sure, no problem,' Richard said. He did not ask what the man had done, why he had to suffer. That was irrelevant, none of his business.

Again, Carmine gave Richard a photograph of the mark, and the address of the place he worked, a used-car lot on Raymond Boulevard in Newark. In the picture, the mark was standing in the lot next to a woman who looked kind of like him.

'You do this right, I pay you very well, capisce?'

'Capisce,' Richard said.

'Maybe you can bring me a little piece a him so I can see for myself and tell my friend how he suffered.'

'A piece of him?' Richard repeated, a little confused.

'Yeah, so I can show my friend.'

'How big a piece?' Richard asked.

'Not so big. Maybe like his hand . . . some toes, OK?'

'Yeah . . . sure, OK,' Richard said. 'No problem. I aim to please.'

'Good,' Genovese said. They shook hands. The contract was sealed.

Glad Carmine was giving him another 'piece of work', Richard left his place, his mind suddenly filled with the job before him. This was, he would later reveal, the part he liked the most: the stalking of a victim. Richard instinctively knew how to do this, and he looked forward to it. Clearly, Richard had grown into a psychotic sadist, one who had discovered a way to hurt and kill people and get paid for it. Life was good.

It was a sprawling used-car lot. Colourful flags were strung across it every which way. Richard quickly found the mark. He was tall and thin and was often walking about the lot with customers. He even went on test drives with people. Before Richard made any kind of move, he surveyed the place for two days, found out when the most people were there, when the mark arrived and when he left. When Richard had a clear plan in his mind, he parked his car a few blocks away, on a quiet street lined with broken-down warehouses. There were fewer people shopping for cars about 11.00 a.m., just before lunch, and that was when Richard walked onto the lot, straight up to the mark, a friendly smile on his high-cheekboned face. It was late March. The weather had become mild. Richard wore a baggy jacket. In one pocket, he had a .38 derringer; in the other, a jawbreaker – a kind of cosh consisting of a piece of solid lead the size of a cigarette packet encased in black leather with a short, thin handle – perfect for knocking people unconscious with one blow. Smiling, Richard told the mark he needed an inexpensive car quickly, that his car had been stolen and he needed wheels for work.

'Something reliable,' he said. 'I'm not handy with engines, and I don't want to get stuck somewhere at night,' he explained, his face suddenly grave. Richard was, in fact, a consummate actor. He had a natural ability, no doubt acquired on the street, to look someone square in the eye and lie through his teeth.

'Got the perfect car for you,' the mark said, and led him over to a two-door Ford. Richard looked it over carefully, kicked the tyres.

'Can I take it for a spin?' he asked.

'Of course,' the mark said. 'Let me get the keys.' He walked into the little office on the left. Richard had set the trap; soon he'd spring it. They piled into the car. Off they went. Richard drove a few blocks, talking about how well the car handled, then headed directly towards his car. Completely unaware of what was about to happen, the mark was no doubt calculating his commission. Richard pulled up to his car and stopped, said he wanted to check under the Ford's bonnet.

'Is that OK?' he asked politely, smiling.

'Sure, no problem. Got nothing to hide here. Clean as a whistle.' The mark was caught up in the moment, having no idea about the hatchet, rope and shovel in the boot of Richard's car. Richard slid out of the Ford and opened the bonnet. The mark, of course, followed. As he was looking down at something Richard had pointed to, Richard struck him with the jawbreaker just above the ear. He went right down, out cold. In seconds, Richard put him in the boot of his car, taped his mouth shut with industrial duct tape and tied his feet and hands behind his back. Calm and cool, Richard got on the freeway and drove south to the Pine Barrens, desolate forests that were perfect for what he had in mind. This was where he had disposed of Charley Lane – the projects bully – so many years ago. Richard had already scoped out a good spot, where he hid his car behind a thick stand of pines. Here he opened the boot, dragged the panic-stricken mark from his car and tied him to one of the trees, his back tight up against it. Richard took a length of rope, forced it into the mark's mouth and tied it tightly to the rough pine tree, forcing the man's tongue up against the back of his rapidly constricting throat. The mark was crying now, trying to talk, to beg, to plead, but he made only muffled, unintelligible grunts. He seemed to know why this was happening, as if, in a way, he had expected it. At this point, Richard actually told him that he had to suffer before he died. He went back to his car and retrieved the hatchet and shovel, very much enjoying the whole thing.

He made sure the mark saw the hatchet and shovel, watched the reality of their meaning in Richard's enormous hands sink in. The man began to scream, to try to break free, but it was impossible. He wet himself, a thing Richard would see many times in years to come. Richard proceeded now to smash the mark's ankles and knees with the hatchet. Then he chopped off his fingers, one at a time. Richard stepped back to see the degree of pain the mark was suffering. He'd been planning to take the fingers back to Genovese as proof of suffering, but he suddenly got *a better idea*, as he put it . . .

When Richard had finally killed the mark, he dug a hole in the pine-needle-covered ground, threw what was left of the hapless man into it, retrieved the proof Genovese had asked for, and returned to Hoboken, carrying it in a plastic bag he'd brought along, listening to country music as he went.

He found Genovese at home.

'Did you do the job?' Genovese asked.

'Yeah, it's done,' said Richard.

'You bring me something good?' Genovese asked.

'Sure did,' Richard said, amused, placing the bag on the kitchen table. Curious, Genovese looked inside, and there was the mark's head. A big smile spread over Genovese's large, round face.

'Son of a bitch! Beautiful . . . you did good, son of a bitch,' Genovese said, realising he had found a rare man in this giant Polack. 'Very good! *Molto bravo . . . molto bravo*!' he added.

'Want me to get rid of it?' Richard asked.

'No . . . leave it here. I want to show it to my friend. Did he suffer?' asked Genovese.

'Yeah, he suffered good,' Richard said, and Genovese paid him ten thousand dollars cash on the spot for, he said, 'a good job well done'.

THE ICE MAN

The cash in his pocket making a pleasant bulge, Richard left Genovese, knowing his reputation as an efficient contract killer was assured.

11

THE ENFORCER

Richard still frequently thought about killing his father, Stanley. He'd start thinking about him, remember the brutal, callous treatment he'd meted out, get all mad inside and want to beat him to death. On several occasions, he actually went to a bar near the projects where Stanley hung out looking to put a bullet in his head, but his father wasn't there.

It was like kind of a spur-of-the-moment thing, Richard explained. *He was lucky because when I was looking for him he wasn't around. Even now, I mean sitting here and talking about him, I regret a lot not capping him – the prick . . . the sadistic prick!*

Stanley never realised how close he'd come to being killed by his second son.

Joseph, Richard's younger brother, was also extremely violent, and in frequent difficulties at school, always getting into trouble, stealing things, drinking excessively. Richard wanted to reach out to him, give him advice, put some money in his hands, but he loathed his mother so much by this time that he wouldn't even go near their apartment any more.

After being given the head of the car salesman, Carmine Genovese took a shine to Richard. Carmine had a lot of money on the street, and he began to use Richard as his chief collector and enforcer, or bagman. Had Richard been Italian, Genovese would surely have sponsored him for induction into the family, but he was Polish, so that could never happen. Still, Carmine gave him a lot of work. Richard was collecting money for him from people up and down the East Coast. He was reliable, honest and very violent when necessary – sometimes too violent. Richard was always knocking on Carmine's door with brown paper bags of money in his hand. He never stole a dime from Carmine; indeed, he never even thought about it, which only made Carmine that much more fond of him. Everyone who borrowed money from Carmine Genovese knew the ground rules out of the gate and paid it back quickly, as agreed. Not to do so, everyone also knew, could be fatal.

For the most part, Richard enjoyed working for Genovese. He made money – most of which he pissed away. People respected him and showed him deference, and his reputation as a dangerous 'mob-connected guy' spread all over Jersey. Nobody fucked with him. Even other mob guys stayed clear of Richard Kuklinski. He became known as 'the Polack'. That became his street name.

Richard took to carrying two guns and a knife whenever he went out. If he wasn't armed to the teeth, he felt naked. He was fond of over-and-under .38 derringers, double-barrelled, with the barrels one on top of the other rather than side by side. They were so small that they could readily fit in the palm of a hand, and at close range they were lethal. Richard enjoyed killing up close and personal, and to kill someone with a derringer you had to be right on top of him; that is why, he said, he also enjoyed killing with a knife.

It's intimate. You can feel the blade going in, the bones breaking, see the shock on the guy's face – watch his light go out.

When asked if he believed in God, believed that it was a sin to kill a human being, he said: *The only God I believe in is a loaded pistol with a hair trigger. Funny how before I killed a lot of guys they'd call me God. 'Oh, God, no! Oh God no!'* he said, smiling, amused by the memories.

* * *

Richard's wife, Linda, gave birth to a baby boy whom they named Richard. Richard senior felt no love for or emotional attachment to his child. He was a natural extension of a sex act – nothing more. Richard didn't even go to the hospital when Linda gave birth, nor did he help bring her home. He acted as though it were someone else's child, not his; but it didn't take long for Linda to become pregnant again.

Linda saw all of Richard's weapons but never questioned what they were for. She knew how violent and psychotic Richard could be and acted as if she were blind. She knew too that if she questioned him, demanded information, he might very well explode and hit her. In this, Richard was a carbon copy of his father – the man he hated most in the world – but he did not, never would, hit his son, or strike any of the five children he would eventually have.

Richard was, for the most part, fond of children; he saw them as put-upon innocents and became enraged when he saw an adult hitting a child. One time, he beat the hell out of a man he saw hitting his kids in a parking lot; in years to come, he'd kill a friend of his because the man asked him to murder his wife and eight-year-old son.

I don't kill women and I don't kill children. And anyone that does doesn't deserve to live, explained Richard. As cold and completely indifferent as Richard was to the suffering of men, he could not stand to see a child harmed. He also hated rapists – *tree jumpers*, he called them – and was always on the lookout for sexual predators. He viewed them as *vermin that need immediate eradication*.

Richard was still taking trips to Manhattan's West Side, where he killed anyone who got in his way, who was pushy or rude. He very much enjoyed killing aggressive beggars, usually so quickly that they didn't even realise what had happened until they hit the ground.

One night, Richard came upon two burly, leather-clad men raping a young boy behind a red 18-wheeler parked close to the Hudson. He was walking along, admiring the way the lights on the Jersey side of the river played on the water, the giant piano keys of light they made, when he heard a plaintive cry, moaning and meaty thumps. He slowly walked round behind the truck, and there he saw the rape: a boy was being forced to fellate one man while the other sodomised him. The men were laughing. They were drunk. They were now in trouble. Richard pulled out a .38 derringer and without a word shot both the rapists dead.

'Thank you, mister, thank you!' the boy said, pulling up his trousers, wiping blood from his nose.

'Get the fuck out of here,' Richard said, and proceeded to cut open the stomach cavities of the two leather-clad men, silently cursing them, before dumping them in the river. Richard knew that if the stomachs were eviscerated, gases could not build up, so the bodies would sink and stay down.

He took great pleasure in killing these two rapists.

Richard had become addicted to killing people. After he committed a murder, he felt relaxed, whole and good – at peace with himself and the world. Richard was very much like a junkie who needs a fix to soothe the pangs of addiction. Murder, for Richard Kuklinski, became like a fix of pure heroin – the best high ever. And the NYPD never suspected that a huge man of Polish extraction from Jersey City was killing the men they kept finding. There were no witnesses, no clues; no one knew anything.

Retired NYPD captain of detectives Ken Roe told me: *Back then there were no citywide records of homicides being kept, as there are today. The local precinct had a file, but that was it, and because most all these killings were of bums, people no one really gave a fuck about, there was no incentive to properly work the case. You see, because he was killing in all different ways, the cops didn't think one guy was doing it. In a sense . . . in a very real sense, they were inadvertently giving him a licence to kill. Hell of a thing.*

* * *

Richard's mentor, Carmine Genovese, had another special job for him. A man in Chicago named Anthony De Peti owed Carmine seventy thousand dollars and wasn't paying as promised, had stories instead of the money. After Carmine explained the facts of life to him, De Peti promised he'd have the money in two days, 'on Wednesday'.

'OK, I'll send Richie to come and get it,' Carmine said, and called Kuklinski.

'You go to Chicago Wednesday. This guy is going to meet you in the lounge bar in the Pan Am terminal, give you the money he owes, seventy Gs, you bring it right back, OK?'

'OK.'

'Be careful. He's slippery like a fuckin' wet eel,' Carmine told him.

Richard enjoyed going out to Newark Airport and flying to Chicago. It made him feel like a successful businessman. These days, Richard sported a Fu Manchu moustache and long sideburns that tapered off at sharp angles just above his jawline. Stern and forbidding to begin with, he looked even more scary and unsettling with the curved moustache and long, daggerlike sideburns. Already his hair was thinning on top, highlighting his high, wide brow and the severe planes of his Slavic cheekbones. He had, of course, a .32 and a knife with him, as well as one of his beloved derringers. Back then, there was no problem carrying weapons onto a plane.

Richard arrived at Chicago's sprawling, very busy O'Hare Airport, went straight to the lounge, sat down and waited for De Peti to show himself, not expecting any bloodshed. This was a simple pick-up, he thought. He sat and looked around, wondering where the hell De Peti was, becoming a little annoyed. Finally, he stood up and walked all over the lounge, making certain every man there saw him. He was hard to miss at 6 ft 5 in. and 250 lb. Nothing, no recognition from anyone. Hmm. He was about to call Carmine when a man who'd been sitting not ten feet away from him all along stood up and said, 'Rich?'

'Yeah.'

'I'm Anthony De Peti –'

'Why the hell didn't you say something? You saw me sittin' here?'

'I wanted to make sure you were alone,' De Peti said.

Richard didn't like that answer. It immediately made him suspicious. He looked at De Peti with a jaundiced eye.

'You got the money?' he asked.

'Yeah, right here,' said De Peti. He was a head shorter than Richard, though wide in the shoulders, with a long, narrow hatchet face and buckteeth. Hairs, like the antennae of an insect, protruded from his narrow nose. He handed Richard a black attaché case.

'But it's not all there,' he said.

'How much is here?' Richard asked.

'Thirty-five. Half.'

'He's not going to like that.'

'I'll have the rest in a day or two.'

'Hey, buddy, I'm here now, and you're supposed to have it all, here now. I gotta get on a plane back to Jersey soon. He ain't going to like this.'

'I swear I'll have it in a day or two.'

'Yeah, well I gotta call him. Come on,' Richard said, and led De Peti over to a nearby bank of phones. Richard got Genovese on the line. 'You find him all right?' he asked.

'Yeah, he's right here, but he don't have it all.'

'Son of a bitch. How much does he have?'

'Half, thirty-five, he says. He says he'll have the rest in a day or two. What do you want me to do?'

'Put him on the phone!'

Richard handed De Peti the phone. Smiling, De Peti explained how he'd have the money soon. 'In a day, the most, I swear,' he proclaimed, making sure Richard saw his smiling face, like all was OK, no problem here – Carmine was his friend, what the hell? He gave the phone back to Richard as flight announcements boomed from a nearby loudspeaker.

'Yeah,' said Richard, not liking De Peti. Richard had an uncanny ability to read people, like some kind of animal-in-a-jungle thing, and he did not like this guy, did not trust him.

'Rich, you stay with him, don't let him out of your sight. He says people owe him money, that he'll definitely have the money real soon.'

'All right. What do you want me to do with what he gave me?'

'You hold on to that! Don't let him out of your sight, understand?'

'Yeah,' Richard said, hanging up.

'See, I told ya,' said De Peti. 'It's all OK.'

'It'll be all OK when you give me the rest of the money,' Richard said.

With that, they left the airport, and De Peti took Richard from bar to bar, looking for various people he could never seem to find. After ten hours of this, in and out of different bars, Richard was thinking this guy was trying to give him the slip, buying time De Peti could not afford. They ended up in a crowded place on the South Side called the Say Hi Inn. It was filled with a rough clientele. They ordered drinks. De Peti went to use the phone; Richard kept an eagle eye on him and saw him talking to a big, burly guy whose face was so pockmarked it looked like gravel. Richard clearly saw something he did not like in the big man's eyes. In his right hand, in his pocket, Richard held the white-handled, chrome-plated .38 derringer. There were two hollow-nosed rounds – better known as dumdums – in the gun, bullets which spread out on contact, making horrific wounds. De Peti came back to the bar, drank some of his drink. 'He'll be here soon,' he told Richard.

'The guy with the money?' Richard asked.

'Yeah, guaranteed.'

Soon, though, Gravel Face made his way over to the bar. Purposely, he shouldered Richard, looking, Richard instinctively knew, to start a fistfight with him so De Peti could slip away. Richard slowly turned to him.

'You like your balls?' Richard asked.

'What? What da fuck?' the guy said.

'If you want to keep your nuts, get the fuck outta here,' Richard said, now showing him the mean little derringer pointed directly at his crotch, 'or I'll blow them both the fuck off here and now.'

Gravel Face turned and left. Richard turned to De Peti. 'So you're looking to play games.'

'No games – what're you talking about?'

'If I start playing games, you are going to end up very hurt. I'm losing my patience. You think I'm a fool?' Richard asked.

'He'll be here with the dough,' De Peti said.

But nobody showed up. The bar was closing. Finally, De Peti said they should rent a room in a nearby hotel, that he'd definitely have the money 'in the morning'.

'In the morning?' Richard repeated.

'I swear.'

Reluctantly, Richard called Genovese, who said it was OK to wait. They checked into a nearby hotel. Richard washed up and, tired, lay down on one of the two beds, as did De Peti. But Richard was wary, and sleep did not come easily. He didn't know how long he'd been lying there, but he sensed, in his half-asleep state, movement near by. He opened his eyes. As they adjusted to the dark, he could just discern De Peti skulking through the room, moving towards him, past him and to the window. De Peti slid it open and began to creep, snakelike, out onto the fire escape. In two swift movements, Richard was up, grabbed him and yanked him back into the room, where he pummelled him. Richard moved shockingly fast for such a big man, which caught many people off guard. Richard turned on the light.

'You slimy motherfucker, you been playing me all along.' Richard kicked him so hard he moved across the floor. Oh, how Richard wanted to kill him, shoot him in the head and throw him out the window; but those luxuries were not his, he knew. This guy owed Carmine a lot of money, and Richard couldn't just go killing him. Instead, Richard called Carmine in Hoboken.

'The fuckin' asshole tried to fly,' he said. 'I caught him sneaking out on the fire escape.'

'Son of a bitch. Put him on'a da phone!'

Blood running from his mouth, De Peti told Carmine that he was only looking to get some fresh air, not escape . . . certainly not trying to get away. 'I swear, I swear on my mother!' he cried, histrionically holding his hand over his heart for maximum effect.

'Where's the money?' Carmine demanded.

'Tomorrow, tomorrow, I swear!' De Peti pleaded.

Richard got back on the phone. Carmine said, 'Give 'im until tomorrow. He don't come up with the money, throw him out a window with no fuckin' fire escape, OK?'

'OK,' Richard said. 'Gladly.'

The next day, it was the same story, running around different bars and lounges, looking for various people who had the money. It was as if, Richard was thinking, De Peti was playing a shell game, a three-card monte shuffle. Again, De Peti went to use a phone. There was a door near the phone, and Richard could see De Peti eyeing it. He hung up, came back, said they had to go to a pizza place. They waited there an hour, then went to two more bars.

Richard was tired of De Peti's bull. 'He'll be here, he'll be here,' he kept telling Richard, and no one showed up.

Pissed off, Richard took De Peti back to the hotel and, without another word, hung him by his feet out of the window. Begging, De Peti now said he'd get him 'all the money', that it was in a place he owned over on the South Side.

'You lying to me, I'll kill you on the spot,' Richard promised.

'I ain't lying! I ain't lying!' he pleaded, cars and trucks and buses moving on the wide avenue ten storeys below.

Richard pulled him inside. 'Let's go.'

It was a kind of go-go place. Half-naked girls who had seen better days danced around, wiggling their breasts and shaking their ample asses in Day-Glo red lights. De Peti took Richard straight to a rear office, opened a safe hidden in a cupboard wall, grabbed a pile of notes, and gave him the thirty-five Gs.

'My God, if you had the money all the time, why didn't you just give it to me?' Richard asked, really annoyed now, anger rising in him.

'Because I didn't want to pay,' De Peti admitted sheepishly.

That made Richard see red; his balls, as he described it, were all twisted already, and this was the straw that broke the camel's back.

'Really?' he said, smiling slightly, making the soft clicking sound out of the side of his mouth.

'Let me get one of the girls in here to clean your pipes out,' De Peti offered.

'Naw, that's OK,' Richard said.

After counting the money, Richard suddenly pressed the little .38 derringer hard to De Peti's chest and pulled the trigger. Boom. The report of the gun was muffled by De Peti's chest and drowned out by the music coming from the club.

With a horrific hole in his chest, De Peti hit the ground hard and was soon as dead as a doorknob.

Calmly, Richard left the club, hailed a cab a block away, went to the airport and caught a flight back to Newark. As soon as he hit the ground, he went to see Carmine Genovese.

'And what happened?' Carmine asked as he opened the door.

'I got two things to tell you.'

'Yeah?'

'First, I got the money – all of it. Second, I killed him. All he did was play me,' Richard said, not sure if Carmine would get mad. After all, he had killed a customer of Carmine's after getting all that was due.

'Good, bravo. We can't be letting these fuckin' assholes

play us for fools. That gets around on the street, we're out of business. You did the right thing,' Carmine said, patting Richard on his enormous back. 'You're a good man, Richie. Mamma mia, I wish you were Italian. I'd sponsor you in a fuckin' minute, in a fuckin' minute,' he said, and paid Richard well.

Carmine, a very rich man, tended – like most Mafia men – to be cheap and greedy. For them, nothing was ever enough.

Content, Richard soon left.

Back in Chicago, one of De Peti's strippers discovered his body. The police were summoned. They questioned everyone in the club and got a vague description of a big man seen leaving the office.

Another unsolved homicide.

12

MOB GUYS AND CROOKED COPS

His name was Jim O'Brien. He was a large, burly, red-faced Irishman, a former police captain out of Hoboken. He was as crooked as a figure-eight pretzel, worked intimately with the De Cavalcante crime family. He'd do anything to turn a buck: pimp women, deal drugs, sell hot merchandise. He, like just about everyone in New Jersey crime circles, knew about Richard Kuklinski, knew how reliable he was, that he was the best bagman in Jersey, how ruthless he could be if and when the job called for violence. O'Brien approached Richard in a Hoboken bar and asked him if he'd pick up a suitcase for him in Los Angeles.

'You interested?' O'Brien asked.

'Sure, if the price is worth my time,' said Richard. He did not usually like cops, crooked or otherwise. He felt they could not be trusted, that they were bullies with badges and guns, but he knew O'Brien worked with the family he was associated with.

O'Brien said, 'It'll take you no longer than a day, and I'll pay you five large and all expenses.'

'Sure, I'll go,' Richard said, and the next morning he was in the first-class section of an American Airlines flight to LA. Richard very much enjoyed travelling first class. It made him feel successful, as if he'd made a notable step up in the world.

Amused, he looked at the other men in the section, knowing they were all civilians, thinking how surprised they'd be if they knew what he really did – that he regularly killed people and enjoyed doing it. Smiling stewards served him a lovely lunch and free drinks, and he soon fell asleep.

Richard took a cab from LAX straight to a fancy hotel on the famous Sunset Boulevard. He checked in under a false name, went upstairs to his room and was admiring the sweeping view of LA when there was a soft knock on the door. He opened it. Two of the shiftiest-looking men he'd ever seen, one resembling a rat, the other a ferret, stood there. 'You Rich?' Rat Face asked.

'I am. Come on in.'

They walked into the room, Ferret Face carrying a suitcase.

'That for me?' Richard asked, friendly enough, but not liking either of these men.

'Yeah, that's for you,' Ferret Face said. 'You got any ID?'

'Do you have any ID?' Richard asked.

'No.'

'Then why should I?' Richard wanted to know.

They all stared at one another. Uncomfortable seconds slipped by. Richard reached inside his jacket and pulled out a short-barrelled pistol.

'This is my ID. It's called .357,' Richard said. 'And in this pocket, I've got some more ID – it's called .38,' he added, showing them both his guns, all solemn-faced, staring at them, deadpan.

'OK,' Rat Face said, and he took the black case from Ferret Face and handed it to Richard; the two men soon left. Good riddance. Richard did not even try to see what was in the suitcase. It was none of his business. His business was getting it safely back to O'Brien in Hoboken. He had a nice lunch in the hotel restaurant, thought he saw John Wayne with some pretty women wearing very short dresses and was soon on his way back to LAX.

In those days, there was no screening for drugs or weapons, and Richard was able to walk onto the plane without being questioned or challenged. He made it back to Hoboken without incident, delivered the suitcase, was paid and, as far as Richard was concerned, it was a done deal.

However, some weeks later he found out that there had been a kilo of heroin in the suitcase. He was furious. If he had been busted with it, he'd have gone to jail, no doubt for a long time. He kept his anger to himself, but when the right time came he did get even with O'Brien. He killed him by shooting him in the head and got rid of his body in South Jersey, not far from the car salesman whose head he had given to Genovese. And no one had any idea that O'Brien was done in for manipulating Richard Kuklinski, putting his life on the line without doing him the courtesy even of telling him. Richard, of course, didn't say a word about what he'd done . . . not even to his mentor Carmine Genovese. The way Richard saw it, a crooked cop had got exactly what he deserved, and he was only too happy to serve it up.

An unusual piece of work now came Richard's way. A mob boss named Arthur De Gillio had to go. He was stealing from his boss, the head of the family, and a death warrant was issued. Carmine tapped Richard to do the job, called him to his home, solemnly sat him down, said: 'This here is the most important piece of work I've given you. This guy is a boss. He's gotta die. You are doing the job. There's a special requirement with this job: you need to take his credit cards, you understand, and after you kill him, you stuff the credit cards up his ass.'

'You're kidding,' said Richard.

'No. That's the way it has to be. That's what the skipper wants. And before you kill him, make him suffer and make sure he knows why he's dying and what you're gonna do,' Carmine said, his meatball-shaped face all serious.

'You're kidding,' Richard repeated.

'I look like I'm kiddin'?'

'No.'

'And so?'

'OK, no problem,' Richard said, thinking these Italians were a crazy lot, had all kinds of nutty rules and regulations. But his job was not to question the ways of the Mafia; his job was to carry out orders. End of story.

'This will be tricky – and dangerous. He always has bodyguards around,' Genovese said, and gave Richard the mark's home and business addresses. 'You do this job good, it'll be a big feather in your cap, OK?'

'OK.'

'Don't hurry it. Do it right. Take'a your time. Make sure no one recognises you. If they do, it'll come right back to me. You understand?'

'I understand.'

'You cap anyone that gets in your way – no matter who.'

'OK,' Richard said, and soon left.

This, he knew, was a very important piece of work, and he felt honoured to be given it; he was moving up in the world. It would put him at the front of the line. It was like an actor being given the role of his life. It was a part that would surely make him a star, a bright light in the galaxy of organised crime.

Richard plotted this murder meticulously for ten days. As Carmine had said, De Gillio always had bodyguards around, but he had a girlfriend in the nearby town of Montclair, and when he went there, every few days, he did so with only a driver/gofer, a skinny kid who was his nephew. The girlfriend lived in a quiet, two-storey yellow building with a parking lot off to the left. The nephew waited outside, in a quiet corner of the parking lot near a wooden fence, as De Gillio, a heavy-set man who had a large belly and short bandy legs, went inside, did the job with his girlfriend and came out. He wasn't inside more than an hour – an afternoon quickie. On the day Richard planned to move, he trailed De Gillio to the Montclair apartment. De Gillio got out of the car and waddled inside.

Richard waited 15 minutes, walked up to the nephew and without a word shot him in the side of the head with a .22 to which was attached a suppressor, better known as a silencer. The small-calibre bullet instantly made mush of the driver's brain, and he was dead before he even knew he'd been shot.

Casually, slowly, Richard walked back to his car, got in, pulled up near De Gillio's car, opened his boot and began to change his tyre, moving slowly, taking his time, not drawing any suspicion to himself, just another guy with a flat in a mostly empty parking lot. Almost like clockwork, De Gillio came waddling out of the house, ape-like, not taking any particular notice of the guy with a flat. When he reached his car, however, his face creased with anger because he thought his nephew had fallen asleep. Richard began walking towards him. As Richard neared De Gillio, he pulled out the .22 with the silencer, an assassin's weapon that immediately stopped De Gillio in his tracks.

'Are you fuckin' kiddin' me here?!' De Gillio demanded. 'You know who da fuck I am?'

'Yeah, I know who you are. You're the guy who's coming with me.'

And with that, Richard discreetly but firmly pressed the .22 up against De Gillio's stomach, took him by the arm and led him towards his car. 'Someone wants to talk to you,' Richard said.

'Yeah, who?'

'A friend.'

'A friend? You're fucking dead! You and your friend are dead!'

Richard's answer was to push the .22 into De Gillio's chest, hard. He pulled back the hammer. De Gillio's face paled. Richard led him to the rear of his car; the boot was already open. Before De Gillio knew it, Richard had pushed him inside. At this point, he tried to resist. Richard cracked him in the head with his jawbreaker, knocking him out cold. He cuffed De Gillio's hands behind his back, put duct tape across his mouth, closed the boot and drove to a desolate area in Jersey City, down by the water.

Here, Richard calmly got out of the car, pulled De Gillio from the boot and laid him on the ground. Richard took a bat from the boot and without preamble beat De Gillio in the legs, breaking bones every time he struck, saying, 'This is happening because you stole from your boss. This is happening because you're a greedy fucking pig.' He smashed De Gillio with terrific force, now in the arms, the elbows, the shoulders, the collar bone. Richard then went to work on his chest and broke his ribs.

Next, he slipped on a pair of blue surgical gloves, took De Gillio's wallet, pocketed the cash he had, found his credit cards and said: 'They want me to stick these up your ass. You believe that? I still don't believe it myself. Fuckin' Italians are crazy.' De Gillio's eyes were bulging with fear and pain; he tried to plead with Richard, offer him money, all the money he had, but the duct tape held. Richard was deaf to his mumbled entreaties.

'Say goodbye to the world,' Richard said, and struck De Gillio square in the head, smashing his skull, destroying his brain – finally killing him.

Richard viciously pulled down De Gillio's trousers and underwear and rammed the credit cards where the sun don't shine. He rolled De Gillio up in plastic sheeting, took him to nearby Bayonne and left him in an abandoned lot down by the water, there for all the world to see.

Finished, Richard went to see Carmine and told him exactly what had been done.

'You're a good man, the best!' exclaimed Genovese, patting Richard warmly on the back and paying him handsomely. When De Gillio was discovered, the police were summoned, but there were no witnesses and no connection to Richard – another organised-crime killing, nothing new in Jersey City, Hoboken or Bayonne.

* * *

Richard's reputation as an efficient, cold-blooded killer spread. He began taking pieces of work from men in different Mafia families, not only the Ponti and De Cavalcante Jersey families, but New York crime families as well. Because he hadn't been 'made', he was able to work as a *giovane d'honore*, an independent contractor, without trouble. He carefully planned each hit and scrupulously followed instructions.

If, he explained much later, *they wanted a guy tortured, I did that; if they wanted a mark to disappear, I did that. I got to really enjoy the planning and the hunt; it was kind of like . . . a science.*

Most of the money Richard earned he still lost gambling. His pockets would be bulging with hundred-dollar bills, then he'd get into a few high-stakes card games and lose it all. Easy come, easy go. That was his attitude. One time, in a card game in Hoboken, he not only lost all the cash he had, he also lost his car and actually had to take a bus back home.

13

INDEPENDENT CONTRACTOR

Linda gave birth to a second male child, and they named him David. Richard was still completely indifferent to his sons. He viewed them as though they were someone else's kids. The relationship with Linda had become more and more strained, and they weren't even having intimate relations any more. Richard gave her some money now and then, but that was the sum of it.

However, he was protective of Linda and the boys in the extreme. He viewed them as his personal property – her especially – and became enraged if anyone abused or took advantage of either Linda or his sons.

In the low-income housing complex where Linda and the boys lived, there was a superintendent who was sweet on her and kept making overtures to her, which became more and more bold. She continued to ignore him. After a time, he became abusive, loud, vulgar. She wanted to tell Richard but didn't want any trouble. She knew he had a fiery, hair-trigger temper, that he could be extremely violent and had all kinds of guns and knives and terrible weapons, so she kept quiet about the abusive superintendent.

But, one day, the superintendent slapped both of Linda's children, claiming they were making too much noise. This was too much for her to bear, and she called Richard at a bar he hung out in, the Final Round in Hoboken. When Richard heard that the super had slapped his kids, he slammed down the phone, jumped in his car and sped to the house. His sons confirmed that the super had hit them for playing in the hall. Richard went looking for him with violence on his mind, planning to kill him and dump his body somewhere no one would ever find it. More and more, this would become one of Richard's noted specialities: getting rid of bodies.

The super, he soon found out, was in a bar that Richard sometimes went to just across the street. It was nearly 4.30 in the afternoon, and the bar was crowded with men having a drink after work before they went home to their families or to empty apartments. His lips twisted to the left, and, making that soft clicking sound through his clenched teeth, Richard opened the door and walked in. The smells of whisky, cigarettes and hard-working men drinking hard liquor greeted him. He spotted the superintendent standing at the bar. He was a large man with a chip on his shoulder – a bully – the kind of man Richard hated most.

Calmly, Richard walked up to him. 'What right you got hitting my kids?'

'They wouldn't shut up –' the super began, but before he could finish, Richard hit him so hard he seemed to fly across the room as if in a cartoon. Richard went after him and beat him to a bloody pulp. The bartender, Richard knew, was a moonlighting cop, but he didn't care. As Richard was making his way to the door, the bartender showed him his badge and demanded to see his ID. Richard answered him with a vicious roundhouse right that knocked him out cold. Richard would surely have killed the super right then and there if there hadn't been so many witnesses.

It didn't take long before angry-faced detectives came looking for Richard because he had punched out the bartender cop. Richard went to Carmine Genovese and told him what had happened, Genovese reached out to some friends in the police department and Richard had to pay three thousand dollars for the matter to be over and done with. The super was in the hospital for three weeks with a broken cheekbone and jaw. Upon release, he quit his job and hightailed it the hell out of Jersey City. Smart move. Richard had planned to kill him.

Some months later, Richard was leaving the Final Round when his brother Joe called to him from across the street.

Joe, like Richard, was now nearly 6 ft 5 in., blond and handsome.

'Hey, Rich!'

'How you doing, Joe?'

'Same old same old.'

'What's up?'

'Rich . . . I have . . . I have something to tell you.'

'About Ma?'

'No . . . Linda.'

'Linda? What?'

Joe stared at his brother. He, like everyone in Jersey, knew Richard was always armed, always dangerous. 'I don't know how to say this,' Joe began.

'Say what?'

'Rich, I saw Linda and Sammy James go into a room at the Hudson Hotel.'

'What?' Richard demanded, his voice rising, his face flushing strawberry red.

'Don't go getting mad at me, Rich. I just thought you should know.'

'What room? You know?'

'Yeah, number 16, on the ground floor, just near the Coke machine.'

'Thanks, Joe,' Richard said, and he jumped into his car and sped over to the Hudson Hotel.

True, Richard and Linda were more or less estranged at this point, but Richard still thought of her as his wife – and his property. He pulled into the parking lot of the hotel, which was in a secluded area near the river. It was a place where people went to have sex, for the most part. Richard knew Sammy James. They had played pool as partners. Richard stormed up to number 16 and smashed the door wide open with his enormous right foot.

There they were, both naked, in bed, actually having intercourse. Linda's eyes nearly popped out of her shocked face. Richard grabbed James, a tall, muscular guy with curly black hair, and pummelled him. Linda, in shock, looked on.

'You treacherous bastard!' Richard told James. 'I'm going to break every bone in your body but one, and you go near her again, I'll find out and break that bone.'

He proceeded to methodically smash and break almost every bone in James's body but the femur of his left leg, repeatedly getting onto the bed and jumping from it onto him, kicking him, stomping him, punching him.

Finished with James, Richard turned his wrath on Linda, drawing out a knife.

'If you weren't the mother of my sons,' he said, 'I'd kill you. But now I'm just going to teach you a lesson you will never forget.' He grabbed for her left breast. She tried to resist him. He slapped her unconscious, grabbed her breast, and cut off the nipple. He then did the same thing to her other breast and left her there like that, storming out of the room like a hurricane.

From that day on Richard had little to do with Linda. He'd see his boys now and then, but that was it. James left town and never came back to Jersey City.

Philip Marable was a captain in the Genovese crime family. He owned a popular Italian restaurant in Hoboken and lived in nearby Bloomfield. The name of the restaurant was Bella Luna. They served good southern Italian food at reasonable prices. There were yellow oilcloths on the tables and candles in empty wine bottles covered with different-coloured wax.

Marable was a good dresser, always perfectly coiffed, handsome with thick black hair and dark menacing eyes . . . a dandy. He reached out to Richard and had him come to the restaurant, greeted him warmly, sat him down, insisted he eat a good meal. Richard kept wondering what he wanted. After they'd finished eating and were drinking anisette-infused espresso, Marable said, 'You know George West, don't you?'

'Sure,' Richard said.

'We have a problem with this guy. He's been holding up my runners [people who collect bets on the numbers racket], and I don't want him around no more,' Marable explained.

'Could be arranged,' Richard said.

'Make sure a message is sent – understand – that this kinda shit can't be goin' on, OK?'

'I understand,' Richard said, pleased, seeing his career horizons broadening.

At that, Marable adroitly slipped a white envelope across the table, as if it were a practised trick. The envelope was filled with cash. Richard pocketed it. Dinner was over. Richard knew that Marable giving him a piece of work was a good opportunity, and he immediately went looking for George West. He searched high and low but couldn't find him. He staked out his house and the bars he frequented but kept missing him. Richard was determined, however, to fill the contract quickly and successfully, and he continued to look for West, like a shark following the scent of blood. Under the front seat of his car, Richard had a sawn-off .22 Magnum rifle with a silencer and a 30-clip magazine. It was a vicious little weapon, an assassin's tool, easy to carry, easy to conceal – deadly. Richard had an unlimited, convenient supply of weapons. He knew a guy named Robert (known as 'Motorboat' because his ears stuck out), who sold all kinds of guns out of the boot of his car, new guns still in boxes. Richard never killed two people with the same weapon. As soon as he used one in a killing, he got rid of it. This habit would serve him well for many years to come, for it kept his activities off the police radar. He would also purposely shoot a person to death with two different-calibre weapons, so it would appear as if there had been two shooters. Motorboat the gun salesman had a big old Lincoln Continental with a huge boot filled with handguns, rifles and silencers. He was a tall, skinny guy with thick rose-coloured glasses. He was also a mechanic and made suppressors for nearly all the guns he sold. When in need, all Richard had to do was call Motorboat, and he'd come around with his wide-ass Lincoln. Richard even bought hand grenades from him. The sawn-off .22 he was going to use on George West he'd got from Motorboat.

For nine days, Richard couldn't find West, no matter how hard he searched for him, yet he knew he was in town because people had seen him. It was the end of April 1958, and it rained just about every day.

By chance, as Richard was driving away from a bar in Bayonne where he'd picked up money for Carmine Genovese, he passed an old-fashioned silver boxcar diner a little way down the road, and George West was sitting there plain as day eating a sandwich. Not believing this bit of luck, Richard nearly hit the car in front of him, he was staring at West so hard. He made a U-turn and pulled into a parking lot next to the diner, found West's car and positioned his own so he'd have a clear shot. It was raining hard. Richard liked to kill in the rain. There were fewer people about. Everyone was in a hurry, not paying attention to anything but where they were going.

Soon, West left the diner and made his way to his car, using a toothpick as he went. Richard calmly took a bead on him, pulled the trigger of the semi-automatic .22 and in two seconds shot West numerous times. Because of the silencer, the gun made only a soft popping sound, *like a ladyfinger firecracker going off*, Richard explained. Wanting to be sure West was dead, Richard calmly got out of his car and walked over to him. No one noticed Richard. No one cared. West was still alive. Blood was squirting from a penny-sized bullet hole in his neck. Richard made sure he was unobserved, put two slugs in West's head, walked back to his car and returned to Jersey City. He would've liked to torture West a bit, that had been the directive, but circumstances hadn't permitted such a luxury. It had taken him nine days to find West, and he hadn't wanted to give him a chance to get away. Richard did not tell Marable of the hit, how it had happened. He'd find out soon enough, Richard knew; indeed, it was bad form to talk about a murder after it was ordered and had gone down.

Marable liked what Richard had done and gave him several more contracts over the next year. One was a man who owed Marable over fifty thousand dollars in gambling debts but refused to pay, was bragging to people all over Jersey that he wasn't going to pay, that he wasn't afraid of Marable – 'Fuck him!' Richard gave this guy a flat and, as he was changing the tyre, crept up on him and struck him in the head with an L-shaped tyre iron so hard he actually opened up the skull and the mark's brain splashed all over the car and onto Richard's trousers. Bummer.

Richard soon began to carry a change of clothes with him at all times because murdering people, he came to know, could be a messy business. The next hit for Philip Marable was a man who owned a boat in Edgewater, New Jersey. Richard didn't know why the guy had to die. He didn't care; that was not his business. However, he had known the mark for a few years and didn't like anything about him, thought of him as a loudmouth braggart. On the evening Richard went to see him, it was the middle of July, a hot, humid night. The boat was moored at a quiet marina, and Richard parked in the dirt lot and found the boat, a small blue-and-white cabin cruiser, in a slipway at the end of the dock. It was 11.00 p.m. Richard could see in the little porthole windows of the boat, and there was the mark, having sex with a young woman, not his wife, Richard knew. He could easily have sneaked up on them, but he did not want to hurt the girl, so he went back to his car and waited for the mark to finish. He sat there for three hours, thinking, *You better enjoy it because it's the last piece of ass you'll ever have.*

By 2.00 a.m. Richard was beginning to think she'd sleep there, but at 2.30 she walked off the boat and got into a red car, and off she went. Immediately, Richard got out of his car and walked to the boat, a .38 with a suppressor he had bought from Motorboat in his pocket. Catlike, silently, as deadly as a puff of cyanide gas, Richard stepped onto the boat, walked to the cabin and inside, the gun in his hand. When the mark saw him, big and mean and deadly serious, he was so stunned he nearly fell over.

'What da fuck?' he demanded.

'You've made some enemies,' Richard said. 'How do you want it, quick or slow?' he asked, subtly tormenting the mark.

'Please, man, I got kids, a wife –'

'That your wife that just left?' Richard asked.

'No, my *gomatta*. Please, Rich, I got money, I'll give it all to you, please, Richie, please . . . you know me, I –'

'My friend,' Richard calmly told him, 'when you see me, it's the end of the line. I'm the grim reaper, my friend.' A nasty, sardonic smile played on his stone-cold face.

'Please, no, please,' the mark begged, now getting down on his knees, his hands in a twisted knot as if he were fervently praying.

'I'll do you a favour,' Richard said.

'What?'

'I'll kill you quickly.' And with that, Richard shot him in the forehead, just above the ridge of his nose. A finger of blood came squirting out of the sudden hole. Richard waited for the blood to stop, for the mark's heart to cease. When that happened, he dragged the corpse, careful not to step in the blood, onto the deck and threw it in the water, cursing the man silently. He then walked back to his car.

Off in the distance, out at sea, a thunderstorm started up, and for a while Richard sat in his car and watched giant lightning bolts dance madly across an ominous velvet-black sky, knowing fish and crabs would eat the mark piece by piece.

He was lucky I didn't torture him. I was in . . . a good mood, I guess, he thought.

14

TOUGH AND ROUGH
AND READY TO GO

It was 1959. Richard was 24 years old and had acquired a serious drinking problem; he often got drunk, became nasty and belligerent – just like his father – and inevitably got into fights, which all too often ended in a spur-of-the-moment murder.

He was in a bar called the Pelican Lounge in Union City, New Jersey, drinking boilermakers. He had words with another man at the bar, and the guy hauled himself off his stool and slugged Richard. Before Richard could do anything, though, the bartender, a guy Richard knew, asked him to 'take it outside'.

'Come on,' Richard encouraged the man. As they made their way onto the sidewalk, Richard took hold of his hunting knife, secreted in his coat pocket, and just as they reached the sidewalk, he turned quickly and in one swift movement, like the strike of a rattlesnake, brought up the blade and stuck it directly into the man's throat, at an upward angle, the blade immediately entering his brain.

Dead, he hit the ground.

Calmly, Richard walked off. When the police came around asking questions, no one knew anything.

On another occasion, Richard was in the Orchid Bar, also in Union City, drunk and a bit rowdy. A huge, burly bouncer made him leave, pushed him outside, which Richard accepted, but the bouncer kicked him in the ass as he went; this outraged him. Knowing, however, that he was too drunk to defend himself properly, he vowed to return. The bouncer spat at him – his second mistake. Richard didn't like bouncers. Most of them, he felt, were bullies: Richard despised bullies. Richard was, in fact, a slayer of bullies.

Two days later, Richard was back, sober, deadly – murder on his mind. He waited in his car for the bar to close, the bouncer to leave, which he did. Richard stepped from his car, carrying a hammer. He followed the bouncer, who got into his car and started it up. Richard approached. 'Hey, big guy, remember me?' he asked.

'What da fuck you want?' snarled the bouncer.

In the blink of an eye, Richard swung the hammer and struck him in the side of the head so hard that the hammer entered his skull. Richard hit him again, again and again. When he finished, the bouncer was dead – destroyed, unrecognisable. Now Richard spat on him and walked away.

No matter how much money Richard made, he was often broke, for he was a chronic, degenerate gambler and most often lost. He also tended to gamble when he was drinking, which only compounded his losing and his problems.

He wasn't happy with his life, with where it was going. Essentially, Richard had come to hate the world and nearly everyone in it. He viewed the world as a mean, hostile jungle crowded with dangerous creatures, a dog-eat-dog place filled with brutal iniquities. He did, however, realise that his drinking and gambling were becoming a problem, though he didn't know how to stop either one. In the circles Richard was moving in, everyone drank and everyone gambled, everyone hustled, everyone lied and cheated and stole. He trusted no one; at the drop of a hat he'd kill. For him, it was a simple equation: kill or be killed, eat or be eaten.

Unsettling rumours about Richard's younger brother were circulating. He kept hearing these stories – that Joseph was taking drugs, that Joseph was gay – and became disturbed. Richard viewed drugs as a one-way trip to nowhere, an early grave.

He heard that Joseph was hanging out in a gay bar called Another Way in Guttenberg, New Jersey.

How could that be? he wondered. He'd seen Joseph with girls on numerous occasions. The thought of this, that his brother was gay, *a fag*, was for him unsettling. Not believing such a thing, wanting to see it with his own eyes, Richard went to the bar on a Friday night. The place was crowded with men and boys who openly showed affection to one another, and there was Joseph, kissing a man dressed as a woman. Richard's face reddened at the sight. He ordered a beer with no glass, not even wanting to drink from a glass in that place. *Back then*, Richard would later say, *there was a big stigma associated with, you know, being homosexual, and I wasn't at all at ease in this joint, where men were kissing and holding hands right out in the open. Probably my own shortcoming, but I couldn't help it; I didn't know any better. I mean, I know people don't really have much say over that, their sexuality . . . but still.*

When Richard looked up, Joe and his friend were suddenly gone. Where had he disappeared to so quickly? Richard looked all over the place but couldn't find Joseph. He wanted to talk to him, tell him he was doing the wrong thing. He went to the bathroom and saw under the toilet stall door that two people were inside. He heard his brother's voice. His stomach turned at the thought of what he was doing. A strange kind of rage came welling up inside him. He kicked open the locked door and there was his brother, performing fellatio on the other guy – an infamy right there before his eyes.

Shocked, Joseph stood. Before he could say anything, Richard struck him and knocked him down to the floor, out cold. He also hit the transvestite, knocking him out, too. Oh, how he wanted to commit more violence, break bones, draw blood; but instead Richard turned and left, his mind reeling with the implications, enraged.

TOUGH AND ROUGH AND READY TO GO

Like some kind of wounded animal, he went back to Hoboken, to the Ringside Inn, in a foul mood. He walked up to the bar and began drinking. He made a rule of never getting drunk here. This was his home base, his regular hangout, and he was afraid he'd hurt someone – maybe kill someone – and not be able to come back, as had happened in numerous drinking establishments.

The Ringside Inn was owned by a cantankerous, tough woman, *ugly as sin*, according to Richard. Her name was Sylvia and she looked like a chimpanzee who'd been struck in the face with the ugly stick a few times. One eye was bigger than the other; her nose was flat like a pancake with two holes – her nostrils. Her face was framed by wiry tendrils of frizzy bleached-blond hair. Sylvia liked Richard because he was handsome and he played high-stakes pool games in her place, which brought in business. Men – and some women – came from all over the East Coast to play pool with Richard for as much as two hundred dollars a ball.

Rather than get into trouble in there, Richard left and found his way to Manhattan's West Side, where he murdered a man for asking him for a light in a belligerent tone.

After the incident in the gay bar, Richard and Joseph did not talk again for several years.

Richard had a long-running streak of bad luck: he lost most of the pool games he was in; he lost at all kinds of bets he made, on football and baseball, on which roach would climb up onto the wall of Sylvia's place first. And he kept drinking more and more.

Angry, Richard made more trips to New York, back to the West Side, where he expressed his rage, where he continued to kill people to vent his hatred for the world. When asked shortly before his death how many men he killed on Manhattan's far West Side, Richard said, deadpan, *All the fingers on both your hands five times.*

I swear, if someone just looked at me the wrong way, I killed 'im, he explained.

And still the NYPD did little to find out who was committing all these murders under the rusting, noisy, antiquated West Side Highway. Because Richard killed in dark shadows in so many different ways, with different-calibre guns, with clubs, bricks and bats, knives and rope and ice picks, the NYPD never thought it was one man; that Richard Kuklinski of Jersey City had created his own personal killing field; that he was stalking and killing human beings as if the West Side were his private hunting reserve. Richard was, of course, deliberately murdering in many different ways, believing that this would confuse and misdirect the police, and he was right. Dead right.

Spurred on by the inner demons that plagued him, the growing, raging psychosis inside him, Richard was hitting bottom. He kept hoping a nice score would come his way, a profitable murder contract, a lucrative hijacking, but business was slow.

Carmine Genovese had been murdered, shot in the head as he was cooking in his kitchen: another unsolved mob hit. Richard had nothing to do with it. He liked Carmine, as much as he could care for anyone. He did not go to Carmine's funeral. He knew the cops would have it staked out, so he stayed away.

Life held little promise for Richard . . .

Richard's friend in the Teamsters union, Tony Pro, managed to get Richard a plum job at the Swiftline Trucking Company in North Bergen. The money was good, the work not that difficult. But still Richard didn't like it. He hated it, in fact. It was a straight job, a thing he always tried to avoid. He was a player, a hustler, an assassin. What the fuck was he doing here? He resigned himself, however, to keeping the job and keeping his eye out for a good load to steal: televisions, jeans, anything he could sell quickly for cash, which, no doubt, he would only gamble away. His plan was to turn this straight job into a way he could make a score by setting up specific trucks to be hijacked.

It was the spring of 1961. Richard Kuklinski was 26 years old and going nowhere fast. He had, by his own account, killed more than 65 men.

It was now that Richard met Barbara Pedrici and everything suddenly changed. The world he had known became a very different place.

PART II

BARBARA

15

BAMBI MEETS
THE ICE MAN

Barbara Pedrici was a tall, curvaceous 18-year-old Italian American with black hair, intense hazel-coloured eyes and a perfectly formed aquiline nose. She was 5 ft 10 in. in her stocking feet, comfortable in her own skin, with a natural air of affluence and superiority about her.

Barbara's father had come to New Jersey from the northern Italian city of Venice; her mother's family hailed from the lovely port city of Naples. Barbara had recently graduated from high school and was not quite sure what she wanted to do with herself. She toyed with the idea of going to college to pursue a career as an artist, but her mother thought that 'a waste of time' and wanted Barbara to get a job, find a man, get married and have children. She even offered to buy her a car if she did not attend college. Barbara refused.

Barbara and her mother did not get along well. Barbara was an only child; her parents had divorced when she was two years old. She was brought up by Nana Carmella (her mother's mother) and her mother's sister Sadie, both of whom doted on Barbara, giving her what she wanted, when she wanted it. Thus Barbara had become a bit spoiled. Early on in life, she learned that if she wanted something, she got it. Nothing was ever denied her. All she had to do was ask, and keep asking, until it was hers.

THE ICE MAN

Barbara's mother, Genevieve, was a cold, austere woman, *a stick-in-the-mud*, as Barbara would later describe her. Genevieve rarely smiled, didn't show much affection. She worked hard as a seamstress in a factory in North Bergen and never seemed to have time or a kind word for her only child. It was as if she had never really wanted a child, as if her daughter was an inconvenience life had dealt her.

Barbara was, however, extremely close to her grandmother and her Aunt Sadie. Sadie had a bad heart condition and couldn't work, and her life was all about pleasing Barbara, giving to Barbara, making sure Barbara had whatever she wanted. Both Carmella and Sadie were warm and effusive, whereas Genevieve was cold and distant, not quite there.

Barbara was popular and gregarious, had a dry, sarcastic sense of humour. She loved music, shopping, going to the movies with her girlfriends. She led a very sheltered life and had never been outside of New Jersey, except to visit her father in Florida; she knew absolutely nothing of the world that Richard Kuklinski came from.

Barbara went along with her friend Lucille that autumn when she responded to an ad for a secretary placed by the Swiftline Trucking Company. As Barbara was waiting for her friend in the lobby, the owner of the company, Sol Goldfarb, saw Barbara and walked over to her.

'You look,' he said, 'just like my daughter.'

'Really,' said Barbara, and they began talking; he explained that his daughter was deaf and mute.

'Oh, I'm sorry,' Barbara said.

He invited her into his office. Goldfarb was a tall, attractive man with dark hair and eyes, a sharp dresser. He worked hard, did well in business, made a lot of money. He was so taken by Barbara and her resemblence to his daughter that he offered her an accounting job there on the spot, which she accepted. Though she had absolutely no office experience, Barbara was a quick learner; she had a high IQ and was readily able to master all that was required. She had always got good grades in school, with little effort. This was her first real job. She enjoyed making her own money, enjoyed entering the workforce, having the responsibilities of an adult and the independence that brought.

There was a drinks machine at the trucking company, and it was there that Barbara first encountered Richard Leonard Kuklinski. They said hello, smiled, and went back to work. They next ran into each other on the loading port, exchanged a few words about the weather; that was it. Mr Goldfarb saw them talking and didn't like it. Right away, he went over to Barbara and, like a concerned parent, warned her to stay away from Richard. He said, 'Look, I know you're a nice girl, an innocent girl. Don't have anything to do with that guy. He's a lug. He's married with kids.'

'Oh, I'm not,' she explained, taken aback. 'We were just, you know, talking about the weather.'

'OK, well, that's good. Just stay away from him.'

'Certainly . . . of course, OK,' she said, caught a bit off guard. She'd had no designs on Richard; the thought of getting involved with him had never even entered her mind. The matter would surely have died right there had Goldfarb not pursued it further. He now called Richard into his office and said, 'Look, Kuklinski, I don't want you associating with the help, see?'

'Excuse me, what're you talking about?' Richard asked.

'Barbara. Stay away from her.'

This caught Richard, too, completely off guard. He hadn't even thought about making a pass at Barbara. She was not his type. He'd never even known a girl like her – a good girl from a nice family, as it were.

Always defiant, always with a chip on his shoulder, Richard said, 'You know, it's a free country. People're allowed to talk to whoever they please.'

'I see you talking to her again, you're fired,' Goldfarb said.

This was like a stinging slap in Richard's surprised face.

'Take this fuckin' job and shove it up your pompous ass,'

Richard said, making that soft clicking sound out of the left side of his mouth, his face flushing.

'Get off this property,' Goldfarb said, standing up.

If Goldfarb had known he was talking to a genuine raging psychopath, he would surely never have taken such an aggressive tone. Richard had killed people for less than this.

'You owe me money,' Richard said.

'Come back later today and you'll get your money. Outta here.'

Richard stared at him long and hard. 'I'll be back,' he said, and left.

Richard's plan was to kill Goldfarb that very night. He was going to follow him home and beat him to death right at his front door. Who the fuck did he think he was? Nobody talked to Richard Kuklinski like that. Without knowing it, Goldfarb had signed his own death warrant.

At four o'clock, Richard was back, looking for his money. As he was waiting for a cheque, Barbara came walking out of the offices to get herself a Coke from the machine. Richard told her how he'd been fired for talking to her.

'What?' she said, not believing this, having difficulty even comprehending such a thing.

'I got fired because I was talking to you,' he repeated.

She felt terrible. The poor guy, she knew, hadn't done anything out of line, had never even intimated he wanted to take her out. 'I'm so sorry,' she said. 'I'll go talk to him right now. I'll get your job back. This is outrageous.'

'That's OK. Forget about it. I didn't want to work here anyway.'

'Jeez, I feel so bad.'

'Don't worry about it.'

'He says I look just like his daughter; I'm sure this is what it's about.'

'To hell with him – the pig.'

'Would you like to have coffee later?' Barbara said, wanting to be nice to Richard because he'd got sacked for talking to her, lost his livelihood because of her, she thought.

'Sure, yeah. I'd like that,' he said.

'Come back at five. I'll meet you out front, OK?'

'OK,' he said, liking the fact that Barbara wanted to stand up for him, was willing to meet him right out front. He soon got his cheque and left.

Had Barbara known who Richard really was, that he was a genuine wolf in sheep's clothing, she would surely have run the other way, had absolutely nothing to do with him. As it was, she got ready after work – combed her hair, put on a little make-up – and went to meet Richard in front of the Swiftline Trucking Company.

Worst mistake I ever made, she would say many years later, still shaking her head in disbelief. *I should've run for the hills, but instead I walked outside like a lamb to the slaughter.*

Richard was tall and exceptionally handsome, shy and respectful, but he was not Barbara's type, and he was too old for her. Still, they did go for coffee that windy autumn day, had a nice talk. He opened doors for her, was truly the perfect gentleman, polite to the point of distraction, even too much of a gentleman. Barbara sensed – mistakenly – that she could readily control him, and she didn't like that. She liked strong men, take-charge kind of men. Be that as it may, after their coffee, he made sure she got home OK. He insisted on taking her. When they reached the house she shared with her mother and grandmother (her Aunt Sadie had moved out and now lived near by with her husband, Harry), he asked her if she'd like to go and see a movie.

'Sure, OK,' she said, as innocent and wide-eyed as a young fawn suddenly caught in the oncoming headlights of a speeding car. A car coming from hell driven by the devil himself.

16

POSSESSION

That Saturday evening, Richard showed up at Nana Carmella's house. Shy and awkward, he met Barbara's mom and grandmother. They thought he was nice enough, certainly tall and handsome, but he was too old for Barbara, and he wasn't Italian. They went to a movie in North Bergen, saw *Godzilla* and a few cartoons, one of which featured Casper the Friendly Ghost. Barbara offhandedly mentioned to Richard that she liked Casper. After the movie, they went for pizza, sat and talked. Barbara still felt bad about Richard losing his job because of her.

'Don't worry about it,' he said, and meant it.

Richard was completely taken with Barbara. He thought she was a perfect lady, all class, polite, well spoken and very funny. She was always making wisecracks that made him laugh – no easy thing. Barbara had no romantic designs on Richard. She did think he was very attractive; he had a lovely smile, engaging honey-coloured eyes. But he was married, he had kids . . . and he was too old for her, not her type.

He told her that his marriage was, in fact, on the rocks, that he barely ever saw his wife and kids, that he was getting divorced, which was essentially all true, and Barbara believed him, took him at his word. Why shouldn't she? There was no reason for him to lie. Plus, lies and deceit had never played a part in her short life. They were foreign to her. When they left the pizza parlour, Richard made sure he opened the door for her, and he hurried to open the door when she got into his car, an old Chevy. In front of Nana Carmella's house, he didn't try to kiss her goodnight, was too shy. She thanked him for a nice evening and went inside, not sure she'd ever see him again.

As Richard made his way back to Jersey City, he couldn't stop thinking of Barbara: her smile, her lovely eyes, how her dark hair contrasted with her fair skin. It was as if someone had put a spell on him, as if Cupid had shot him with an arrow, a particularly sharp arrow. Until then, Richard had only known 'bar women'. Women who were loose, *whores and tramps*, as he thought of them. He also met many married women who *fucked like rabbits in heat when their husbands weren't around*, he said.

Richard had grown to think of most women – certainly his own mother – as whores. He would never forget his mother screwing the next-door neighbour, a slovenly guy with three kids, right in the middle of the afternoon. That image – her naked with her legs wide open, her feet up in the air – was seared into his strange mind.

But not Barbara; she was different. She was good and innocent and pure as the driven snow. He wanted her, he resolved. He'd move heaven and hell to get her. But how? he wondered. How could he get her to fall for him? He didn't have much to offer her. This was a dilemma. Still, he wanted to own her, possess her, to make her his.

But how?

That night, when Barbara went inside, her mother immediately started complaining about Richard: he was too old for her; he lived in Jersey City; he seemed rough around the edges; he was not Italian (the biggest sin of all). Nana Carmella had nothing to say. If Barbara liked him, he was fine with her. Aunt Sadie, however, would have much to say. She would hire a private detective to look into this Richard Kuklinski of Jersey City.

* * *

THE ICE MAN

It was Sunday morning, an unusually cold autumn day. Barbara liked to sleep late on Sundays. She was still sound asleep when her mother shook her awake with some urgency.

'That man you went out with last night is here,' she said, obviously not pleased about it.

'Here? Where?'

'Downstairs!'

'Richard?'

'Yes.'

Surprised to the point of shock, Barbara climbed out of bed, freshened up and went downstairs. She found Richard sitting in the living-room. He popped up when he saw her. In his left hand he had a big bouquet of flowers and in his right hand a white stuffed toy: Casper the Friendly Ghost.

Speechless, though touched, Barbara just stood there, her mouth slightly agape. No one had ever paid such attention to her. What was this about?

'I'm sorry I woke you up,' he said. 'I didn't mean to –'

'That's . . . that's OK. How thoughtful of you,' she said, taking the flowers and Casper, smiling politely.

Richard had never courted a girl in his life. He had no idea how it was done, what was good form and what was not. Barbara offered him some coffee and put the nice roses in a vase. This was another first: no boy had ever given Barbara flowers.

It was painfully obvious to Genevieve that this Polish guy from Jersey City, certainly an undesirable place filled with ruffians, had designs on her daughter – her only child – and she didn't like it. Her daughter was good girl, a virgin . . . Where did this guy get off coming around early Sunday morning with flowers and lovesick eyes? Genevieve believed an older guy like him was after one thing – sex – and he wasn't going to get any of that from her daughter, her Barbara. Forget it.

Genevieve was cold and indifferent to Richard, and Barbara knew it was best to get him out of the house, away from her mother, ASAP. She showered and dressed, and she and

Richard left. They went to Journal Square in Jersey City, a main shopping street lined with beautiful old art deco movie houses – the Loews and the Stanley – and all kinds of nice shops. They went for a Sunday brunch at an Italian restaurant called Guido's, walked up and down the wide street looking in shop windows and talking.

Richard felt close to Barbara, as if he'd known her a long time. For some inexplicable reason he . . . he trusted her. They even talked about sex that day, and Barbara told him she was a virgin and proud of it. This really bowled Richard over. How could a girl so attractive, so sexy and desirable, still be a virgin? That didn't make sense, he thought, and told her so.

'Yeah, well I am,' she said, adamant, not pleased he hadn't taken her word. But in truth he did believe her, and that made him want her all the more. She really was, he was surer than ever, a good girl – someone he could trust. They saw another movie, Otto Preminger's *Exodus*, and Richard took Barbara back home. He tried now to kiss her goodnight, but she wouldn't let him. She didn't invite him inside; she wanted to keep him and her mother apart.

That Monday, when Barbara left work, Richard was outside waiting for her, and he had more flowers with him.

This all caught her off guard, made her . . . a little uneasy. There was no plan for him to be here, but here he was, insisting on taking her home, and of course she had to get into his car; after all, he was only being nice. How could she decline? She did have plans to meet a girlfriend and go to the record shop, but now that had to be scrapped.

Barbara recently explained: *If I'd had any sense I would've seen the handwriting on the wall then and there and ended it. But I'd never met anyone like Richard . . . so . . . attentive, and I had no real point of reference.*

Barbara went to the record shop in North Bergen with Richard, and he insisted that she let him buy her the records she wanted. She tried to pay, but he wouldn't let her.

'Forget it, let me . . . I want to,' he told her.

When he took her home, Nana Carmella saw them and made him come in for dinner. Barbara had to go along with this, though she felt his presence was being forced on her. Genevieve worked hard all day and had no real interest in cooking, but Nana Carmella was an amazingly good cook, and she served up aubergine alla parmigiana, no big deal, but Richard raved about how good it was.

Genevieve was not thrilled he was there – she knew what he was after – but she tolerated him and was . . . pleasant enough. After dinner and some sweets Nana Carmella had made, they sat in the living-room and watched *The Sid Caesar Show*, everyone but Genevieve laughing out loud. Though he was shy and awkward, Richard felt oddly at ease, at home. He'd never in his life been around a family that wasn't severely dysfunctional, and he admired the warmth in Barbara's home. He wanted this for himself. He'd do anything he had to do to get it. Nothing would stop him from having Barbara – from having his own family with Barbara.

He came to view Barbara as a valuable means to an end, became sure she could show him a part of life he knew nothing about. He could, he was equally sure, know real love if he made Barbara his. He didn't so much see her as an intelligent, independent woman; he saw her as a potential possession, a thing to acquire, own and control, to hang above the mantelpiece – a prized trophy everyone could admire.

Outwardly, Richard was a perfect gentleman, soft-spoken, fervently polite; inside, he was a churning volcano, intent upon owning and possessing Barbara Pedrici, no matter what. His wife, Linda, was forgotten, a thing of the past.

Every day when Barbara left work, Richard was there. She quickly became so used to his presence that she began to take it for granted, to accept it. She didn't tell him she had other plans; she didn't tell him that she wanted to go shopping with her friends, hang out and talk and have fun with the girls. She didn't want to hurt his feelings. As it happened, Richard didn't even give her the chance to protest; he was just always there with that handsome face and those intense almond-shaped eyes, flowers, his shy smile, his polite ways. How could she say no? How could she resist him? In fact, she began to grow fond of his undivided attention. After all, he was a handsome older guy, obviously nuts about her, and she felt . . . well, she felt flattered. The attention and the admiration appealed to her ego; none of her friends had a tall, gorgeous older guy waiting on them, always there, opening doors, being polite, a caring, considerate gentleman out to please.

Little by little, Barbara was becoming more and more fond of Richard. His seduction was bearing fruit. Now when he kissed her she let him; indeed, she kissed him back . . . passionately. But that was it. She refused to have sex with him. Her mother had warned her many times over the years to never, *never* have sex before being married. That had been ingrained in Barbara since she was a young girl.

But the more she resisted Richard's impassioned pleas, the more he wanted her, had to have her. He began to tease Barbara about her virginity, said the reason she wouldn't have sex with him was because she wasn't really a virgin at all, that she was 'hiding the truth'. At first, he said this jokingly, toying with her, but the more she said no, the more he teased her and dared her to show him. Prove it.

Barbara, a strong-willed, independent young woman by nature, finally gave in to Richard's entreaties, more to shut him up and prove she was a virgin than anything else. The first time they were intimate was in a motel in Jersey City, and it was not a particularly pleasant experience for Barbara. In fact, it hurt. But Richard had reached the top of Mount Everest, and Barbara proved there in the hotel that she was indeed a virgin, for her blood was there to show it. This made Richard want her all the more. Barbara was the only virginal woman he'd ever known, and he was intent upon making her his.

He was intent upon marrying her.

17

AUNT SADIE

Barbara's Aunt Sadie was more like a mother to Barbara than Genevieve had ever been. Cold and aloof, Genevieve was not a people person. She didn't seem to like anyone. She'd go to work, come home, eat, watch a little TV and go to sleep. That was her life; that's what life was all about.

Aunt Sadie, on the other hand, was outgoing, warm and friendly, loved movies, loved opera, enjoyed going out, had a giving, effusive southern Italian way about her. Sadie was also a crafty, cunning woman, as is also the way of southern Italians, of Neapolitans. If Barbara, who was surely more like a daughter than a niece, wanted to be involved with this big Polish guy, that was OK with her. But Aunt Sadie wanted to know more about him: who he was, where he came from, what kind of family he had. Whenever the subject of his family came up, Richard became quiet and changed the subject. Sadie wondered why, and she resolved to make it her business to find out. Her brother Armond was a part-time cop in nearby Cliffside Park, and, with his help, Sadie found a private investigator who, for a fee, went to Jersey City and Hoboken and began snooping around and asking questions about Richard Kuklinski.

It didn't take long for him to find out that Richard was a player, that he hurt a lot of people, that he hijacked trucks, that he had a hair-trigger temper, that he had drinking and gambling problems – and that he had associations with organised crime. He even heard rumours that Richard had murdered people in sudden bar altercations, and for money! Mamma mia! Richard had no kind of police record, but he had a reputation as a dangerous guy: a thug, a hustler with a violent streak, who carried a gun and a knife. All this, Armond summarily reported back to Sadie. She was appalled and immediately dispatched Armond to go and talk to Richard, intent upon ending the relationship before it went any further. Armond found Richard in a Jersey City bar and said he needed to talk to him . . .

'Sure,' Richard said, wary because Armond had suddenly come to Jersey City to talk to him, 'what's on your mind?'

'Barbara,' Armond began, 'is a good girl –'

'Yeah, I know. That's why I like her,' said Richard.

'Look, I found out all about you, Richard. I know who you are. And me . . . me and the family want you to stay away from Barbara.'

'Really?' Richard said, his lips tightening, his eyes narrowing.

'Yeah, really,' Armond told him, acting tough.

'And what if I don't?' Richard asked.

'It won't be good for you,' Armond said.

'You threatening me? Are you threatening me, Armond?'

'I'm telling you to leave Barbara alone. She's a good girl.'

'My intentions toward her are only honourable.'

'You are married with two kids. What's honourable about that?'

'I'm getting a divorce.'

'You aren't for her.'

'Says who?'

'Me. Says me. The family wants you to steer clear of Barbara. Don't you get it?'

'Yeah, well I ain't, OK?'

'That wouldn't be . . . good for you.'

'You are threatening me. Look, Armond, if you wanna go

to war over this, that's fine with me, but I can tell you right now, right here, like a friend, that only one of us is going to come out of it, and it ain't – listen to me – it ain't going to be you. Take that to the bank.'

Richard let his words sink in. Armond was not a particularly tough man. He was tall and thin, not powerful. But he had fought in the Second World War, was highly decorated, had killed a lot of Japanese soldiers, and he did carry a gun. He had one on him right now, a .38 with a four-inch barrel, his service revolver. Richard had two guns on him. They stared at each other.

'My niece is a good girl!' Armond repeated with firm conviction. 'Don't you get it?'

If Armond hadn't been Barbara's uncle, Richard might've taken him outside and shot him there on the spot, then got rid of his body. Instead, he said, 'Like I told you, my intentions toward Barbara are only honourable. Tell the family that. Tell them I'm getting a divorce. Tell them I love Barbara and'll never do anything to hurt her. Tell them that. OK?'

'OK, I will,' Armond said, seeing clearly the resolve in Richard's face, and he went back to his sister Sadie and told her what Richard had said.

'I'll talk to Barbara,' Sadie said, and she sat Barbara down and told her all she had learned, none of which was particularly troubling to Barbara. Whatever Richard had done, she said, was in the past. 'He's nice and kind and real good to me,' Barbara said, trying to defend the indefensible.

'He's married with children,' Sadie said. 'He's a gangster.'

'He's getting divorced,' Barbara said. 'He's no gangster. When I met him he was working. Working hard. He got fired for talking to me. You believe that? For just talking to me.'

'He's hurt a lot of people,' Sadie said.

'I'm sure they deserved it,' Barbara said, having no idea of how severely Richard had hurt a lot of people, that indeed he was a full-blown serial killer.

'Barbara,' Sadie said, 'I love you. I'm only telling you this because I care. I don't think you know what you're getting involved with here.'

'I know, and I love you too, and I appreciate your caring, your looking out for me. Listen, we're only dating, OK? I mean, I'm not marrying him; we aren't going to rush off and elope. Don't worry. *Please*, don't worry.'

'But I do. I don't want to see you hurt. You can do better than this guy, I promise you.'

'We are only dating,' Barbara repeated.

'OK . . . but you be careful. Don't go falling in love with him. Don't go letting him make you pregnant.'

'Of course not,' Barbara said, and hugged her Aunt Sadie long and hard. 'I love you.'

'I love you,' Aunt Sadie said, with a very bad feeling deep inside her gut about this Richard Kuklinski from Jersey City with the shy, crooked smile and shifty eyes.

That Christmas, Barbara decided to invite Richard to join her family for both the Christmas Eve fish dinner and the Christmas Day meal, which would be the customary five-course feast lasting all day and part of the night. For Barbara's family, as for most Italian-American families across the country, Christmas was a special time of year – a wonderful opportunity to give and laugh and sing and eat and bring everyone together. Barbara, a talented artist, painted colourful Christmas scenes on the windows with watercolour paint, and there was a big tree in the living-room.

Barbara saw this as a good opportunity for her family to get to know how kind and polite and sweet Richard really was. When Barbara told her mother she wanted to invite Richard for the holidays, Genevieve was not happy, but she reluctantly accepted it, as did the rest of the family. If that's what Barbara wanted, so be it. Unless she had her way, she'd have a long, sour face, and would let everyone know she wasn't happy.

THE ICE MAN

When Barbara told Richard she'd like him to join her family over the holidays, he was caught off guard, but he was pleased, too, and readily accepted the gracious invitation, looking forward to it. He knew Barbara was close to her people, and if he wanted her, he knew, they had to accept him. Simple. But he was nervous. His family had never had a Christmas tree or any special food; for him, Christmas had meant nothing – zero. He usually went to a diner to eat, and that was it. No big shakes. This would be a whole new experience.

18

THIS IS FOR YOU, RICHARD

Christmas Eve, December 1961, Richard arrived at Barbara's house in North Bergen.

This stone-cold, remorseless killer was nervous, indeed had butterflies in his stomach; he'd never been to such a function, had no idea what to expect, what to do, how to act, what was expected of him. Barbara's whole family was there, 15 people in all. Grandma Carmella had been cooking non-stop for days. Huge, colourful platters of food were ready to be served. Barbara introduced Richard, awkward and painfully shy, to cousins, aunts and uncles he'd not yet met. It was now that Richard met Barbara's cousin Carl. 'He's my favourite cousin,' she told Richard. Of course her Aunt Sadie was there, and she was warm enough to Richard, but she didn't like him, didn't like anything about him – what he did, where he came from, where he was going. Still, she resolved to be nice, to make him feel welcome no matter what. After all, it was Christmas Eve, the time of love and family unity, and if her Barbara wanted him there, so be it. She'd make the best of it, hoping it was only a passing phase.

Drinks were soon poured. Toasts were made. The smell of delicious southern Italian food permeated the air, mixing with the strong smell of pine coming from the Christmas tree. Richard knew better than to drink whisky, and he had only a glass of white wine, to be social.

THE ICE MAN

When they all sat to eat at the long, glorious table that Barbara and Nana and Aunt Sadie had carefully set, Richard sat next to Barbara. They started with colourful platters filled with antipasti: red peppers in oil, salami, prosciutto, all kinds of cheese, stuffed peppers, olives, artichoke hearts. They then had the customary spaghetti and clams, followed by fried fillet of sole, stuffed shrimp and scampi, stuffed calamari and grilled lobster tails. This was followed by fruits and nuts and more cheese, and finally by Neapolitan stuffed artichokes, to help with digestion. Then, of course, the desserts.

Richard had never even seen a home-cooked Italian meal like this, let alone eaten one, and he was amazed at how good everything was. Warmed and flushed by the beautiful meal, he was even more touched by the way the family openly showed affection, readily touched and kissed and hugged, the constant banter and laughter. He was seeing something he had never known existed: a tight-knit family enjoying one another's company, openly showing tender feelings. By the time espresso was served, with sweets Carmella had made – also sambuca and grappa – it was almost twelve, the time when gifts were given. Richard hadn't brought any gifts. He didn't know you were supposed to, and when Aunt Sadie handed him a carefully wrapped present and said, 'This is for you, Richard, merry Christmas,' he was touched. He was speechless. And there were still more gifts for him, from Barbara, from Nana Carmella, even from Barbara's mother. Richard was so moved that tears actually filled his eyes, and like this he opened his gifts: a sweater, some cologne, a nice suede jacket from Barbara. All choked up, Richard tried on the jacket. It fitted perfectly. It was the nicest gift anyone had ever given him.

'Is it always like this?' he asked Barbara.

'What do you mean?' she asked, smiling.

'Everyone so nice and warm and giving,' he said.

'Of course! It's Christmas-time,' she said. 'It's always like this, Richard.'

* * *

The following day, Richard returned to Nana Carmella's house carrying gifts. He had shopped all morning and made sure he'd got something for everyone who would be there. He gleefully handed out the gifts, receiving thank yous, kisses and hugs. He never knew people could be so warm and effusive, readily expressing their feelings.

Soon, they all sat down to eat again, and this meal was even larger than the one the night before. There was antipasti, lasagna and aubergine alla parmigiana, followed by ham and lamb with three different kinds of potatoes, stuffed mushrooms, rice balls, huge bowls of salad, and fruit, sweets and fennochio (fennel). They ate for hours, taking a break after each course; much wine was poured, toasts were made, there was laughter, and old and new jokes were shared, some a little bawdy. They also sang Christmas carols.

That Christmas, Barbara's family came to accept Richard; his shyness, how much he obviously enjoyed being there, the considerate gifts he'd brought won them over. Though he was not Italian, they made him feel welcome and loved, as if he were truly one of them. Part of the family. He wanted to reach out and hug them all, wrap his powerful arms around them and hold them tight. With a warm glow, he sat there eating and smiling, and maybe – truly for the first time in his entire life – Richard was glad to be alive. Richard felt . . . *loved*. He was so moved, so touched, that he went out onto the screened-in patio at the back and cried in his cupped hands. Barbara found him there like that and she took him in her arms and held him tight, thinking he was just a big baby.

If she'd only known.

After the holidays passed and the New Year began, Richard and Barbara saw each other more and more. But Barbara was beginning to feel stifled, boxed in. Richard was always there. No matter which way she turned he was there, waiting for her, opening doors for her, demanding her undivided attention. He had cut her off from seeing her friends, certainly from dating anyone else, and she felt that she was trapped. She had grown very fond of Richard, but she wanted a little room to breathe, to go for sodas, to go shopping and have long talks with her girlfriends. She resolved to tell him. She had the right. She was only 19 years old and couldn't do anything on her own any more. She thought of the best way to do this, turned it over in her mind. She did not ask any of her friends or anyone in her family for advice because she didn't want to let anyone know how hemmed in she felt.

Meanwhile, Richard decided to take her to his favourite haunt in Hoboken, Sylvia's Ringside Inn. Richard had told Sylvia all about Barbara, the wonderful time he'd had over the holidays, the feast they'd served. Barbara didn't particularly want to go to the Ringside Inn. That was a part of Richard's life she wanted nothing to do with. But, being polite, she agreed to go, and Richard proudly introduced Barbara to the crowd there and to Sylvia. Sylvia was outright rude, even hostile. She felt Barbara had been keeping Richard away from the place. Richard's pool playing had been a draw. She'd been making money because of him. Sylvia resented Barbara and had no reservations about letting her know. The feeling was mutual: Barbara thought she was the rudest, ugliest person she'd ever met and told Richard so. 'I don't like being here,' she said. 'It's dirty, it smells. I don't like the people. I don't like this Sylvia character! My God, what a face! It could stop a clock, stop Big Ben! I want to leave, Richard.'

For the life of him, Richard couldn't understand Barbara's animus or why Sylvia was so unfriendly, and the couple left.

'I don't ever want to go back there,' Barbara said, 'and truth is, I don't see why you would either. It's below you, Richard.'

'OK, guess it was a bad idea to bring you,' Richard said. They never went back as a couple, and soon Richard stopped going altogether.

* * *

THIS IS FOR YOU, RICHARD

Several days later, Barbara finally mustered up the courage to tell Richard how she felt. He had come to pick her up at work. When she got in the car she still had no idea how dangerous Richard was, that he carried a gun and a knife with him all the time. However, she would soon learn.

'Richard, I need to talk with you,' she began.

'Sure,' he said, sensing he was about to hear something he wouldn't like.

'Look, Richard, I'm very fond of you. You know that. It's . . . well, I feel trapped. Everywhere I turn, you're there. I want some space; I want to hang out with my friends. I'd like to go out on a Saturday night with my girlfriends like I used to do.' She went on to describe, her voice kind and considerate, warm and sincere, how she needed space. She was very young and didn't, she said, want such a 'serious commitment'.

Maybe, she said, she'd even like to . . . you know, date other guys.

Barbara's words cut Richard like broken glass. They hurt. They made him bleed. As she talked, he actually began to pale, and his lips twisted off to the left. Barbara did not see him reach down and pull out the razor-sharp hunting knife he always kept strapped to his calf. As she talked, he reached out his arm and held it behind her. He looked at her and smiled as she prattled on about freedom and space and her being so young. He raised his hand and jabbed her in the back, just behind her left shoulder, with the knife.

'Ow!' she said. 'What was that?' Then she saw the glistening knife in his hand. 'My God, you stabbed me. Why?' Seeing the blood, her eyes filled with shock and dismay.

'Why? As a warning,' he said, in a sickeningly calm voice. 'You're mine . . . understand? You aren't seeing anyone else, understand? You do what I tell you!'

'Really, that's –'

'Listen, Barbara, if I can't have you no one can. Got it?'

'That's what you think. Who the hell do you think you are? How could you stab me like that? What kind of person are you? Where'd this knife come from?' She was aghast. 'I'm going to tell my family. I'm going –'

'Really?' he said, his voice calm and icy cold, a voice she'd never heard before, detached, inhuman. 'How about this: how about I'll kill your whole family, your mother and your cousins and Uncle Armond. How about that?' he asked.

Now really angry, she began to yell at him, to berate him. He grabbed her by the neck and throttled her until she was unconscious. When she came to, he was driving along as if nothing had happened, calm, cool, collected . . . as if they were on the way to a movie.

'Take me home,' she said, making a point of not being too aggressive. Aggression obviously didn't work. Barbara now viewed him as a very dangerous man, a nut, a psycho; she didn't trust him, was deathly afraid of him. She had to get away from him. But how? When she arrived home, he warned her again that he'd kill 'anyone who meant anything to you . . . understand?'

'Yes, I understand,' she said, her mind reeling with the dire consequences of his words. Dizzy, nauseated, she got out of his car and slowly walked inside. He pulled away.

That day, Barbara's life took an irreversible turn for the worse. Indeed, her life was about to become a long series of nightmares, of terror, and there was nothing anyone could do for her.

Not her family.

Not the police.

Not Jesus Christ himself.

Richard was outraged. How could Barbara want to stop seeing him, feel hemmed in by him? He'd been nothing but kind and gentle to her. Where had he gone wrong? What could he do to win her back? His mind turned like an out-of-control merry-go-round. He felt dizzy; his head throbbed. He resolved he would murder her and bury her in South Jersey if she left him. If she was dead, she couldn't hurt him.

Murder, as always, was the answer.

The following day, when Barbara left work, Richard was waiting outside. He had flowers for her, a cute little teddy bear, an abundance of sweet words. He told her how sorry he was, that he loved her too much, that was the problem.

'Barbara,' he said, 'I never felt like this for anyone. The thought of losing you . . . well, it just makes me, you know, crazy. I'm sorry.'

'And the threats?'

'I just can't lose you. I . . . I couldn't handle it,' he said. 'I'd go over the deep end. Please let's make this work, let's try. I love you. I want to marry you.'

'Richard, you're already married, with children!'

'I'm getting a divorce. I promise. I swear. My word.'

And in this way, Richard convinced Barbara, gullible and young, that they would have a wonderful future together. The truth was Barbara did want children, did want to have a family and a loving, dedicated husband, and she knew that no one could ever be more dedicated than Richard.

Had Barbara been older, more mature, had she seen more of the world, known herself better, she would have found a way to end it then and there. But she truly believed Richard would hurt the people she cared for the most, and she succumbed to his sincere, seemingly heartfelt, endless entreaties.

That night, Richard had dinner at Nana Carmella's house. He had grown to love Nana Carmella's cooking and really enjoyed eating there. He was, in a sense, making Barbara's family his own family; he was co-opting them for himself, filling a deep void he had inside. Barbara's mother had learned to accept Richard, and he felt at home and at peace when he was there.

Over the coming weeks and months, as spring grew near, Barbara was caught up in a kind of sticky spider's web she could not get out of. The more she twisted and turned, the more entangled she became. Most of the time, Richard was nice enough, fawningly polite. He could be very funny and good company. But he had no reservations about striking her, choking her, threatening to kill her – and her family. Barbara's mindset became: *it's better he hurts me than anyone in my family.*

At one point, she did go talk to the police, she says, and learned that if he was arrested for assaulting her, he'd soon be out of jail, and she believed he'd come looking to kill her. She knew now he carried guns as well as a knife.

Barbara repeatedly thought about telling her Uncle Armond and Nana Carmella's brother, the chief of police in North Bergen, but Barbara was absolutely convinced that if she told them about Richard's abuse, they'd surely confront him, and just as surely Richard would end up killing them and burying them somewhere. He flat-out told her he would. She believed him. She stayed quiet and endured the abuse, which only became worse and worse still.

Barbara came to realise that Richard could be sadistic in the extreme, *as cold as ice*, as she puts it. Richard had, in fact, all the worst qualities of both his parents, magnified many times over. He had Stanley's capacity for prolonged, sudden cruelty and Anna's indifference to people's feelings. Richard had taken those elements to new, staggering heights; he was far more dangerous and cruel than Stanley Kuklinski had ever been.

When, conversely, Richard was kind, he was the nicest, most easygoing, giving guy in the world: attentive, polite, considerate and very romantic. On a regular basis, he brought Barbara long-stemmed red roses and loving cards with romantic sayings. Barbara felt like she was on a roller-coaster. A roller-coaster she desperately wanted to get off. But she did not know how.

The couple were now having intercourse on a regular basis. Richard had rented an apartment, and they went there for romantic interludes. Richard refused to wear a condom, Barbara didn't have access to any kind of birth control, and the inevitable happened: Barbara became pregnant. It seemed that was what Richard had been planning all along – to make her pregnant, to force her deeper into a relationship with him.

Barbara became despondent. She was normally an upbeat, optimistic woman; she was now depressed, cornered . . . *trapped*, she explained later.

Richard talked about getting married. He said he was glad she was pregnant, that he'd wanted to have children with her all along, from their first date. Barbara decided she didn't want to marry Richard, did not want to have his child, and finally – after much soul-searching – she went to her mother and told her the truth . . .

'I knew it!' Genevieve said, her face stern and cold and angry. 'I told you. I warned you. That's all he wanted, and you gave it to him – a married man with kids. How could you? How could you allow this to happen? You know better. I taught you better –'

Disgusted, Barbara turned away from her mother.

Nana Carmella was far more understanding. She didn't know anything about Richard's past. His shy, polite ways had grown on her. True, he wasn't Italian, but she had, with some difficulty, learned to accept that, to accept him. Nana Carmella hugged Barbara and assured her everything would be OK.

But Barbara knew better. She knew she was in quicksand and sinking rapidly. She was a good Catholic and did not believe in abortion. Even if she had, that would have been, back then, a hard thing to come by. She'd have the baby, she resolved. But she wanted nothing more to do with Richard. That was, she was sure, a one-way ticket to a place she didn't want to go. She'd make the best of this bad situation she'd got herself into. How right Sol Goldfarb had been about Richard. If only she had listened to him, she mused over and over again.

Barbara went to the bank, withdrew all her savings and took off, left town without telling Richard anything. She went to the only person in the world who would understand, who would protect her, who loved her unconditionally and didn't judge her no matter what: her father, Albert Pedrici. Mr Pedrici lived in Miami Beach, and when Barbara boarded the plane and it taxied and took off, she felt as if she were leaving a bad dream, a nightmare, behind. Little did she know that she was actually speeding towards the nightmare her life would become.

19

BETRAYAL

Al Pedrici was a tall, handsome Venetian who loved life and made the most of it. He was quick to laugh, quick to make friends, a naturally gregarious man – the exact opposite of Barbara's mother. Albert's father had come to America through Ellis Island in 1906 and bought a house in the Italian enclave of Hoboken, on the same block where the Sinatras lived. The Pedricis opened a small food shop in Hoboken, and the family did well, never wanting for anything. Albert met Barbara's mother when he was 22, she 19. It was a kind of love at first sight, which resulted in an ill-conceived marriage that did not work out. Albert and Genevieve were divorced when Barbara was two years old.

During the years when Barbara was growing up, she saw her father as much as circumstances allowed. Albert gave Barbara whatever she wanted. All she had to do was point and it was hers. He spoiled her. Barbara was much closer to her father than to her mother, even though they lived apart. When he moved to Miami, they spoke on the phone often and wrote detailed letters to each other. Albert very much enjoyed living in Miami: the fair weather, the glorious sunshine, being near the sea, the city's bustling nightlife. He and his second wife, Natalie, socialised a lot, went to parties and clubs all over Miami. Albert liked to dance, and just about every weekend the couple went out 'high stepping', as Albert was fond of saying.

When Richard learned that Barbara had fled New Jersey, he was distraught. He kept asking Genevieve and Nana Carmella where Barbara had gone. They wouldn't tell. Richard became obsessed. He kept coming back to the house. He wouldn't leave them alone. He did not get aggressive, rude or threatening, but Genevieve sensed he could very well become violent. Extremely violent. She had heard stories about his violence from Sadie and Armond. Nevertheless, in no uncertain terms, Genevieve told Richard to forget Barbara, to get on with his life, to find a nice Polish girl his own age.

'You don't understand,' he said, shaking his head in dismay. 'I love Barbara, I love her with all my heart. I've never – never – cared for anyone like I care for Barbara –'

'Richard,' Genevieve interrupted, 'you're a married man.'

'I'm getting divorced. That woman, that marriage, never meant anything to me.'

'You've been saying that for months now, and you still aren't divorced. What's that about?'

'I'm . . . I've had a run of bad luck. I need money for the lawyer. I already spoke to him, a lawyer over in Hoboken, and he won't do it until I pay him. Linda, my ex, she doesn't mean anything to me. I met her when I was a kid. I never loved her. The children, they just happened. I wasn't planning that – you know, to settle down, anything like that. Barbara is pregnant with my child. I want to marry her. I wanted to marry Barbara and have a family with her from the first time we went out, I swear. Barbara is all class. I never met anyone like her.'

There was a long, heavy pause. Finally, Genevieve said, 'If I give you the money for the Hoboken lawyer, you'll get a divorce?'

'Right away, like tomorrow.'

'Promise?'

'On my life!'

Genevieve looked at him long and hard; he was a very handsome man. She was, in fact, beguiled by Richard.

When he wanted, he could be extremely charming, indeed disarming.

'How much?' she asked.

'A thousand,' he said.

'Come back tomorrow and I'll give it to you,' she said.

'No . . . really?'

'Yes. Really. I wouldn't kid about something like this.'

Richard picked up Genevieve like a doll and hugged her so hard he nearly broke her ribs. 'Then you'll tell me where she is?' he asked, all hopeful.

'Yes, only after you've gotten a divorce – and you prove it.'

'I will, I promise I will,' he said.

He came back the next day, got the thousand dollars from Genevieve – every dollar hard-earned – hurried to Hoboken and paid the lawyer. The papers were drawn up, and Richard had Linda sign them. He gave her no option. He then signed them, and, with the lawyer's help, Richard and Linda were soon legally divorced. Richard had never loved Linda, and he'd hated her since he caught her in the hotel. He was glad to be rid of her.

Proof in hand, Richard went back to see Genevieve, and she then told him where Barbara was – a thing Barbara would hold against her mother for the rest of her life.

That May was unbearably hot and humid in Miami. When the sun went down, mosquitoes filled the air. You couldn't go outside, there were so many of them. Barbara didn't like Miami. She wasn't used to the heat, and the pregnancy was making her particularly uncomfortable. She was afraid Richard would hurt her family. He'd said a dozen times that he would, and she was haunted to distraction – sleepless – by the idea that at any moment the phone would ring and she'd hear the terrible, unspeakable news: *Richard killed your family. Nana, your mother, your Aunt Sadie . . .*

What, Barbara wondered, had she done to deserve such a

fate? She'd been a good, God-fearing person all her life. Since she'd known the difference between right and wrong, she'd always done right. And now this. This living, breathing, snake-eyed nightmare. She began to think she had to have committed some heinous, terrible crime in another life to be condemned to such an unjust state of affairs. God . . . there was no God. What kind of God would sentence her to such a fate?

She began to wonder if it was all because she'd had sex with Richard – wanton, lustful sex whenever he pleased. Surely that was it. That was what had brought this black curse, this psychotic Polack from Jersey City, down upon her. He was, she came to think, punishment for her carnal passions.

Barbara very much enjoyed the company of her father. He was supportive and loving and didn't criticise her at all, had nothing negative to say. He kept telling her everything would work out well, that she had her whole life before her, that she could stay with him and his wife as long as she wished. No pressure. Just love. Unconditional love, given without expecting anything in return.

Aunt Sadie called her every day. She too was supportive and optimistic, and they talked about the joy of having a child. Aunt Sadie said she'd be more than happy to babysit for the child – she was sure it was going to be a girl – when her niece was ready to go back to work. With each passing day, Barbara became stronger and more resigned to her fate. She stopped beating herself up. She began going for long walks along the glorious Atlantic Ocean, and she enjoyed swimming in the early morning as the Florida sun slowly climbed out of the east. She got dark with the sun and looked quite beautiful with a radiant tan, the baby rapidly growing in her ever-expanding stomach.

A storm from the south came tearing into Miami. The sky abruptly darkened, became the deep grey colour of gunpowder. Strong winds bent palm trees, making them seem as if they were dancing to Latin music. Lightning bolts tore the darkening sky apart. Thunder trembled the air. Since she'd been a little girl, Barbara had not liked storms. They seemed to her to be harbingers of bad things to come.

Barbara was sitting on the screened-in porch of her father's house, watching the storm, the lightning bolts, the wind abusing the palm trees, when she saw, out of the corner of her eye, a taxi come to a slow stop in front of the house. A lone man, a large man, got out of the cab. He carried one piece of luggage. He began to walk up the path to the house. Barbara suddenly realised, as if she'd been struck by a thunderbolt, that it was Richard. She wanted to get up and run, but where could she go? Where could she run? He walked up to the screen door and knocked. Barbara went to the door, not pleased, actually scowling.

'I found you,' he said.

'Yes, I see that.'

'Why'd you run away?'

'Why do you think I ran away?'

'You look so beautiful. You've changed. Guess it's true.'

'What's that?'

'That women become more beautiful when they're pregnant.'

'So you say.'

'Can I come in?'

'I'd rather you didn't, if you want to know the truth.'

They stared at each other through the screen. It began to rain. He just stood there in the rain getting wet.

'I got divorced,' he said, taking out the divorce papers so she could see. 'See, they're signed by a judge.' The papers were getting wet.

'I'm shocked . . . I didn't think you would.'

'I said I would and I did. I love you, Barbara. I love you so much it hurts,' he told her. And thus Richard insinuated himself back into Barbara's life, a storm-filled purple sky and lightning bolts behind him, as if nature were trying to send Barbara a message.

THE ICE MAN

When Barbara found out that her mother had paid for Richard's divorce and told him where she was, she called her mother and berated her non-stop for 15 minutes. Genevieve's answer was, 'I don't want you to have a child without a husband. How would that look? It's not right. It's not . . . natural.'

'I don't care how it'll look! You had no right telling him I'm here. No right – no right!' Barbara hung up on her mother.

Young and inexperienced and particularly vulnerable now with this sudden unwanted pregnancy, Barbara was soon convinced that Richard would change, that his love for her would make everything good and right, and they would be happy.

Al Pedrici readily accepted Richard. He could see that Richard was nuts about his daughter and resolved not to do anything to get in their way. He figured things would work themselves out, that Barbara – whose pregnancy was more evident every day – was certainly better off with a husband than without. Al had no idea about Richard's violence towards Barbara, his homicidal threats, how calm and cold he was when he made them, or that he was always armed. Even now, she was sure, he had a gun with him.

Barbara and Richard went for long walks and talked. Barbara, aware now that Richard had drinking and gambling problems, made him swear off those vices, which he readily did. Al managed to get Richard a job driving a delivery truck, and he dutifully went to work every day, not complaining, toeing the line, intent upon proving that he would be a good provider. A good husband. A better man. He resolved also to stay away from crime. Killing people. The Mafia. Days quickly melted into weeks then into months. Florida's summer arrived with even more thick, stuffy humidity, as well as more giant mosquitoes. As Barbara's stomach grew, the heat and humidity bothered her more and more. Richard kept insisting that they get married, Barbara finally agreed and, as the summer grew to a close, they were married by a justice of the peace at Miami's

City Hall. Al and his wife attended. That night, they went out for a nice dinner in a fish restaurant. Toasts were made. There was no honeymoon (no money for that) and suddenly Barbara Pedrici was Barbara Kuklinski.

That was, she recently confided, *the worst day of my life. Now that I think of it I should have thrown myself in the ocean and drowned rather than marry Richard. But I did, and the die was cast.*

When, one evening after dinner, Richard saw his new wife smoking a cigarette, he became disproportionately angry. He ripped the cigarette from her hand and stomped on it.

'I'll smoke if I want to,' Barbara said, annoyed.

Richard's answer was to step on her right foot with all his weight and turn it, fracturing her big toe.

'Are you crazy?' she asked, grimacing with pain. 'What's wrong with you?'

'You aren't smoking,' he said. 'You will do what I say!' And that night Richard would not even allow Barbara to come to bed. He made her sit on a grey metal stool on the screened-in patio the whole night.

'You move, I'll kill your father in front of you,' he said, dead serious, and left Barbara there like that.

Convinced that Richard would truly kill her dad, Barbara sat on that hard metal stool *the whole friggin' night*, as she put it. The temperature dropped suddenly, as it always did, and she was so cold she began shivering. Certainly, Barbara should have hurried to the police, told them what Richard had done, what he was making her do; but she was so frightened for her father that she sat there shivering and freezing all night long, silently cursing heaven and hell, and her mother for telling Richard where she was.

Barbara lost the baby the next day. She was sure what Richard had made her do was the reason. Whatever affection Barbara had once had for Richard was inexorably being replaced by another emotion entirely – and that emotion was hate.

20

LOVE AND MARRIAGE
AND A BABY CARRIAGE

On 15 October 1962, Barbara and Richard Kuklinski returned to New Jersey. It was a bitterly cold night. Uncle Armond met them at the airport, all smiles, hugs and kisses. Barbara was overjoyed to see her uncle and be back home. When Barbara saw Nana Carmella they both cried, they were so happy, and hugged each other for a long time. Now that Barbara and Richard were married, the family readily accepted him, for better or for worse. Richard's dream of making Barbara's family his family came true. That was what he'd wanted, and that was what he'd got. As the newlyweds had little money and nowhere to live, Genevieve graciously invited them to stay with her and Nana until they 'got on their feet'. Richard was quite serious about his marriage with Barbara working. He swore off drinking hard liquor and gambling, and he stuck to his word . . . for the most part. Barbara still had no true idea about Richard's involvement in crime, in murder, and Richard knew that if he was serious about the marriage and having a family with Barbara, he had to give all that up. He had to go straight. *Become a working stiff, a civilian*, he said.

Because he had no education and no skills as such, Richard's opportunities for employment were limited.

LOVE AND MARRIAGE AND A BABY CARRIAGE

However, Barbara's Uncle Tony managed to get him a job at the Twentieth Century Deluxe Film Lab off Eighth Avenue in Manhattan. Richard didn't like having to go to the city every day, but he dutifully took the bus, carrying his lunch, prepared by Barbara, in a brown paper bag. The job consisted of lugging and shelving boxes and large reels of film, getting things for people, cleaning up discarded pieces of film. He was beginning at the bottom of the totem pole. The Twentieth Century Deluxe Film Lab made prints from masters to be distributed to movie theatres across the country. Richard, being a quick learner, always looking for angles, wanting to move up within the company, began to watch carefully how the printers made copies on the machines. There was a redheaded printer named Tommy Thomas, who patiently showed Richard how to make prints, step by step. After a few months, Richard did in fact begin working as a printer. He received a raise and was making ninety dollars a week. He had grown to like the job. And it didn't take long for Richard to find a way to make some extra cash: by bootlegging masters and selling them on the black market. The lab printed all of the Disney Company's masters for the East Coast, and Richard began running pirated prints of *Cinderella*, *Bambi* and *Pinocchio*, for which there was a ready market. It was now already the spring and Richard made pirating Disney cartoons a business.

Richard and Barbara's mother didn't get along. She didn't like the way he treated Barbara. Richard did, however, like Carmella. It was hard not to; she was gracious and kind and exceedingly giving.

Time seemed to fly by. Soon the holidays were upon them, and Richard very much enjoyed being at the festively decorated Christmas dinner table with Barbara's family, now as Barbara's husband. Proud and content, he ate and drank and laughed and even sang along with the family. He was one of them.

Sexually, Richard couldn't get enough of Barbara. The

couple did not practise any kind of birth control, and it didn't take long for Barbara to become pregnant again. But she lost this child too, a miscarriage through natural causes. Doctors told her she had weak muscles along the vaginal canal and her muscles weren't giving the proper support to the foetus, a condition none of the other women in her family had. But both Barbara and Richard wanted children, a family of their own, and they quickly set out to make that happen.

Richard had no reservations about hitting Barbara in front of Nana or Genevieve. He viewed a man striking his wife, physically dominating her at will, as the normal order of things. That was all he'd ever known growing up, and he slapped and pushed Barbara right in front of her mother. 'Richard, don't do that!' Genevieve would admonish him, but he couldn't care less. He even once threw a pillow at Genevieve and told her to mind her own business.

The couple finally rented a small apartment in West New York. What little money they had saved up was quickly exhausted. Richard hated being broke, wanting for things – furniture, clothes, a new car, a larger TV, a stereo player. It reminded him of the suffocating poverty and sacrifice of his youth. He became depressed, mean and short-tempered, and vented his rage on Barbara, who had grown to view his abuse as a twisted but intrinsic part of her marriage, and she stoically learned to accept it. But Barbara grew further and further away from Richard. At times, she felt she was a prisoner, not his wife, and, surprisingly, she often stood up to him, answered him back, disagreed with him, lashed him with her sharp, acerbic wit, which only fuelled his anger. Barbara had always been an outspoken, independent person with an edge to her personality, and her overbearing husband wasn't about to take that away from her. He broke her nose for smoking; he fractured ribs when she didn't spread peanut butter on his sandwich the way he liked; he gave her black eyes. Yet she stood up to him, her courage astounding given Richard's size and near-superhuman strength. Barbara was continually amazed by his strength, how he could carry a refrigerator, a stove, a porcelain sink up to their second-storey apartment all by himself, easily.

Barbara's third pregnancy occurred, and, under doctor's orders, she took it easy and did exercises to strengthen her weak muscles. Richard was attentive, would not let her carry anything heavy. But he still struck her, abused her, if she angered him or gave him lip.

'Big man, tough guy. You're nothing but a bully,' she'd say.

Often when Richard came home from work, he talked about the film lab and his gay colleague Tommy Thomas. Though Barbara had never met him, she knew what he looked like because Richard had described him; he had a freckled hatchet face and carrot-red hair.

One evening when the couple were in bed watching *The Milton Berle Show* on TV, a funny-looking man with bright-red hair appeared. Barbara offhandedly commented how odd he looked, that she imagined that was how Tommy looked. Without warning, Richard gave Barbara a beating, breaking her nose, beating her so violently that she began bleeding from her vagina. He called her mother. Genevieve hurried over, took one look at her daughter and called an ambulance. Barbara was now five months pregnant. The baby was coming out prematurely. Its leg was actually sticking out of Barbara when the emergency doctors examined her. They helped the baby out. It was a boy. It was dead.

Barbara was distraught. She hated Richard. She so wanted to have a child, a boy; she was inconsolable. She thought about telling the authorities what had happened, but was deathly afraid of what Richard would do to her family, to her mother, to her cousin Carl, whom Barbara was very fond of, Richard knew; so she kept her mouth shut about the beating and how she had really lost the child.

In the afternoon, Richard showed up at the hospital as if nothing had happened, carrying beautiful fresh red roses and a big box of expensive chocolates. He didn't say anything about what had occurred other than that it was Barbara's fault, to which she said, 'Yeah, sure, I beat myself up, I'm responsible for losing the child. Bullshit!' He ignored her. She came home two days later. She was quiet and sullen and wondered about her life with Richard, how she could deal with this violent madman she had married. The thought of suicide played in her head. She wondered if he'd physically abuse children they might have.

When Richard wanted to have sex with Barbara, she flat-out refused for a long time, but he was not about to take no for an answer, and Barbara became pregnant yet again, for the fourth time. Richard promised he wouldn't hit her, but if he came home in a bad mood, and something she did didn't please him, he'd slap her. As Barbara's stomach began to grow again, she summoned up the courage to tell him, 'Richard, listen to me carefully . . . real carefully. If God blesses us with a child, and you hurt that child, hit that child, I swear I'll kill you. I'll cut your throat while you're sleeping. I'll poison your food . . . I'll kill you. Hitting me, abusing me, is one thing. You ever so much as lift a finger to my child, you're dead.'

Strangely enough, Richard readily accepted this; he didn't even answer her.

Barbara and Richard moved again, to a cute little garden apartment in Cliffside Park. The fourth pregnancy was very difficult for Barbara. For the last several months, she was bedridden. She saw an obstetrician every week. Between doctor visits and everything else, money was short. To help make ends meet and save a little nest egg for the baby's arrival, Richard took a second job driving a delivery truck. He worked all day at the lab, took the bus home, had a quick dinner, and went and drove the delivery truck most of the night; then he would sleep for a few hours before he had to go back to the lab. He was always tired, in a bad mood, his body aching, and still he was coming up short. Having a child was an expensive proposition. *The harder I worked, it seemed, the less we had. I felt like I was . . . I was drowning, and no matter how hard I tried, I couldn't stay afloat*, Richard explained.

Against his better judgement and the solemn promise he'd made to himself, Richard decided to become a player again; now, however, he would be much more careful and judicious, not take any undue chances, he vowed.

And he soon turned to his old friend: crime.

Richard contacted a couple of fellows he knew back in Jersey City, two hard-boiled Irishmen who were quiet and stand-up, discreet and tough, professional hijack artists. One was John Hamil, the other Sean O'Keefe. They had contacts with guys who worked in different trucking companies and sometimes got tips about good loads. They knew that Richard was reliable and tough, that he kept his mouth shut – and that he was deadly. The three of them, tipped off by a loader, staked out a trucking company in Union City.

They saw how truckers just pulled into the yard, hooked up to a rig and drove away, waving to the security guard as they went. This, they decided, would be an easy way to get their hands on valuable loads without so much as a 'how do you do?' Richard even went to a truck-driving school to learn the intricacies of handling an 18-wheeler. He was the only one who had the balls to just drive onto the lot and hook up to a rig as if he had every right, so outright bold no one even thought of questioning him.

When the newly formed gang learned that there was a load of valuable jeans, they stole a cab. Richard dressed up as a truck driver, even donned a truckers'-union cap, drove the cab onto the lot, hooked up to the rig containing the jeans and pulled away, making a point of waving to the security guard, who smiled and waved back. It all went like clockwork. Now all they had to do was get the rig to a buyer in nearby Teaneck and get paid, and the job was done. Richard was pleased with how well the heist had gone. But he was still nervous: now, for the first time in his life, he had something to lose – a wife he loved and a child he would love unconditionally. The plan was for John and Sean to follow Richard to the Teaneck warehouse, but to keep up with Richard they went through a light and were pulled over by a New Jersey state trooper. Richard drove on, apprehensive and unsure of this huge rig on the open road. He calmed himself, reminded himself to drive slowly, to not do anything to get pulled over. The rig and cab were stolen and he had a gun on him, a .38 revolver with a two-inch barrel. If a cop did pull him over for some reason, he'd kill him and continue on. He would not, he vowed, go to prison, be taken away from the only person he'd ever cared for . . . and his unborn child. This child he would love and cherish, make sure it wanted for nothing.

As Richard thought about the future, hoping no cops came along, he inadvertently cut up a red Chevy. There were young men in it. They pulled alongside him and began cursing him, calling him names, then drew ahead of him and slowed, forcing him to jam on the heavy air brakes. Richard made a fist at them. They gave him the finger, a thing that always enraged Richard. They kept it up. He figured they were drunk and hoped they would leave him alone. But they continued forcing him to slow up and slam on the brakes. This went on for miles. Richard was concerned now that a state trooper would see him driving erratically and pull him over, and he'd have real trouble. He decided to pull over himself and stop, let the two jerks go on their way, which is what he did. But the car also stopped and backed up. Oh shit, Richard thought. All I'm trying to do is avoid trouble, but trouble won't leave me alone.

Shaking his head, Richard got out of the cab, hoping his huge size would calm the situation, but the two guys got out of their car, cursing Richard. One had a cut-down baseball bat.

'Look, fellas,' Richard said. 'I don't want no trouble here. Go on your way. I'm just trying to do a job here.'

'Fuck you, fuckin' asshole!' said the guy with the bat, who kept coming at Richard.

LOVE AND MARRIAGE AND A BABY CARRIAGE

'Fuck me? No, fuck you,' Richard said, and he pulled out the .38 and shot them both down. He walked up to them and put a bullet in each of their heads, wanting to be sure they were dead, could tell no tales. With that, he calmly got back into the cab and pulled away. Without further incident, he made it to the warehouse, received his end of the money and went home.

Always tight-lipped, he said nothing to Sean and John about what had happened.

With the proceeds of the job, twelve thousand dollars, Richard bought a nicer car, a large colour TV and some things they needed for the house and put a little something on the side. Barbara didn't ask him where he got the money; she knew better than to question him . . . about anything. If he had something to say, he'd tell her.

Richard was pleased. He had put it on the line, made a score; he was a man, a good provider. He'd prevail.

He didn't even think about the two men he'd killed. They were, for him, like two insects who had smashed up against the windscreen; they were roadkill, nothing more. But he did get rid of the gun he'd used to do the job.

These two murders were never linked to Richard – no witnesses, no clues, just two men shot to death on the road.

As Barbara's stomach grew, Richard tried to control his temper. He didn't want to hurt her, cause her to lose another child. He didn't want to become, he explained towards the end of his life, what his father had been. *When I get mad, I just see red and go off like a bomb. I didn't like that about myself. Still don't. I didn't want to hurt Barbara. I loved Barbara. Problem was, I guess I was obsessed with her. After I . . . after I struck her or became abusive, I was always mad at myself. Real mad. I'd look in the mirror and I really didn't like what I saw.*

Richard still had the gambling bug inside him.

Wanting to parlay the money he had made in the hijacking into more, he went to a high-stakes card game in Paterson,

New Jersey. When Richard arrived, he had six thousand dollars in hundred-dollar bills in his pocket. He had a golden winning streak for a few hours but wound up losing the whole six grand. Mad at himself, he went back home. Barbara had no idea about the money he'd had and lost. In a foul, dark mood, he walked in the door. It was just getting light out, but Barbara knew better than to question her erratic husband. She made him some eggs. He said they were overcooked, threw them on the floor and went to bed. *Good riddance*, thought Barbara.

Barbara's Aunt Sadie passed away. Her bad heart finally failed, and she died peacefully in her sleep. Barbara was devastated. She'd been very close to Sadie. Richard had liked Sadie – he didn't care for many people – and he attended the funeral with Barbara, dutifully sat there with the appropriate demeanour. When Barbara cried, he consoled her. He had never seen the way Italians openly express their grief, and he was taken aback by it. For Richard, death was just a process of nature – nothing to fall apart about. He seemed oddly removed and detached from the normal grief people experience after a loved one's passing. It was a classic symptom of his psychotic personality: no empathy. Stanley Kuklinski had, very successfully, beaten that out of Richard. Richard had never seen Barbara so upset, not even when she had lost the baby the year before.

When, that evening, they had to go for the final eulogy by the parish priest, Father Casso, Barbara and Richard were late because he went somewhere and picked her up after the service began. She was upset. He couldn't understand why.

'She's dead, isn't she?' he asked.

'That's not the point. The point is to show the proper respect.'

He had no good answer, no point of reference, no real concept of this kind of respect.

* * *

LOVE AND MARRIAGE AND A BABY CARRIAGE

Merrick Kuklinski was born in March 1964, a seemingly healthy baby girl. Barbara was overjoyed. She'd lost three children, and, with Richard's irrational explosions, who knew what could happen? Richard viewed this child, unlike those he had with Linda, as a prized blessing, and he was very attentive to Barbara. He couldn't have been more considerate about everything. Did she want something to drink, to eat? What could he get her? Barbara was beginning to think she had, in fact, married two distinctly different men, *the good Richard and the bad Richard. When*, she explained, *he was the good Richard, he couldn't have been nicer, more giving and considerate. When he was the bad Richard, he was the meanest bastard on the face of the earth . . .*

When it was time for Merrick to come home, Richard proudly carried his little girl to the car, being ever so careful, a big smile on his high-cheekboned face. He'd wanted a little girl, and he had her. Strangely enough, he felt a male child would eventually have competed for Barbara's affection, so he wanted only female children. At this point, he saw very little of the two boys he had with Linda. It was as though a different man had fathered them, not Richard. He felt no tie to those children as he did to Merrick.

When Merrick was brought home, Barbara's whole family came over to see her. Everyone was thrilled for Barbara, knowing that she'd lost three children in a row. Barbara's Nana Carmella went to church to light candles, to thank God, sure he had intervened and blessed her granddaughter with a beautiful, healthy baby girl. Drinks were poured. Expansive toasts were made. Richard proudly gave out cigars, the beaming father. Life was good.

Soon, however, they realised that Merrick wasn't as healthy as she seemed. She had a urinary block, which quickly caused kidney problems, high fevers, convulsions. She was in constant pain, and she had frequently to be taken to to the doctor's office to undergo numerous procedures and surgeries.

Meanwhile, Barbara became pregnant again. Her fifth

pregnancy was a comparatively easy one, though during the last several months she was again bedridden. This was a difficult time for her. She was not easy to get along with, was sometimes demanding and short-tempered. She had to make frequent trips to the doctor. Bills piled up. Richard felt as if he were swimming upstream and could make no headway no matter how hard he tried. He hustled, took chances, but still had difficulty making ends meet. He felt trapped. Barbara gave birth to a second girl, whom they named Christin.

As Merrick grew into an attractive child with large round eyes, she frequently had to stay in the hospital. Richard could not have been more attentive. He stayed by his first daughter's side, stroked her hair, hurried to get her anything she needed. He even slept, as did Barbara, in her hospital room with her, on the floor with just a pillow and a thin blanket. Barbara was pleasantly surprised at what a caring, devoted father Richard was. For the first time, she realised what a truly good man Richard could be, and she was glad he was her partner in this crisis.

Doctor and hospital bills mounted up. The couple were soon deep in debt. Though Barbara's mother and grandmother did what they could, Richard was forced to work more and more hours at the lab. Sometimes he'd do his shift, then stay the whole night printing pirated copies of popular films and cartoons. But no matter how hard he worked, how many hours of overtime he put in, how many pirated films he printed and sold, there was never enough money. Barbara became pregnant yet again. The family moved to a larger apartment in Cliffside Park. Bills kept coming. Richard later put it like this: *I felt like I was in a sinking hole, and the more I worked, the harder I tried, I was sinking deeper and deeper. This straight life wasn't working for me!*

Richard called John Hamil in Jersey City. 'You guys got anything good coming up?' he asked.

'Fact is, we do, Rich.'

* * *

LOVE AND MARRIAGE AND A BABY CARRIAGE

This job involved a truckload of Casio watches, which were popular and easy to turn into cash. There was a guy in Teaneck who'd buy the whole load. Richard, John and Sean went to see him. He had a warehouse just off Route 4. He was a big, burly individual who talked out of the side of his mouth as though he had lockjaw. He confirmed that he'd take the whole load; a price was agreed upon. 'Everyone wants one of those fuckin' watches. I'll take five truckloads if you guys can get your hands on 'em,' he assured them.

With that settled, Richard and his partners went about hijacking the load of Casio watches. They'd gotten a tip about the load, when and where it would be; they followed the truck and made the driver pull over and stop by showing phoney police badges. Richard got in the cab, and off they went, leaving the driver tied up by the side of the road. As always, Richard was wearing gloves. No matter what he did, if it was illegal, he wore gloves. They managed to get to the warehouse in Teaneck. The man who had agreed to purchase the load was all smiles. But he insisted his crew of three guys unload the truck to make sure there was a full load – one hundred thousand watches.

'Hey, my friend, they're all there,' Richard said. 'We didn't even open the rig.'

'I've gotta check,' was his answer.

'OK,' Richard said, 'no problem, my friend,' wanting to get this over with, to get the money and go home to his family. He was, of course, armed. He had two pistols stuck into his waistband under his jacket.

The three other guys used two fork-lifts to unload crates off the rig. Richard, Sean and John watched them, not pleased. When they had the load on the ground they proceeded to open the crates and actually count the boxes; there were exactly one hundred thousand watches. This took two full hours.

Richard was becoming impatient. 'See, I told you, my friend,' he said, knowing the more time he spent there, the greater the risk. Richard was becoming tense, and when that happened people often suddenly died.

'Come on in the office,' the buyer said. Richard had a bad feeling – something unsavoury was in the air.

'Wanna drink?' the buyer offered, speaking out of the side of his mouth.

'No thanks, just the money,' Richard said.

'You know, I wanted to talk to you about that,' said the buyer, who looked more like a weasel by the minute.

'About what?' Richard asked, knowing the answer.

'The money.'

'What's there to say, my friend? We agreed upon a price. You have the watches. Time for us to have the money. Simple.'

'Not so simple. I'm thinking I'd like to . . . renegotiate.'

'Come again?' Richard said, his high, wide brow creasing, his eyes growing cold, icy, distant.

'Fifty large instead of seventy-five. I'm more comfortable with that,' said the weasel.

'My ass!' said Richard. 'We agreed upon seventy-five. And now after you had your guys unload the watches you want to renegotiate? Funny guy . . . You know you're a funny guy, my friend.' Richard looked at Sean and John, his eyes telling them to get ready because there was going to be trouble. Gunplay.

'You know Tommy Locanada from Hoboken? He's my goombah. Let's call him and he'll tell you fifty is a good price.'

This really disturbed Richard. 'You can call Jesus fuckin' Christ himself if you want. We ain't taking fifty. We agreed upon seventy-five. That's what it is.'

'No it ain't,' the buyer said, and at that, Richard ran out of patience, whipped out the pistol, and shot the buyer in the head. He was dead before he even hit the ground, before he even knew his life was over. Richard hurried back into the warehouse and quickly killed the three other guys – bullets to the head.

LOVE AND MARRIAGE AND A BABY CARRIAGE

'We can't have witnesses,' he said, and they put the watches back in the truck and split, making sure they left no clues. When the bodies were discovered the next day and the police summoned, the murders were put down as 'mob related' and were never solved, never attached to Richard Kuklinski.

They managed to sell the load to Phil Solimene, a player Richard had known well for many years now. Solimene was a feral-looking man with thick dark hair, slicked back. He was charming and affable. Solimene had his fingers in many pies, all of them illegal. He had a discount store in Paterson with no sign out front. He sold everything, and everything he sold was stolen: small appliances, perfume, coffee and dried fruits, all kinds of canned goods – all hijacked stuff. Above the store he had a few girls who worked as prostitutes, and he sold porno movies too, even ones involving hard-core bestiality, any kind you wanted – women screwing and fellating dogs and Shetland ponies. There was a big market for that stuff, and Solimene was happy to fill it. He'd sell anything, including his own mother. He also ran a burglary gang, acting as a fence for all kinds of thieves who stole from people's homes all over New Jersey. He was, in a sense, the Fagin of New Jersey. On weekend nights, Solimene hosted poker games in the back of the store. Richard liked him because he was a born outlaw, a slick operator who would do anything to turn a buck; they spoke the same language. Though Solimene was not a born killer, as Richard apparently was, he had no qualms about setting someone up to be robbed and killed. Solimene was one of the few friends Richard ever had – which proved to be a fatal mistake.

Now the idea of returning full-time to a life of crime loomed larger every day, like a glistening pot of gold at the end of a long rainbow. Richard wanted more out of life. A bigger, juicier slice of the proverbial American dream. He even thought about 'hurting people' for money again – contract killing. It was something he did well, enjoyed and found challenging; but now he had a family, something to lose.

He continued to go to work every day at the film lab, stealing more and more from it. He noticed, he said, that the three men who owned the place were all stealing from one another, absconding with stock (huge cans of films) and masters they could make copies from and sell on the side.

Once Richard sniffed what was in the wind, they suddenly had a fourth partner – him. He became bolder and bolder and began to sell expensive rolls of film as well as the movies and cartoons he was pirating.

The lab, as a matter of course, also printed and developed X-rated movies. They were perfectly legal, and the lab processed most of the porno movies produced on the East Coast.

Richard began pirating these productions and would sometimes stay all night, running four or five machines at a time. He partnered with another guy in the lab, a developer, and together they printed and developed all kinds of pornography.

For the first time in his life, Richard was seeing hard-core porn on a regular basis. He said little of it turned him on; he viewed the women in these films as whores and sluts and was not aroused by them at all. He did, however, get a rise out of the 'girl-on-girl' productions. They also processed porn movies involving bestiality, one of which starred the not yet famous Linda Lovelace, giving a very happy German shepherd a lustful blowjob. Richard sold some of these films to Phil Solimene, and they seemed to fly off the shelves. He never mentioned any of this to Barbara. She knew he was bootlegging cartoons and thought nothing of it, didn't see it as any big deal.

Wanting to earn still more money, Richard spoke to a 'connected guy' he met at the labs, Anthony Argrila, an associate of the Gambino crime family. Argrila said he and his partner, Paul Rothenberg, would buy all the films Richard could pirate, and in this way, overnight, Richard fell into selling bootleg porn to the Gambino crime family, who had a lock on porn shops all over the entire country.

John Hamil called Richard to tell him that a load of television sets was leaving a trucking company just across the state line, in Pennsylvania. 'We got the number of the truck and everything,' John explained.

'Count me in.'

'Rich, we have to move quickly.'

'I'm ready to go,' said Richard, and the following night Richard, Sean and John headed to Pennsylvania. Rather than drive a hot rig to New Jersey with no buyer lined up, they decided to find a safe stash for the rig while they found a buyer. It was always better to sell the whole lot at once: wholesale, not retail, was the way to go. John knew a guy who had a farm and barn in Bucks County, and this man agreed to let them stash the rig in his barn for five hundred cash, no questions asked.

The truck was hijacked without difficulty. The driver had a gun put to him as he stopped for a traffic light on a lonely stretch of road. He was tied to a streetlamp and left there for the authorities to find. Richard and his partners wore masks. The driver couldn't give a description even if he wanted to, which he didn't. Nothing of his had been stolen. Why put his head in a noose? Richard drove the load to the farm. They left it in the barn and went to find a buyer. This was always the best way to off a hot load – not in a hurry, shop it around. In fact, it took them eight days to find a guy who'd buy the entire load at a fair price, COD. They returned to the farm for the load. The barn was empty, the truck gone. The man who owned the farm – a tall, skinny dude who needed a shave and a bath, had long hair, was missing front teeth – said he had 'no idea' where the truck was, looking the three hijackers square in the eyes, scratching his head as he did so.

'What?' Richard said.

'I have no idea what happened,' he said.

'My friend, there is no way anyone could have driven off with that load without you knowing. Do I look stupid here?'

'I have no fuckin' idea what happened to it,' the owner repeated. 'I swear!'

'We paid you good to stash the truck here. We want it. Where is it?'

'I don't know. I swear on my mother's life, I don't know,' he said, adamant.

Richard took a long, deep breath. 'Don't make me hurt you – I will hurt you bad,' he said. 'Where's our truck?'

'Honest, guys, I don't know! It was just suddenly gone.'

'My friend . . . this is your last chance. Where's our truck?'

'I'm tellin' you, I don't know!'

Richard had John and Sean tie the guy to a tree near the barn. This was a very desolate place, no other houses around for miles. That was one of the reasons they had chosen it. Now the skinny guy was pleading and telling them he knew nothing. Richard slapped him a few times.

'I swear I don't know!' he wailed, a little blood streaming from his lip.

A diabolical idea came to Richard; he calmly walked back to the car. He had two red flares, the kind used for road emergencies, in the boot. He grabbed one and returned to the guy. 'I'm telling you, I'm going to hurt you bad. Where's our load?' he asked, showing the man the flare.

'Buddy, I don't know!' The skinny man's bleeding lower lip was quivering now.

Richard had Sean and John take off the guy's shoes and socks. It was a nice spring day. Birds chirped. The sky was clear and friendly. The sun shone. Butterflies danced in the air. Richard lit the flare. A sudden tongue of white-hot flame leaped from it. Richard brought it to the man's left foot, just close enough to blister the flesh, not burn it. He was trying to give the guy a chance to talk, to spill the beans.

'Please, I'm telling you, I don't know. I swear!'

At that, Richard shoved the burning flare against his foot. The guy screamed and screamed, but denied any knowledge of the truck. The smell of burned flesh filled the air. Richard knew how intensely painful this was, and he was beginning to think that maybe the guy really didn't know. To be sure, he kept it up. When the guy's left foot looked like a charred piece of meat, Richard stopped. The bones of his toes were plainly visible; most of the flesh was gone. It didn't quite look like a foot any more.

'Where's our truck?' demanded Richard.

'On my mother's life, I don't know, on my mother's life!' he screamed, crying, his face a mask of tormented sincerity.

'Tell us and we'll take you to a hospital, you can get your foot taken care of and we'll be on our merry way. There's no way anyone could have gotten that rig off this farm without you knowing. It sounds like a fucking jet taking off.'

'I wasn't here 24 hours a day, I swear I don't know!'

Richard smiled his deviant wolf grin and went to work on the other foot, soon burning that to a bloody, seared mess, the guy screaming bloody fucking murder all the while.

By now, the first flare was all used up. Richard, John and Sean walked off to confer.

'I think if he knew, he'd've told,' said Sean.

'So do I,' John agreed.

'Yeah, I'm beginning to think so too,' Richard said, watching the guy crying like a baby. 'Maybe he really don't know,' Richard said.

But something, a sixth sense, told him the guy did know. Richard walked back to the car, retrieved the second flare, and went back to the distraught farm owner.

'Why,' Richard asked, 'are you causing yourself to suffer like this? Tell us. We'll drop you off at the hospital and it'll all be over and done –'

'But I don't knooow!' he pleaded.

Richard lit the second flare. 'OK, here goes, now I'm

through playing fuckin' games here. No more games. You tell us where our fucking load is or I'm burning your balls off.' He brought the white-hot flare to the guy's crotch.

'Jesus, Mary, Mother of God, I don't know!' he wailed, his eyes popping out of his head, cartoon-like.

At that, Richard calmly pushed the flare up against his crotch. The intense flame quickly burned through the fabric, and Richard held the searing heat to the man's suddenly exposed testicles. He screamed and wailed, begging, promising, swearing he didn't know. When the man's balls were burned to a shriveled knob of flesh, Richard took away the flare. The guy was so distraught now he could hardly talk.

Richard, a bona fide sadistic psychopath, felt no sympathy for the guy. John and Sean were slightly appalled. It was hard not to be. The man was a sorry sight.

'Where's our load, my friend?' Richard asked. 'This is just the beginning.'

'I . . . I . . . I . . . don't know,' he managed to cry.

'OK, here goes your dick,' Richard said. 'I'm going to burn your fucking cock off.' He brought the flare to him –

'Don't! I'll tell you! I'll tell you!'

'Where is it?' Richard asked, really pissed off now.

'On a farm down the road. My friend Sammy has it.'

'Sammy has it,' Richard said. 'You fuckin' moron. Why didn't you tell us in the first place and avoid all this?'

'Because I thought . . . I thought I could fool you,' the farm owner gasped, as if he'd been running full out.

'Does it look like you fooled us?' Richard asked.

'No.'

'You could have avoided all this pain.'

'I didn't want to do it. My girl needed an abortion. I was desperate for money.'

'You think money is worth your balls . . . My friend, you don't have any balls any more.'

'I knooow,' he wailed.

'Idiot,' Richard said, 'fuckin' idiot!'

Richard sent John and Sean to the farm while he stayed with Burned Balls.

Sammy came walking out of the door of the farmhouse when they pulled up.

'You got our truck?' Sean said.

'What truck?' came the reply.

'Here we go again,' John said.

'Jon Atkins says you got our truck.'

'Jon said that? I don't have any truck,' said Sammy. He was a short burly guy with a big round head. There were food crumbs in his beard. Flies buzzed around his huge head. If you looked up 'white trash' in the dictionary, you might very well see a picture of this individual. Sean called Richard and told him what Sammy had said.

'Put some hurt on him,' Richard suggested. They whipped out their guns and began to pistol-whip Sammy. He immediately gave it all up, said the truck was behind a stand of trees out back, took them there, and, lo and behold, they finally found their truck.

Back at Burned Balls' farm, Richard decided both of these guys had to die. He figured it was just a matter of time before the guy whose feet and balls he'd ruined would come looking for revenge. Without a moment's hesitation, he shot them both in the head, and off the hijackers went, back to New Jersey, where they sold the load at the agreed-upon price.

Money, however, seemed to burn a hole in Richard Kuklinski's pocket. He took the family on a holiday to Florida, and he lost a lot of money at poker and baccarat tables. Nevertheless, with some of the proceeds from the score and money Barbara's mother and Nana Carmella gave them, Richard and Barbara managed to buy a new home, a two-family house in West New York. Richard had always wanted a house of his own, a castle he could be king of. He finally had it, and he would rule his castle with an iron hand.

21

ENTER THE
LONE RANGER

It was late 1970, and a young man who would eventually play a pivotal role in Richard's life was just finishing a four-year stint in the air force. His name was Patrick Kane.

Kane was a tall, handsome 22 year old with a wiry, muscular body and a thick head of dark hair, which he combed straight back. He had large walnut-shaped brown eyes, filled with hope and optimism, set in a symmetrical, oval-shaped face. Kane had been brought up in Demarest, New Jersey, a small town where everyone knew one another. The youngest of three boys, Pat was an upbeat but pensive young man, still not quite sure what exactly he wanted to do with his life. He was thinking of working on a 250-acre farm a friend of his owned in Pennsylvania. What drew him to the farm was the fact that he'd be outdoors all day. Ever since Pat Kane had been a kid he had always craved the open air.

Kane was a superb athlete and excelled at all the sports he played: wrestling, baseball, football and basketball. He was very fast and strong and had excellent natural reflexes and coordination. But his favourite sport was fishing. He loved to fish on quiet, out-of-the-way lakes and streams, eating what he caught. He did not like hunting, because he felt it was inherently unfair to shoot an unsuspecting, unarmed animal that couldn't defend itself.

ENTER THE LONE RANGER

Kane had been stationed in Sacramento, California, and in Iceland. He met his sweetheart, Terry McLeod, while stationed in California. They met on a blind date, and it was love at first sight. Pat had just left her and already missed her a lot.

The day Pat returned home, his brother Eddie, a New Jersey state trooper, came to pick him up at Newark Airport. Ed was wearing his immaculate gold-and-black uniform and driving a shiny state-police car. The two brothers hugged long and hard. The Kane family were all very close. While Eddie was driving him to their parents' home, he said, 'Pat, the test's next Tuesday.'

'What test?' asked Pat.

'To be a state trooper.'

'Eddie, I'm not sure what I want to do yet.'

'Pat, it's a great job. The money and benefits are good, and you've got a chance to make a difference, to make this world we live in a better place. You'd be a good cop, Pat, I'm sure.'

'I'll think about it.'

'The test is next Tuesday,' Eddie repeated. 'Pat, we are the first and last defence against the bad guys. Without us, society would fall apart.'

Pat knew his brother had a point; he just didn't know if he wanted to live the regimented life of a state trooper. The New Jersey State Police was, he knew, run like a military operation. You had to follow strict guidelines, rules and regulations, something Pat had been doing now for the last four years. He wanted some space, room to breathe, not to jump from one uniform to another.

When Eddie and Pat reached the Kane home, Patrick senior and Helen Kane, Pat's parents, came hurrying out of the front door, both of them hugging and kissing Pat and welcoming him home. He was their youngest, and they'd been worried about him; he had never lived away from home before he left for the air force. Now he was back safe and sound, and they were very pleased.

'Welcome home, son. Welcome home,' Patrick Kane said, holding his last-born hard. Pat was so happy to be home and with his parents that tears came to his eyes.

'Come on inside, son. I've cooked you a wonderful meal,' Helen Kane said.

As it happened, it took a full year for Pat to decide what he wanted to do with his life. During that time, he worked in menial jobs, did a lot of fishing, spoke to his sweetheart on the phone several times a week, went to visit her when he had the funds. Pat had little money; his parents weren't wealthy people, and cash was tight.

Several factors finally convinced him to become a state trooper. First and foremost was his brother Ed. Just about every day, Pat saw Ed in his slick uniform, his gun prominent on his right hip. Second, Pat came to realise just how vitally important law-enforcement officers really were. They were, just as Eddie had said, the first and last defence society had against the rapists, murderers, thieves and desperadoes. Every day, Pat heard about the unspeakable atrocities people committed on one another. You couldn't read a newspaper or watch the news without learning about another heinous crime. The third reason Pat was drawn to becoming a state trooper was the challenge. The physical tests and requirements were extremely difficult. You had to be in tip-top shape to qualify. On average, only 50 out of 5,000 applicants met the physical mandates. Last, he was attracted to the state police because he'd be working outdoors most of the time.

In the spring of 1971, Pat Kane applied to be a state trooper. He easily passed both the written and physical tests, and towards the end of that winter he became a Jersey state trooper. His parents and brothers came to the graduation ceremony. Pat Kane cut a dashing, handsome figure in his spanking new uniform, and he looked forward – *in a big way*, he recently explained – to making a difference, *to trying to make this volatile world we live in a better place, keeping the wolves at bay.*

ENTER THE LONE RANGER

One of the first things Pat did after graduating from the trooper academy was to ask Terry to marry him. She said yes, and soon she moved up to Demarest, leaving her family and all her friends behind, and married Pat.

Pat Kane now felt he had everything a man could hope for: a good job that was meaningful, rewarding and challenging, and which kept him outdoors, and a beautiful, devoted wife who thought the world of him.

Terry, Pat recently explained, *gave up everything, her family, her home, her friends, surroundings she was familiar with, to be with me. To be my wife. As far as I was concerned I was the luckiest guy in the world.*

Thus the die was cast, the stage set for one of the most important, shocking murder investigations in the annals of modern crime history in America, indeed in the world.

PART III

VERY BAD GOODFELLAS

22

MAKING ENDS MEET

Richard Kuklinski was still putting in a lot of overtime, though at another film lab. Now he was pirating mostly porno movies; there was a large and ever-expanding market for porn, and Richard was dutifully filling it.

All the hours of overtime he was putting in, however, were causing guys in the lab to complain to the film printers' union, and a delegate came to the lab to talk to Richard. The delegate was a broad-shouldered Irishman with an attitude problem, the type of guy who doesn't know how to wield authority – a bully. He stopped Richard as he was leaving work. The lab he was working at now was on West Fifty-fourth. They went into the DeWitt Clinton Park on Twelfth Avenue to talk. By now it was dark.

'We got complaints,' the union guy began, 'that you're taking all the overtime.'

'Hey,' Richard said, 'they ask me if I want the time, I say yes. I got a wife and child. What's the problem?'

'Problem is you're stealing from the other guys.'

'My ass! They're saying they don't want the work. I do. Take a walk.'

Richard started on his way. The union guy grabbed his shoulder, and Richard spun and hit him a solid roundhouse right. As the union man went down, he struck his head hard on the edge of a park bench. Unmoving, he stayed on the ground.

Richard checked for a pulse. There wasn't one. *Oh shit!* he thought. *I'm in hot water now.*

He knew people had seen them together and figured someone at the union knew the guy had come out to talk with him, and now he was dead. Not good. Richard quickly hid the body in some bushes there, went to a nearby hardware store, bought some strong rope and hustled back to the park. He spotted a wooden milk crate in front of a grocery store and grabbed it. Richard made sure no one was watching, dragged the guy to a tree, tied the rope around his neck, threw the other end over a thick branch, hoisted the guy up, tied the loose end of the rope to a park bench, put the milk box under his dangling feet and left him there like that, quite dead, swinging in a breeze off the Hudson River, no one the wiser.

When the police found the body of the union official, they first believed that it was indeed a suicide, but soon suspicion fell upon the notorious Westies gang. This was their turf, the heart of Hell's Kitchen. The leaders, Mickey Featherstone and James Coonan, were picked up and questioned. They said, truthfully, that they knew nothing. Richard was never even suspected, let alone questioned. He had amazing luck when it came to killing people.

For the most part, Richard now stayed clear of his mother and his sister, Roberta. He had grown genuinely to hate his mother – he thought of her as 'cancer' – and he despised Roberta, considering her to be a whore; however, after several years had passed, he did have some contact with his brother Joseph. What had happened in the bathroom stall was forgotten. Richard felt he could have done more to help Joseph: given him advice, direction, a brotherly helping hand. Richard now saw his brother once a month or so. They'd meet in a bar for a drink, Richard would give Joseph a few dollars, and that was it. Though he didn't like it, Richard had learned to accept his brother's homosexuality.

Joseph, like Richard, had a hair-trigger, homicidal temper, and hurt people with broken bottles, chains and stools in bar fights. Several times, Richard had to go to Jersey City to get Joseph out of jams. Each time Richard helped Joe, he warned him it was the last time, said he had a family now and couldn't be coming to get him out of trouble all the time.

Richard received a call from Joe late one Saturday afternoon. 'Richie, I got a problem,' Joseph said.

'Yeah, what now?'

'I'm in a bar. There's four guys here and they won't let me leave.'

'Why not?'

'They say I owe them money.'

'Do you?'

'We were playing cards, and I guess I lost.'

'How much?'

'Not much.'

'Just walk out, Joe.'

'They won't let me. I tried. There's four of them. They got . . . bats.'

'Bats?'

'Yeah.'

Richard took a long, exasperated breath. 'This is the last time I'm going to help you. Understand?' he said.

'Yeah,' Joe said.

Richard hung up.

Everyone knew Joseph Kuklinski was his brother, and Richard didn't like the idea of a group of guys holding him hostage, threatening him with bats. Where did they get off thinking they could get away with such a thing?

Richard had a locked attaché case that he kept hidden in the garage. From it, he retrieved two .38 over-and-under derringers loaded with dumdum bullets and put them in his jacket pockets. Then he put a hunting knife in his sock and drove to Jersey City, getting angrier with each mile. Angry that his brother was such a fuck-up, angry that these guys would dare to hold him hostage. Richard parked his car a few blocks away from the bar, made sure no one was lying in wait for him and walked into the bar. His brother was sitting at a table off to the left. There were indeed four burly guys sitting around him. One of them, Richard could see, had a bat under the table.

'Come on, Joe, let's go,' Richard ordered. Joe began to get up. The largest of the four guys walked over to Richard.

'He ain't goin' anywhere till he pays what he owes. I'm glad you came, Rich. We know you're a stand-up guy.'

'How much does he owe?'

'Five fifty.'

'I'll make sure he does his best to pay you back. Come on, Joe, let's go,' Richard ordered again.

'Hey, I says he ain't goin'.'

'Joe, walk toward the fucking door,' Richard ordered.

'We know all about you, Rich, that you always carry a gun. Why don't you pay what he owes?'

'I ain't paying you anything. If you know all about me, you know I'm not going to let you hold my brother against his will. Joe, come on over here!' Joe began to stand.

'Stop him,' the one close to Richard said.

Richard ran out of patience. He pulled his right hand out of his pocket, let them see the gun in his hand.

'I got a slug for each of you,' Richard said. 'Come on, Joe!'

At that, the four guys backed down. Joseph joined Richard. They both walked out the door.

'Thank you, Rich,' Joe said.

'This is the last time. You gotta stop this shit.'

'They cheated. That's what this is all about – they set me up.'

'I don't give a hoot. Joe, I can't be doing this stuff. I got a wife and two kids. Merrick is sick. She needs me. I can't be doing this any more . . . OK?'

'OK . . . I understand,' Joe said.

By now they were half a block away from the bar. They began to cross the street when a car, the four guys in it, came barrelling down on them. The driver tried to run the brothers over. Richard pulled out one of the derringers and fired two shots. One of the bullets hit the boot lock, and the boot popped open. Within seconds, it seemed, police sirens filled the air. Richard tossed both the derringers away. Police cars blocked off each end of the street. The driver of the car told them that Richard had shot a gun at them. Richard, of course, denied it.

'What gun, where?' Richard said.

But the cops found the two bullet holes in the car and began looking for the gun, and they found one of the derringers. Everyone was cuffed and arrested. Richard was fit to be tied. He needed this like a hole in the head. At the police station, Richard denied having any gun, and he warned the four guys in the car to keep their mouths shut.

'You don't say anything and we'll all walk, got it?'

They nodded, but Joseph again began arguing with them, saying they had cheated him, they had set him up, they had called the cops.

'Shut up! All of you shut the fuck up,' Richard demanded. 'The cops are listening.' They became quiet. Detectives interrogated them. Everyone kept his mouth shut, but the detectives knew what had happened and kept badgering Richard. He wouldn't even talk to them. Richard didn't like cops; they were corrupt bullies with guns and badges, and he had no reservations about letting his animus show.

Finally able to make a call, Richard phoned a criminal attorney in Jersey City and told him what had happened. The attorney came over to the jail and told Richard he needed money to 'resolve the matter'. Jersey City was one of the most corrupt municipalities in America. Cops and judges could be bought and sold for little more than a song and dance. Richard quickly made another call, got John Hamil on the phone, told him what had happened and asked him to get three grand to the lawyer.

'Done, brother,' John said.

Richard and the others stayed in jail overnight. Richard called Barbara to say he was working at the lab. Richard often stayed at the lab overnight, doing overtime.

In the morning, they were all taken to court for arraignment. In a foul mood, Richard made sure no one said anything. His lawyer found them in the holding pen, winked and said, 'Everything is taken care of.' They soon appeared before the judge – who had been given the three Gs by Richard's lawyer. The judge said he didn't see 'reasonable cause' to hold over the case, levied a small fine and dismissed it on the spot.

As Richard and the others were walking out of the courtroom, one of the detectives – not a happy camper – walked up to Richard. 'Here's your gun back,' he offered, holding out Richard's derringer.

'That's not my gun,' Richard said, and walked out of the courtroom.

Outside, he told his brother: 'This is it. Get yourself in another jam, I am not going to help you. You understand?'

'Yeah,' said Joseph sheepishly, 'I understand.'

23

MURDER RUNS
IN THE FAMILY

The dog had a broken leg and was in shock, shaking and trembling and barking non-stop in the yard of a building on Jersey City's Central Avenue, number 438. It was 12.30 a.m., 16 September 1970, and the dog was disturbing people trying to sleep. It belonged to Pamela Dial, a 12-year-old girl, small for her age and thin. Pamela had black hair and large, round, dark eyes. She was a straight-A student at nearby St Anne's Parochial School. She lived at 9 Bleeker Street with her mother and father and brothers, John and Robert, just around the corner from Central Avenue, the block on which Joseph and Anna Kuklinski lived.

Pamela loved her dog, Lady, a little black-and-white mutt. They were always together; wherever Pam went, the dog was with her, wagging its tail and unusually attentive to its owner.

Earlier, shortly after eleven o'clock that fateful Tuesday night, Pamela had left the house looking for her dog. She had not finished her homework yet; it was still spread out on her bed. Nor did she tell her family she was going out to find Lady. Her parents were watching the eleven o'clock news when she left and didn't even know she'd gone.

Pamela did find her dog and was walking home when she ran into Joseph Kuklinski.

Joseph and Pam knew each other from the neighbourhood.

Joseph was tall and handsome, thin and muscular, had glistening, long blond hair, a Fu Manchu moustache. He was now twenty-five years old. The two talked. Joseph asked Pamela if she'd like to be alone with him. Not knowing exactly what he had in mind, she innocently said OK and followed Joseph Kuklinski into a four-storey building, 438 Central Avenue, and up to the roof. Joseph lived at 434 Central Avenue with his mother, just two doors down. Joseph had used the roofs along Central Avenue for sexual liaisons many times over the years, with both girlfriends and boyfriends. Pamela had no idea of what Joseph was after. He was known in the neighbourhood as 'Cowboy Joe', and she thought he was cute. She liked the idea that he was paying attention to her, that he wanted to be alone with her. Unaware of the demons inside of Joseph Kuklinski's head, Pamela willingly went up to the roof.

Joseph had been drinking. He was buzzed and smelled of alcohol. On the roof, he quickly came to the point and tried to have sex with Pam. She refused. He wouldn't take no for an answer. He forced himself on her, sodomised her, then choked her to death; all the while, little Lady was barking like mad. Joseph tried to catch the dog but couldn't.

When Joseph was finished with Pamela, he picked up her lifeless body as if it were a rag doll and tossed her off the roof. She hit the cement back yard of 438 Central Avenue with a meaty, bone-breaking thud. Joseph then managed to catch the dog and tossed it off the roof, too. The hapless animal landed near Pamela, and its legs and several ribs broke. Lady crawled to Pamela's lifeless body and began to cry, then howl and bark non-stop. People called the police to complain about the insistent barking and howling. A squad car was dispatched. The police discovered Pamela Dial's lifeless, broken body.

The murder of a child, even in rough-and-tumble Jersey City, was a rare event, an outrage. Early that morning, every available detective and uniformed cop in Jersey City was looking for Pamela's killer, canvassing the neighbourhood, knocking on doors, stopping people driving by. Detectives soon learned that Pamela had been seen talking to Joseph Kuklinski the night before. When Detective Sergeant Ben Riccardi came knocking on the Kuklinskis' door, Joseph was still sleeping and hung over. When he was taken to the police station and threatened by angry Jersey City detectives, he admitted what he'd done.

'I threw her off the roof,' he said. At that, Joseph was roughly handcuffed and placed under arrest.

Later that day, Anna Kuklinski called Richard and told him that Joseph had been arrested for the killing of a 12-year-old girl. This bowled Richard over. He couldn't conceive of his brother doing such a thing. It had to be some kind of mistake. As much as Richard wanted nothing to do with his mother, he hurried to Jersey City. Just the day before, Richard had gone to see Joseph. He'd waited in a bar on Central Avenue for him, but he hadn't shown up. Richard had known that Joseph was at home, out of work, but he hadn't knocked on the door to get his brother because he didn't want to see his mother; he had grown to despise Anna to that degree. The few times she had come to his home, Anna had always tried to instigate trouble with Barbara, who also grew to loathe her mother-in-law, although she tolerated her. Barbara had no choice; Anna was Richard's mother, after all.

My mother was cancer; she slowly killed whatever she touched, Richard said shortly before his death.

At first, Richard was willing to try to help Joseph, to get him a lawyer. He found his younger brother at the Jersey City jail, and Joseph admitted at once to Richard that he had raped and killed the girl and thrown her and her dog off the roof.

'Why the fuck would you do such a thing?' Richard demanded, so angry he wanted to beat his brother, beat him to death. Richard had two daughters, and the thought of someone doing that to either of them left him cold and empty inside – outraged.

'Because,' Joseph said, 'she wanted it.'

At that, Richard stood up and walked away; he would never talk to his brother Joseph again.

That day, I washed my hands of him, wanted nothing to do with him any more. As far as I was concerned, I didn't have a brother. I didn't have a family. To hell with them all . . .

Within several months, Joseph Kuklinski was convicted of Pam Dial's murder, given a life sentence and sent to Trenton State Prison. To Richard, he had no brother. No mother. No sister. No family.

24

LET'S DO THE TWIST

The film lab where Richard worked now moved to a
new space on Forty-sixth Street, not far from the famous
Peppermint Lounge on Forty-fifth Street, the place where
Joey Dee and the Starliters started the world-wide craze
for the Twist. Richard sometimes liked to go there in the
early evening, before he started a double shift bootlegging
porn, for a cocktail or two. Richard well knew he shouldn't
drink hard liquor, but it mellowed him. He was, in a sense,
self-medicating, for the liquor tended to calm him; but he
also became nasty when he drank, just like his father and
brother. On this night, he made an off-colour remark to a
woman at the bar; she took offence and complained to her
boyfriend, who in turn said something nasty to Richard. The
guy was a friend of the bartender. Soon in an argument with
the bartender, Richard reached over the bar and grabbed
him by the tie. He was going to sock him, but the bouncer
interceded, coming out of nowhere, and made Richard leave,
said he'd call the cops.

On the sidewalk outside, Richard was talking to the
bouncer, trying to explain how the bartender had a big mouth,
when suddenly the bouncer sucker-punched him.

'Why'd you do that?' Richard asked, more shocked and
embarrassed than hurt.

''Cause you got a big fuckin' mouth. Come back and'll send
you to the hospital,' the bouncer promised.

'Thanks for the warning,' Richard said. 'I will be back. Count on it, my friend.' Richard went back to the lab, fuming. The punch had cut his lip, and he was bleeding slightly. He wasn't really physically hurt, but the incident ate at him. He couldn't forget it. Another guy might have written it off as a stupid occurrence that meant nothing.

But not Richard.

His mood fouled.

He couldn't think of anything but this bouncer and getting even. Having revenge. Killing him. But how? Forty-fifth Street was a very busy thoroughfare. The club was popular, people were always there, moving in and out.

Richard took out his anger on Barbara, abused her for not making a sandwich correctly, not cutting off the crusts just so, the way he liked. Though Richard never touched either of his daughters, he frequently abused Barbara or broke furniture in front of them.

That night, Richard couldn't sleep; he couldn't stop thinking about how the bouncer had embarrassed him, disrespected him, hit him with a sneaky punch. Richard resolved to murder the bouncer. Come hell or high water, he was dead.

Some three days later, Richard was ready. He had it all worked out. He left the house that morning carrying a change of clothes, those of a labourer. He had a .22 with him, in a paper bag with his lunch – two turkey-on-rye sandwiches with extra mayo, his favourite.

Late that afternoon, Richard went to the bathroom, which was in the hall. He changed into the clothes he had brought, put a peaked cap on his head, pulled the brim down in front of his face and went downstairs. He knew the bouncer began work at about 4.00 p.m. Richard stood in front of the building with the gun in his coat pocket, staring, waiting, looking for an opportunity to strike, like a hungry predatory cat with its eyes on a potential meal. The club had a large picture window, and he could clearly see inside. It was a chilly autumn day in 1971, and Richard had murder on his mind.

What this bouncer had done was, for Richard, exactly what his father had done to him – struck him for nothing when he least expected it – and as Richard stared at the club, memories of Stanley's brutality, in stark, harsh black-and-white images, flashed before his eyes. These memories often came back to Richard like this, as if he were watching an old silent movie.

A band began to rehearse inside the club. Richard could hear the music across the street. Everyone at the bar looked towards the stage. This was the moment to move, to strike. Quickly, catlike, Richard crossed the narrow street and opened the door. The bouncer was right there. Perfect. Without a moment's hesitation, Richard put the .22 close to his head and fired, turned and calmly walked out, not looking back. He took a right, grabbed a cab on the corner and had it take him to the Port Authority Bus Terminal on Forty-first Street. There, Richard changed back into his clothes, threw away the outfit he had been wearing and walked back to work. Now there were cop cars and ambulances in front of the Peppermint Lounge, spinning red lights. A big crowd had gathered. Richard stopped and looked for several moments, just another curious guy, then went into the building where he worked, feeling good and whole – at peace. He wasn't even remotely suspected of the killing, was never questioned about it, never connected to it.

A change of sorts had come over Richard: these recent killings reminded him of his past, and he coveted having power over life, deciding who would live and who would die, when and where and how.

Murder, Richard knew, was one of the few things in life that he truly excelled at. It seemed, he mused, that he had a gift for it, and he began to think seriously of hiring himself out as a contract killer again, making that his profession, his job, his speciality, committing himself as a killer for hire.

But now, he reminded himself, he had a wife and two adorable little girls. He couldn't do anything to jeopardise them. Yet he believed that if you planned a killing carefully, meticulously, didn't hurry it, it was relatively easy to get away with it as long as there was no tangible link between the killer and the victim. This, he knew, was the reason serial killers were so hard to catch: the randomness of the crimes made it nearly impossible for the police to connect the killer to the victims. Richard would exploit this element over and over again.

With these life-and-death musings in his head, Richard returned to Jersey City and Hoboken and let it be known that he was available for 'special work'. He also went to see Tony Argrila, the porn distributor. He found him at his office on Spring Street in downtown Manhattan. Argrila was in his mid-40s, balding, short and heavy, with a thick Brooklyn accent. He and Paul Rothenberg were responsible for almost all the porn produced in New York. They had a silent partner named Roy DeMeo.

'I need to make some serious money,' Richard began. 'I want to get back in the life. I –'

'Listen to me,' Argrila stopped him. 'You really wanna make money, get into porn. There's truckloads a money to make. We'll front you whatever you want. No problem.'

Richard didn't see much of a future making porn movies. He thought of it as dirty and didn't want to get that involved in it. Pirating it was one thing; making it himself was another. Murder – murder was OK, nothing wrong with that. But producing porn movies was sleazy . . . beneath him, as it were.

'I'm tellin' you, there's a ton a fuckin' money in it,' Argrila repeated.

'Really?'

'Abso-fuckin-lutely. No fuss, no muss and it's perfectly legal. We'll give you all the product you need. I know you're a stand-up right guy. Just pay us for what you take when you get paid, and you're in business.'

'I'll think about it,' Richard said, ultimately warming to the idea because it was, in fact, perfectly legal. The more he thought about it, the more appealing the idea seemed, and he decided to try it, what the hell. But he knew that if he did delve into this, he would have to make a go of it, not fuck up, because the money involved was mob money, and he had to pay it back in a timely fashion. He didn't like owing mob people anything, but for such an enterprise, he also knew, there was nowhere else to turn. *I couldn't go to a bank and say, 'I got three naked girls and two guys with hard-ons and I want to make movies'*, he explained.

So Richard began taking large shipments of porn on consignment from Argrila and Rothenberg and wholesaling it all over the East Coast. Money began pouring in. Richard was surprised at how much in demand porn was, and the dirtier and kinkier it was, the better. Because he was selling most of the product he was getting from Argrila on consignment, the bill he had with Argrila quickly grew to seventy-five thousand dollars, since Richard was spending money he should have been giving Argrila.

Richard wasn't even sure Argrila and his partner were really mob connected. Guys were always saying they were 'mobbed up'. Richard kept taking product and was slow in paying it back. He also got it into his head to make his own movies, to have his own line, and decided to use the money he owed Argrila to start his own business. This proved, as Richard would soon find out, to be a near-fatal error in judgement.

Richard quit working in the film lab and immersed himself in the porn business full time. Argrila and Rothenberg kept asking for money, and he kept stalling them. From working in film labs over the years, Richard did know quite a few people who made porno movies: line producers, camera people, even directors. He began talking to some of these individuals and quickly realised that he could indeed make his own porno movies from scratch. Using Argrila's money, that's exactly what he did – he began producing porno films, hired directors he knew, made deals with them and let them run the show. He was only interested in the end result: making money.

Richard's daughter Merrick's health was not improving. She was frequently in pain and had raging fevers, sometimes up to 106 degrees. Her sickness and distress embittered Richard even more. Her suffering, any child's suffering, was so unfair that surely, he thought, there was no God. How could any God allow a child to suffer? Richard had great empathy for children, though absolutely none for adults. He and Barbara did all they could for Merrick, but nothing they did worked. At least he was making money now and had the funds needed for Merrick's care.

Richard was thinking he'd deal in porn for a short while – a few years at the most – make some serious money and get the hell out of the business. Maybe move to the West Coast, buy a house on the beach and relax. That was Richard's dream: to have a first-class white house on a beach and enjoy the view, the glorious sunsets, watch the girls frolic in the surf.

Richard said nothing to Barbara about what he was doing or his plans for the future. He knew she wouldn't like it. As much as Richard dominated and abused Barbara, he had much respect for her; he valued her opinion and her judgement. She often explained things to him that he read in the newspapers and didn't understand. An avid reader, Barbara told him about books she enjoyed. She was always reading a book, both popular novels and classics. Richard was, of course, still dyslexic and had comprehension problems when it came to the written word. The only thing he ever truly enjoyed reading were the true-crime magazines; those, for some reason, he never had any trouble understanding.

The movies Richard was producing were shot in dilapidated warehouses – no doubt now fashionable lofts – in SoHo. Richard never went to any of the shoots. He was not interested in seeing the films being made. He thought little of the people who did such things and didn't want to be around them. For him, this was strictly a money-making proposition. He had no prurient interest at all. He was, when it came to sexual matters, a bit of a prude. Because all the films Richard was distributing were given out on consignment and were paid for after the retailer sold them, there was a mandatory period of time that the producers had to wait to get paid. There was no getting around that.

When Richard was sober and not in a bad mood, he was relatively easy to get along with. People he did business with tended to like him. He had a keen sense of humour and would readily pay for drinks and meals. For the most part, he tried to keep his word. Because of that, he expected others to keep their word, which all too often didn't happen. One individual who let him down was named Bruno Latini. He was a short, balding, mobbed-up guy who owned a bar on Eighth Avenue. Richard had given him fifteen hundred dollars' worth of films on consignment. Because the 52-year-old Latini had mob connections (his brother was Gambino captain Eddie Lino; it would later be alleged that Lino's murder was committed by crooked cops Louis Eppolito and Stephen Caracappa at the behest of Anthony 'Gaspipe' Casso), he thought he could get away without paying. He kept stalling Richard, then stopped returning his calls. This incensed Richard, ate at him.

Christmas was still very much a big deal to Barbara and she went out of her way to make the holidays special; she bought dozens of wonderful gifts, had a huge tree, decorated the house beautifully. That Christmas Eve, Richard was quiet and morose. He was thinking of Latini, not his family. When everyone went to bed, he quietly got into his car and drove to the city looking for Latini, looking to kill him. It was snowing hard but that didn't stop Richard. When he reached Latini's bar, he learned that he had just left. Richard went to the lot on the corner of Forty-ninth Street and Tenth Avenue and found Latini sitting in his car. He invited Richard into the car and gave him a song and dance about the fifteen hundred dollars.

Richard pulled out a .38 and shot him twice in the head. For a minute or two he was blinded and couldn't hear because of the report of the gun in the enclosed space. Richard found Latini's wallet. There were several thousand dollars in it. He took his fifteen hundred and put the wallet back with the rest of the money still in it. Odd. He finally stepped from the car, went back to his Cadillac and returned to New Jersey.

In the morning, on Christmas Day, a parking attendant found Latini with his destroyed head, quite dead. Police discovered his wallet on him and there were sixteen hundred dollars in it. This murder was never linked to Richard by the police or by the mob.

I killed him, Richard explained, *out of principle. He thought he could treat me like a piece of wood.*

Though Barbara made a big deal of the holidays, they tended to depress Richard. They reminded him of his childhood, and that always made him . . . angry. He still thought about his father, about killing him.

Tony Argrila kept hounding Richard for the money he owed. Richard kept stalling, giving excuses, not money, to Argrila. Just when Argrila began getting hot under the collar, Richard would give him some money – although not the amount he said he would – to shut him up. Richard was planning to pay him and was doing his best, but his best wasn't good enough. Finally, Argrila lost his patience and called his silent partner, Roy DeMeo, and suddenly everything took a serious turn for the worse.

Roy DeMeo was an out-of-control psychopath, an associate of the Gambino crime family who would eventually become the subject of a popular true-crime book by journalists Jerry Capeci and Gene Mustain appropriately entitled *Murder Machine*.

25

THE GAMBINOS

Roy DeMeo was born and raised in Canarsie, a tough neighbourhood in one of the toughest towns anywhere in the world: Brooklyn, USA. As a boy, Roy had been overweight, Humpty Dumpty-like, and was regularly put upon and abused by neighbourhood bullies. He had thick black hair, dark eyes, olive skin and a huge belly, and he waddled like a penguin. His older brother Anthony, known as Toby, was a tough, muscle-bound kid – always there to protect Roy – but he joined the marines, went to fight in Vietnam and never came back. Thus fat little Roy was left to fend for himself on Canarsie's mean streets.

The young Roy DeMeo always admired neighbourhood mob guys, of whom there were many. They were all over Canarsie, mostly members of the Lucchese crime family, with their fancy cars, fancy women, fancy clothes and huge rolls of hundred-dollar bills. That was what Roy wanted for himself; that was Roy's dream; that's what Roy saw in his future. Roy's heroes were Lucky Luciano, Al Capone and Albert Anastasia, infamous killers all. Those were the people Roy looked up to, wanted to emulate. He longed to be respected and feared like them.

Though a bright child and good with numbers, Roy did not do well in school. School didn't interest him in the least. He knew that what he wanted he could never get in any classroom. What he wanted you could learn only on the street, so that's where Roy spent his time; that's where he went to school; that's where Roy DeMeo applied himself.

The first order of business was to lose weight and get muscular. The young DeMeo began to diet and lift weights with a vengeance, and soon enough he lost the puppy fat and protruding stomach and his muscles became large and rock hard. Now when anyone bothered him, Roy gladly beat him to a pulp. He was an extremely dirty fighter, biting and gouging people's eyes, and soon – as he had planned – he secured a reputation as a tough guy, as someone who was stand-up, dangerous, no one to trifle with – not an easy task in Canarsie.

As a young teen, DeMeo began lending (loan-sharking) the money he earned working at a supermarket. If someone didn't pay back on time, Roy took apparent delight in beating him up. He quickly became a loudmouthed bully, mean and sadistic, swaggering around with his mouth twisted up as if he'd been sucking on lemons. He had a chip on his broad shoulders and dared people to try and knock it off. He was trouble looking to happen.

DeMeo loaned money to a kid named Chris Rosenberg, who sold nickel bags of pot. With the money Roy loaned him, Chris was able to buy weight and was soon selling ounces and even pounds. Roy made Chris his partner, co-opted him and his pot business. This would be a recurring theme in DeMeo's bloody, infamous life of crime: he made people who owed him money and couldn't pay him on time his partners. This was, in fact, a classic Mafia ploy, used from its very inception. The word 'mafia' in lower case means a man of respect, an individual who has pride and honour and walks with his head high. 'Mafia', capitalised, has come to mean the criminal enterprise that began in Sicily in the mid-1800s and spread its insidious tentacles all over the globe. For many years, the Mafia was a highly secretive, highly successful criminal enterprise the likes of which the world had never known. All its members took a blood oath to the particular family into which they were inducted. Until Joe Valachi, at the 1963 McClellan Senate hearings in Washington, told of the intricacies of the Mafia – where it began, how it worked, its structure – law enforcement had no comprehensive understanding of the Sicilian Mafia. In fact, there are three distinctly different criminal organisations in Italy: the Camorra from Naples, the 'Ndrangheta from Calabria and the Mafia from Sicily. Of the three, the Camorra was – and still is – the most violent and vicious.

The infamous John Gotti was one of the few Neapolitans who was allowed into the ranks of the Sicilian Mafia, into the Gambino family, which many say was a fatal error in judgement on Carlo Gambino's part. An exceedingly cunning individual, Carlo Gambino was a small, frail, unassuming Sicilian who dressed and acted like a simple peasant from Sicily, when in truth he ran the largest and most successful of the five New York crime families. Carlo opened the books to John Gotti because Gotti killed a man who was stupid enough to kidnap Carlo's nephew Sal and murder him after a ransom was paid. That, of course, was a one-way ticket to the graveyard, and John Gotti gladly killed the jerk who masterminded this ill-conceived kidnapping and killing.

Carlo would later make a second grave error, and that was appointing his brother-in-law, Paul Castellano, the head of the family shortly before his death in October 1976.

Castellano was a tall, gaunt, sallow and dark-eyed man who had a butcher's shop on Eighteenth Avenue, just off Eighty-sixth Street, in the Bensonhurst section of Brooklyn, another very tough, Mafia-ridden neighbourhood. If the Mafia had a graduate school, it was surely Bensonhurst. Made men – soldiers, lieutenants, captains, underbosses and bosses from all the five families – lived in Bensonhurst. Here they bought homes, baptised and married off their children, celebrated holidays, lived their lives. The Bensonhurst schools were filled with children who were the offspring of made men.

Paul Castellano was a good businessman but a very bad mob boss. He parlayed his butcher's shop into a large chicken and meat wholesale business that made him a wealthy man. Paul married Carlo's sister, Kathy, and it was largely that marriage that caused Paul to rise quickly within the Gambino hierarchy.

Paul was a notoriously greedy individual, did not come from the street as such and was resented by most of the 21 captains in the Gambino family. Resentment of Castellano's greed eventually caused him to be killed in front of Sparks Steak House in December 1985. He and his bodyguard/chauffeur, Tommy Bilotti, were killed at the behest of John Gotti and Sammy 'the Bull' Gravano by a hit team; one of those men was, in fact, Richard Leonard Kuklinski.

In theory, Roy DeMeo should have been associated with and inducted into the Lucchese family. They were centred in Canarsie and had scores of junkyards and chop shops – where hot cars were disassembled for resale – in the area. But Roy wanted more for himself; he wanted to become a member of the Gambino family. They were Mafia royalty, and that was where Roy wanted to be made. DeMeo was an excellent money-maker: he had interests in unions, stolen cars and credit cards, drugs and loan-sharking, had partnerships in restaurants and bars, had a lot of money on the street. But DeMeo was loud and boisterous and drew attention to himself, all traits shunned by mob guys, and he had a very bad temper . . . would scream and yell and pull guns at the drop of a hat. He believed the best way to get people's respect was to bully them, to beat them up, to make them bleed.

'I don't give a flyin' fuck if anyone likes me; what I care about is that they fear me,' was a favourite saying of his, and people did fear him, with good cause, for Roy DeMeo was a bona fide raging psychopath. Besides all his other enterprises, he killed people for both sport and money. He filled mob-sanctioned hits as well as hits civilians wanted done and were willing to pay for. Essentially, he retailed murder. Roy had worked as a butcher in Key Food, a Brooklyn store, and he was particularly adept at cutting people up to get rid of bodies.

'Disassembling,' he called it, laughing. With expert knife work he dismembered those he killed, cut them up into six convenient pieces – the head, arms, legs, and torso – all of which he cleverly disposed of in different places, the head in a garbage bin, the arms in the nearby Atlantic Ocean, the legs in the mountain-high Canarsie garbage dump over near the Belt Parkway.

DeMeo put together his own little killing crew – a bunch of cold-blooded serial killers named Joey Testa, Anthony Senter, Chris Goldberg, Henry Borelli, Freddy DiNome and Joe Guglielmo, DeMeo's cousin, who was known as 'Dracula' – and they shot and stabbed and bludgeoned their way to prominent positions in the Mafia homicide hall of fame. Before they were finally brought to justice, the DeMeo crew murdered over 200 people. Many of the murders were carried out in the rear apartment of a bar DeMeo owned called the Gemini Lounge on Troy Avenue, Brooklyn.

DeMeo made the acquaintance of Nino Gaggi, a made man in the Gambino family and a close personal friend of Paul Castellano. Both Gaggi and DeMeo dealt in stolen cars. DeMeo had a contact in the Department of Motor Vehicles and provided Gaggi with clean vehicle identification numbers (VINs) and paperwork for stolen cars. DeMeo was only too happy to help Gaggi in any way he could. He saw Gaggi as his entrée to the Gambino family.

Nino Gaggi lived at 1929 Cropsey Avenue in Bensonhurst. It was an apartment in a three-family red-brick house, with small yards in front and out back. Gaggi was from the old school, quiet and reserved, a slight man with small, seemingly frail hands, but he was tough like coarse sandpaper, with a bad temper. Everything about him was understated. He didn't particularly like DeMeo, because he was so loud, so bold, so in your face. But DeMeo was a hell of a money-maker, so Gaggi tolerated him and, as time passed, did more and more with him. During the Christmas holidays, DeMeo brought carloads of gifts for Gaggi's three children and diamond bracelets and watches for Nino's wife, Rose, an attractive blonde who was fiercely loyal to her husband. Gaggi had a vicious German shepherd named Duke. He loved the dog because it was tough and wanted to bite everyone, man or beast. Duke was so vicious that he used to climb up the eight-foot chain-link fence around the back yard, using his teeth and paws, to get at the garbage collectors on Bay Twenty-second Street. Gaggi had to have a chain-link overhang installed so Duke couldn't escape and wreak havoc on the neighbourhood. Duke's tenacity gave Nino a big kick, and he loved that dog as much as one of his own sons.

It was an inconsequential incident on Bensonhurst's Eighty-sixth Street that eventually caused Roy DeMeo to be inducted into the Gambino family: when a neighbourhood tough, a Golden Gloves amateur boxing champion named Vincent Governara, known as 'Vinnie Mook', hit Gaggi and broke his nose, Gaggi turned to DeMeo and asked Roy to kill him. Whatever Nino asked of DeMeo, Nino got; and he later sponsored DeMeo to be made by the Gambino family, making his long-cherished dream come true.

Because DeMeo lived and worked out of the Canarsie section of Brooklyn, a few miles away from JFK International Airport, he had a lot of contacts at the airport and helped mastermind numerous cargo thefts, heisting all kinds of merchandise from all over the world: wines and champagnes from Italy and France, exotic foods, jewellery, cash and guns. Lots of guns. Crates of pistols, revolvers and even machine guns, Berettas from Italy, Walther PPKs from Germany, Uzi machine guns from Israel.

Roy was a genuine gun fanatic and truly loved firearms. He had an extensive collection of them, enough guns to arm a small army, and he happily and easily sold all the stolen armaments from Kennedy Airport to men involved in organised crime. Because of Roy DeMeo, crates upon crates of clean, untraceable guns found their way to the New York and New Jersey underworld, and thus DeMeo was inadvertently responsible for scores of mob killings all across America.

When Tony Argrila, a friend of DeMeo's, went to Roy and told him that Richard Kuklinski was behind on his payments and had an 'attitude problem,' DeMeo said he'd talk to Kuklinski.

26

PARTNERSHIP
BORN IN HELL

It was a blistering hot August day, 1973, the humidity near 100 per cent, the temperature in the low 90s. No one was in a hurry to go anywhere. People seemed to move in slow motion. DeMeo was in a foul mood, on his way to the office/film lab of Argrila and Rothenberg to collect his end of the business.

A year earlier, DeMeo had gone to see them and told them he was their new partner. Rothenberg laughed. DeMeo took out a pistol and slapped the shit out of him. Argrila and Rothenberg had a new partner. Theirs was a quasi-legal business, and neither Argrila nor Rothenberg had the balls to go to the police at that point.

That August day, all DeMeo knew about Richard was that he was big, acted tough and was behind on his payments. DeMeo was at the office when Richard showed up for some product. Acting tough, DeMeo was heavy-handed with Richard. Richard had no idea who DeMeo was or that he was truly connected, and he was curt and nasty with him. Richard didn't like this loudmouthed Italian guy trying to strong-arm him.

'I'm a friend of Tony's here,' DeMeo said.

'And so?' Richard said.

'And so I'm here because you're behind and you got a bad attitude, I hear.'

'Like I told them, I'll pay back everything I owe when I have it.'

'Yeah, and when's that?' Roy demanded, getting mad, not liking this big Polish guy's attitude one bit.

'Hard to say,' Richard said, a slight smirk on his chiselled face. 'You know how it is. The product's out there. I'm waiting to get paid; when I get paid, they'll get paid. Simple.'

'You think you're cute?' DeMeo asked.

'I think I don't like you coming around and trying to put the squeeze on me,' Richard told him, and these two very dangerous men – neither knowing anything about the other yet – stared at each other with angry, homicidal eyes, like two white sharks eyeing each other, sizing each other up.

DeMeo could see that Kuklinski was not scared of him and would readily fight. Like all bullies, DeMeo was not about to tangle with a guy as big and tough as Richard apparently was.

'We'll see,' DeMeo said, and he turned and stormed off.

'Yeah, we'll see,' Richard said to his back.

Argrila now, for the first time, told Richard who DeMeo was, that he was a connected guy. 'I don't wanna see you hurt, Rich. Leave, leave before he comes back.' At that, Richard turned, went into the hall and pushed the elevator button.

DeMeo was fuming. There was no way he was going to let this big Polack trifle with him, disrespect him. Downstairs, in his white Lincoln, were his cousin Joe Guglielmo, Anthony Senter and Joey Testa. Guglielmo was grey-haired and resembled Bela Lugosi, hence his nickname, Dracula. Anthony and Joey looked so alike that they appeared to be brothers, but they weren't. They were both dark-eyed and handsome, with a thick head of black hair, each 6 ft, muscular and athletic.

Now, with his guys behind him, DeMeo went back upstairs to see Richard, and they found him in the hall waiting for the elevator. Richard was suddenly surrounded, guns pointing at him.

'So, tough guy,' DeMeo said, 'you wanna die? You fuckin' wanna die?' And with that, he struck Richard hard in the head with the butt of his gun. Knowing his life was on the line here, Richard did nothing. He had a .38 derringer in his pocket, but he didn't draw it. DeMeo hit him several more times. Richard went down. Guglielmo hit him in the back of the head and kicked him in his right knee. Now they all proceeded to pummel Richard. Though they didn't knock him unconscious, they beat him good. Richard had never taken a beating like that in his entire life. He was angry beyond words, but he knew that DeMeo would kill him on the spot if he fought back. He had only a two-shot derringer on him. DeMeo found Richard's derringer and took it.

'You come up with the money or you're fuckin' dead – fuckin' dead, motherfucker!' DeMeo said, and they left.

Richard was suddenly alone, bleeding all over the floor. He stood up, went into a bathroom off the hall and looked at himself in the mirror. He was a mess.

Cursing out loud, using paper towels to wipe away the blood, Richard vowed to kill DeMeo. The wounds he'd got from the pistol-whipping were deep, and Richard had to go to St Vincent's Hospital on Seventh Avenue to have them stitched up. He received thirty-eight stitches on three different nasty gashes on his head. His eyes blackened, his lip swollen, all stitched up, Richard slowly went back to New Jersey. He was so beat up that he didn't want Barbara and his daughters to see him, so he went to his mother-in-law's house. Shocked when she saw him, Genevieve let him into the house and got an ice pack for him. He told her, and later Barbara, that he'd been mugged, jumped by four guys and robbed. He slept at Genevieve's house that night, mostly tossing and turning, planning how he'd torture Roy DeMeo.

It didn't take long for Richard to find out who Roy DeMeo really was: an associate in good standing of the Gambino family, who ran a ruthless band of serial killers. Richard knew that if he killed Roy now, he'd surely be killed in turn, and quickly. He was so mad over what DeMeo and the others had done that if he hadn't been married with children, he might have gone and found DeMeo and killed him anyway. But because of Barbara and his family, he had to play it cool – for now. No easy thing for Richard Kuklinski. But he knew that there would be, in the future, an opportunity for him to get revenge; he'd bide his time. But, he vowed, he would one day pistol-whip and kill Roy DeMeo.

The first thing Richard did was make arrangements with Tony Argrila to pay him back the money. That done, Richard went to Brooklyn, to the Gemini Lounge, and asked for DeMeo. DeMeo was shocked to see Richard at the bar by himself.

'I hear,' DeMeo said, 'you're doing the right thing. You got balls coming here like this.'

'I wanted to talk with you.'

'Yeah, well talk.'

'First off, I didn't know who you were,' Richard diplomatically, and uncharacteristically, said. 'Second, Rothenberg and Tony are stealing from each other. I've seen it myself. Sure, I'm a little behind but nothing like they're saying. All the time, Rothenberg is trying to give me material on the side. That's the truth, Roy.'

Richard figured, correctly, that it was Rothenberg who had sicced Roy on him, and now he was returning the favour.

'I'll tell you, big guy, you got balls. You got some pair a nuts coming here like this. I'm thinking maybe we got off on the wrong foot here. I got mad when I shoulda been talking. I asked around 'bout you and I know you're a stand-up guy. You had a gun on you and didn't use it . . . you got balls.'

'Roy, I want to make money with you, not fight with you. That's all I want to do here is make money . . . do business.'

'I hear you got contacts all over the place. We can do something together. You just play straight with me and you'll make money – a lotta money.'

'Sounds good.'

'Let's shake on it,' Roy said, and these two killers shook hands, a slight smirk on each of their faces.

'I hear,' Roy said, 'you got an Italian wife. Take a ride with me.' They got into his car and drove to an Italian food shop a few blocks away.

'Come on,' Roy said.

They went inside. The place had sawdust on the floor, salami and giant rolls of provolone hanging from the ceiling. Roy picked out all kinds of meats, Italian sweet sausages, giant blocks of different cheeses and a head-sized piece of mozzarella in water.

'They make mozzarella fresh a few times a day,' he told Richard. Roy paid for everything – a hundred and fifty dollars – and gave Richard four big bags.

'You bring this stuff home to your wife. She'll like it, I bet you. Call me in a couple of days and we'll do business, OK? I got a few lines of my own and I'll front you all you want.'

'OK,' Richard said, genuinely taken aback by this little-seen generous side of Roy DeMeo. 'Thanks, Roy,' he said, and it was done.

27

FORGIVE ME, FATHER, FOR I HAVE SINNED

Anna McNally, Richard's mother, was terminally ill, dying of liver cancer. When Roberta, Richard's sister, called to tell him of their mother's impending death, he didn't even want to go and see her. *Finally*, he thought, *she's getting her due.* But Barbara convinced him that he should see his mother one last time, so he and Barbara went. Barbara had no use for Anna; she knew what a rotten mother she'd been to Richard. But still Anna was his mother, and Barbara felt he should see her one last time before she died. It was the right thing to do.

As the years had gone by, Richard had grown to despise his mother more and more. He pretty much blamed her for everything: for marrying Stanley; for having children with Stanley; for how Stanley mercilessly beat Florian – killed Florian; for how Stanley beat him.

When they arrived at the hospital, however, Anna did not even acknowledge his presence. She was facing the wall, holding blue rosary beads, repeating 'Forgive me, Father, for I have sinned' over and over, non-stop, as if it were a Tibetan chant. Richard spoke to her. He tried to say goodbye. But she wouldn't even look at him. It seemed as though she were already dead and gone but her body didn't yet realise it. She had shrunken to a mere shell of the robust, attractive woman she had once been. For Anna McNally, life had been cruel:

a constant, bitter struggle filled with heartache, hard menial labour, pain, suffering and want. For Anna, death would be a blessing, certainly better than her life had been, and she welcomed it.

She did in fact die later that night. Richard reluctantly went to the wake, only because Barbara convinced him he should go. He did not cry. He showed no emotion.

Stanley Kuklinski also came to the wake, and Richard didn't even say hello to him. It was all he could do to keep from taking Stanley by the neck and choking the cold, heartless bastard to death, right there in front of everyone. With great effort, he held himself back. Barbara could see he was getting all bent out of shape at the sight of his father, his lips twisting up, his face flushing. Sitting there next to Barbara, all Richard could think of was killing Stanley; harsh black-and-white images of what Stanley had done to him moved in his head like a grainy old slow-motion film. It took much restraint for Richard not to take his father outside, put him in his car, kill him and dump him down a Pennsylvania mine shaft. Richard told Barbara he wanted to leave. In the car on the way back home, she said, 'You OK, Richard?'

'I'm fine,' he said. 'I just . . . when I see Stanley, it all comes back. That man should never have been allowed to have children.' Here he stopped talking. He didn't want Barbara to hear the truth, what Stanley had done to him, how he had murdered Florian.

28

THE PORN KING
OF NEW YORK

True to his word, DeMeo gave Richard, on consignment, all the pornography he wanted. Richard bought himself a van, went to Brooklyn and picked up boxes of porn produced by Roy, 100 films per box. By this time, Richard had many contacts in the porn business across the country. He was distributing porn – both his and DeMeo's – to wholesalers everywhere, and business boomed. For the first time, Richard was making good money on a steady basis.

Richard was scrupulously careful about giving Roy all he was due, on time as promised. Roy began to take a shine to Richard. He admired his temerity, the fact that he had taken the beating 'like a man', as he told his crew. The fact that Richard had had a gun in his pocket and hadn't used it. The fact that he came to the Gemini by himself – that, he knew, took balls.

DeMeo's crew, however, didn't like Richard. They thought he was aloof and unfriendly (he was) and disliked the fact that he was a non-Italian. They made fun of him behind his back, told one another silly Polish jokes at his expense. Richard sensed the hostility, the cold stares, the sneers, but he didn't care. He figured they were just jealous of his relationship with Roy, and he was right.

As the months passed, Roy and Richard's 'friendship' grew.

Roy learned that Richard had killed well and discreetly for the De Cavalcante family, and one day when Richard went to the Gemini to drop off some money, Roy sat him down in the rear apartment.

'I hear,' Roy said, 'that you are cold like ice and do special work. That true?'

'Sure, no problem.'

'I have a lot of special work . . . you interested?'

'Definitely.'

'Definitely?'

'Sure.'

'You'll do it with no questions asked?'

'I'm not a curious man.'

Roy stared at Richard. Being stared at by Roy, with his penetrating black eyes, was like having two drills bore into you.

Roy had to see for himself if, in fact, Richard could do a piece of work, coldly and methodically.

'OK,' he said, 'let's take a ride. You game?'

'Sure,' Richard said, and Roy, Joe Guglielmo and Richard piled into Roy's car. Joe was driving. Richard sat in the back.

'Let's go to the city,' Roy ordered. He always ordered people to do things, never asked. In silence, they drove to Manhattan. It was a nice, cloudless day. The sky was blue. The sun shone. Someone was going to die. As they were going through the Brooklyn–Battery Tunnel, Roy turned around and handed Richard a short-barrelled .38 with a suppressor on it.

'Use this,' he said.

'OK,' Richard said, and casually slipped the gun into his waistband. They continued uptown and wound up on the west side of Greenwich Village, on a quiet tree-lined street. Richard's old hunting ground. They passed a lone man walking a dog.

'Pull over,' Roy ordered. 'See that guy with the dog?' he asked Richard.

'Yeah.'

'Cap him.'

'Here, now?'

'Here, now.'

Richard calmly stepped out of the car and walked towards the man with the dog, who was to the rear of the car, maybe 20 steps. After Richard passed him, he stopped and turned around and tailed the hapless man. He wanted to do the job right in front of Roy and Joe. Just as the dog walker passed the Lincoln, Richard caught up with him, made sure he was unobserved, quickly pulled out the gun and fired, shooting the man in the back of the head.

He never even knew he died, or why.

He went down like a laundry bag, Richard confided.

Richard calmly walked back to the car and got in. 'You're fuckin' cold like ice. Well done,' Roy said, smiling. 'You're one of us.' And they went back to Brooklyn. Richard had just proven to Roy, beyond a shadow of a doubt, that he was a stone-cold killer, and that murder that day cemented their bloody relationship. When they arrived back at the Gemini Lounge and went into the rear apartment, Joey Testa, Anthony Senter, Chris Goldberg and Henry Borelli were all there.

'The big guy,' Roy announced, 'is fuckin' cold. I just saw him do a piece of work right in the middle of the fuckin' street. He's one of us.'

Thus, Richard became part of a coven of serial killers the like of which has never been seen before or since; they would, in years to come, make homicide history.

Richard, however, didn't like any of this. He didn't want any of these guys knowing about him, what he did, what 'special work' he performed. He didn't trust them and didn't like them; he thought it was just a matter of time before they caused problems, for themselves, for Roy and for him.

Richard needed to use the toilet and went to the bathroom. There was an odd, thick, fetid smell hanging in the air. As he was taking a leak, he looked around the shower curtain and there, hanging over the tub, was a dead man. His throat had been cut and there was a black-handled butcher's knife sticking out of his chest. His blood, rubbery and thick, was slowly draining into the tub. They were bleeding him.

These fucking guys are really into it, Richard thought, and went back inside.

'You see the guy taking a shower?' Roy asked, laughing out loud at his joke. The others laughed too.

'No, I didn't see anything,' Richard said, and they sat down and had a meal of spaghetti olio and broccoli. Roy enjoyed cooking and loved to eat. As they sat there and ate, drinking red wine – with the guy hanging over the tub – they made jokes, talked about sports, about a girl both Joey and Anthony had fucked the night before.

After they'd had espresso, Chris and Anthony spread blue plastic sheeting on the floor. They brought the guy out of the bathroom and proceeded to cut him into 'manageable pieces', as Roy put it. 'Makes getting rid of him easier,' he told Richard. They had a professional autopsy kit, with razor-sharp saws and knives made for the sole purpose of cutting up bodies. Within minutes, they had cut him into five pieces. Each piece was wrapped in brown paper, then put into heavy-duty black garbage bags. Richard watched this through amused eyes, thinking, *These guys are something else*, admiring how easily and expertly they disassembled the body. They'd obviously had a lot of practice and knew what they were doing. Chris Goldberg especially seemed to enjoy taking apart the body.

When Richard was ready to leave and go back to his family, he asked to speak to Roy on the side. They went outside. By now, the sun was setting. A nice breeze blew in from Jamaica Bay.

'Look, Roy,' Richard said. 'Don't get me wrong here, but I'd rather just work with you on any special jobs.'

'You're reading my mind,' Roy said. 'Big guy, you are my secret weapon. I ain't mixing you up with my crew. Don't worry. They are all good, very fuckin' stand-up guys – Chris is like my son – but I ain't mixing you up with them.'

'OK,' Richard said. They hugged and kissed on the cheek, and Richard went back to his family in New Jersey. In this way, Richard Kuklinski became Roy DeMeo's 'secret weapon'.

The police could find no witnesses to the murder of the man walking his dog in the Village, no likely suspects, no rhyme or reason for the killing: yet another unsolved New York homicide Richard Kuklinski had committed.

29

FAMILY MAN

Richard was scrupulously careful to keep what he was doing far from his family. Barbara had no idea what he was really up to; she didn't ask, and he didn't tell her.

Besides distributing porn, Richard rented a warehouse in North Bergen and from it sold counterfeit sweaters, handbags, jeans and even perfumes. He bought large lots of these knock-off goods, had women sew brand-name labels into the clothes and sold them to wholesalers, who in turn sold them at flea markets all over the country. Money was rolling in. Richard still dabbled in hijacking, acting as the middleman between the hijackers and the buyers and always making a profit. He stopped drinking hard alcohol and tried not to gamble. He loved his family deeply and profoundly and didn't want to do anything to undermine it. On the one hand, he was the perfect husband and father, considerate, loving and generous to a fault. He'd gladly drive his daughters and their friends to movies and to restaurants they liked; he took great joy in buying them nice clothing, two of everything. Nothing was too good for his children. He constantly bought Barbara clothes and shoes and jewellery, mink coats – whatever she wanted. They went out to fancy restaurants every weekend. Richard always made sure a bottle of Barbara's favourite wine, Montrachet, was already at the table in an ice bucket waiting for her. He opened doors for her. He graciously pulled out her chair so she could sit down.

On the other hand, he could lose his temper over some little thing and become tyrannical, mean, a menace. The Kuklinski home could be one moment a tranquil Shangri-la, the next a storm-besieged island in the middle of a dangerous, turbulent sea.

When my dad was normal, he was golden. When he lost it he was . . . he was a maniac, his daughter Chris explained.

Richard bought himself a new white Cadillac. The family began looking for a new house in a better part of Jersey. West New York, Hudson County, was changing; many minority groups were moving in, and Richard and Barbara wanted to move to 'greener pastures'.

They wound up buying a split-level ranch-style home in Dumont, New Jersey, with a garage and three bedrooms. This was a nice, upper-middle-class neighbourhood, a good place to bring up children, a reasonably juicy slice of the American dream come true. Barbara wanted a pool and the grounds covered with bright-green, healthy turf – no problem; whatever Barbara wanted, Richard was anxious and only too happy to provide. He still had no concept of money and spent it as quickly as it came in.

At weekends, the Kuklinskis had extravagant barbecues, invited everyone on the block. Richard was, for the most part, outgoing and friendly – a good neighbour, quick to offer a helping hand. He'd don a cooking apron and happily grill burgers and frankfurters for his children and all their friends. He watched them play in the pool, making sure no one was hurt. He gladly doled out towels and helped dry his children off, happily cleaned the yard after a day of the kids playing. The Kuklinskis had also been blessed by the birth of a son. Barbara had always wanted a boy, and her dream had come true. They named the boy Dwayne, after a country singer Richard was fond of.

When Richard did get mad, however, he'd explode. He didn't seem capable of controlling his anger, and when he became angry, his cruelty knew no bounds. It was as if Richard became a different person; he'd break his children's toys and keepsakes, smash chairs and tables and knick-knacks. After Barbara had the kitchen redone, all new appliances and cabinets installed, Richard lost it and actually tore the cabinets right off the wall. He pulled the kitchen sink out and tossed it through one of the windows.

Afterwards, he always felt bad, indeed hated what he'd done. He was so angry with himself that he couldn't even look at himself in the mirror. When he was like that, in one of his out-of-control tirades, all Barbara and the children could do was stay the hell out of his way, and they did, as best they could.

Also, when Richard was mad at Barbara, he had no reservations about abusing her in front of the children. It was as though he didn't even know they were there. He slapped her, pushed her, beat her. Horrified, his daughters watched this, begging him to stop, screaming and crying and pleading with him. If not for his daughters' intervention, their pleas, he might well have killed Barbara in a fit of rage. If he had killed her in such a fit, he would also have killed his children.

'If Mommy dies, Merrick,' he actually told his first-born, 'you know I'll have to kill you and your sister. I couldn't leave any witnesses . . . you understand?'

'Yes, Daddy,' Merrick said.

Barbara was, she said, trapped. There was nowhere for her to turn. If she went to the police and showed them her injuries, her black eyes and bruises, he might be arrested; but she knew that he'd be out on bail soon enough, and he'd come looking to kill her. He had told her as much in plain language on numerous occasions.

And she believed him.

In her heart, Barbara was certain, she explained, that Richard would destroy her if she ever went to the authorities or did anything to cause him to lose his family. Before he allowed that to happen, he'd kill them all.

However, as odd as it sounds, Barbara was not cowed by

Richard. She'd stand up to him, defy him, point her finger in his face and dare him to hit her again – which he usually did. 'Big shot, think you're so tough, beating up a woman – you aren't tough. You ain't tough at all!' she'd say, right in his face.

If, Merrick explained, *my mom had kept her mouth shut, it wouldn't've been so bad. She made things worse – a bad situation even worse. It was like she wanted to egg him on. I used to tell her to be quiet – 'Mommy, be quiet' – not to answer him back, not to stand up to him – 'Mommy, shut up' – but she didn't.*

Barbara's only way of fighting back, of not losing her own identity, who she was, was to stand up to her husband, and she did, and she regularly suffered the consequences.

Chris explained it this way: *My father married the wrong woman. If, say, Mom was more meek, I mean less outspoken, the tirades would've ended much more quickly. But she wouldn't keep her mouth shut and made it worse. Even when he was actually striking her, beating on her, my mom would taunt, berate and belittle my dad. My mother . . . my mother encouraged it.*

Barbara, however, does not feel that way. *There was no way*, she explained, *that I was going to allow him to walk all over me and I was going to keep my mouth shut and let him abuse me. I had nowhere to turn, no one to ask for help, and so I told him . . . I told him how I felt. Maybe, I mean now looking back on it, I was encouraging him, enabling him, but I was not about to let him make a doormat out of me and keep my mouth shut. Forget that.*

Afterwards, Richard was always angry with himself for terrorising his daughters. Dwayne was still too young to know what was going on. Yet Richard never said he was sorry or that it wouldn't happen again. He acted as though nothing had occurred; everything was just peachy and dandy. It was as though a terrible storm had come and gone and the destruction was just a natural consequence of the storm. Nothing more. He had nothing to do with it. It was all the storm's fault.

Chris took to calling the operator after one of her father's tirades and hanging up when she heard their voice; she somehow felt comforted and reassured knowing that there was someone at the other end of the phone, someone out there who would help. Chris and her sister began to pack an 'escape bag', as they called it. In it were some clothes, a favourite toy or two, an extra pair of shoes for each of them. They figured it was only a matter of time before their father really did kill their mother, and they wanted to have an escape kit ready so they could run out the door when the time came.

In no uncertain terms, Barbara again told Richard that if he ever laid a finger on her children, she'd cut his throat when he was sleeping. She said this with such cold, calm sincerity that he believed her. Besides, he would cut his hands off before he ever physically hurt any of his children.

Barbara . . . Barbara was another matter entirely.

Sometimes, when Richard was losing it, his face paling, his lips twisting up, that terrible clicking sound coming from his lips, he'd actually strike himself with his fist so hard he'd knock himself out cold. This was, he confided, the only way he could avoid striking Barbara and terrorising his little girls: to knock himself out. So he did.

Richard beating himself unconscious was a frightening, unsettling, sobering thing to see. Not only did he hit himself, he banged his head against the wall so hard he'd knock himself out cold, come to after a while and silently leave the house, like a tornado going away, quietly disappearing over the horizon.

True, Richard did not strike his children or physically abuse them in any way, but he was causing them great anxiety and pain inside . . . a thing Barbara seemed oblivious to. Outwardly, Chris and Merrick appeared well adjusted and happy, but inside they were in turmoil. They did, however, make friends easily, were outgoing and gregarious and did reasonably well in school.

Merrick, though, was still plagued by kidney and bladder problems, high fevers, infections and convulsions, and spent a lot of time in the hospital, consequently missing an inordinate amount of school, several months of every year.

When Merrick was hospitalised, her father was always there, getting her whatever she needed and making sure she was comfortable and receiving good treatment. He catered not only to his daughter but to all the other children on whatever ward she was housed. He was always bringing dolls and toys and sweets to the kids on the ward. He had tremendous empathy for these sick children and would gladly do anything he could, including paying for procedures and medication children needed that their parents could not afford. One child, a seven-year-old girl in the room next to Merrick's, was dying of cancer and had only a few days left. Her parents could not afford the hospital TV, and it was disconnected. When Richard came to see Merrick and heard what had happened, he was outraged. He went and found the technician, paid him and made him immediately activate the child's television. Richard was a true Dr Jekyll and Mr Hyde character. No matter what he did, however, what kind of outburst he had, no matter how afraid of him she was, Merrick always forgave her father, never ever held anything against him. These two, Richard and Merrick, had some kind of special bond that neither Barbara nor Chris had with Richard.

Both Chris and Barbara held Richard's outbursts against him, would never forgive or forget what he did. But not Merrick. To this day, after all that has happened, Merrick does not have a bad word to say about her dad, holds nothing against him. He was her sunrise and sunset, and she was there for him to the very end, no matter what, no matter where, come hell or high water.

Richard was somewhat jealous of his son, Dwayne, because of the attention he received from Barbara. He confided that he didn't actually want a boy because he felt somewhere deep inside that a son would become competition for Barbara's attention, even for his daughters' attention. Richard was jealous in the extreme of any other male.

30

HIT MAN

'Can you meet me at the diner on my side of the Tappan Zee Bridge?' Roy DeMeo asked.

'Sure, be there in an hour,' said Richard, and he was soon on his way to meet Roy, in his flashy new white Cadillac El Dorado. Roy and Richard had developed and perfected a simple clandestine way of talking: Roy would call Richard on his pager and punch in the number of a Brooklyn phone booth, and Richard would use a phone booth near his house to phone him back. In this way, they managed to talk without fear of an FBI tap – a constant, very real concern among mob guys. Goodfellas were falling like flies because of the newly developed and cleverly applied Racketeer Influenced and Corrupt Organizations (RICO) Act. All anyone had to do to be convicted of RICO and go to jail was talk about committing a crime, or 'conspire', as the statute says. No crime actually had to be committed.

As Richard drove to his meeting with Roy, he wondered what piece of work he had. Since the day Richard had blown away the dog walker in the Village, he had undergone a radical metamorphosis; he had now totally committed himself to murder, to killing for profit.

Cold, detached and exceedingly calculating – sober now – Richard was about to embark on a violent journey that would leave scores of people dead, mangled, tortured, buried and burned alive, thrown into bottomless pits, fed while still alive to ravenous rats, fed to crabs along the abandoned piers of Manhattan's West Side.

Whatever murders Roy DeMeo was committing with his Brooklyn crew of serial killers, he kept his promise and never involved Richard in any of those. No, DeMeo would use Richard for 'special jobs', as he thought of them. DeMeo had become the premier assassin for the Gambino family. He was undertaking hits for them – and other families – left and right, several a week. His reputation as an efficient, brutal killer had grown to monumental proportions. Even the notorious Gotti brothers, Gene and John, steered clear of DeMeo and his serial killers. His bar, the Gemini Lounge, had become known, aptly, as 'the Slaughterhouse'.

Richard and Roy met in a busy diner near the Westchester side of the Tappan Zee Bridge. They greeted each other with a hug and a kiss on the cheek, as is the Italian way. Roy had chosen this place because most people who went to a diner were on their way somewhere and probably wouldn't come back and because this one was off the beaten path of mob guys; here, it was highly unlikely that anyone in 'the life' would see them together. Their business was the business of murder – a serious, life-and-death enterprise for all involved. There was no room for mistakes or oversights, for bad timing or miscalculations.

'I got a piece of work for you,' DeMeo said. 'Nothing fancy, just make sure it's done quickly and that no one knows about it. Got it?'

'Got it.'

DeMeo handed Richard a photograph with a Queens address on the back. 'This is him. He always carries. Be careful.'

'I'll take care of it,' Richard said. Roy handed him an envelope. There was twenty thousand dollars cash in it. Nothing else had to be said. The less said the better. They hugged and kissed each other goodbye and went their separate ways.

Still, in the back of his mind, Richard remembered the beating Roy had given him.

The following day, Richard was parked on a residential street in Queens, two blocks from Calvary Cemetery. The mark lived in a two-family red-brick house, on the ground level. He had, Richard quickly discerned, a pretty wife and two little boys. The fact that the mark had a family didn't matter to Richard, had nothing to do with the job at hand, though he would not kill him in front of his family. After a time, the mark left his house, got into his car and drove off. Richard followed him to a multi-storey car park on Queens Boulevard and parked in the space just next to the mark's car. When he'd gone, Richard first flattened the front left tyre of the mark's car, then he unlocked the boot of his Caddy, sat in his car and calmly waited for him to return. Richard had unusual patience in these situations. He could sit still for hours on end, his mind drifting all over the place but never losing focus on the job. This time it didn't take long for the mark to return, carrying packages. When he saw the flat, he grimaced, then opened the boot of his car. The moment was perfect. Richard moved quickly, silently sliding out of the car.

'Got a flat?' Richard asked the mark, stopping and looking as if he cared, as if he were a concerned Good Samaritan.

'Yeah,' the mark said, and before he knew it, Richard had a gun to his head and made him get in the boot of the Caddy, on his stomach. Richard now handcuffed him, taped his mouth shut and warned him to be quiet. He closed the boot and drove out of the car park. He had a pistol under his seat and one in his pocket. If a cop pulled him over, he'd kill him – simple.

Listening to country music, Richard made his way to the bottomless pits in Pennsylvania. When he arrived there, at that desolate area he knew well, he pulled the mark from his car, marched him to a mine shaft, shot him once in the head and let him drop down the gaping hole, which seemed to swallow up the hapless man. Richard casually disposed of him as if he were discarding a bag of trash. He turned, went back to his car and drove home to his wife and children . . . just another guy returning home after a day's work.

It didn't take long for people in organised crime to learn that Richard was available for hire, up and running and particularly reliable. The fact that he was non-Italian and could never be made was a plus because it enabled him to work for any of the seven East Coast crime families – the Pontis and the De Cavalcantes of New Jersey and the Gambino, Lucchese, Colombo, Genovese and Bonanno factions of New York – without conflict, problems or needing to explain to anyone. He did not have to ask permission to fill a contract. He was a freelance agent and was soon receiving contracts from skippers (captains) affiliated with different families.

Richard carried out each hit with great care, with patience and cunning, never in a hurry. He didn't tell anyone what he was doing, when or where or how; that was his business. He kept to himself. He didn't hang out with mob guys and always went home to his family.

Barbara had no idea where he was going when he left home. She learned not to question her mercurial, exceedingly moody husband. Barbara had learned to live with Richard, accept him for what he was, stoically tolerated his mood swings, his temper, even his abuse. She had, in reality, no other choice. As long as he didn't hit her children, she accepted his abuse. It was blatantly obvious to Barbara, even at this early stage, that Richard resented Dwayne. He was not nearly as warm to him as he'd been to Merrick and Chris, and this greatly concerned Barbara. She knew that in a fit of rage, Richard could very well hurt Dwayne . . . accidentally break his neck . . .

For Richard, killing by contract became a kind of life-and-death cat-and-mouse game, a lethal chess match that he was intent upon winning. He knew that if he was caught and exposed, he'd lose his family, truly the only thing in the world he'd ever cared about. Yet he continued taking contracts and filling them. He would *go talk to anyone*, as he put it. He figured if he was careful, meticulous and sober, he could earn enough money to retire, buy a mansion on the beach somewhere and live well, provide all his family needed. They would want for nothing.

It didn't, of course, work out that way.

Through his new friend, partner and crime associate, Roy DeMeo, Richard managed to secure all kinds of handguns, shotguns, and semi-automatic .22 Magnum rifles, which Richard cut down – both the stock and the barrel – creating a perfect weapon with which to kill human beings at close range. Roy had an inexhaustible supply of armaments, which were regularly pillaged from Kennedy Airport, conveniently located a mere ten minutes from the Gemini Lounge.

DeMeo had weapons all over the Slaughterhouse. He often held them, fondled and caressed them like a woman's breast, as though they were warm, cute, cuddly teddy bears, not instruments of sudden death. A gun, in DeMeo's hands, was a means to an end: dead people.

One day when Richard went to the Lounge to drop off money for Roy, his end of porn profits, Roy was all smiles and hugs and happy to see him. The usual group of serial killers was present, Anthony and Joey, Chris and Freddy DiNome and Roy's cousin Dracula. They all sat around the big round table and had steak and potatoes and home-made red wine. Off to the left there were weights and a heavy bag.

Richard didn't like any of these people, but he sat there like one of the boys, bantering and laughing and eating. Roy ate like a slob, talked with food in his mouth, a real *gavone* (an ill-mannered man).

At the end of the meal, Roy's mood suddenly changed – he was even more mercurial than Richard – and he picked up an Uzi with a long, ominous-looking silencer, a weapon that fires fifteen nine-millimetre parabellum rounds per second.

'Beautiful fuckin' piece,' he said, suddenly pointing the

gun at Richard and chambering it, a sickening metallic sound – *click-click*.

Everyone around the table quickly moved back, as if on cue, no one smiling or laughing or merry now. In the blink of an eye, Richard knew, his chest could be filled with gushing bullet holes. He stared at Roy curiously.

'Why you coming at me like this, Roy? What the fuck?' he said.

'I hear,' Roy said, 'you're saying shit about me.'

'That's bullshit. I have anything to say about you, I'll say it to your face. Bring the motherfucker here who said that. I want to hear this for myself. It's bullshit!' Richard said, getting hot. The Uzi still pointing at Richard's wide chest, Roy stared at him with his black, white-shark eyes. Outwardly, Richard appeared tough and defiant, but inside he was anxious. He well knew Roy was a psychotic killer, that the Uzi could literally tear him apart in seconds. Roy's finger was, he could see, actually on the trigger. The silence in the room – the Slaughterhouse – became thick and heavy. Stark images of the guy they had bled over the tub came to Richard.

'Yeah, you would,' Roy finally said, lowering the Uzi. 'You got balls, big guy. I know you got balls.' He laughed his sickening hyena-like cackle, and everyone moved back to the table. The moment passed as quickly as it came. Roy put down the Uzi as if it had never happened. Soon, Roy and Richard moved outside. Roy sort of said he was sorry. Richard assured him of his friendship. The two hugged. Richard was soon on his way back to New Jersey. As he went, he cursed DeMeo under his breath; he had pulled a gun on him twice, bullied him – embarrassed him. All the way back to Dumont, Richard vowed to kill the prick.

When Richard arrived home, Barbara immediately knew he was in a foul mood, and she and the girls steered clear of him. Barbara made sure Dwayne stayed in his room. Richard put on the television and watched a cowboy movie – his favourite kind – and seethed about Roy DeMeo. Yes, he would kill Roy;

but he'd wait, he'd be patient. He'd do it when the right time came. Meanwhile, he'd use him.

Just as Richard had thought she would, Barbara fussed constantly over their son. She couldn't get enough of him, and Richard did outwardly resent little Dwayne. He never felt like that about his daughters, but he did about his son. Barbara tried to play down Richard's jealousy, but inside she worried that Richard might actually do something to hurt Dwayne; she worried that he'd explode over an inconsequential event and vent his anger on the boy.

'Hurt my son and you're dead,' she told Richard on numerous occasions.

If Barbara had known to whom she was talking, she would, she says, have packed, grabbed her children and run for the hills. Still, she knew no matter where she fled, he'd find her, he'd never let her go. She became so concerned about Dwayne that she began taking him to her mother's house for the weekend so he'd be 'out of harm's way', as she put it.

The porn distributor Paul Rothenberg, Tony Argrila's partner, was becoming a problem. Rothenberg was an in-your-face guy, pushy, belligerent and curt, a stocky individual with a potato-like nose. He had been arrested numerous times over the years for making and distributing pornography, which in itself was not illegal, but Rothenberg pushed the envelope and sold bestiality films and films involving minors or heavy sadism – films in which blood was drawn, golden shower films – and was arrested for the distribution of these types of products.

'If people didn't want to see them, I couldn't sell them,' he was fond of saying, and he went on selling these exceedingly hard-core, kinky productions, which were generating a lot of profit. The more perverse they were, the more they sold, indeed they flew off shelves in shops across America.

Richard had a grudge against Rothenberg: he blamed him for his initial troubles with DeMeo and was biding his time to take his revenge. Richard firmly, obsessively, believed in revenge. He could never turn the other cheek. That was as foreign to him as the moon. If someone did him a disservice, he didn't feel complete until he hurt that person.

The NYPD raided the film lab and confiscated truckloads of porn, valued by Rothenberg's lawyer at a quarter of a million dollars. The NYPD well knew that organised crime had muscled into the porn business, and the police and District Attorney Robert Morgenthau were intent on exposing this insidious business. They were sure that the Gambino family was deeply involved – everyone on the street knew that – but they needed proof, tangible evidence that they could use in a court of law. No easy task, for someone would have to be willing to take the stand and point the finger.

The police also confiscated Argrila and Rothenberg's books, and there they found cheques made out to Roy DeMeo, who had cashed them through the Borough of Brooklyn Credit Union – the first direct connection to the Gambino family.

The cops suspected Roy had links to organised crime, but they had no proof. Detectives began trailing DeMeo all over, though he often managed to lose them. 'He was wily like a fox during the first days of hunting season,' an NYPD detective later confided.

Roy obviously knew that if Argrila and Rothenberg cooperated with the police, he'd be in trouble. Not only him, but Nino Gaggi as well: Gaggi had been there the day Roy strong-armed Rothenberg. Roy knew he had to protect Gaggi at all costs: if Gaggi was busted because of this shakedown, Roy would be in deep shit, might very well have to be killed. Nino Gaggi had murdered people for a lot less.

DeMeo didn't think Tony Argrila would talk, but he didn't trust Rothenberg. DeMeo contacted Rothenberg and took him for a nice dinner in an Italian restaurant in Flatbush, Brooklyn, to feel him out, and he didn't like what he felt. Roy, like many people who come from and are educated on the street, had an overly developed sense of danger, and he sensed that Paul Rothenberg couldn't be trusted, that he was resentful of the money Roy had been shaking him down for, that he felt his, Rothenberg's, troubles with the law were being disproportionately magnified because of Roy DeMeo. Acting like a concerned friend, Roy gave Rothenberg a few thousand cash to help pay his lawyers, saying he'd be there if in fact Rothenberg needed more money. For Rothenberg, it was not about money. He'd always resented Roy, the beating he'd given him, and felt no kind of friendship or kinship at all with DeMeo.

'He's a fuckin' punk and I ain't taking any heat for him,' he told one of the girls who worked in the lab. When asked if he felt in danger, he said, 'I know too much for anyone to hurt me' – a fatal error in judgement. It didn't take long for this quote to reach DeMeo.

The Manhattan district attorney's office urged Rothenberg's lawyer to convince his client that he should tell about how the Mafia was shaking him down. The district attorney's office didn't give a flying fuck about the porn Rothenberg and Argrila were making and distributing: they wanted the mob. That's where the headlines were, and all prosecutors in all places love headlines. A good example of this would, of course, be former federal prosecutor Rudolph Giuliani: 'He never saw a camera he didn't like' was a running joke among reporters covering Giuliani's much publicised war against organised crime.

There were several meetings between Rothenberg's lawyer, Herb Kassner, and assistant DAs. DeMeo, who had extensive connections in the NYPD – i.e. crooked cops who sold him information – soon learned what was in the wind. He immediately called Richard to a meeting in Brooklyn.

When Richard arrived, Nino Gaggi himself was there. He was wearing a short-sleeved yellow shirt and large aviator-type glasses. Introductions were made. What Roy wanted done, the murder of Rothenberg, he would not entrust to any of his guys. Rothenberg knew them all, and Roy wanted a professional to do this job. His guys were great for killing and dismembering in the Gemini apartment, but Roy knew better than to involve them in a job that required finesse, careful planning . . . discretion.

Roy, as usual, got right to the point: 'This fuckin' Jew Rothenberg's a problem,' he said. 'Did you hear what he said about knowing so much we couldn't hurt him?' he asked, incredulous.

'I heard,' Richard said.

'Our friend here is concerned. It's because of him that we're able to earn. It's because of him no one bothers us.'

Richard nodded respectfully; he understood.

Gaggi spoke now for the first time. 'I made the mistake of letting this kike see me. He knows who I am. It's a problem. The cocksucker can put me away.'

Nino Gaggi dreaded the thought of going to jail. He viewed himself as a businessman who just happened to rob and kill, and jail never came into the equation. Most mob guys know – never forget – that jail is an inherent part of the territory, but not Nino Gaggi. He was above that. Jail wasn't for him.

'I can take care of this problem,' Richard offered. He now knew why he'd been called to Brooklyn, and he knew this was a good chance to get in good with Gaggi and the Gambino people. 'I'll be happy to go see him,' he added.

'Good,' Roy said, and told Richard where Paul Rothenberg lived, the type of car he drove, even the licence-plate number. Nothing else had to be said. Now it was just a matter of time.

When Richard went out on a 'piece of work', he usually took his van with tinted windows. He brought a supply of bottled water and a plastic container he could use to relieve himself.

Being an efficient contract killer was all about planning and patience – being able to sit and watch and wait for the right moment to strike; this was the part of a piece of work that

Richard enjoyed the most, what he excelled at, the stalking and planning.

Sunday, 29 July was a hot, humid day. Richard discreetly parked his van a block away from Rothenberg's house and sat there waiting. Roy had told him that Rothenberg was married and that he often took his wife shopping. Rothenberg also had a black girlfriend, whom Richard had met several times. Richard had with him a .38 with a silencer. Patient and calm, he sat there in the July heat waiting for Rothenberg, listening to country music.

When Rothenberg finally walked out of the house, he took a rag from the boot and began cleaning the windows of his car. Roy had asked Richard to call him when he spotted Rothenberg, which Richard now did, from a phone booth on the corner. He paged DeMeo with the number. Roy called him right back.

'What's cookin'?' Roy asked.

'I'm looking at him right now. He's in front of his house cleaning the windows of his car,' Richard said. 'Looks like he's going somewhere.'

'Call me and let me know where he goes. If possible, I want to see this go down.'

'Roy, that complicates –'

'Rich, just call,' Roy insisted, always the bully, always the boss.

Richard hung up. He didn't like the idea of letting Roy know when and where the hit would go down, but he'd do as Roy asked.

Soon, Rothenberg's wife came out of the house. They both got in the car, and off they went, Richard following. He did not know the area well, but he managed to trail Rothenberg to a mall. Because it was the weekend, there were many shoppers. Rothenberg parked, his wife got out of the car and went into a store. Rothenberg began reading the sports section of the *Daily News*. Richard called Roy and told him where he was, that he was planning to pop him right there. Because of the silencer he'd be able to do the job if the right moment presented itself.

'I'm on my way,' Roy said. 'Wait for me!' he added.

'Are you nuts?' Richard began, but Roy hung up. Angry about this, Richard went back to his van. Shaking his head in disgust, he sat there, watching Rothenberg read the paper. He knew that once his wife came out of the store, the moment would pass. He would not kill him in front of his wife. Rothenberg was parked off to the left of the large lot, near an alley between two concrete buildings where goods were unloaded from trucks.

Sure enough, Richard spotted DeMeo's white Lincoln come speeding into the lot, tyres screeching. Richard rolled his eyes. There were three guys in the car: Freddy, Dracula and Chris. Freddy spotted Richard's van and pointed to it, Richard saw. Roy got out of the car and walked over to the van.

'Where is he?' Roy asked.

'There, but I don't understand – what's this all about? Why'd you bring your army?'

Before Roy could answer, Richard watched Rothenberg get out of his car and start towards the alley, moving quickly, looking over his shoulder, fear on his face.

'He spotted you,' Richard said, pissed off. He stuck the .38 into his pants, got out of the van and went after Rothenberg, who now began to run into the alley. When Richard reached the alley, he pulled out the .38, aimed carefully and fired two times, shooting Rothenberg down. He hid the gun, turned and made his way back to the van.

Roy approached him. 'Fuckin' great shot, Rich,' he said, smiling.

'Yeah,' Richard said, getting into his van, keeping his anger to himself.

'You mad, Rich?'

'Roy, come on, I just popped someone, I want to get the fuck outta here,' Richard said, and pulled away.

Richard got lost but soon found his way to the Belt Parkway

and headed for home, thinking that Roy DeMeo was nuts, that he had watched too many gangster movies. And Richard didn't like the fact that three other guys had seen the hit. This was yet another thing Richard had against Roy DeMeo. The list was growing.

As Richard drove back to his family, a man in a red Mustang cut him up. Richard pulled up alongside the car and began to curse the guy, made a fist at him. The driver of the Mustang gave Richard the finger. Incensed, Richard followed him off the Parkway and caught up with him at a light. Just the two of them were there. The guy jumped out of his car. Richard shot him dead, made a turn and left him there by his car, another unsolved murder committed by Richard. With no witnesses and no apparent motive, the police could do nothing. He soon dropped the .38 in a creek, but he kept the silencer. He had used the gun to kill two people within the span of forty minutes.

Richard returned home, had a turkey-on-rye sandwich, sat down in the living-room and watched TV with Barbara. The children were sleeping.

Angry, serious-faced detectives immediately went and picked up Roy DeMeo and questioned him about Paul Rothenberg's murder. He had nothing to say other than to give his name and address. Anthony Argrila – lucky for him – had been boating when his partner was murdered by Richard. He swore he knew nothing about Roy DeMeo, nothing about anything, said that his partner had 'a lot of dealings with people I know nothing about'.

'Truth is,' he told sceptical detectives, 'he dealt with people I never even met. Truth is, I think – no, I'm sure – he was stealing from me, you know.'

However, the police trailed Tony Argrila and actually saw him meet with DeMeo several times, proving that he lied through his teeth. However, there wasn't much they could do about it at this point.

More than anything in the world, Roy DeMeo wanted to be

made, and he was hoping this murder would do the trick. A big smile on his pudgy, dark-eyed face, Roy went to Nino Gaggi at his Bensonhurst home on Cropsey Avenue and proudly told his boss, hopefully his sponsor – the man who could have him inducted into the Gambino family – that Rothenberg was dead and that he'd actually seen him go down. Gaggi wanted all the details, which Roy gladly regaled him with.

'Good, good job!' Nino told Roy, proud of him. How quickly he had disposed of this potentially serious problem. He hugged and kissed Roy, as is the custom. Little did Nino Gaggi know that Roy DeMeo would soon bring his world crashing down on his balding head.

Richard did not ask for or receive any payment for this hit. It was a favour. But Roy later told him, 'The slate's clean between us,' forgiving Richard fifty thousand dollars he owed him for porn. All nice and neat and tidy, it seemed.

31

'LADY' AND POUILLY-FUISSÉ

Barbara Kuklinski both dreaded and looked forward to weekends. Though she never knew when Richard would be home – he often left the house without any notice, at the drop of a hat, at all times of the day and night – she tried to make plans that included him. Barbara enjoyed getting dressed up and going to nice restaurants, enjoyed good food, good company, good conversation. Unlike her mother, Genevieve, Barbara was outgoing and gregarious and liked the company of friends and other couples on Friday- and Saturday-night outings. In this, she was just like her father.

When they went out, Richard always ordered the best of everything. Money was no object. As far as he was concerned, money was for spending, and he spent as if he had a tree in the back yard that grew crisp new hundred-dollar bills every time you watered it. Chateaubriand, lobster, three-hundred-dollar bottles of wine were the norm. Richard also enjoyed putting on hand-tailored suits, silk ties, expensive Italian shoes. Barbara picked out most of his clothes. He trusted her taste; he trusted her social graces and direction. If another couple joined them, as often happened, Richard picked up the tab. He wouldn't let anyone else pay. Barbara tried to explain that he didn't have to pay every bill, that it was OK to split tabs or let others pay. But he didn't see it that way, and her words fell on deaf ears.

'LADY' AND POUILLY-FUISSÉ

Barbara didn't know where all the money was coming from. She figured he had finally found his way in business and didn't question him. If she had questioned him, his answer would have been a blank stare, a stone face, as though he hadn't heard her. Barbara learned to accept, like everything else, her husband's tight lips . . . and generous ways. When Barbara and Richard went out for a night on the town, he was usually quiet, didn't talk much. He just sat there, taking everything in. Barbara, however, talked enough for both of them, and that was fine with him. She'd even answer questions for him. Richard now drank only a little wine. He knew hard alcohol made him mean, and he had the good sense to steer clear of it. He was mean enough without it.

Richard was not only generous, he could be amazingly considerate, an incorrigible romantic. He had, for instance, nicknamed Barbara 'Lady' and often called her that, and he'd arrange for Kenny Rogers' song 'Lady' to be playing when they entered favourite restaurants – Palisadium, Archer's, Over Rose's Dead Body, Le Chateau and Danny's Steakhouse – and he made sure Barbara's favourite wines, Montrachet and Pouilly-Fuissé, were in fancy ice buckets next to their table. He even arranged for freshly cut long-stemmed red roses to be placed on their table before they arrived.

Nothing was too good for Lady.

This Richard – the good Richard – Barbara loved in her own quiet way. The other Richard, however, she had grown to hate, and often the bad feelings she harboured for him far outweighed the good ones. Like a pendulum, her feelings swung back and forth: love, hate; love, hate.

When they dressed up and went out, Richard was usually polite, a gentleman. But he was obsessively jealous. If a waiter or any man paid too much attention to Barbara or stared at her, Richard's face iced over, and he didn't have the slightest compunction about becoming rude, aggressive . . . even violent. More than ever, he viewed Barbara as his personal property, a treasured bauble, and it was a dangerous enterprise paying her too much notice.

One Saturday evening, they went to a movie in Dumont. As they were leaving, Richard abruptly walked away from Barbara, went over to some guy Barbara hadn't even noticed and demanded to know why he was staring at Barbara. The man told Richard he was crazy, that he wasn't staring, to 'shove it'. Richard punched the guy and knocked him out cold.

'Why, Richard?' Barbara asked when they got outside.

'I saw him staring *disrespectfully*.'

'At me?'

'Yeah.'

'I didn't even see him.'

'This was between me and him,' he said.

Barbara loathed being in the car with Richard, for he often got into arguments with people about how they drove, which inevitably caused him to lose his temper, get out of the car, berate people, break windscreens with his huge ham-hock fists. Barbara knew that when Richard was like this she could do nothing to reason with him. No one could. Not even a cop with a drawn gun. It was best she just kept quiet because his rage could suddenly be turned on her. Richard was a walking time bomb. When he was mad and you looked at him, you could almost hear the ticking. He could go off at any moment. That was reality. That was what she had to live with. Even when he was in the car with his daughters, he'd get into these nutty, nonsensical, violent disputes with men and women about their driving. He was even arrested for breaking the windscreen of a woman's car when his daughters were with him. However, the woman refused to press charges. She was – correctly – deathly afraid of Richard. To see him in one of his rages was a frightening experience. No one who saw it was apt to forget.

Dwayne was still too young to comprehend fully what a madman his father could become, but both Merrick and Chris well knew how volatile and violent he was, and both of them were terrified of their father, scared to the cores of their little beings. Merrick took to trembling when Richard lost it. But he never laid a finger on either girl. Even many years later, both Merrick and Chris paled and trembled at just the sound of Richard's voice.

Yet when Merrick had to be hospitalised, as she often was, Richard could not have been more solicitous and caring. Oh how Merrick loved that daddy, and oh how Merrick feared the other daddy. It was during the quiet times at the hospital, when Richard and Merrick were alone in the early-morning hours and late at night, that Richard began telling his first-born about his childhood. How he, his mother and his brother Florian were brutalised by Stanley; how poor they were; how there was never enough of anything; how he stole to eat. He never spoke like this to Chris or even to Barbara, only to Merrick. She'd look at him with her huge, honey-coloured fawn eyes and silently listen to him, having an understanding beyond her years. It wasn't as though he was trying to rationalise or make any kind of excuse for his temper tantrums and his violence against Barbara. He just wanted her to know the truth, how it had been. But after hearing these things, Merrick only loved her father all the more.

There were times at home when Richard would have one of his outbursts, break things and then lock himself in his office. Merrick would go to him, ask him to calm down, to 'please relax, Daddy'. During these episodes, Richard would explain in a matter-of-fact way, 'You know if . . . if I kill Mommy, if something happens and she dies, I'll have to kill you all . . . I can't leave any witnesses.'

'Yes, Daddy. I know, Daddy,' she said.

As strange and horrible a thing as this was to tell a child, Richard was trying to let Merrick know in advance – out of consideration – what might happen. He wanted her to understand that his doing such a thing was out of . . . love. Only out of love.

He loved Barbara too much.

He loved his children too much.

That was the problem. The only way he could deal with their loss, if he inadvertently killed Barbara, was to kill them. Essentially, that was how Richard had dealt with all his problems since he was a child. Kill it and the problem goes away. Richard had a unique ability to compartmentalise emotional pain and turmoil. He was like two different people who didn't know each other, two strangers in the same body.

'But you, Merrick . . . you'll be the hardest to kill. You understand?' he'd tell his daughter, she recently explained.

'Yes, Daddy,' she said, and she did understand and accept this. She was, she knew, his favourite, and she was glad of it.

That August, Richard and Barbara – with her cousin Carl and his wife, Nancy – rented a nice beach house in Cape Cod for two weeks. Barbara was still very close to Carl. Richard had grown to accept and even like Carl, though, because he was a man, Richard would not let Barbara kiss him hello or even hug him. She could only shake his hand. Carl and Nancy had two children, and all the kids loved playing on the beach, making sandcastles and frolicking in the surf. Richard enjoyed playing with the kids. He helped them with their castles and sea walls, dug deep holes for them, let them cover him in sand, though his skin was fair and he always ended up sunburned. Barbara would warn him about the sun as if he were a child, remind him how sensitive he was to it, but Richard enjoyed playing with the children so much that he'd inevitably end up burned red like a steamed lobster.

They had barbecues on the beach, everyone happy and smiling and having a good old time. To look at Richard there on the beach with the children, you'd think he was the best dad in the world. A wonderful, devoted family man who surely wouldn't hurt a fly.

That summer, the family also went down to Florida to visit Barbara's father. Little Dwayne couldn't fly because he'd get ear problems from the altitude of the plane, so the family drove.

They got up early – all the kids excited about the trip, about Disney World and seeing their grandpa – piled into the car and headed south on the New Jersey Turnpike. During this Florida trip, Richard did not lose his temper at the way anyone drove. They stopped at a restaurant for lunch on their way down. Barbara and the children sang and played licence-plate poker, seeing who could find the most matching numbers on any given plate, and they looked for animal-shaped clouds. They stayed in a good hotel, where the kids played in the pool, and they continued on their way in the morning. Richard even sang along with the family as they went.

As fun and good as the trip was, both Chris and Merrick were wary and on their guard; they never knew when their father would go off, when Barbara might say something to upset him. Barbara had a sharp tongue and would use it to cut Richard if she had a mind to. It was, in a sense, her way of getting back at him for bullying her.

In Florida, they stayed with Barbara's father. He now had a house on the Intracoastal Waterway and a 22-foot Chris-Craft fishing boat. He gladly took the kids out on fishing trips – Barbara did not go because she became seasick – and they gleefully caught snappers, blue runners and blowfish, which Al cleaned and grilled in the evenings. Barbara's dad was an excellent cook, and it was always a big treat to eat anything he prepared. Chris recently observed, *Never on any of these fishing trips would Dad go off, because my mom wasn't there to upset him.*

Sometimes they saw sharks in the water, a very dramatic thing. Once a small tiger shark took a snapper Richard was reeling in. The children were both horrified and fascinated; the sharks gave Richard macabre ideas.

Barbara very much enjoyed going to fine outdoor restaurants along the waterside in the nearby resort of Naples and having sumptuous meals. Like most married women with three children, she liked to be waited on. The children were all exceedingly well behaved, like three small adults. They never acted up or made any kind of fuss. Richard always insisted on taking care of the bill. He wouldn't even let Al put his hand in his pocket. Richard paid with cash, never by credit card. He carried around a roll of hundred-dollar bills that could choke a horse. All his money was earned illegally now. He had no 'straight employment' and there couldn't be any record of the money he spent so readily. There was one fancy restaurant, Philippe's, that Barbara particularly liked. All the waiters wore stiff white shirts, black bow ties and jackets. Al would inevitably get the children in trouble by making them laugh: he'd hang onion rings on his ears, tickle them and grab their feet under the table. Al Pedrici loved his grandchildren no end and couldn't get enough of them.

After a few days at Al's house, the Kuklinskis drove to Disney World and stayed in the Contemporary Hotel, the best one in the Disney complex. It was expensive, but you could get the monorail from there straight to the rides, where all the action was. The family would get up early so they could enjoy as much as possible before it became too hot. As much as Barbara loved Florida – going for long swims, watching the children play on the beach – she didn't like the heat or the humidity. It made her tired and irritable, and when Barbara was irritable, she and Richard inevitably clashed. Still, the Florida vacations were great fun.

They were, Merrick explained, *some of the best times of my childhood . . . but you never knew when Dad might go off, so it was always – well, there was always this kind of tension lurking.*

32

BLOOD MONEY

For Richard Kuklinski, money mattered. With money, you were a successful man; without it, you were a failure, a needy no one who had to watch the good things in life go speeding by.

After Richard killed Paul Rothenberg, he was in good with DeMeo, but, more importantly, he was in solid with Nino Gaggi and by extension the Gambino family. Roy invited Richard to dinner with Gaggi at an Italian restaurant called the Villa in Bensonhurst. It was on Twenty-sixth Avenue, in an old-fashioned house with large pillars out front. The restaurant served first-rate home-style Neapolitan cooking, Nino's favourite. Everyone there knew who Nino was, and he was waited on as though he were Italian royalty; the best of everything, food and wine and service, was immediately his. Richard was impressed. It was hard not to be. Nino was obviously pleased that Richard had done away with Paul Rothenberg, and he promised that Richard would 'earn with us'.

DeMeo acted as if he had created and moulded Richard ... a kind of secret Frankenstein's monster killing machine who would faithfully carry out any contract, no questions asked, no piece of work too dangerous.

Because of DeMeo, Richard would become an integral part of the killing arm of the Gambino crime family. The fact that he was not Italian and did not hang out with wiseguys proved to be a big plus and would eventually get him involved in taking down the heads of two different crime families – a unique distinction.

After the sumptuous dinner with Gaggi and DeMeo at the Villa, Richard headed back to his family in Dumont. Dumont was as different from Bensonhurst as the sun is from the moon. In Dumont, Richard was able to wrap himself in a cloak of respectability: he was the good neighbour, the guy who drove his daughters' friends all over, a faithful, stoical usher at Sunday Mass. Richard had no use for the church or its hypocritical teachings, but Barbara insisted that all her children attend private Catholic schools, which were quite expensive, and that the family attend Sunday Mass together every week. In these things, Barbara was the boss. Richard had nothing to say. He acceded to all of Barbara's demands and directives when it came to the children – where they went to school, how they dressed, who their friends were, their table manners.

The following week, Richard was beeped by DeMeo and went to meet him at the diner near the Tappan Zee Bridge.

'Hey, Rich,' DeMeo greeted him, and they warmly hugged and kissed, these two stone-cold killers, and began to walk around the parking lot.

'Got a special piece a work for you. This Cuban cocksucker down in Miami beat up and raped the 14-year-old daughter of an associate of ours. She couldn't pick him out in a line-up because he wore a fuckin' bandanna, but we know who he is. He works as a maintenance guy in the complex where they have a place. It's called the Castaway, right in Miami, on Collins Avenue. Richie, you go see him and make sure he fuckin' suffers . . . really suffers! You understand?'

'My pleasure,' Richard said, and he meant it.

'This is from our associate,' Roy said, and slipped Richard an envelope with twenty thousand dollars in it. Mob guys make trainloads of money, and twenty thousand was a mere

Third Street, Jersey City, New Jersey, where Richard Kuklinski was born.

Richard the day he received his First Communion at age eight. (Courtesy of Barbara Kuklinski)

Anna McNally Kuklinski, Richard's mother, with Richard and Barbara, Christmas 1961. (Courtesy of Barbara Kuklinski)

Richard at work in the lab, 1962. (Courtesy of Barbara Kuklinski)

Oh bliss! Barbara has just learned she is pregnant (with Merrick), in 1963. (Courtesy of Barbara Kuklinski)

Richard and Barbara with newborn Merrick in March 1964.
(Courtesy of Barbara Kuklinski)

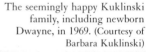

In front of their West New York home at Christmastime 1969. (Courtesy of Barbara Kuklinski)

The seemingly happy Kuklinski family, including newborn Dwayne, in 1969. (Courtesy of Barbara Kuklinski)

Richard and Dwayne in 1973.
(Courtesy of Barbara Kuklinski)

Richard with Chris and
Merrick in 1973. (Courtesy
of Barbara Kuklinski)

Carmine Galante lies dead in the garden of Joe and Mary's Restaurant in Bushwick, Brooklyn, in 1979. A cigar remains clenched between his teeth. (Courtesy of the *New York Daily News*)

The *Daily News* front page after the 1985 murder of Paul Castellano. (Courtesy of the *New York Daily News*)

MANHATTAN ★ ★ ★ • SPORTS FINAL

LET THEM EAT HORS D'OEUVRES
A guide to New York office parties
In Tuesday Business

DAILY ◉ NEWS
NEW YORK'S PICTURE NEWSPAPER®

35¢   Tuesday, December 17, 1985

RUBOUT

MOB HITS BIG PAUL Body of Thomas Bilotti lies by his car on E. 46th St. after Bilotti and Paul (Big Paul) Castellano, 70, were shot to death by three men who fled last night. At the time of his death, Big Paul was reputedly the boss of the nation's biggest crime family. **Stories start on page 2; other pictures in centerfold.**

The park near his Dumont, New Jersey, home,
where Richard enjoyed feeding the ducks.

A drawing Richard later made of one of his victims
being eaten alive by rats. (Courtesy of Barbara Kuklinski)

Richard and Barbara exchange gifts on their last anniversary before his arrest. (Courtesy of Barbara Kuklinski)

Richie goofing around with his 'favourite possession', Barbara, during 1981. (Courtesy of Barbara Kuklinski)

MANHATTAN ★ ★ ★ SPORTS FINAL

COLOMBIA'S REIGN OF TERROR:

COCAINE KILLS

PART 4 OF WHY THE SMUGGLERS ARE WINNING — Starts on Page 7

DAILY●NEWS

NEW YORK'S PICTURE NEWSPAPER®   Thursday, December 18, 1986.

BURGER MURDER

N.J. man held in killings of 5 with gun & cyanide

Story on page 2

ncy:
hey
ceived
Ron

HASENFUS IS FREE

Nicaraguan President Daniel Ortega as he handed over gunrunner Eugene Hasenfus (left) to Sen. Christopher Dodd (right) in Managua yesterday. At far right is prisoner's wife, Sally. Hasenfus will arrive home today and may be summoned

The *Daily News* headline on 18 December 1986. (Courtesy of the *New York Daily News*)

Trenton State Prison, where Richard was incarcerated until his death.

Richard during the period of his famous HBO TV interviews. (Courtesy of HBO)

Richard and the author, discussing this book.

Merrick and Chris at a Hallowe'en party. Even after all they have been through, they love life and are quick to laugh. (Courtesy of Barbara Kuklinski)

drop in the bucket, though it was enough for Richard to leave for Miami the following day. Now he did not stop for lunch or stay at a nice hotel on the way down. He drove straight through. When he bought gas and oil he paid cash. Even if Richard had had a credit card, he would not have used it, because he wanted no record of this trip. There was no photo of the mark, but DeMeo told him the kind of car he drove and that he parked it in the designated area for hotel employees; he even gave him the licence-plate number.

The only people Richard hated more than bullies were rapists. As he drove, he thought about how he'd feel if one of his girls was attacked that way . . . the rage and hatred he'd know. As cold and indifferent as Richard could be to human suffering, he had great empathy for a young woman who had been raped. This killing was a piece of work he'd enjoy. This was a piece of work he'd gladly have done for free.

As always, Richard was careful about not speeding, even though he was in a hurry to do the job, indeed looking forward to it. He had with him a .38 loaded with hollow-point rounds and a razor-sharp hunting knife with a curved blade and a hardwood handle. The handle had four notches on it. Richard liked to notch his knives when he used them to kill someone. He explained, *I didn't know how I picked up the habit, but I always liked to notch my knives. Like gunfighters used to. Over the years, I had dozens of knives I used to kill. Some of them had ten to fifteen notches on them. Then I'd just get rid of them.*

Richard planned to use a knife for this particular job. He very much enjoyed, he said, killing with a knife because it was so personal; you had to be close to the victim. He liked to see life leave the eyes of those he killed – especially a rapist. This would be . . . fun.

The Castaway was a sprawling three-storey apartment complex on Collins Avenue, near Seventieth Street, on both the ocean side of the street and the inland side. Richard checked into a hotel near the place, had a nice lunch and drove to the parking lot, looking for the mark's car. It wasn't there. Richard quickly found out there were two shifts, 8.00 a.m. to 4.00 p.m., then 4.00 p.m. to midnight. It was now the middle of the winter, 1974, and the parking lot was full. He would have to be careful, he knew, about being seen taking the mark.

He left, returned at 3.30 p.m. and waited. He didn't have to wait long, for the mark soon pulled into the lot and parked, not a care in the world, singing to himself. He drove a beaten-up red Chevy. The licence plate matched. Richard smiled when he saw the guy, a tall, skinny Latino with a thick, greasy head of black hair, combed straight back. Richard quickly saw how the job should be done and soon left.

Now it was only a matter of time.

At 11.30 that night, Richard was back in the parking lot of the Castaway. Just across the street was a hangout for young people called Nebas, and a huge crowd of kids were mingling. Richard parked his van as close to the mark's car as possible, got out of it, walked to the red Chevy, gave it a flat, then calmly returned to the van. This was a tried and proven method, which Richard would use many times over. He already knew where he'd take the mark once he snatched him: a desolate stand of palms about half an hour north of the hotel, right by the ocean.

Near midnight, the mark came bopping over to his car. He spotted the flat, cursed out loud and opened his boot. As he bent to pull the spare out, Richard stole up behind him and put the .38 in his lower back.

'My friend, I need you to come with me,' he said, his voice faraway and detached, as if it were coming from a machine, a telephone recording. Richard let him see the gun now, took his skinny arm and marched him to the van, put him inside, handcuffed him, put a sock in his mouth and taped his mouth shut with heavy-duty grey duct tape. Richard calmly got behind the wheel and pulled out of the lot. The whole thing took less than two minutes. As Richard drove north on Collins, he talked to the mark.

'My friend,' he said, 'I want you to know that I've been sent by friends of the girl you beat up and raped.'

At that, the mark began to moan and flop around like a fish suddenly out of water.

'If you don't stop making a fuss, I'm going to hurt you.'

The mark became still, silent. What was so unsettling about what Richard said was not so much the words. It was the cold, detached way he said them, each one like the cut of a jagged knife.

'So, my friend, I want you to know that you have to suffer before I kill you. They paid me well for that, but truth is I'd gladly do this for free. I want you to know that.'

'Hmm! Hmm!' the mark mumbled, panic-stricken.

'If you believe in God, my friend, you better start praying because you've reached the end of the line. The train is going to soon stop, and it's time to get off.'

Richard was purposely tormenting the mark, letting the caustic words be the last he heard in this life.

'Did you really think you could do such a thing and go about your business like nothing happened? Well, my friend, you picked the wrong girl this time.'

Richard turned right, switched off the lights and made his way onto a rough road that went all the way down to the beach. There was a nearly full moon in a velvet black sky. The moonlight, white and clean and lovely, reflected off the calm sea, laying a glistening lunar highway on the still surface of the water. Richard stopped, sat and listened. All was quiet and still. No sound but the gentle lapping of small waves on the fine white sand of the beach.

Richard put on blue plastic gloves, pulled the rapist from the van, dragged him to a wide, particularly curved palm and tied him to the tree with yellow nylon rope. Now the mark was in a frenzied panic. Richard showed him the gleaming curved blade, the moonlight reflecting ominously on the razor-sharp steel.

'So, my friend, let's get started.'

And with that, Richard roughly pulled down the mark's trousers, took tight hold of both his testicles and pulled so hard he literally tore them off.

White-hot pain exploded where his testicles had just been. His eyes burst open. Richard showed him his balls.

'How's that feel?' he asked, smiling. 'My friend.'

Richard allowed time for the shock to wear off a bit and for the pain to set in.

'Nice night, isn't it?' he asked. 'Look at the moon. How pretty.'

Now he used the knife; he grabbed hold of the mark's penis – 'This is what got you in all the trouble, you don't need it any more' – and easily cut it off. He showed it to the rapist as blood gushed from the sudden fleshy stump Richard had created. He went back to the van and put the severed member in a ziplock sandwich bag he'd brought for this purpose.

He returned to the mark, ripped all his clothes off him and began slowly slicing away fillets of flesh – kind of like pieces of skirt steak – making sure to show him the pieces he was methodically taking away, smiling as he worked.

The mark was soon a monstrous sight, terrible to see in the pale silver light of the Miami moon. Richard again returned to the van. He had brought along a large container of fine kosher salt, and he now poured the salt all over the exposed flesh. It would bring, Richard knew, a whole new symphony of pain. He allowed time for the salt to work.

Now Richard forced the blade into the mark's lower abdomen and slowly pulled it up with his superhuman strength. The man's guts spilled forth and were suddenly just hanging there like a nervous cluster of blue-red snakes.

Richard cut him free, put a life jacket on him, grabbed his ankle and dragged him down to the water's edge, talking as he went: 'My friend, I know the tide's going out now, I checked, and you're going out with it. I put the life vest on you because I don't want you to drown. I'll bet you my last dollar that the sharks'll find you in no time. I hear there are big nasty tiger sharks here.' And with that, Richard swung him up and around, tossed him into the water and watched him drift out. Then he turned and went back to the van, retrieved what he had cut from the mark, threw it all in the water and returned to his hotel, where he had a nice sandwich – his favourite, turkey and mayo on rye – and slept like a baby. Richard always slept particularly well after a good piece of work.

In the morning, after a leisurely breakfast and a nice walk, Richard started back home, calm, relaxed, listening to country music as he went. He had very much enjoyed this job and wondered how long it had been before the sharks had found the rapist. He knew they prowled the shoreline at night and was sure it hadn't taken long at all.

As Richard was going through South Carolina, a van with a rebel flag in the window pulled up alongside him. There were three guys in it. They began to taunt Richard, called him a 'nigger lover', gave him the finger. Of all the people in the world to pick on, they chose the wrong guy. Richard told them to fuck off, to get lost. They again gave him the finger, all serious-faced, as if they had bad intentions, wanted to hurt him. He pulled ahead of them, spotted a lay-by off the highway and drove into it. They too pulled into the lay-by. Richard retrieved his gun from under the seat. The three of them got out of the van. One of them had some kind of club. Richard got out of his van and without so much as one word shot all three of them dead, got back into his van and pulled away. In less than ten hours, he had killed four people without a second thought, other than to wonder how long it had taken for the sharks to find the rapist; he was proud of his work, his imaginative ingenuity, the justice he had served up. When the police found the three dead men in the lay-by, there was little they could do with no tangible link – witnesses, clues, tyre marks – between these bodies and the person responsible for the three homicides.

* * *

Back in Brooklyn, Richard went to see DeMeo. He met him at the Gemini Lounge, told him what he had done and gave him the severed member.

Roy smiled. This he liked. 'Good, great!' Roy exclaimed. 'I'll show it to our friend. He'll be pleased. Excellent job. Fuckin' beautiful. You're the best. D'you eat yet, big guy?'

'No, you?'

'Let's go grab a bite,' Roy said, and they went and had a good meal in a restaurant Roy liked in Coney Island called Carolina's. Over a large, colourful platter of antipasti, Richard provided more details of how the rapist had met his end. Roy just loved it, smiled and laughed and had a new-found respect for Richard.

'You're fuckin' one in a million!' he exclaimed happily.

Richard smiled along with Roy, ate with gusto; but he had not forgotten the beating Roy had given him or how Roy had pointed the cocked Uzi at him. It would be, Richard knew, just a matter of time before he had revenge. For now, he'd wait, bide his time, smile and be friendly and make money with Roy. He'd profit. Richard was, in fact, a very good actor; he could effortlessly sit and eat and drink and laugh along with a man whom he knew he would surely kill. Until he killed DeMeo, however, he wouldn't quite be whole. That's how he looked at it. That's how it was.

Because of DeMeo, news of Richard's homicide acumen quickly spread in the circles all mob guys frequented. Made men are a clannish lot, a close-knit society, and they talk incessantly among themselves; like old washerwomen, they are incorrigible gossips.

Richard began keeping a record of new ideas he had about ways to torture and kill people, writing down these inspirations in a small spiral reporter's notebook. He'd be sitting at home watching TV, see something and write it down: the idea of using salt on the rapist had come from a pirate movie he'd seen; the idea of using wet strips of rawhide and pouring hot water into people's noses also came from a film. Richard even took inspiration from cartoons, especially those featuring the Road Runner with Wile E. Coyote: the use of heavy weights, fires, booby traps, throwing people out of windows, these all came from Road Runner cartoons. He also found inspiration for mayhem and chaos in Popeye cartoons.

Meanwhile, Richard's porno business was thriving. He consigned almost everything that he produced or that Roy fronted him within a day or two of receiving it. Now that Paul Rothenberg was gone, Richard and Roy were filling the vacuum created by his sudden demise. Richard only wished he had killed Rothenberg sooner.

The next job he did for the Gambinos was in Los Angeles. As usual, Richard travelled first class. He got a big kick out of the fact that he was a professional killer, sitting there like all the other businesspeople, except that his business was the business of taking life, quickly or slowly, whatever the client preferred.

Through Gambino family ties in Los Angeles, Richard secured a .22 with a silencer, rented a van and went to fill the contract. He had a photo of the guy and his address, and he knew he used the same phone booth at the same time every day. The mark was a made man, and this was a sanctioned hit. He was giving information to the feds and had to go.

Like clockwork, the mark, a burly, big-bellied Italian, left his apartment, made his way to the phone booth and started talking animatedly, waving his free hand as if he were conducting an orchestra. Richard had been told to call Roy when he spotted the guy, which he now did. As usual, Richard used a phone booth, beeped in the number, and Roy called him back.

'You find him?' Roy asked.

'I'm looking at him right now. He's on the phone. Loves to talk.'

'He's talking to a guy I'm with right now.'

'You want me to move?'

'Hold off. We need to find out something first,' Roy said.

Every day for nearly a week, Richard was in position and would call Brooklyn as the mark talked up a storm and was told 'not yet'. Richard didn't like all this hanging around, but he would do what the job called for. Several times a day, he'd call home, make sure everything was OK – the concerned dad and husband just checking in.

Finally, Richard was given the green light. It was raining that day. He positioned the van where he knew the mark would walk, opened the side panel an inch or so and waited. The mark had, Richard knew, broken the cardinal rule: he'd fallen into the same pattern every day, making Richard's job that much easier. Sure enough, the mark came walking towards the van, his mind preoccupied. Richard raised the .22 and waited for him to be in position, and when he was in the precise line of fire, Richard pulled the trigger – a soft pop, hitting the mark in the side of the head, a little left of the temple. He went right down, brain-dead before he hit the wet pavement. Richard used a .22 Magnum hollow-point round, which entered the skull and bounced about inside the mark's head, making instant mush of his brain.

Richard got behind the wheel and headed to LAX, pleased that this piece of work was finally done. He hadn't liked having to hang around for several days. But he was a hunter and knew that with all hunting, patience was a prerequisite.

As always, Richard got rid of the murder weapon quickly, on his way to the airport, and he soon boarded a flight back to Newark. He took a cab home and walked into the house in a good mood. He had been paid thirty grand for this job. The Los Angeles police knew nothing about Richard, and the murder was never linked to him.

Barbara was in the kitchen preparing dinner; the girls were setting the table; Dwayne was reading a book. Richard kissed everyone hello, got hugs and kisses from his children.

'How was your trip?' Barbara asked, having no idea what

Richard had just done; she only knew he'd been in LA 'on business'.

'Good,' he said, no more.

The family soon sat down for dinner, roast beef and potatoes, one of Richard's favourites. He sliced the meat carefully, just so, not too thin, not too thick. The girls talked about school. Dwayne talked about the book he was reading. Richard, as always, sat quietly and listened.

Merrick was enrolled in the prestigious Devonshire Academy, an extremely expensive private school. Chris was enrolled in Holy Angels, also an expensive school. That's what Barbara wanted; that's the way it was going to be. Barbara was, for the most part, oblivious of the cost, certainly of the chances Richard was taking to earn the kind of money needed for the private schools and for all the trappings required to attend such schools.

Young Dwayne, Barbara had realised early on, was a gifted child, and she could not have been more proud of him. He had an IQ of 170 and loved to read; he'd much rather read a book than watch cartoons or play with toys. He loved the Golden Books series, quickly burned through them and went on to the classics: *The Jungle Book* and *Treasure Island*, *A Tale of Two Cities*, *Moby-Dick*, *Oliver Twist*. Books fascinated him. Barbara would often catch him in bed, under the covers, with a book and a torch to read by. She treated Dwayne as if he were royalty and repeatedly let Richard know how smart the boy was, this without any malice. She was just a proud mother effusively expressing herself. But Richard didn't take it that way. Yes, Dwayne was his son, yes, he was pleased the boy was obviously gifted; but he was still a male, and Richard didn't want any other males stealing away Barbara's attention. Richard inevitably became jealous of Dwayne and was, for the most part, stand-offish and somewhat aloof from his last-born, his own son, he readily admitted.

Barbara did not want any more children with Richard. She already had serious misgivings, she says, about having had three children with him. She'd had a sterilisation to make sure she could never become pregnant again. Richard was a very sexual man. The older he became, the more he wanted to make love to Barbara, every day . . . sometimes twice a day, even more. She wasn't always receptive to his overtures, which would immediately infuriate him, and he'd take her whether she wanted to or not. That was his nature. That's what he did. This was a frequent source of friction between them because Richard would not take no – 'I'm not in the mood' – for an answer. If she said, 'I have a headache,' he'd say, 'I don't want to make love to your head.'

He'd even become violent with Barbara if she said no. He took it as rejection – a thing he would not tolerate, on any level, for any reason. Even if she was menstruating, he didn't care. For him, it was irrelevant. Richard was obsessively loyal to Barbara, would never ever go with another woman, *wouldn't even think about it*, he claimed later, and thus he felt he had the God-given right to have his wife whenever the hell he pleased. He was, for the most part, a gentle, considerate lover; he never hurt her during sex, never wanted to bind her or dominate her or anything like that. He was conventional, indeed a bit puritanical, when it came to sex. Yet, he was hot-blooded, like a dedicated Latin lover, and often wanted to make love to Barbara.

Like all things, Barbara had to learn to accept this, make the best of it. But Richard always made sure she too was satisfied. In that way, he was *quite considerate*, she recently revealed.

Because of financial pressures, Richard was always looking for more ways to make more money. There was never enough money. But as word of Richard's dedication, expertise and efficiency spread, more and more people contacted him to do hits, and blood money came rolling in. He took pieces of work all over the country, indeed the world. Wherever the Mafia had interests, did business, there was conflict, disagreements, back-stabbing, the disrespecting of wives, girlfriends, daughters, there were people who had to die. Richard filled the bill. He travelled to Wisconsin, Florida, Hawaii, Maryland, North and South Carolina, Georgia, Las Vegas, Mississippi, Chicago, Arizona, Los Angeles, San Francisco, Wyoming, Indiana – all over the place – and killed people. Some he left where they dropped. Others disappeared forever . . . were buried, squashed in the boots of cars, thrown down bottomless pits in Pennsylvania, fed to rats in Bucks County.

A man in Brooklyn owed the Bonanno family $140,000. Instead of paying, he figured he'd go to the feds and talk, get the people he owed money to arrested. He had a garage. Richard was called there. The people owed the money were already there, waiting. They wanted to see it done, a skipper and four associates. Richard was given the nod. He knocked the guy down and, with a pistol equipped with a silencer, shot him in the arms, elbows and knees, then in the genitals, drawing out the death for his customers to see and know and enjoy. After shooting him seven times, Richard tortured him with a knife, then finally slit his throat. Everyone was happy. Richard received twenty-five large. He liked to please his customers.

A guy in Tennessee owed money, would not pay. He had been given porn by the Gambinos and thumbed his nose at them; told his friends, 'I ain't payin', fuck 'em.' Richard was sent to see him. He gave Richard cheques that proved to be worthless. Richard threw him out a window – eight storeys up.

A big heavy guy who was thought to be talking to the cops got into his car and drove off, listening to music as he went. Richard followed him on a motorcycle. He had a sawn-off double-barrelled shotgun with him, hidden in his leather jacket. The mark stopped at a red light. He began to light a fat cigar, looked at the large biker who had just pulled up next to him. He didn't give him a second thought. A moment later, Richard pulled out the shotgun and let loose both barrels, holding it with his enormous hand, completely taking the mark's head off. The light turned green. The motorcycle pulled away slowly, not in any hurry. No witnesses, no connection to Richard.

THE ICE MAN

An Asian man in Honolulu also owed money and wouldn't pay. He made excuses; he thought he was above reprisal. Richard was dispatched. His orders were: 'Get the money or make him dead.' Richard met him in his room in a very expensive five-star hotel. No money. Plenty of lame excuses. Richard was fawning and excessively polite. They moved out onto the terrace. 'What a nice view,' said Richard, looking out at the wonderful vista.

'Yes, yes it's lovely,' said the mark, and before he knew it he was plummeting to the ground. A big, bloody, meaty thud, broken bones, smashed beyond recognition or repair. Richard calmly turned and left. Whenever he killed, he never hurried. This killing was thought of as a suicide by the authorities, as Richard knew it would be, he claimed.

Shortly before his death, Richard said, *I felt I had no friends because I thought everyone was against me, always against me, no real ties to anyone. Rage, hate, that's what I walked around with. That's what I brought to the job. I used bats, tyre irons, rope, wire, knives, guns, bow and arrow, ice picks, screwdrivers, poison, explosives, my hands, just to mention a few . . .*

Interestingly, when Richard filled contracts he felt no animus towards the marks. Except the rapists. For him, killing people was as easy as breaking wind. He felt no empathy or sympathy or anything like that. Stanley Kuklinski had, quite successfully, beaten those things out of Richard many years ago . . . lifetimes ago.

Richard viewed himself as a champion gladiator in an arena of death, simply doing what was his calling in life. Richard had accepted – indeed grown to relish – the fact that he was part of an elite underground society: people who killed for the sheer fun of it; and people who killed for profit. What made Richard unique, however, was that he was doing both: he killed for both personal enjoyment and profit, on an unprecedented scale, the police having no idea he even existed.

* * *

Richard was not averse to working with other killers. Sometimes the job called for that and he readily did it; but he always preferred to work alone. One such hit was on a man in Detroit, a union guy involved with the mob. The mark had a big mouth and a bigger ego, was always saying that he wasn't scared of the mob, wasn't scared of anyone, that he would do this and he would do that if they ever tried to make a move on him. This was a genuinely tough individual with tight, narrow lips and high cheekbones, thinning hair greased straight back. As well as having a big mouth, he had serious delusions of grandeur.

The order for the hit came from Tony P., a made man in the Genovese family who held court in Union City, New Jersey. At the behest of Russi Bufalino, temporary head of the Genovese family, Tony P. was given the job of getting rid of this union guy.

Tony P. had known Richard since he was a kid back in Jersey City. He knew he could be trusted and would keep his mouth shut, so he made Richard part of a four-man hit team that included two brothers, Gabe and Sal, and a guy named Tommy. Of the four, Richard was the only one who was a bona fide professional killer, who had a doctorate in murder. Richard didn't know who had to die and he didn't particularly care. *I could give a flying fuck less*, he explained. *The who and why is never any of my business.*

It was 29 July 1975. Richard drove to Union City while it was still dark out and met the others. They got on Route 80 West and made their way towards Detroit, always staying within the speed limit. Richard sat in the back seat. Tony P. was with them. He was to lure the union guy to a lunch. Richard had a .22 auto with a silencer on it and a razor-sharp hunting knife. Both weapons were strapped to his massive calves. He also had a jawbreaker with him. The plan was to quickly snatch the mark. It would be Richard's job to make sure this went smoothly, without a commotion, and to actually kill the mark, who had then to disappear 'forever'. That was mandatory.

THE ICE MAN

The drive to Detroit took almost ten hours. Everyone but the driver slept most of the way. Richard did not drive. When they arrived in Detroit it was already mid-morning, a hot, humid day. Quiet and stoical and serious – few words said – they checked into a hotel, freshened up, had a light breakfast. They had walkie-talkies with them, which they would use in the taking of the mark. Richard would have preferred to do this alone, but he accepted the fact that it had to be this way. Murder, he knew, can be a very complicated, political business.

A phone call came. They left and went to the parking lot of the Machus Red Fox restaurant in Bloomfield Hills, a well-to-do suburb of Detroit. As they pulled into the restaurant, a man who looked vaguely familiar to Richard was standing there waiting for them. Tony P. got out of the car. The two shook hands and talked for a minute, and the mark got back into the car with Tony P. He sat up front. He didn't seem too happy. They started out. Richard was going to use the knife in a special way. He was just waiting for the nod from Tony P. After they'd gone a few miles, Richard was given the signal. He first knocked the mark unconscious with the jawbreaker. So there would be little blood, less of a mess, Richard pulled out the hunting knife, leaned forward, grabbed the mark's wide chin, and pulled him up so he'd have access to the lower back of the mark's head. Now Richard positioned the knife just at the base of his skull, slanted it upward, and with his unusual strength he thrust the blade directly into the mark's brain. The man shook violently, became still; his last breath came as a rattle. Because of the upward motion directly into the brain and the fact that Richard left the knife in the skull, there was little bleeding. They soon pulled over in a lay-by and put the mark in a body bag in the boot. Richard agreed to take the body back to New Jersey. He would have preferred to dump it in Michigan, but they wanted it back in Jersey. The others were going to take a bus. Richard dropped them off at a bus depot and headed for Jersey. Now that the job was successfully done, he was relaxed and sang along with the radio as he went.

Back in New Jersey, Richard went straight to a junkyard under the Pulaski Skyway in Kearny, just along the road from Newark. The junkyard was owned by a mob associate. Here the mark was placed in a black 50-gallon drum. Gasoline was poured all over him. He was set on fire, and they let him burn for half an hour or so. The fetid stink of his burning flesh and organs and bones filled the air. The junkyard dog was howling and salivating for some meat. They then sealed the drum carefully, welded it and buried it there in the junkyard.

The job, for now, was done. Richard was paid forty thousand dollars, a good score. Before he left the junkyard, he made sure to wipe away any fingerprints he might have left in the car; couldn't be too cautious. Though none of the hit team except Tony P. knew who Richard was or where he lived, he knew who they all were. They only knew him as 'the Big Guy'.

Tired but pleased with how well the job had gone, Richard returned to Dumont, to his family. Dwayne had a new kite, and Richard showed him how to fly it. Barbara was in the pool with Chris and Merrick and some of their girlfriends. It was a very hot day and the cool pool was a welcome reprieve from the stifling heat. The family had a barbecue. Richard did all the cooking, gladly served up burgers and frankfurters for the kids, steaks for the adults. 'Well done or rare?' Richard always asked. He very much enjoyed doling out the meat the way people – even the kids – liked it. As the meat cooked, he was reminded of the burning union guy.

Later on, one of the brothers, Sal, began talking to the feds, and, because he might try to use this murder to get out of trouble on an unrelated problem, the drum was quickly dug up and placed in the boot of a car, which was smashed down to a four-by-two-foot cube of metal in a giant car compressor. It, along with hundreds of other compacted cars, was then sold to the Japanese as scrap metal and shipped off to be used in the making of new automobiles that would compete with Detroit manufacturers' products.

And that, according to Richard, is what happened to Teamsters union boss Jimmy Hoffa.

He's part of a car somewhere in Japan right now, Richard confided, a slight smirk on his high-cheekboned face.

33

THE BIG GUY

Mob guys and their associates, allies, affiliates and friends are, for the most part, a bitter, vengeful lot. They do not believe in letting bygones be bygones. Thus, Richard's murder business flourished. The more he worked, the more successful his game, the more new contracts came rolling in from all over the country, then even overseas: in South America and Europe, Richard murdered for profit.

More often than not, the job required a quick murder, nothing elaborate. But Richard was killing so many people, he inevitably received *special requests*, as he referred to them.

A made man in New Jersey had a very lovely daughter, innocent and wide-eyed, drop-dead gorgeous. She was 19. She started seeing an older guy, a particularly handsome fellow. The father tried to stop his daughter from seeing this older guy, an obvious playboy type with big white teeth and flashing dark eyes, an earring in his left ear, too good-looking for his own good.

In frustration, the father took the boyfriend aside and politely asked, 'What're your intentions regarding my daughter?'

'Intentions?' the playboy asked, perplexed. He had no idea the father was mobbed up.

'Yeah, we'd like to know, me and her mother.'

'Just to have some fun, you know.'

'Fun?' the father asked.

'Yeah, you know, fool around. Some fun!' the playboy volunteered, smiling his big, toothy, beguiling grin.

The father, a Sicilian, turned beetroot red, though he didn't say another word.

Through some friends, this Sicilian father reached out to Richard, told him that he wanted the guy to disappear, but that first 'he must suffer!'

'My pleasure,' Richard said, and he meant it.

Within two days, Richard snatched the playboy and took him to the caves in Bucks County where he knew the rats lived. Richard had with him thin strips of rawhide. He wanted to try out something new. He stripped the playboy, wet the rawhide strips, wrapped one around his testicles, one around each arm, one around his forehead. It was a mild September day. As the rawhide grew taut, Richard watched the playboy suffering, amused, detached, telling the guy why this was happening. Richard took some Polaroid photos of the playboy's distress, his now tomato-red balls. He stayed there for some time with the mark, watching him suffer, hearing his pleas. Unfazed, Richard studied the man's suffering as a scientist doing research would examine infectious bacteria under a microscope. For Richard, this was a learning experience, seeing how the rawhide strips cut into his flesh . . . how the rats began to gather near the mark. So many rats appeared that Richard was finally forced to leave, though he took more Polaroids of the playboy before he left.

He returned two days later. There was nothing left of the man but some of his gnawed skeleton. The rats had even eaten the rawhide strips. The fetid smell of the rats and their grisly droppings filled the air. Richard threw the paltry remains down a mine shaft.

When he showed the Sicilian father the Polaroids, he was quite pleased, smiling from ear to ear, and, with new-found respect for 'the Big Guy', he gave Richard an extra ten grand. Another happy customer.

Richard took to wondering why seeing and doing such

things – committing such barbarous acts – didn't bother him in the least. He thought long and hard on this. It was troubling and, to some degree, disconcerting to him.

Why, he wondered, could he be so cold, so indifferent to people's suffering? It made him feel, for a while, that there was something wrong with him. He explained: *Since I was a kid I always felt like an outsider, like I didn't belong, and now, because of these things I did, I was really feeling that way again. But from another angle, for the most part, it didn't bother me . . . I got used to it. But why – why, I wondered, am I like this? I mean so cold, so indifferent to people's feelings. Their pain. Was I born like that, or was I made that way? Even my own family – how mean I could be to them, the only people I truly ever cared for. I didn't like that; I didn't want to be that way, I mean to my family.*

I thought about going to see a psychiatrist, seeing if I could get, you know, some help, maybe some medication, but of course I couldn't do that. I mean, what would I say to a shrink: I torture and kill people for money and I like my work? I don't think so.

This 'introspective Richard' was much in contrast to the stone-cold killer whose reputation as a homicide superstar was clearly established in mob circles across the country. The Big Guy was becoming a much sought-out killer. He was efficient and tight-lipped and did not hang out with wiseguys. He was a true 'family man' who happened to be a contract killer. For a long time, this kept Richard off the police and FBI radar. Very few people even knew his real name. He did not socialise with mob guys. He did not go to their weddings, funerals or family functions.

People, even Roy DeMeo, had only his pager number. That was the only way he could be reached, and that was the way he wanted it. He never brought any mob guys to his home or told them where he lived. He kept all that far away from his family.

One of the few people that Richard had a personal relationship with was Phil Solimene over in Paterson. Richard considered Solimene a friend, didn't have designs to kill him (rare for him) and did a lot of business with him: sold him porn, bought and sold hijacked goods from him, murdered people Solimene set up in bogus business deals and rip-offs. Barbara and Richard even socialised with Solimene and his wife, Anne. It would be this one relationship – this one friendship – that would ultimately make Richard vulnerable. It was a chink in his carefully constructed and well-worn armour. The Achilles heel of his size-14 foot.

Meanwhile, Roy DeMeo was out of control, a runaway train heading for disaster. He had taken to thinking of himself as invincible, above the law, believing that he could do anything when and how and where the fuck he pleased. The small apartment in the back of the Gemini Lounge was now truly a slaughterhouse. DeMeo and his crew of serial killers were murdering, cutting up and dismembering scores of people; several a week; sometimes two a day. All these murders were going to Roy's head. He began to think of himself as untouchable, a god among mortals. He had several NYPD detectives on his payroll and thus was given frequent information he was able to use to stay out of trouble, avoid arrest. One of these crooked cops was a beady-eyed detective out of the Brooklyn hot-car unit. His name was Peter Calabro. He had dark, receding hair, dark, hooded eyes, full lips, and was in his mid-30s, relatively young to be a detective.

Peter Calabro was in deep with Roy DeMeo. When Calabro wanted to get rid of his estranged wife, Carmella, Roy did the job for him, had her abducted in Brighton Beach, Brooklyn, drowned and left in the ocean. But, by chance, her body was discovered floating near New Jersey's Sandy Hook by the Coast Guard. Carmella's mother, Antonia, was positive Calabro was responsible and told every cop who would listen to her that Peter Calabro killed her daughter, that he was a low-life murderer, 'a scumbag', she said. The case was even presented to a Brooklyn grand jury, but Calabro had an airtight alibi and there was insufficient evidence to indict. It couldn't clearly be established if Carmella's death was in fact a homicide or a suicide.

Richard had nothing to do with the murder of Carmella Calabro, but DeMeo personally drowned her and left her body adrift. DeMeo, unlike Richard, had no qualms about killing women.

This murder, DeMeo knew, would cement for ever his relationship with Calabro, and because of it he had an everlasting inside track into most of the investigations into his exceedingly nefarious business dealings – particularly his booming, very lucrative stolen-car operation. DeMeo was like a greedy octopus – he had his tentacles in everything. He also paid Calabro handsomely for his assistance. One of the many 'favours' Detective Calabro did for DeMeo – and others in the Gambino family – was to provide him with clean VIN numbers for stolen cars.

Richard's business with the very busy Roy DeMeo was twofold – murder and porn – and they were now both making money hand over fist. When DeMeo had a special 'piece of work', he called upon Richard, the Big Guy. Richard also became known as 'the Polack'. He didn't particularly like that nickname, though any name, he knew, was better than his real one. It's no accident all mob guys have nicknames.

With Richard's deadly assistance, DeMeo became the well-oiled killing apparatus for the Gambino family, and because DeMeo was not made yet, he was filling murder contracts for almost anyone who wanted someone dead.

Nino Gaggi, Roy's mentor, kept telling Roy to cool it, to be more discreet, to stop killing so many people; but the huge amounts of cash DeMeo was giving Gaggi put to rest most of his concerns. Gaggi was absolutely money hungry, greedy to a fault, and Roy DeMeo regularly gave him brown paper bags filled with cash. At Christmas, DeMeo still showed up at the Gaggi home with truckloads (literally) of presents, expensive jewellery for Nino's wife, Rose, toys for all the kids. A kind of Italian Santa Claus from hell.

* * *

During the months after the Hoffa hit, Richard met with DeMeo a dozen times at the diner near the Tappan Zee Bridge, and every contract DeMeo gave him, he carried out successfully, without problem or repercussion, complication or mishap.

It was during this time that Richard brought more and more marks to the caves for the rats to eat and filmed their deaths. He even took to sitting down in his house when everyone was asleep and watching these ghastly videos as he had a late-night snack – turkey on rye, a bit of mayo. He wasn't so much viewing the films for entertainment as trying to understand himself, his reactions to them . . . why, he said, such things didn't trouble him in the least; this . . . *concerned* him, he explained.

He even showed one of the films to DeMeo, a bona fide psychopath, to see his reaction – and even DeMeo couldn't stand to see it. Because of the films, DeMeo knew that Richard was a rare individual, indeed a man – as he thought of him – with no soul.

'He's fuckin' ice,' he told his crew. 'I . . . mean . . . ice.'

And, too, these films created a perverse bond – 'friendship' – between Roy and Richard, and they actually enjoyed each other's company . . . two peas in a bloody pod.

Still, though, Richard was waiting for the chance to kill Roy, to beat him and humiliate him and end his life. For Richard, that was the ultimate cure-all. Richard used murder to get rid of his problems the way people use aspirin to get rid of headaches.

Besides contract killing, Richard was murdering people he did business with, men he fronted porn to who decided they were not going to pay him. One such individual had a porno shop in downtown Los Angeles, a bear of a man who prided himself on being tough, independent, not afraid of anyone. He owed Richard ten thousand dollars and, arrogantly, stopped even taking his calls.

Angry, Richard got on a plane and went to see the guy. He

had brought with him in his luggage two fragmentation hand grenades that he'd got from DeMeo. A grenade in each pocket, Richard walked unannounced into the guy's store. The mark was behind the chest-high counter, sitting on a tall, upholstered stool, big and heavy and mean faced, not liking the world or anyone in it.

'Hello, my friend,' Richard said, approaching him, walking on the balls of his feet, his mouth twisted off to the left, that soft clicking sound issuing from it.

'Hey, Big Guy,' the mark said, not pleased to see Richard suddenly in his shop.

'Been trying to reach you, my friend,' said Richard.

'Yeah, well I been busy, you know how it is.'

'You have a bill with me, my friend.'

'Yeah, well I don't have all the money just yet.'

'What do you have?' asked Richard.

'Nothing.'

'Nothing?'

'Yeah, zero,' he said, smiling, showing cigar-stained crooked teeth. As if he had just heard a joke, a joke Richard was deaf to.

'Funny guy,' Richard said.

'A real comedian: I used to do stand-up before I got into this,' he said, expansively indicating the shop, as though it were an accomplishment of note, something to write home about.

'What about my money? I need it,' Richard said.

'How about you come back in . . . in, say, a month.'

'That wasn't our agreement.'

'Yeah, well it is now.'

'Say you?'

'Say I.'

Richard smiled. It was not a pleasant smile to see. *Ti-ti-ti* came the clicking sound from his lips.

Richard took out a grenade and pulled the pin, though the shop owner didn't see it because of the high counter. Richard handed the pin to the guy behind the counter.

'What's this?' he demanded.

'A surprise,' Richard said as he began walking out of the store.

'What surprise?'

'This one,' Richard said, and tossed the grenade behind the counter just next to the guy. Richard exited the store. The grenade went off and blew the belligerent guy to pieces.

This incident, like many others Richard was involved in, was not so much about the money as about the principle of the thing. If one guy on the street could get one over on you, everyone would soon be doing the same thing. True, by killing this man Richard lost ten thousand dollars, but he figured in the long run he'd earn much more because people would pay what they owed. On the street, as Richard had learned so many years ago in Jersey City, might was truly right.

I didn't give a flying fuck about the money, Richard explained. *I wasn't about to let this stiff make a fool out of me, and I capped him to make a point. An exclamation point, I guess you could say.*

Again, the cops did not tie Richard to this *homicide by hand grenade*, as Richard referred to it.

Richard grew to like Los Angeles, the accommodating weather, the relaxed lifestyle, the palm trees. Porn was very popular in Southern California, and Richard made more money distributing there than on the East Coast. He liked going to the 'porn conventions', thought they were fun, he said. He had a lot of business there and enjoyed spending time in Los Angeles. He enjoyed LA so much he rented an apartment in West Hollywood, just off Sunset Boulevard. He liked to sit at outdoor cafés in the warm weather and watch the world go by – the colourful circus that LA always is, the fancy cars, the fancy women, the fancy clothes. Barbara knew nothing of this apartment. She didn't even know where Richard was when he went off on 'business trips'. Barbara's only concern – her whole life – was her children, especially Dwayne. She focused all her energy on them. When Richard wasn't home, the house was peaceful, calm . . . normal. Only Merrick missed Richard when he wasn't home, though she was not encouraged to express such emotions.

When Richard returned from Los Angeles, he was given a contract by the Gigante family that had to be filled at a chain hotel just off Route 46. No problem. The mark was going to a breakfast meeting at this hotel, a set-up. Richard chose a .22 Ruger rifle, cut down to a mere 15 inches and equipped with a blue-black silencer. He was in the parking lot when the mark arrived early that morning for his meeting with a Gigante lieutenant. Richard watched the two of them have breakfast, pancakes, shake hands and part in the parking lot as if friends. As the mark reached his car, Richard raised the weapon and shot him nine times in two seconds, in rapid succession. The mark fell to the ground, dead. Richard calmly pulled away. It looked as if the mark had had a heart attack until you saw all the blood coming from those sudden little holes. Another job well done. Another murder never linked to Richard by police.

It didn't take long for a host of new contracts to come in from the Gigante people, which Richard gladly filled. There was no contract he would not take – except, of course, the killing of a woman or a child. That was taboo for Richard, a line he would not cross.

There were, however, female contract killers, lethal femmes fatales who could easily get close to a mark, offering warm embraces, hot sex, a lustful blowjob, but delivering sudden death. These women, Richard felt, were fair game, and he would kill one as quickly as any man. But this had not yet come to pass.

When, in the autumn of 1976, Carlo Gambino died of natural causes, everything suddenly changed, and the stage was set for a tumultuous earthquake that would rock the very foundations of Mafiadom.

34

ROLLING OVER IN HIS GRAVE

Because Carlo Gambino so fervently believed in family ties – fidelity and loyalty – he appointed his brother-in-law, Paul Castellano, as his successor as the head of the family, now the biggest, most successful crime family in history. This would prove to be a monumental error in judgement.

Paul Castellano was not cut out for this position; he did not have the inherent instincts, the cunning or the street smarts to master the multifaceted operation he was suddenly put in charge of. Yes, Castellano was a good businessman, but the head of a crime family – no.

His first in a series of serious blunders was demanding that all 20 captains in the Gambino crime family come to see him once a week at a social club called the Veterans and Friends Club he began on Brooklyn's Eighty-sixth Street, just off Fifteenth Avenue. This directive enabled the FBI to take extensive surveillance photos and video footage of who came and went, and thus the government suddenly knew who all the Gambino *capos* were, which proved to be the beginning of the end – the very unnecessary exposure of the family's star players, the inner circle, the engines that ran the family.

The second fatal error Castellano made was not detecting the FBI's listening devices in his fortress-like Staten Island home. Because of these bugs, the FBI – for the first time ever – got a fly-on-the-wall view of all the inner workings of a Mafia chieftain: who did what, when, where and even how.

The third fatal error Castellano made was having a carnal affair with the Colombian housekeeper his wife, Carlo's sister, had hired, while his wife was actually in the house – an unspeakable thing that surely caused Carlo Gambino to roll over in his grave. This, for a Sicilian, was the ultimate infamy, unforgivable – a blasphemy!

And because of the excellent listening devices in the Castellano kitchen, the FBI heard all the ridiculous syrupy conversations Castellano had with his lover while his wife was in the house. These conversations would eventually be made public, printed in a book, excerpts of which appeared in *New York* magazine, making Paul Castellano a despised laughing-stock for every made member of all crime families in all places, even in Sicily, which sealed Castellano's fate. Interestingly, Richard Kuklinski would play a large role in that fate.

The only capo pleased about Castellano's promotion was Nino Gaggi. Gaggi had for 30 years been a very close personal friend and confidant to Castellano, and this put him – and, by extension, Roy DeMeo, too – in an excellent position.

DeMeo still wanted more than anything to be made, get his button, and now, with Castellano as the boss, that possibility loomed large in the very near future.

Castellano, like Gaggi, was a particularly greedy man – whatever he got, it was never enough. DeMeo was a money-making machine, and Castellano was impressed with the money he was receiving – via Gaggi – from DeMeo. Gaggi kept petitioning Castellano to make DeMeo, but Castellano was reluctant. He thought DeMeo too loud, too brash – a psychopath who would eventually draw police attention – and said no.

Then DeMeo really stirred up a hornets' nest when he brought the infamous Westies into the Gambino fold – another large mistake.

The Westies were a loose-knit group of Irishmen who ran Manhattan's Hell's Kitchen on the West Side. They specialised in shakedowns of local stores, bookmaking, loan-sharking, numbers running – and murder.

The leaders of the gang were James Coonan and Mickey Featherstone, two stone-cold killers. Featherstone was a rather frail-looking guy, about 145 lb, with little baby hands and a baby face, but he'd shoot someone in the head as readily as blink. Coonan was just the opposite, broad-shouldered, big-boned, square-jawed, red-faced, with a bulbous nose; he had whitish blond hair in a military-style crew cut.

DeMeo liked these guys because they were utterly ruthless. At his suggestion, they began cutting up their victims and burying dismembered bodies in the abandoned railroad yards on the far reaches of the West Side of Manhattan.

One afternoon, when Richard went to drop off some money at the Gemini Lounge, DeMeo asked him to go up to Harlem with Freddy DiNome and see a black guy who owned a bar there. He owed DeMeo a lot of money and wasn't paying it back as promised.

'Big Guy, I want you to go see him and let him know he's walking on thin fuckin' ice here, OK?'

'No problem,' Richard said. 'Sure.'

'You go pick up Eddie Mack. He knows the guy, and he's got brass balls. OK?'

'Sure, Roy,' Richard said, and he and Freddy DiNome, an ugly guy with curly brown hair and a giant potato for a nose, left to go to the city. DiNome was a car freak who helped Roy give stolen cars legit makeovers. He had a pet chimpanzee which one day punched DiNome and knocked him out cold. Richard had no monetary interest in this business; he was just doing DeMeo a favour.

These days, DeMeo was very 'up'. He was figuring he'd surely be made soon, the thing he had coveted since he was a little fat kid victimised by neighbourhood bullies. For him, in a sense, being made was the holy grail and winning the lottery rolled into one.

Eddie Mack was part of the Westies gang, a tough Irishman and another stone-cold killer. Richard liked the Westies, thought they had balls. But he also thought they were out of control, should be kept on leashes, indeed in cages. Be that as it may, he went to the city with DiNome and picked up Mack, a stocky guy with long blond hair, and together they went up to Harlem. The bar was on Third Avenue. Eddie said he'd go in and talk to the owner, said that they knew each other from jail.

'I'll go in with you,' Richard offered.

'Nah, that's OK,' Mack said, and got out of the car and went inside.

As always, Richard was armed. He sat there wondering why the hell he'd been asked to come along if Mack didn't want him to go in. Within minutes, however, there was a commotion inside, things breaking, a shot fired. Richard jumped out of the car and hurried inside. Just as he entered the place, he got struck in the forehead with a bat. He fell back but didn't go down. Chirping birds moved before his eyes. The sidewalk spun. He drew a .38 derringer and started back in, pissed off. Eddie Mack came out. He was holding his stomach.

'The fuckin' nigga shot me,' he said.

'Let's go get 'im,' Richard said.

'Forget it. There's a whole fuckin' tribe a them,' Mack said, getting back in the car. 'The motherfuckers.'

'What happened?' Freddy asked.

'He got cute, I went after him and one of them shot me in the side. It's dark in there and all I saw was teeth and eyes. I ain't laying down on this. Take me home. I got some serious heat – I wanna get it and come right fuckin' back.'

'Let's go,' Richard said.

They returned to Hell's Kitchen. Freddy called Roy and told him what had happened, said they wanted to load up and go back. Cursing, DeMeo gave them the green light. Eddie Mack had an old trunk filled with weapons – heavy-duty armaments he'd got from DeMeo. Richard chose a street sweeper, a twelve-gauge shotgun with a large round clip, like an old-fashioned tommy gun. Both DiNome and Mack grabbed Mac-10s, machine-gun pistols that fired thirty nine-millimetre rounds a second. Richard helped Mack put a bandage on the bullet hole, which was on his extreme left side, level with his belly button, and off they went, straight back to the bar, and parked in front. Richard, his forehead all swollen, burst from the car, was the first in and let loose with the shotgun. Soon, both Freddy and Mack cut loose with the Mac-10s, and they literally blew the place apart and shot whoever was standing.

Satisfied, they left and went back to Brooklyn, making jokes about how you couldn't see the black guys in the dark bar. At the Gemini, DeMeo got a doctor he knew to treat Mack's wound. The bullet had apparently passed right through his side. Freddy told everyone how Richard had gone in with the shotgun and let loose.

'The Big Guy's got elephant balls,' DeMeo proudly said.

Richard now had a lump on his forehead the size of an orange. He also had a splitting headache. DeMeo thanked him half a dozen times and gave him a big basket filled with Italian delicacies. 'Your wife'll love this,' he said, and Richard went home, angry the whole thing had happened. He could have been killed, he knew, for nothing, a thing he had no stake in. He now had something else against DeMeo.

Barbara's eyes got wide when she saw Richard's head. 'What happened?' she asked, concerned.

'I fell,' he said, nothing more. She prepared an ice pack for him. He took a few aspirin and sat in his easy chair in the living-room, watched a Clint Eastwood movie and stewed. His favourite actors were, not surprisingly, Eastwood and Charles Bronson.

* * *

Word quickly spread in mob circles that the Big Guy went up to Harlem and blew apart a bunch of 'uppity niggers' who needed to be put in their place, to be killed, and Richard was more in demand than ever. His murderous exploits were taking on legendary proportions; yet, still, few people even knew his real name.

Also, stories of how he was feeding live people to ravenous rats were making the rounds, both amusing and appalling those who heard them.

The Big Guy was much in demand.

It began as an insignificant event on Bensonhurst's Eighty-sixth Street. Nino Gaggi was sitting in his car, double-parked in front of the Hy Tulip, a popular Jewish deli just off Twentieth Avenue, under the West End elevated train. Gaggi was waiting for his brother Roy's wife, Marie Gaggi. Marie was a dark-haired beauty with blue eyes. When she walked down the street just about every man's head turned. When Marie left the deli that day – 14 February 1975 – a few neighbourhood youths made some inappropriate comments, wolf-whistled. Seeing this, Nino Gaggi leaped from his car with a hammer and started swinging it at the youths, looking to break some heads. From the old school, Nino Gaggi could not tolerate such disrespect. One of the teenagers was named Vincent Governara. He did not know who Nino was – a capo in the Gambino family – nor did Nino know who Governara was – an excellent boxer, a Golden Gloves champion. Governara, a wiry, muscular youth, ducked the hammer and hit Nino with a left hook, knocking him right down and breaking his nose.

This was an insult Nino would never forget, and he vowed to kill Governara.

Word quickly spread all over Bensonhurst that Gaggi wanted Governara, wanted blood. Vinnie Governara was known as Vinnie Mook because, mentally, he was not the swiftest guy, but he was a truly superb athlete, a great handball and baseball player, as well as a champion boxer. He looked like an Italian Jerry Lewis, had a wide mouth. Vinnie Mook was also an excellent dancer. He'd go to the Hollywood Terrace on Eighteenth Avenue on Latin night and dance up a storm. He was such a good dancer that people always moved out of his way to give him room to tear up the dance floor. Vinnie was also a vicious fighter, would hit people with extremely fast combinations. He never lost a street fight. When Vinnie heard whom exactly he had hit, he left Brooklyn and went down to Florida. He had been born and raised in Bensonhurst, and he well knew the consequences of punching out a made man: death.

Vinnie Mook would end up playing an instrumental role in Roy DeMeo finally aquiring his much coveted button.

Some months after Governara broke Nino's nose, he returned to the neighbourhood, and his car was spotted parked on Bath Avenue, just a few blocks south of Eighty-sixth Street. Nino Gaggi had his nephew Dominick Montiglio, a Vietnam War vet with Special Forces training, rig up a concussion grenade to go off when Governara opened his car door. Roy DeMeo happily provided said grenade.

However, when Governara opened the door, releasing the pin from the grenade, he didn't close the door right away, and when the grenade went off most of the concussion escaped out of the open door. Nonetheless, the explosion broke Governara's leg and threw him across Bath Avenue, a main thoroughfare running directly through Mafiaville.

Needless to say, Governara again hightailed it out of Bensonhurst, went back to Florida and wisely stayed away for a while. Not long enough, however, and when he returned to Bensonhurst his car was spotted on Twentieth Avenue and Eighty-fifth Street, just two blocks away, coincidentally, from the Hy Tulip, where it all began.

It was now 12 June 1976, the birthday of Dominick's wife, Denise. In the Gaggi house, birthdays were always a big deal. Roy DeMeo happened to be there that day, and he gave Denise

– a beautiful neighbourhood girl of Neopolitan extraction with long black hair and a big, lovely smile – a diamond-studded watch. Denise was Nino's niece by marriage, and Roy would do anything he could to please Nino, to ingratiate himself with him.

When word reached Nino that Vinnie Governara's car had been seen on Twentieth Avenue, he, his nephew and Roy DeMeo quickly left the house and Denise's birthday party to go and kill Vinnie Governara for a slight, a broken nose, made now some 15 months ago. Nino's nephew Dominick had dark hair, dark eyes, high cheekbones. He had seen a lot of action in Vietam, and since he'd returned he was quiet and sullen and seemed to walk around with a dark cloud hanging over his head.

Nino put on a ridiculous false moustache, and he, Dominick and Roy drove over to Twentieth Avenue in Roy's car and waited for Governara. It was the middle of the afternoon, a Saturday. A lot of shoppers were out. None of that was going to stop Nino Gaggi from getting his revenge. This was, in fact, a stupid, very risky enterprise, killing a man in broad daylight near Eighty-sixth Street, but that wasn't about to dissuade Nino. He was willing to sacrifice all he had to get even with Vinnie Governara, just a young man struggling to find his way in life with a good punch.

Nino Gaggi didn't have to wait long. They soon spotted Governara walking to his car, an old Plymouth, without a care in the world. Nino and Roy were soon behind him. Governara spotted them and began to run. Right there, in broad daylight, Roy and Nino took aim at the fleeing Governara and let loose a fusillade of .38 bullets, shooting him down. Dominick did not fire the .22 he had. As they were hurrying back to Roy's car, bystanders began to chase them. Gaggi raised his .38. Everyone hit the ground. The killers quickly got into DeMeo's car, and off they went, making a clean getaway. Governara died of his wounds a few days later at Coney Island Hospital.

Now, with new-found intensity, DeMeo petitioned Gaggi to talk to Paul Castellano about getting him made. Gaggi promised Roy he would; he would see to it that DeMeo finally got 'straightened out', as they said.

This incident with Governara and Nino Gaggi concerned Richard Kuklinski only because it would ultimately cause Roy DeMeo to become made, which meant that Richard made more money with DeMeo and DeMeo sent more murder contracts Richard's way.

The next hit Richard performed for DeMeo was again in Los Angeles. The mark owed money to wiseguys, wasn't paying, seemed to be daring the wiseguys to do something. DeMeo paged Richard, they met at the diner near the Tappan Zee Bridge, Richard was given the contract, and he was on a plane back to LA the following day.

This mark was very cagey. He knew people were looking for him and moved with caution. For days, Richard staked out his home. He lived in a pink apartment complex in Sherman Oaks. The two times Richard saw him, he couldn't make a move. There were witnesses. Richard did not like hanging around to do a piece of work. The chances of something going wrong became greater by the hour. In frustration, Richard tried something he'd seen in a Bugs Bunny cartoon. He boldly went and knocked on the mark's door. He could see light through the peephole and he put his eye up against it. When he saw the shadowy figure of the mark approach and reach the door, Richard put the barrel of a .38 up to the peephole, waited for the right moment, and fired, shooting the guy directly in the eye, instantly killing him.

Another job well done, Richard went for a nice meal in West Hollywood, had a long walk, got a good night's rest and headed home, back to his family.

Money kept rolling in, but no matter how much Richard earned, it never seemed to be enough. *It went out*, he said, *faster than it came in.*

ROLLING OVER IN HIS GRAVE

Richard was now filling, on average, four to six contracts every month. He was a very busy, dedicated man, always scrupulously careful, always successful. He even began using poison to kill. He also began to gamble heavily again – not a good thing. Old habits die hard.

35

DOUBLE SUCK

It was the spring of 1977, a time of rebirth and renewal, the end of the bitterly cold East Coast winter. All over Bensonhurst's quiet tree-lined streets and avenues – this unassuming place with the world's greatest concentration of serial murderers – green leaves and grass on small lawns returned. Birds chirped. Flowers bloomed. The sun shone. Kids returned to the streets and played boisterous games of stickball, Johnny-on-the-Pony and Ringalevio. Young girls jumped rope. Except for the mob rub-outs that occasionally occurred here, Bensonhurst was a safe place, a good place to bring up children, OK for women and girls to walk about without worry.

Because of Nino Gaggi's constant campaigning, the never-ending lovely stacks of hundred-dollar bills DeMeo was sending to both Gaggi and Castellano, and the Vinnie Mook killing, Paul Castellano had finally relented and agreed to make DeMeo. That spring, Castellano was 'opening the books' and allowing new members into the fold, and Roy DeMeo was one of them.

For DeMeo, this was like receiving a doctorate after a lifetime of earnest studying. It was the highlight of his life, what he had always wanted, a dream come true. As is the mandated custom, word went out to every made man in all the families that Roy DeMeo was being 'straightened out', and if anyone knew something about DeMeo that was reason for him not to be made, they had to speak up and let the Gambino people know. No one spoke against DeMeo's induction.

The simple but deadly serious ceremony was held in the converted basement of a Gambino lieutenant who lived on Bay Seventeenth Street in Bensonhurst. Castellano and Gaggi, DeMeo and old-timer Jimmy Esposito were there. Gaggi, of course, was sponsoring DeMeo. The ceremony was made, a little blood was drawn from DeMeo's finger, the oath was taken, all comically solemn. Gaggi and Castellano kissed DeMeo on both cheeks and gave him a big bear hug, and now Roy DeMeo was officially, formally, a made member of the Gambino crime family . . . a *sgarrista*.

Afterwards, they went for an elaborate four-course meal at Tomaso's on Eighty-sixth Street. After dinner, there were toasts and more hugs and kisses, and Roy DeMeo headed back to the Gemini on the Belt Parkway – a made man.

Now, he knew, many more doors would open to him. He would finally get the respect and fear he had always yearned for. Now he'd be able to move up the ladder. DeMeo had big, expansive plans that included getting his crew sanctioned by the mob, being made a capo and, perhaps, eventually, head of the family. Why not? As far as DeMeo was concerned, he had more going for him than anyone else in the whole Gambino family or, for that matter, any other family. And, too, he was ruthless, a stone-cold killer, a very necessary attribute if you wanted to ascend in organised crime in New York.

By now, DeMeo's reputation for murder had spread far and wide; he was considered the undisputed assassin of the Gambino family, its lethal arm. No other Gambino crew (there were 20 altogether) even came near the extraordinary killing acumen of Roy DeMeo and his gang of serial murderers. And Richard Kuklinski was always lurking in the background, like some supernatural, malevolent spirit ready to come out of the shadows and create chaos when DeMeo summoned him.

Richard Kuklinski was Roy DeMeo's Luca Brasi.

Back at the Gemini Lounge that evening, there was

another celebration. All DeMeo's people were there. Bottles of expensive champagne were opened and numerous toasts were made. Glistening piles of cocaine were on the kitchen table for anyone who wanted to partake. Some loose women were brought in to entertain, put on a cunnilingus show, perform virtuoso blowjobs. AIDS was not an issue yet and the women happily swallowed all.

Roy considered himself quite the ladies' man, did not get along with his wife, was always horny, and tonight he got a double-header: two women sucking and licking his penis and testicles at the same time. 'A double suck', as the crew called it.

Life was good. Life held much promise. Roy DeMeo was a very happy man. Roy DeMeo had been made. Roy DeMeo was at the top of Mount Everest. He came, he saw, he conquered.

Drugs were just one of a host of problems that began to plague the Gemini crew. Henry Borelli, Chris Goldberg, Joey Testa and Anthony Senter were all doing a lot of cocaine. Anthony Senter was becoming rail thin, paranoid and unreliable. Because of their success so far, the Gemini crew had come to believe nothing could ever hurt them – not the police, not the FBI, certainly not another Mafia crew or crime family. They were invincible. They were deadly. They were Murder Inc. and the Purple Gang all rolled into one, the kings of a mountain strewn with dismembered bodies.

Roy DeMeo walked around – *really* swaggering now – as if he were 10 ft tall, the king of Brooklyn, his egg-shaped head the size of a watermelon, filled with himself. With careless abandon, he killed or had killed anyone that got in his way, anyone he believed might be a problem; anyone who disrespected him, whom he perceived as a threat, a source of dismay. He took no chances.

'Dead men tell no tales,' he'd say. His answer to any concerns he had about someone was to kill him. Like Richard, he acted as if he had the God-given right to kill human beings. Unlike Richard, however, Roy DeMeo had surrounded himself with a bunch of psychotic coked-up serial killers, which would prove to be a grave error in judgement.

Richard left his house carrying a wrinkled brown paper bag of money for DeMeo, his cut of the porn business. They were fully fledged partners now.

Richard knew that DeMeo had been made, that he was no longer a *picciotto* but was now a sgarrista. He knew, too, that DeMeo had grand plans. Richard believed DeMeo would ascend quickly within the Gambino family, would surely have his own sanctioned crew within a few years. But he firmly believed that DeMeo was too temperamental, was an out-of-control maniac, had too volatile a temper to last very long and reach his full potential. Richard also believed it was just a matter of time before DeMeo's crew of crazies, as he thought of them, set fire to the bridge DeMeo was building for himself.

Richard still planned to kill DeMeo when the time was right. DeMeo's being made would not stop that. Indeed, nothing would. It was just a matter of time before the proper elements were all in play. Richard had come to know that it was OK to cap a made man, provided no one knew about it. To murder a made man without the hit being sanctioned and letting anyone know about it was a ticket to the grave . . . certain death.

Richard hugged and kissed DeMeo at the club, effusively congratulated him, playing the part of a loyal friend, a good partner: an Oscar-winning performance. Richard gave Roy his share of the money. Richard was scrupulously honest with DeMeo. He made sure he got every dollar due.

Roy surprised Richard by inviting him to go fishing on his boat, a new toy he was proud of. It was a nice day, Richard liked to fish, so he agreed to go along. They got into DeMeo's Caddy and headed over to the nearby Sheepshead Bay Marina.

THE ICE MAN

The serial killers Chris Goldberg, Joey Testa and Anthony Senter were already at the marina waiting for Roy. They had a fourth guy with them, Bob, whom Richard didn't know. Introductions were made. They got on the boat, a fast, 30-foot gleaming white cruiser outfitted with a few fishing rods, and off they went. DeMeo had brought along a big box of Italian sandwiches, chunks of provolone and mozzarella and thick links of pepperoni. He obviously loved the boat and was proud of it – like a kid with a new bike, the best bike on the block, which everyone envies. The sky was clear and very blue. It was unusually warm and the ocean was calm and friendly. When they were a little way out, DeMeo full-throttled the boat, and off they went, straight out to open waters. Richard sat and enjoyed the ride, the fresh air. Though Roy's guys still hadn't warmed to Richard – nor he to them – they had learned to accept him. But they were wary of him.

Since he was a kid in Jersey City, Richard had loved the ocean, and he enjoyed being on a boat, the clean, fresh smell of the Atlantic coming to him. Joey and Anthony were talking to this Bob guy, making jokes with him, telling him how these two gorgeous girls had given Roy a double suck.

When they were way out, Roy slowed the boat, shut off the engines and announced that this was a good place to fish, but first they had to put chum – a type of groundbait – in the water.

'What are we fishing for?' Bob asked.

'Sharks,' Roy told him.

Bob was a short, square guy with the face of a bulldog. He had a slight accent, which Richard couldn't place. Maybe Canadian. After lowering a chum basket in a net into the water and putting a couple of baits on big hooks, Roy broke out the sandwiches and they had lunch, drinking beer and white wine and telling dirty jokes. There were no other boats to be seen. Richard was curious about seeing sharks up close and personal, though he didn't really believe there were sharks in these waters. He had an open mind, though, and was excited by the prospect. Roy, however, was sure there were sharks here, said he'd caught a lot of them in this very spot.

Richard sensed something in the air – danger – but he didn't know why. All seemed OK. He was, as always, armed, had a gun and a knife on him. DeMeo was in a great mood. As they were finishing lunch, Chris spotted a shark, its cobalt blue dorsal fin cutting the water. They all stood to see it as it moved closer.

'See, I told ya!' DeMeo announced. Soon there were other sharks; they suddenly seemed to be all over the place. DeMeo moved to where Bob was standing. DeMeo said, his demeanour suddenly changing, 'I know you're a fuckin' rat. Calabro told me what you've been up to,' and with that, DeMeo pulled out a pistol and shot Bob in the face. The hapless man screamed and fell down. The others grabbed him and tossed him in the water.

Wide-eyed and screaming, he tried to keep afloat, but was having difficulty. Chris wanted to shoot him again, but Roy wouldn't let him.

'Let the sharks do him,' Roy said. Bob was bleeding profusely; his heart, no doubt, was pumping away furiously, and blood came from the hole in his face in a pulsating torrent of red. It didn't take long for the sharks to gather near him, swim around him, as Bob screamed and flailed about wildly. This Richard watched in awe, amused, enjoying it. Soon the sharks, no doubt stirred on by the blood, began taking nips then bites out of the screaming, pleading, begging Bob, and before long he went under and didn't come back up. DeMeo and the others thought it was entertaining, great fun, better than any Broadway show; they high-fived one another, laughing and smiling. Richard too thought it entertaining, liked its originality.

'Fuckin' rat got what he deserved. I only wished it lasted longer, you know,' DeMeo said.

They all agreed. They caught a few sharks, shot them in the head when they were close to the boat, then headed back to the marina. As they went, the sky abruptly changed, became grey and dark. It began to rain. With the rain came wind, thunder, lightning. The water grew choppy. Whitecaps hurried across the suddenly rough sea. Richard began to feel seasick and wanted to get back on solid land. They arrived at the dock all right. Richard thanked Roy for a 'very entertaining afternoon'.

'You're full of surprises,' Richard said.

'Got a million a them,' Roy said.

As Richard made his way along Flatbush Avenue – it was dark by now – a car filled with black guys wearing red bandannas on their heads pulled up alongside him and for no reason began harassing him, calling him 'cracker' and 'honky'. They reached a red light.

'Hey, motherfucker!' one of them said, only a few feet from Richard now. 'Get the fuck outta this neighbourhood.'

'My seven friends don't like that talk,' Richard said.

'What seven friends?' the driver demanded, looking at Richard as if he were nuts.

'These seven friends,' Richard said, showing them his gun, which contained seven bullets. The guy went through the red light, tyres screaming, burning rubber. Richard drove onto the Belt Parkway and headed west, back to Dumont, his wife and children, turning over the day in his mind. He liked the idea of feeding people to sharks, thought it was a novel way to get rid of a body.

He began thinking of new ways to kill, of expanding his repertoire. He wondered about poisons. He knew assassins had successfully been using poisons for many years. Deciding it was something he needed to look into, he began across the wide expanse of the Verrazano Bridge, admiring the view as he went, the way a multitude of coloured lights shimmered on the water. He remembered how he used to admire the way the lights of Manhattan glistened on the Hudson River when he was a boy back in Jersey City.

* * *

Richard's one friend, Phil Solimene, could get his hands on anything if he put his mind to it. Richard was still going to Solimene's store on Friday nights to play high-stakes games of poker, and he usually stopped in a few times a week to shoot the breeze, see what was in the wind, have some coffee. Richard was gambling again, more and more.

If New Jersey had a Fagin it was Philip Solimene. It seemed every thief and larceny-hearted hustler knew Phil. Richard asked Phil offhandedly if he knew where he could get some poison.

'What kind?' Phil asked.

'To kill rats – big rats, ha ha – cyanide, strychnine, arsenic.'

'I'll ask around,' Phil said. That's what he always said when people asked him for various items. Solimene never said no, and he most often came through.

Solimene had seen at first hand just how deadly Richard was. He had set up people for Richard to rob and kill. He would offer merchandise for sale – perfumes, drugs, blank tapes, porno, guns – and when the people showed up with the cash, Solimene would call Richard, who'd come over, bullshit the buyer, get him alone, kill him and split the cash with Solimene. Solimene had actually seen Richard kill people.

Solimene liked Richard, thought he was stand-up, always kept his word, was tight-lipped and steely-eyed and had balls. If, of all the people in the world, Solimene had to be in a foxhole with someone, he would want it to be Richard – hands down.

Four days later, Solimene called Richard and asked him to come by that night. Richard made his way to the store, and Solimene told him that he had a friend, a Union City pharmacist and player, who'd sell him all the poison he wanted. Thus Paul Hoffman entered, for a relatively short while, Richard Kuklinski's life.

Hoffman was average in size, overweight, a particularly

greedy individual. He was always looking for an angle, a way to get one up, more than what he was fairly and equitably entitled to. He had a good profession, a successful business, but it wasn't enough; he always wanted more. He had been buying hijacked loads of drugs from Solimene for years. He'd buy anything – aspirins, barbiturates, diet pills, antibiotics, ulcer medication, perfume, razor blades – for a fraction of the real worth and then sell it at retail prices, making a big profit. When Richard first met Hoffman at Phil's store, he didn't like him. Of course, Richard liked very few people.

Not only would Hoffman sell Richard all the poison he wanted, but he told him how to administer the proper dose for the desired – for the maximum – effect. He actually sat down with Richard and gave him detailed instructions, insights and pharmaceutical advice on the proper application and use of the most dangerous toxins known to man, warning him that if he used too much the police could determine the cause of death, too little and it wouldn't work at all. He even gave Richard a tiny measuring spoon for doling out proper dosages. Richard first bought cyanide; it came in a thick glass vial adorned with a skull and bones. Richard got the strangest sensation when he held the deadly little vial. It gave him, not surprisingly, a feeling of power and omnipotence.

This, indeed, was a very dangerous combination – Richard Kuklinski and cyanide.

The hit was on a lieutenant in the Bonanno family, a paranoid, crafty individual – a hard man to kill because he knew people were looking to do him in and because he always went around with two grim bodyguards. His name was Tony Scavelli. He was known as 'Dapper' because he always dressed to the nines. He was quite the ladies' man, had a beautiful girlfriend who liked to go to the best restaurants, out clubbing afterwards . . . to the upscale Regine's on Park Avenue and Xenon on West Forty-fifth Street. For ten days, Richard stalked Dapper but could never get close enough to make a decisive move.

DOUBLE SUCK

Richard decided to do it in one of the clubs – with poison. Paul Hoffman showed him how to mix the cyanide with a special liquid and put it in a hypodermic needle.

'A lethal hot shot,' he called it.

Using the thinnest, least detectable needle he could find, Richard mixed the liquid and cyanide carefully until all the poison blended and became one with the liquid.

Regine's was, he decided, too small, not crowded enough for him to get close to the mark unobserved. But Xenon was another story – it was perfect: crowded, noisy, strobe lights blinking on and off. To blend in, Richard put on a garish outfit that he believed made him look gay.

It was a Saturday night. The mark, his girlfriend and his bodyguards ate in a popular French restaurant called Un, Deux, Trois, then headed over to Xenon. Wearing a red peaked cap, pink pants, a yellow vest, beads around his neck and platform shoes, Richard managed to get in the club, which in itself was a feat. The place was packed with dancers – an upscale, chic crowd – music blared, the bass thumped, disco lights swirled madly. The lights confused Richard. He didn't like them. People, he could see, were openly snorting cocaine. Richard managed to find the mark. He was dancing on the edge of the floor, off to the right.

Moving with the music, shaking his huge body as he went, Richard shimmied past the mark, and as he went he stuck him with the needle while moving towards the exit. Within a minute, the mark went down, and he was soon quite dead. Everyone believed he'd had a heart attack. At the autopsy in the medical examiner's office, the poison was not even detected.

According to Richard, one of the guys on the Jimmy Hoffa hit, Sal Briguglio, got into some trouble with the law, and word spread that he was trying to use what he knew about the Hoffa murder to get himself out of trouble. This is what caused Hoffa's remains to be dug up, compacted in the boot of a car and exported to Japan. Richard was given the contract to kill Briguglio. He and another Jersey assassin, Paulie Salerno, tracked Sal to Little Italy. As he was walking near Mott Street, Richard struck him from behind with a jawbreaker, knocking him down, and shot him numerous times with a .38 equipped with a suppressor, then quickly walked away. The cops were called. Detectives questioned neighbourhood people. No one saw anything. Another mob-related murder in Little Italy . . . nothing new.

Poison and Richard Kuklinski went together like peanut butter and jelly. For one of the few times in his life, Richard bought books and carefully studied them, medical texts about poisons. For several weeks, he was reading and taking notes, teaching himself the subtleties and finer points of killing people with poison. He learned about cyano, prussic acid, hydrocyanic acid, hydrogen cyanide, aniline and cyanic acid, and their proper applications. Whenever he saw Paul Hoffman, he asked him questions, and Hoffman gladly answered Richard's queries and provided him with the actual poisons. Hoffman, of course, was charging him exorbitant amounts, but Richard didn't care; it was just the price of doing business.

Like a child with a new toy, Richard was anxious to try out these new killing tools. He loved, he said, the subtlety of poison: that there was no violence, guns, blood, broken bones; that it was odourless and colourless, yet as lethal as – perhaps more lethal than – a bullet to the head.

With vials of poisons in his pocket, Richard went out into the world to fill murder contracts. In many instances, he could get close to a mark, invite him for a meal, a drink – and use *my new friends*, as he called the poisons.

His name was Billy Mana. He was a made guy in the Genovese family. His boss wanted him dead. Richard contacted Mana and invited him for a drink, saying he had a load of fur coats he wanted to sell 'real cheap. I'm in a hurry to move the load.'

DOUBLE SUCK

Like all mob guys, Mana was money hungry, and he met Richard for a drink in a Union City bar. Richard had a pinkie-sized vial of cyanide with him. When Mana went to the toilet, Richard quickly and discreetly – like a magic trick – dumped the poison in Mana's drink. Mana soon came back and knocked off his drink. Richard graciously ordered another round. Before the drinks were served, however, Mana choked, held his throat, his eyes swelling, and soon fell over.

'Heart attack, call a doctor!' Richard called out, and soon disappeared, as if he never was there.

Pleased, Richard made his way home, back to his family, like Dracula returning to his lair. Over the coming months, whenever possible, Richard used poison to kill, in food, in drinks, on pizza. He became quite the expert in the application of deadly substances.

This, of course, only bolstered his reputation as an assassin, and even more murder contracts came his way. He was travelling all over the country now to kill people the mob wanted dead. He'd go anywhere to do a piece of work. He was very busy – too busy. He knew this could not go on forever; but he greatly enjoyed the work, the challenge, a successful outcome. It made him feel godlike, a truly lethal force. Richard became the brightest star in a rogues' gallery filled with stone-cold killers. As Richard's reputation spread, people 'in the life' didn't like to be around him, looked at him warily out of the corners of their eyes. Even Roy DeMeo was wary of Richard. DeMeo was one of the few people in the world who knew how truly dangerous and diabolical Richard was. When DeMeo had a beef with John Gotti and his brother Gene, he asked Richard to come to a meeting with them and watch his back.

The Gotti brothers and their crew also had a reputation for being dangerous, ruthless – quick to kill and ask questions later. But even they wanted nothing to do with DeMeo and the Gemini gang. True, DeMeo and John Gotti were in the same family, but there was friction between them. Yet, because they were members of the same family, disputes and disagreements had to be settled, in theory anyway, with talk, amiably, not by murder. When DeMeo and John Gotti – these two ruthless men with oversized egos – had a disagreement over how merchandise stolen from Kennedy Airport was to be divvied up, who would get what, there had to be a 'sit-down', the mob term for resolving disputes with reason and conversation, not violence.

John Gotti, like DeMeo, had a reputation as a no-nonsense, two-fisted, dangerous man with a volatile temper. He had recently been released from jail, having done time for his involvement in a murder: Gotti had killed Jimmy McBratney, the man rumoured to be responsible for the abduction and murder of Carlo Gambino's nephew. Gotti hired to defend him the famous Roy Cohn, who made a sweetheart deal for Gotti – four years for attempted murder, a cakewalk.

Gotti had done the time and was out now and making waves in the Gambino family. He, like many in the clan, hated Paul Castellano, for a host of reasons: Paul's greed; his insistence that all the captains come to pay homage to him once a week at the Veterans and Friends Club; the fact that he was appointed because of family connections; the fact that he failed to prevent the FBI from bugging his home; the fact that his affair with the housekeeper had become a public scandal, much talked about in Mafiadom.

DeMeo didn't like or trust John Gotti, and when the sit-down occurred DeMeo brought along Richard as his bodyguard. As they drove to the meeting, held in the home of another Gambino captain, Roy said, 'Big Guy, we can't trust this fuckin' Gotti. Keep your eye on him, and don't let me out of your sight, got it?'

'Got it,' Richard said.

Richard had three guns on him and a knife strapped to his calf.

Richard enjoyed being taken into DeMeo's confidence like this. Of all the killers in his crew, DeMeo had chosen Richard to watch his back. DeMeo knew that Richard was the coldest, most dangerous killer he had ever come across, and he trusted him. Over the years they'd been doing business together, Richard had been scrupulously honest – always kept his word. DeMeo still had no idea that Richard was waiting for the right opportunity to kill him; that Richard never forgot the beating he'd given him, how he pointed the cocked Uzi at him and laughed. On the one hand, Richard liked Roy, his gregarious, generous ways when he was in a good mood; on the other, he despised him, his loud, bullying ways, the way he went from hot to cold in the blink of an eye.

Roy and I were alike in many ways. When I was in a good mood, I was the nicest guy – give you the shirt off my back. When, however, I was on a tear . . . I scared myself, he explained in all sincerity.

The site was a red-brick two-family house on Brooklyn's Mill Basin, a simple, unassuming structure. A three-foot statue of the Virgin Mary, dressed in blue and white, stood in the front yard, as though to scrutinise visitors with a critical eye. Richard was pleased – proud in his own way – that DeMeo was trusting him like this, counting on him to watch his back. This could, Richard well knew, turn into a life-and-death situation, and DeMeo wanted Richard to be there to protect him.

I was, you know, kind of honoured, Richard explained.

As usual, Richard was wearing a large, baggy short-sleeved shirt, the tail out. The shirt covered the guns he had in his waistband. He had extra clips in his trouser pocket.

John and Gene Gotti were already there, as were a few soldiers from John's crew and Aniello Dellacroce, the underboss of the Gambino family, John's mentor, an old-school diplomatic man. Everyone within La Cosa Nostra had believed Aniello would take over the Gambino family after Carlo's death. He'd been the most likely choice. By rights, he should have succeeded Gambino, but that hadn't happened. Still, in many of the captains' minds, Aniello Dellacroce was the real head of the family; he had kept a tenuous peace within the family after Carlo's death. Dellacroce seemed sickly and frail, as if he might keel over any moment. He had large, aubergine-coloured circles under sad blue eyes, thin grey hair, a flattened nose. But this was a strong-willed individual, a tough Sicilian with a backbone of steel, who believed it was better to make money than war but would kill in a heartbeat if and when necessary. This meeting was an informal get-together. It was not, as such, a formal sit-down. Hellos, handshakes, reserved, respectful hugs and kisses on both cheeks, in an age-old tradition, were exchanged. The smell of Old Spice and Canoe hung in the air. Richard was introduced. He respectfully nodded, shook hands; no hugs or kisses for him. Everyone knew who he was – Roy's secret weapon, a virtual killing machine – and resented that DeMeo had brought him. It was an affront. But DeMeo had purposely brought Richard for just that reason. He wanted to make a point; and he did, without saying a word.

This was all before John Gotti became a Mafia superstar, a legend in both his own mind and the public's, but even then he was ambitious in the extreme and quite deadly, everyone knew. Yet Roy DeMeo had a far-reaching reputation as a very dangerous man that overshadowed John Gotti's.

As the meeting began, Richard stood stiffly in the living-room as the others moved to a large, dark-wood dining-room table. DeMeo sat with his back to Richard, who carefully watched what was happening, studying eyes and hands as a tennis umpire observes a championship match. He couldn't hear exactly what was being said. John Gotti expansively made his case, Roy made his, Dellacroce had a say, and soon they all shook hands. A deal had been struck. Richard could see that the Gottis were wary of DeMeo. Who could blame them? It was no secret that Roy had turned the apartment in the back of the Gemini Lounge into a slaughterhouse, that DeMeo and his crew were murdering scores of people, cutting them up and getting rid of body parts all over Brooklyn. Gotti thought of DeMeo as an out-of-control ghoul who would eventually make trouble for everyone in the family with all these murders.

Whatever the dispute had been about, it was obvious to Richard that it had been peacefully resolved. The meeting was soon over. DeMeo and Richard left. In the car on the way back to the Gemini, DeMeo said, 'This fuckin' Gotti can't be trusted. Mark my words, he's gonna be trouble. I don't like him. He thinks he's hot shit. He ain't nobody. If it wasn't for Dellacroce he wouldn't even be made.'

Richard just listened. Back at the Gemini, he did not go into the club. He knew DeMeo's people were inside, and he didn't want to be around them. DeMeo thanked Richard for coming and hugged and kissed him, and soon Richard was on the way back to his family, feeling in his gut that there really would be trouble some day because of John Gotti. It was clear in Gotti's eyes, the way he moved, his body language, even the way he gestured with his hands. He was, Richard thought, a storm waiting to happen.

Richard never drove straight home any more. He always took roundabout routes, would suddenly pull off the road and wait for cars to pass him. He didn't want to be followed home. He didn't want anyone to know where he lived. Above all else, Richard wanted to protect his family, to keep the street and what he did far away from them.

Barbara still had no idea what Richard did, that he was one of the most proficient killers organised crime had ever known. However, one time she did find a gun wrapped in a rag in the garage, up on a high shelf. She put it right back, didn't even mention it to him, not sure how he would react.

36

THE OFFICE

Richard was still losing his temper and abusing Barbara. He would often come home in a bad mood and get into an argument with her over something small and inconsequential, she'd get in his face, he'd lose it and do damage – slap her, rant and rave, break things with his superhuman strength.

Barbara had bought a gorgeous dining table. It was made of thick Italian marble and had wide marble legs. It cost a fortune, but she wanted it, so they bought it. What Barbara wanted, Barbara got. The table was so heavy it took four burly men to pick it up and carry it into the house and place it where Barbara wanted it. One afternoon, Richard came home in a foul mood. He and Barbara got into an argument; he started to lose it. He wanted to slap her, wring her neck, throw her up against the wall. But rather than hurt her, he actually picked up the beautiful marble dining table and tossed it right out of the large bay window that faced the street.

Aghast, Barbara berated him, having no idea just how truly dangerous Richard was, whom she was arguing with.

She would later say, *Mind you, we are talking about a table that took four men to bring in the house. He picked it up like nothing and tossed it right out the window*, shaking her head at the memory, smoking.

Unfortunately, this kind of outburst was happening in front of Merrick and Chris, though not Dwayne. It was Merrick who would usually calm her father down. She had a soothing effect on him. She talked softly to him, got him to leave the house, got him to take her to feed the ducks.

Over in the town of Demarest, a ten-minute drive away (the place where Pat Kane was born and raised), there was a small freshwater pond in the centre of a park, called the Demarest Pond. Flocks of wild ducks always gathered there. Richard enjoyed going to this tranquil pond and feeding the ducks. He'd buy bread in a nearby shop, sit on a green park bench just near the calm water's edge and feed the ducks. He often took Merrick there with him, and together they'd toss the ducks small pieces of bread, which they quickly gobbled up, and as they sat there Merrick would calm her father, talk to him about his childhood, make him forget his anger at Barbara, his anger at the world. Merrick had, for some unfathomable reason, a very calming, soothing effect on her dad. Chris rarely did this with her father, though Barbara did often come here with Richard too. They both enjoyed sitting on the bench, close to the calm pond, feeding the different ducks, talking quietly . . . at peace. The pond truly had a calming effect on Richard. The ducks knew him and would come waddling over at the first sight of him.

Richard's daughter Chris drew further and further into herself, away from her father – away from the family. For Chris, the arguments and violence were extremely upsetting and debilitating.

Chris was now a very attractive twelve-year-old. She had a long, slender body, long, thick blond hair and a sweet, heart-shaped face, with big blue eyes. One summer evening, Barbara and Richard were arguing after dinner, and he began to break things. Chris silently got up and left the house. As she would later relate, she couldn't deal with the violence, the yelling, her father's temper, her mother's 'big mouth', as she thought of it. She walked to the corner and sat on a wooden bench near the bus stop there, trying to figure out what to do, to whom she could talk, where she could get help, where she could turn.

Once, Chris had thought that all parents argued, that surely all dads tore the house apart; but now she knew that wasn't the case at all, that her father was unique, and her mother too. As she sat there, dusk coming on quickly, fireflies starting to appear, a man in a red van pulled up and said hello to her, offered to take her where she was going.

'I'm not going anywhere,' Chris said in a small voice, knowing she shouldn't be talking to a stranger. Barbara had warned her many times about talking to strangers.

'Would you like to go for a ride?' the man asked. He was in his mid-30s, had blond hair, was attractive, seemed nice – seemed . . . interested in her.

'OK, sure,' she said, and got in the van with the stranger, knowing she shouldn't, knowing her parents would be angry, would punish her severely for such a thing; but she didn't care. She was taking control; she was in charge; that was it.

It didn't take long for Chris to find out exactly what the blond man was interested in: he asked if she'd like to go to a secluded place he knew of and 'fool around'.

'OK,' she said, even before she realised she'd said it. He took her to a small clearing in some nearby woods and began kissing her. She let him; she didn't resist him. He took her into the back of the van, undressed her and proceeded to have all kinds of relations with her, including intercourse, which she willingly let him do. This was Chris's way of taking control of her life. Her body was hers, hers only, nobody could take that away from her – and she was going to use it, let it be used, any way she wished. She certainly didn't enjoy what he was doing, what he had her do. She was doing it to assert her individuality, to rebel. Chris knew that if her father saw such a thing he would probably kill her, and would surely tear this man apart, literally. But she didn't care . . .

When it was over, when he was done, he thankfully took Chris back to the bus stop, the bench where he had found her, and she got out of the van, thanking him as she went, polite and sweet, not traumatised at all. He didn't ask to see her; she didn't volunteer any information. She didn't want to see him again. They both knew what had happened was wrong – very wrong, sinfully wrong, against-the-law wrong.

Chris slowly walked back home, a virgin no more. Barbara asked her where she'd been.

'At a friend's house,' she said.

Richard knew his violent outbursts were wrong, and he didn't like himself because of them. He knew he shouldn't be violent with Barbara, but he had no control over his volatile temper. It was as if a bomb exploded inside him. Richard decided to rent an office, to have a place he could go when he wasn't in a good mood, a place where he could prepare himself for hits, calm himself after a job was done. He had come to realise that he shouldn't be around his family at such times. It wasn't fair to them. It was outright dangerous, he also knew.

From Argrila the porn producer Richard heard that there was office space available in a commercial building on Spring Street, just off Lafayette, perfect for what he had in mind, and it was in the city. Richard was often in the city now on business, and this little office would serve him well. He rented it and proceeded to buy some office furniture, a bed, a big desk, a safe, a fridge. He had phones installed, and suddenly Richard Kuklinski had an office – a place from where he could conduct business, his criminal dealings, murder contracts. He stashed a host of weapons in the safe, as well as hand grenades, handcuffs and some of his expanding library of poisons.

Now, when he knew he had a job to do early in the morning, a contract that had to be filled in the city, he'd sleep at the office, his *war room*, as he thought of it. There was even a bathroom with a shower stall. He didn't tell Barbara about it. He told Barbara very little.

Another piece of work came Richard's way, the killing of a Genovese soldier. He was using drugs, making mistakes, compromising the family; he had to go. Richard knew that the mark, Henry Marino, was a coke hound and decided to use that as a way to kill him. Richard bought a few grams of pure coke and carefully laid it out on his desk in his new office, on a piece of mirror. Richard did not use coke; he didn't do any drugs. But he knew about drugs, their applications and effects. After chopping up the coke with a razor, he put on white plastic gloves and carefully mixed enough cyanide with the coke to kill a man. That done, he put the drugs in a vial, and he was soon on a plane to Las Vegas. Richard had always loved Vegas, ever since he was a kid, and now he was going there to do a piece of work and get paid well for it. As far as he was concerned, he had it made in the shade.

Richard knew the mark was staying at a swank hotel on the Strip. He checked into the hotel, went down to the bar around 9.00 p.m. and had a beer. Richard rarely, if ever, drank when on a job, but he knew Henry Marino liked to hold court at the bar, pick up babes, that he'd show up sooner or later, and Richard wanted to look as if he belonged, act as though their meeting were purely coincidental.

It didn't take long. Henry Marino soon came strolling in, a tall, thin man with thinning hair. He saw Richard; they shook hands, said hello. Richard bought him a drink before he had a chance to say no. They began to shoot the breeze. After a time, Richard offhandedly mentioned that he had just ripped off a Colombian coke dealer and had a few keys of high-grade coke he wanted to unload.

'You know anyone?' Richard asked, somewhat con-spiratorially; this immediately caused Henry's ears to perk up.

'Good stuff?' he asked, equally conspiratorially.

'Pure, straight from Medellín,' Richard said.

'Yeah?'

'Yeah.'

'What happened to the Colombians?'

'Went fishing.'

'Sure, I might be interested – if it's really good and the price is right.'

'I got some with me. Wanna taste?' Richard innocently asked, springing the trap.

'Sure,' Henry said.

Richard discreetly handed him the vial. Henry smiled, winked and walked off to the bathroom, new-found purpose in his hurried step. Richard paid for his drinks and left.

Henry Marino was found dead in the bathroom, a vial of coke on the floor near by, and his passing was written up as a heart attack, not a homicide.

Later that same evening, Richard went out gambling. He was again beginning to gamble large amounts of money. Money was rolling in. He had it; why not? he reasoned. He enjoyed the thrill of gambling, the challenge of it, so much. The higher the stakes, the more he got out of it. He won sometimes, but mostly he lost. He didn't know when to quit. That was his problem in a nutshell. He lost, in fact, all the money he had earned killing Henry Marino. He felt doubly bad about losing because he had a family now, a wife who wanted and demanded nice things: that the children go to top private schools, that everything was the best, their clothes, their cars, the restaurants they went to, the wine they drank. Angry with himself for losing forty thousand dollars in a few hours, Richard went back to New Jersey in a foul mood.

Richard came to truly enjoy killing with poison. He now used it whenever possible. Most often, these hits were written up as suicides or natural deaths, mainly because Richard was scrupulously careful about using the right dosage: just enough to kill, not enough to be easily detected. But in one interesting instance, the cause of death could not be put down as natural.

Richard was still involved with hijacks and B&E (breaking and entering) jobs. He'd do pretty much anything to turn a buck. His life was all about crime, and there was nothing he would not do except kill women or children. This particular job involved six people all told: a B&E crew of four (with

Richard, five) and the insurance guy who spotted the job, the 'inside man'.

A wealthy businessman in Montclair, New Jersey, had an expensive collection of coins and rare stamps. He kept them in a tall, narrow safe in his house, built into a fancy cedar closet. The insurance guy knew about the coins and stamps because the company he worked for had insured the collection. He also had the combination of the safe.

Richard knew this B&E crew from his wild and woolly days back in Jersey City. There was a possibility that the owner would show up unexpectedly, and it would be Richard's job to take him out quickly and quietly. The gang met in Jersey City, got into the house without trouble, opened the safe without incident, found the coins and stamps and made a clean getaway. So far it was a perfect job; it had gone like clockwork.

Back at the home of one of the gang, Ralphie the Snake, they looked over their loot, the rare coins, the precious stamps. Beforehand, all had agreed to a six-way split. But they got to arguing among themselves about who would and should get what. This was exactly why Richard hated working with other people, this kind of ridiculous bickering, back-stabbing . . . greed.

Losing patience, Richard said, 'Hey look, guys, this all went perfectly, a piece of cake, let's not fudge it up by arguing amongst ourselves. The deal was a six-way split; that's it, OK? I mean, come on.'

Still, they argued on: about who had the largest part, about how the split should be made. Richard became more and more annoyed.

One of the guys said he was hungry; another said Harry's was still open. Harry's was a small takeaway restaurant in Jersey City, little more than a greasy spoon, but they made great sandwiches with a renowned 'special sauce'. Richard magnanimously said he'd go and get the sandwiches, diligently wrote down what the others wanted, and off he went. These days, Richard had taken to carrying around, especially when he went on a job, a vial of cyanide. He had it with him now.

He later explained: *So I'm driving over to get the sandwiches, when the idea first came to me. I mean, I was going to completely play it straight here with these guys, but now . . . now I'm thinking to myself they're all a bunch of greedy stiffs and I decided it was going to be a one-way split – one way my way. I'd show them what greed really was.*

Richard dutifully ordered the sandwiches, some soft drinks and coffee.

Outside, in the quiet solitude of his car, he put his sandwich on the side and put on plastic gloves (Richard always kept an economy box of plastic gloves in his car), opened each of the other four sandwiches and ever so carefully sprinkled cyanide on them in such a way that anyone who ate one would get a full dose, each dose being about the amount you'd find in a salt packet at any McDonald's. He put the sandwiches back in the bag, his own right on the top, took off the gloves and returned to the house and the still-squabbling gang. Richard took his sandwich, announced he was starved, went into a corner and ate with gusto – he really was hungry; and as he ate, he watched the others consume their delicious Harry's sandwiches with the special sauce as they continued to bicker. Within minutes, the poison took effect; suddenly they were all frozen in position, eyes wide open, spittle coming from suddenly lax mouths, which actually hung open as though their jaws had become unhinged. Richard carefully watched them, eating his sandwich, got up and looked at them closely, learning by experimentation the effects of the poison, like a scientist in a lab observing monkeys. One of them tried to stand, but that was impossible. Motor movement was gone. Richard carefully put all that was left of the sandwiches, the drinks and the coffee back in the bag. He then wiped away all his fingerprints, moving slowly, methodically. Satisfied, he took the loot and the garbage and left, closing the door softly as he went.

The following day, he went to meet the insurance appraiser who had turned them on to the job. They met in a crowded bar in Teaneck. When he wasn't looking, Richard put *a boost*, as he calls it, in the insurance guy's drink. Within minutes, he fell to the floor – yet another heart attack in a Jersey bar; how sad. Yet another murder not attached to Richard Kuklinski.

Richard wound up selling what they stole to a fence he knew in Hoboken. Altogether, he earned $400,000 dollars. He put it in one of the two safety deposit boxes he rented in different Jersey banks.

Most of that money, however, was soon gone – Richard gambled it away. As far as he was concerned, it was *easy come, easy go*.

Barbara would have been livid if she'd found out he was squandering amounts of money like that. He never told her about it, or even about the safety deposit boxes. They were, like much of Richard's life outside the home, his secret. His business.

That Sunday, Richard was watching *Wild Kingdom*, one of his favourite programmes. Richard liked animals far more than people. When he saw a large male lion subdued by a tranquilliser gun, he got an idea. *Why not use such a gun on humans*, he thought. It would be, he reasoned, an ideal way to snatch people marked for death. On Monday morning, Richard went to see his buddy Phil Solimene and asked him if he could get him a tranquilliser gun, with the darts and tranquilliser.

'Sure, I'll ask around,' Solimene said, and within two days Richard had the gun, thirty-five darts, and enough tranquilliser to put a football team to sleep.

37

MISTER SOFTEE

Richard was given a contract to kill another mob guy by the notorious De Cavalcante family. The job specifically called for torture. The mark had to suffer severely; that was a prerequisite.

This was a particularly difficult job because the man knew he'd been marked for death and was wary and paranoid, as skittish as a house cat around a crazed junkyard dog. The mark often doubled back for no reason when driving, would suddenly pull over and let the cars behind him pass. Richard followed him for eleven days and could never get the opportunity he needed. Then he figured out that the mark met a woman at a Marriott Hotel in Queens, either a nurse or a beautician, because she wore a white uniform. They would spend afternoons and evenings in one of the deluxe rooms. Richard began hanging around the hotel, looking for a clear chance to snatch the mark, waiting for the right moment.

While in the elevator, coming down from the floor where the mark was having his romantic tryst, Richard first ran into him – a small, dark-haired man with shifty eyes, a thin, nasty mouth and bushy eyebrows who was definitely up to no good, Richard was sure. They smiled at each other. Richard knew the guy was a player. The elevator opened. They went their separate ways. A few hours later, Richard went to use the hotel bathroom (he had taken a room in the hotel), and as he was standing at the urinal taking a leak, the shifty-eyed guy walked in and took the urinal next to him. Richard thought this guy was stalking him and got ready to draw his gun, do battle, kill him right there.

'How ya doing?' Richard asked, looking down at him, a tight smile on his face.

'Yeah, OK.'

'We keep running into each other.'

'I know.'

'You following me?' Richard asked, facing him head-on.

'No . . . you me?' the guy asked.

'No. I'm doing a piece of work, that's all. You've nothing to do with it.'

'So am I.'

'You sure your business isn't with me?'

'Positive. Yours with me?'

'Absolutely not.'

They stared at each other.

'OK.'

'OK.'

They both finished their business and washed their hands. Richard reached out and shook the guy's hand.

'OK,' he said, 'good luck to you.'

'And to you,' the other said, and they parted.

Richard had an uncanny way of discerning immediately other contract killers. He knew intimately the moves, the looks, the eyes, the body language. He could spot another killer a mile away, hands down, with one eye closed, and he was sure the little guy was stalking someone to kill him. Richard even contacted the people who'd given him this job to ask if they'd given it to more than one person. He was assured they hadn't.

Hmm . . .

Several days later, Richard was sitting in his van (these days he generally used the van for stalking marks). He had with him the animal-tranquilliser gun and four darts filled with tranquilliser. If the mark was true to form, he'd soon be showing up at the hotel. Richard was planning to snatch him right from the parking lot, if circumstances permitted such a move. It was a warm day. Richard was thirsty. He had already drunk the sodas he'd brought from the house and eaten a turkey on rye Barbara had prepared for him. Richard heard the familiar jingle of a Mister Softee ice-cream van. He saw in his rearview the white van slowly coming down the block. Richard stepped from his van and waved the ice-cream van down, sweat beading on his high, wide brow. He walked up to the window and was stunned to see the guy from the bathroom inside the Mister Softee van.

'You again,' Richard said, amused though suspicious and on guard.

'You again,' the guy said.

'What're you doing?' Richard asked.

'This is what I do. I'm Mister Softee . . . I use the truck to do, you know, surveillance, to follow people,' he said.

'Really . . . fucking clever!' Richard said, impressed, admiring the originality of it. Who would ever suspect a Mister Softee? Brilliant.

'You still working?' this Mister Softee asked.

'I am.'

'You want something?'

'Yeah, how about a Coke?'

'Sure thing,' he said, and gave Richard a cold can of Coke. Richard tried to pay.

'It's on me.'

'I like this,' Richard said. 'Great idea. Talk about blending.'

'My name's Robert, Robert Pronge,' he said, offering his hand.

'How you doing? I'm Richard.' They again shook hands. 'Funny how we keep running into each other,' Richard said.

'I keep my van in a garage near by. So you're doing a piece of work?'

'Yeah. Guy's very hard to pin down.'

'Does he drive?'

'Yeah.'

'Use the car.'

'Can't be that way – there's a special request involved here.'

'Got you. Look, if you can come over to the garage I'll show you some interesting stuff.'

'I'll come now. I'll follow you,' Richard said, and he got into his van and, curious but on guard, followed Pronge to a garage in a quiet Queens neighbourhood.

Pronge parked his van and opened a battered grey locker in the rear corner of the garage. It was filled with weapons: rifles, pistols, hand grenades, boxes of ammunition. Richard was impressed. He'd never heard of an ice-cream man who killed people. What better disguise could someone take on? He showed Richard a hand grenade he had wired up so it could be detonated by remote control. Robert Pronge, as it happened, was also a contract killer.

'What I do,' Pronge said, 'is put the grenade under the driver's seat of the car and set it off when the moment's just right. It's got a radius of about two blocks.'

'Very clever,' Richard said, noticing a bottle of poison. 'I see you use poison.'

'Absolutely. I use it whenever possible. I made a spray, but you gotta be real careful about the wind.'

'How do you mean a spray?'

'I mixed cyanide with DMSO [dimethyl sulphoxide, a solvent easily absorbed through the skin] and put it in this,' he explained, showing Richard a sturdy white spray bottle.

'It works?'

'Abso-fuckin-lutely. Watch this,' he said, obviously proud of his creation.

There was a stray cat lolling about by some garbage cans. Pronge walked up to it, acting as if he had something to eat for the cat. When he was close enough, he checked the wind, held his breath, sprayed the cat right in the face and quickly backed off. The cat immediately went down and started to die.

'Fuckin' amazing,' Richard said. 'I never knew something like that existed. Will it work on a human?'

'Abso-fuckin-lutely,' Pronge said, and the two of them shared war stories about how they killed people. This was a one-in-a-million coincidence – that Richard Kuklinski and Robert Pronge would run into each other. It seemed like some kind of ungodly, unholy contrivance Satan had to have a hand in . . .

Robert Pronge was a former Special Forces soldier. He had one passion in life, and it was killing people. He was 36 years old, a guy with an extremely diabolical mind, a seemingly normal man who drove an ice-cream van but in truth was an unhinged psychopath. Richard would later say of him, *The two most dangerous men I ever met in my life were Roy DeMeo and Bob Pronge. Pronge was completely nuts. At least Roy had some semblance of being normal, but Pronge was way, way out there . . . dangerous beyond belief. Far more dangerous than Roy.*

Robert Pronge was an obsessed assassin. He hated the world, everyone in it, and nearly all his waking hours were devoted to devising new, unorthodox ways to murder people. In his garage, he had stacks of Special Forces and survivalist magazines, boxes of books about how to kill people . . . how to use explosives, poisons, booby traps, pistols, rifles equipped for night-time use.

Pronge, like Richard, filled contracts for the Mafia, and these two hit it off like long-lost relatives. Richard took an immediate liking to Pronge, who in turn liked Richard. After sharing notes with each other for a while, Richard said he had to get back to work, and he left after they'd made plans to meet again soon.

The following evening, Richard managed to park his van close to the mark's Lincoln. He had the tranquilliser gun close at hand. He had practised with it and was sure he could score a bullseye at close range. A little after midnight, the mark left the hotel and approached his car. Just as he reached it, Richard shot him with the dart, hitting him in the left buttock. Startled, the mark turned, began to reach for a weapon but never made it. He went right down. Richard picked him up, put him in the van, handcuffed his hands and feet together, put duct tape over his mouth and headed for the caves in Bucks County.

This job required torture, and Richard was going to feed him to the rats. He was very pleased at how well the dart gun had worked and planned to use it again. By the time he arrived in Bucks County, it was almost 4.00 a.m. Richard parked the van, pulled the mark out, uncuffed his ankles and walked him to the cave. The guy was hysterical now, crying like a baby, but his mouth was taped and all he could do was grunt and moan. Richard didn't want to hear anything he had to say. He had heard it all before and didn't want to hear it again.

Richard said he didn't get any particular kick out of doing this. It was just a job, nothing more, he said. In the cave, using a powerful flashlight, Richard made the mark lie down, again cuffed his ankles together. He used his knife to cut the man's arms so he'd bleed. The blood, Richard knew, would quickly draw the rats to him. He set up the camera and light and left.

When Richard returned two days later, the mark was completely gone. There was only a stain on the ground where he had been. This time the rats took even the bones.

Richard retrieved the camera and that night he watched the video in his war room on Spring Street, and sure enough it was, again, all on film: how the rats first approached, took tentative bites, soon completely covered the mark. Richard proceeded to take the video to Hoboken and showed it to the De Cavalcante captain who had ordered the job. He loved it. Clapped his hands, patted Richard on the back.

'You're the fuckin' best!' he proclaimed, and gladly gave Richard forty thousand dollars.

Another job well done, another customer satisfied, Richard headed back home, looking in his rear-view mirror as he went, pulling off the highway suddenly to make sure he wasn't being trailed. Besides country music, Richard was fond of oldies, and he sat there listening to 'Blue Moon'. The oldies, he said, relaxed him.

Somewhere in the back of his mind, Richard knew this couldn't go on forever, that sooner or later, if he didn't stop, there would be trouble. He didn't worry for himself but for his family, his children. If what he was doing came out, it would be a terrible thing for them to have to live through. He shook his head at the thought of the embarrassment and humiliation they'd suffer if he was ever exposed. The thought of it shook him to the core of his being. He would, he resolved, make enough money to retire, then walk away from the life and go straight.

He still had a fantasy, a daydream, of having a house on the beach in Southern California. He had mentioned it to Barbara numerous times, but she didn't want to leave Jersey. She liked Jersey. It was where she'd been born and raised, where most of her family lived, where her children went to school and had friends.

'I'm not moving to California. Forget it,' she said, with grave finality. But still Richard had this hope . . . this dream.

What I wanted to do was walk away from it all, go to LA, only deal in porn out there – it's big out there – but Barbara wouldn't go and so that was that. Barbara made all the decisions when it came to those things . . . about the family and all.

Richard and Barbara's son, Dwayne, was a truly gifted child. He was always first in his class, and this in the prestigious Elisabeth Morrow School. Dwayne had grown into an intense dark-haired boy with curious eyes, intelligent beyond his years. His eyes seemed like the eyes of a middle-aged man who had been around the block a few times, not those of a child.

Barbara, Chris and Merrick still did their best to shield Dwayne from Richard's tirades and outbursts. Most weekends, he was sent to stay with Barbara's mother. Richard did try to exhibit more control when Dwayne was around. He seemed to know instinctively that if Dwayne saw him be violent towards Barbara, as the girls did, it would be only a matter of time before Dwayne attacked him, and he'd have to hurt his son.

Dwayne was painfully shy around strangers, but he was open and gregarious once he got to know someone. Dwayne was endlessly curious, still always reading, a polite, very well-behaved boy of whom any parent would be proud. Barbara and the girls thought they had protected Dwayne from Richard well and that little if any damage had been done to him, his development, the way he viewed the world, his take on life, his psyche.

But in truth, Dwayne knew what was going on. This was a very sharp little guy. He saw the marks on his mother, the black eyes and bruises, the broken furniture, and he well knew his father was responsible.

At first, this exceedingly bright, curious child accepted what he saw, thinking such things were normal. But it didn't take Dwayne long to piece together the reality of his father's actions, and it made him terribly angry. Dwayne loved his mother and sisters deeply, and the thought of his father hurting his mom, terrorising his sisters, left him cold and angry deep inside. Dwayne started planning how he'd defend himself against his father, what he'd do if Richard went to hurt him, even kill him. He began leaving knives and swords Richard had given him in strategic places in his room. When Richard gave him an airgun, Dwayne plotted how he could use it to blind his father. Surely, if he blinded his father the way Ulysses had blinded the Cyclops, Dwayne could handle Richard, do him in if it came to that. When Richard gave Dwayne a bow-and-arrow set, Dwayne made it part of his arsenal. He practised with the bow to be able to hit his father if necessary.

Barbara was effusively, gushingly proud of Dwayne and let Richard know every chance she had how smart the child was, implying that Richard couldn't hold a candle to his son. This, of course, caused Richard to resent Dwayne, and sometimes, when angry, he'd stare at his son with a dreadful gleam in his eyes. In fact, one time, just after dinner, Richard grabbed Barbara, manhandled her in front of Dwayne, and the boy immediately got up and put himself between Richard and Barbara.

For a second, it appeared that Richard might clobber him, but he turned away, saying, 'I knew it would come to this.'

'Don't . . . don't do that,' Barbara warned Dwayne. 'Never do that!' He didn't answer her, but no matter what – even if he died – Dwayne would not allow Richard to hurt his mother. Thus the stage was set for a terrible tragedy, with dire, Shakespearean implications.

In no time, Richard and Robert Pronge became . . . friends. The more Richard learned about Pronge, the more he liked him . . . at first. In addition, Richard had been looking for an out-of-the-way garage he could rent; he needed a place to stash stolen items and sometimes kill people, and he wound up renting a garage near where Pronge kept his van.

Pronge told Richard he had a job that he had to do in Connecticut and invited him to come along. He wanted to show Richard how well the cyanide spray worked. This was, he explained, something he had personally developed, and he was obviously proud of it.

The mark lived in a nice stone house on a quiet street. He went to work at the same time every day and returned at the same time every night. This kind of pattern made an assassin's work relatively easy. Pronge parked about 100 feet away from the mark's home. He and Richard sat there, waiting for the man to arrive home. There was, Pronge pointed out, no wind. 'You cannot ever use this stuff in the wind – don't forget that.'

When the mark pulled onto the block, Pronge slipped on a pair of gloves and boldly got out of the car, saying, 'I'll be right back.'

As the mark parked, Pronge was nearly at his car. The

mark opened the door and stepped out of the car, and at just that moment Pronge sprayed the man right in the face. Pronge turned and calmly walked back towards his car. He hadn't taken ten steps when the mark fell over. He was soon dead.

Richard sat there quite amazed, impressed – and impressing him was not an easy task. Pronge got back in the car, and off they went.

'Wow,' Richard said. 'So he's dead?'

'He is by now.'

'Smooth. Very smooth. I like it.'

'Just never use it in the wind if you're outdoors.'

'Of course,' Richard said, feeling close to his new-found friend, Robert Pronge, who had, before they left, put another licence plate on his car with magnets. He now removed the bogus plate.

Richard had to have one of these cyanide sprays, and back at the garage where Pronge kept his Mister Softee van, he showed Richard how to mix it and put it into the special spray bottle he had. Richard couldn't wait to use it; he was a kid with a new toy.

But on the next job that came his way, he would not be able to use this unique killing tool. It would have to be done the old-fashioned way, with guns and bullets at close range. This would be the most important murder contract Richard had filled to date: the killing of the head of a Mafia family – a milestone in his bloody career.

38

JOE AND MARY'S

Just how the Gambino family became involved in the murder of the notorious Carmine Galante is a long, convoluted story with many twists and turns, betrayals and colourful characters.

Carmine Galante was 'one tough cocksucker', as a rival boss put it. He was born in Riva del Gotta, Sicily. As a young man, he had thick, wavy black hair and the dark, fearless eyes of a predatory killer. Galante came up the Mafia ladder the hard way, gleefully breaking heads and killing people as he went. His early association with the Mafia began with Vito Genovese, whom many say Mario Puzo used as a model for his immortal Don Vito Corleone.

The young Galante was a hit man for Genovese. When someone had to die, Genovese sent Galante. Genovese was a staunch Fascist, an ardent fan of Benito Mussolini, and he ordered Galante to kill an Italian journalist, Carlo Tresca, who worked for *Il Martello* and was an outspoken critic of Mussolini. Galante shot him four times, twice in the head, twice in the chest.

Eventually, however, Galante was inducted into the Bonanno crime family, not the Genovese clan. Joe Bonanno was a far less volatile and violent man than Genovese, but he used Galante to commit murder when necessary. In the early 1950s, Joe Bonanno sent Galante to Montreal. Though Bonanno openly condemned dealing in drugs, he put Galante in charge of the

Bonanno family's Montreal rackets – extortion, loan-sharking – and Galante soon turned Montreal (with Bonanno's silent blessing) into the main transit point for heroin coming out of Marseille into America, instigating and encouraging the so-called French Connection. Thus Galante worked his way up in the Bonanno family, and by 1962 he was the underboss of the family. Thinking he was above the law, invisible (very much like Roy DeMeo), Galante ran afoul of the law, was arrested in Brooklyn for drug trafficking and sent away for 20 years. While he was in prison, a psychiatrist announced that Galante was a psychopath ... no shit, Sherlock. In prison, Galante methodically plotted and planned his ascension to the very top position of La Cosa Nostra: *capo crimini*, or *capo di tutti capi*, the boss of bosses.

Tough as rusted nails, Galante picked fights with large black guys in prison, got in front of them on food lines, saying, 'Get the fuck outta my way, nigger.' From prison, he boldly let it be known that he planned to take charge of the Bonanno family, that he planned to be capo di tutti capi. By now, Carlo Gambino was the boss of bosses, and Galante regularly told anyone who would listen how he would get rid of Gambino, that Gambino was afraid of his own shadow, that Carlo Gambino was a 'spineless prick'.

No one looked forward to Galante's release, least of all his own crime family, but he was let out of prison in the autumn of 1974, having served twelve years. He never testified against anyone. He never tried to cut a deal. He kept his mouth shut and did his time. Not like the mob guys of today.

Now Galante was balding, wore large black plastic glasses, had a perpetual scowl on his hard face, as if he'd been sucking on lemons all the years he'd been away. Bitter, angry and very dangerous, Carmine Galante quickly managed to take charge of the Bonanno family. By now, Joe Bonanno had effectively retired and lived in Tucson, and Galante quickly bullied the family leadership away from Rusty Rastelli.

Galante immediately plunged the family into heroin

distribution. He believed that was where the most money was, and that was where he concentrated the family's resources, energy and power. This was the beginning of the end: Galante was recklessly leading the family down a ruinous road. He also began ordering the murders of other mob members who, he felt, were competing with his interests. In one year, he had killed nine Genovese people (all made men) who dealt in drugs; it was painfully clear to anyone who looked that Carmine Galante would not stop killing until he completely dominated and controlled the exceedingly lucrative drug trade and the entire American Mafia. Yes, he and his family were making truckloads of money, but he was also writing his own death warrant.

Galante became so out of control, so greedy, so violent, that the heads of the other four families, as well as the powerful Florida boss Santo Trafficante, secretly met in Boca Raton, Florida, and decided that Galante had to go or he would eventually destroy La Cosa Nostra single-handedly.

Thus, with the full commission's backing, the contract to kill Galante was issued. This was a first. The full commission had never ordered the death of a family head. It was now the summer of 1979.

Bonanno captains and people Galante trusted were contacted and told what was about to happen, and they agreed to do nothing (they actually had no choice). They would even cooperate in the hit.

It was decided that people from several families would be used. Genovese killers were tapped. Paul Castellano had committed the Gambino family; he sent Nino Gaggi to see Roy DeMeo, and Gaggi told DeMeo what was in the wind. DeMeo immediately suggested his premier killer – Richard Kuklinski – for the job. 'He's by far the best we got, and no one will suspect him. He ain't one of us. He's off the map. I mean, we can put him right fuckin' there close to Galante.'

Nino agreed and told Paul Castellano, Paul gave the green light, the proverbial nod, and it was done.

DeMeo soon called Richard, they met near the Tappan

Zee Bridge and DeMeo told Richard they wanted him to cap the head of a family – kill Carmine Galante. 'He's gotta go,' DeMeo said.

'No problem,' said Richard. He knew all about Galante, thought of him as a loudmouthed bully, and would gladly blow him away. 'Be my pleasure.'

'Paul himself OK'd you.'

'Really, I'm honoured.'

'This will be very important for you, Big Guy. They'll owe you huge after this.'

'Like I said, it'd be my pleasure,' Richard said. Galante was a notorious bully, and Richard had been a bully slayer ever since he killed Charley Lane back in the projects. He hated bullies, truly enjoyed killing them. Richard knew too that this would put him in good with all the families, that this was a hit sanctioned by the commission itself. For Richard, this was the job of a lifetime, a homicide milestone.

It was now late June. The wheels that would result in Carmine Galante's murder were oiled and inexorably turning. Galante, however, was not an easy man to take out. He was cunning and very dangerous, and he knew that a lot of people wanted him dead. He was a professional assassin himself and knew what to do and what not to do. He never adhered to any set routine. He always travelled armed. He always had two stone-faced bodyguards with him, Caesar Bonventre and Nino Coppola.

But Galante had no idea that his death had actually been sanctioned by the full Mafia commission, that bosses all over the country, in Philadelphia, California, Detroit – even Joe Bonanno – had given the nod that he had to go.

One of Galante's bodyguards was also brought into the hit, and he readily agreed to help set up his boss. He really had no option: if he didn't agree, his days would be numbered. By cooperating, he assured his own ascension in the family; he'd have his own crew in no time.

The hit was going to go down in a restaurant on

Knickerbocker Avenue in the Bushwick section of Brooklyn, a heavily Sicilian enclave. It was called Joe and Mary's Italian-American Restaurant. They served real home-made Sicilian dishes. It was owned by Galante's cousin Mary. For that reason, Galante felt safe there and often had both lunch and dinner at the restaurant.

On 8 July 1979, Richard met DeMeo at the Gemini, and they headed over to Bushwick for lunch. DeMeo wanted this to go down flawlessly. For him too, it was the biggest job he'd ever taken part in and would guarantee his moving up quickly in the Gambino family. Both his reputation and his life were on the line. This was going to be an inside job, and DeMeo wanted Richard to see the layout, 'the lay of the land', as DeMeo told him that morning.

The restaurant was a small, family affair. An inexpensive sign over the front door said: 'Joe and Mary's Italian-American Restaurant – Special Attention to Take-out Orders'.

It had a large window from one end of the room to the other, a good 20 feet, with thin, inexpensive curtains covering the window. DeMeo and Richard entered, took a table and ordered lunch. The food was good and cheap. The two men ate quietly, started with antipasti, then shared some pasta, thinking about murder, sudden death in the afternoon. Richard then had veal and peppers, Roy a prawn dish covered with hot marinara sauce. Richard did not like the set-up at all. The place was small, long and narrow, with one way in and one way out. Out the back, there was an outdoor patio with some tables, enclosed by three-storey buildings. It was there, DeMeo said, that Galante liked to sit. He felt secure back there because he could see anyone coming his way in time to make a move; you had to walk the full length of the restaurant to reach the patio.

'It's tight,' Richard said in little more than a whisper. 'I don't like it.'

'This,' Roy said, 'is how it's set up. See what you think. Keep an open mind here. His people will be with him when he comes in and while he eats. Two guys. One is with us. After they eat, our guy is going to excuse himself to make some calls. You're going to be the inside guy. You'll be having lunch when they come in. He'll never suspect you. You obviously aren't Italian, see. He always has a cigar after he eats. So you sit as close to the back as possible, facing the street, and order food. Our guys will pull up right out front, double-park and get out of the car. You'll be able to see them through the curtains. Because the place is long and narrow, he'll be able to see them right off, and this guy will start shootin' and ask questions later. That's why there has to be a guy inside, in position – and that guy is you.'

Richard looked towards the street. Through the curtains, he could easily see the sidewalk and Knickerbocker Avenue, people and cars passing; he heard the rumble of trucks, the sound of horns.

'So,' Roy continued, 'soon as you see them, you move. Get up calm, real calm, walk toward the patio and let him have it. Don't give him the chance to reach for a piece. They'll be right behind you, with shotguns. This cocksucker can't live. He can't survive this . . . What do you think?'

'It's tight,' Richard repeated. 'But doable.'

'You OK with it?'

'I'm OK with it. Just make sure the guys that come in know I'm on the team.'

'They'll know. You should be firing at the scumbag when they first see you. When you're done just turn and walk out. Don't run. I'll be in a car waiting for you. OK?'

'OK. When?'

'Thursday, the 12th. I'll pick you up that morning. Say 10.30. You gotta be here, you gotta be inside, sitting down, at 12.15. Use something that'll definitely do the job . . . maybe a .357.'

'OK,' Richard said, calm, cool, collected, taking a drink of water, thinking the food was good.

* * *

JOE AND MARY'S

On 11 July, Richard called Barbara from the war room and told her he wasn't coming home, that he had business. As always, she said OK. Barbara never questioned Richard. He did what he wanted to do. By now, she had come to realise that he was involved in 'shady dealings', and she simply accepted what he said. He had some Chinese food in nearby Chinatown, watched television in his war room, called Barbara to say goodnight, talked about the children, a planned trip for the family to go to Disney World. He went to sleep after watching the news and Johnny Carson's *Tonight Show* monologue.

Thursday, 12 July was a clear, typically hot, humid day. Richard showered and dressed for the day's events. He put on plain green trousers and an oversized short-sleeved shirt that would easily cover the three pistols he would bring to lunch. He went and had an omelette in a Greek coffee shop nearby, bought the three New York newspapers, took a walk, went back to the war room and opened the safe. He would use the newspapers as props. Inside the safe, he had an extensive collection of weapons. He chose two six-shot .357s and a .38 with a four-inch barrel. One of the .357s had a hair trigger. Richard had filed down the firing mechanism so the gun would go off with just the slightest pressure applied to the trigger. He put the guns in a black sports bag and went downstairs carrying the bag and newspapers. As planned, DeMeo picked him up on the corner of Spring and Lafayette. They barely spoke on the trip to Brooklyn. Richard was, as always before a hit, oddly calm; he knew he could very well be killed today, that any one of a number of things could go wrong and it would be over for him. However, this didn't unduly trouble him. In an odd way, Richard Kuklinski had a death wish, which would become stronger with each passing year. He listened to golden oldies as they went. Roy liked oldies too.

Richard was looking forward to confronting Galante. He knew this would be up close and personal – what he liked best. He knew, too, that Galante would definitely try to defend himself, that he had finely tuned killing instincts and skills. In a sense, Richard viewed this as his *High Noon*. He was Gary Cooper, and he was going up against the baddest outlaw in town, a black-hearted bastard who had to die – who needed killing the way a rabid dog needs killing.

No, Richard was not nervous at all. Near Knickerbocker Avenue, he took the three guns from the bag and carefully stuck them in the waistband of his trousers, in the positions they needed to be in. Roy said he'd be out front when he came out, in front of the car that would bring the two other shooters, whose job it was to deliver the *coup de grâce*.

'Make sure I don't come out of there and I'm stuck.'

'I'll be there!' DeMeo promised. They shook hands, kissed on each cheek. DeMeo wished him luck. Richard stepped from the car into the fierce mid-July sun. He was carrying a copy of the *Daily News*, a handy prop. Rubbery waves of heat rose from the ground in sinuous currents. Richard slowly walked to the restaurant, passing Italian cafés, pizza shops, Italian food stores with salamis and giant logs of provolone hanging in the windows. The smell of freshly baked bread permeated the air. He opened the door and went inside. He took a table towards the rear, but not too far back because he didn't want to draw undue attention to himself. He greeted the waiter in a friendly manner, ordered some lunch, a meatball sandwich, something he could eat without using utensils. He didn't want to leave prints on anything. He opened his paper and paid attention to it, looking down, acting as though he were reading something of great interest. His sandwich was served. It looked and smelled delicious. He didn't, however, touch it. He'd wait.

Soon, Carmine Galante appeared at the door. Loud and gruff, he and his two guys entered and made their way straight to the rear patio. There was a long table already set up for them, adorned with a spanking new tablecloth. The patio was shaded by the surrounding buildings. Fawningly, waiters hurried to serve Galante. Everyone knew who he was, and he was treated like the pope himself. Bottled water, wine and food were hustled to the table. Still reading the *Daily News*, Richard now casually began to eat his sandwich. At one point, he dropped the paper and, as he picked it up, turned for a brief moment and saw where Galante was seated. It was set in his mind. Now he kept his eyes on the street. The car with the other assassins could pull up at any moment. Richard slowly ate the meatball sandwich and read the paper, keeping his eyes on the street. DeMeo had told him one of the bodyguards was supposed to leave Galante at one point and that was when the hit team would show up; but he was thinking that they could come sooner. Calm and relaxed, feeling no anxiety – in his element – Richard waited, eating slowly, reading the paper after each bite.

Then, sure enough, one of the bodyguards got up and walked out of the restaurant. It was Caesar Bonventre.

It would be any moment. Richard prepared himself. He moved his feet to be in position to quickly stand. True, Richard was a huge man, but he had the quickness of a lithe cat – a giant pale-coloured panther.

The car pulled up right out front. Richard saw the assassins getting out. This was it. Time to do it. Richard immediately got up and, not hurrying, walked straight towards the patio, straight towards Galante, his eyes now riveted on the mark. All of Richard's senses were heightened. He heard the front door open. Galante now saw Richard coming; they locked eyes. Galante immediately knew what was up, clearly saw his own death fast approaching. He knew the dance; he knew the look; he knew the beats, the steps, the body language. He began to stand. Richard pulled out two guns, the .357s, aimed and fired repeatedly, emptying the guns in seconds; he hit Galante and shot Coppola too. Richard turned, and the hit team immediately let loose on Galante, one with a shotgun. It was deafeningly loud in the enclosed space. Richard grabbed his newspaper and walked out of the restaurant, the sounds of all the shots ringing in his ears. The car was there. He walked to it and got in, and off they slowly went.

'How'd it go?' Roy asked, his face all creased with curiosity.

'Like fuckin' clockwork,' Richard said.

'You're the best, Big Guy.'

Richard went straight back to the city. He was pleased at how well it had gone; it really had been like clockwork – perfect. He and Roy went to a Little Italy outdoor café and ordered coffees, and Richard told him all the details – how Galante saw him coming and knew right off the bat what was up. Roy shook his hand several times. He was as happy as a kid on Christmas morning. The two walked back to Richard's office. Roy hugged him and kissed him, and they made plans to meet soon. Richard went up to the war room. Pleased, he felt as though he had just run a gruelling marathon race and come in first. He planned to stay in the office, in the city, for a few days. He would not go home until he was sure it was truly over and done. For all he knew, someone would now come looking to kill him, to silence him, to close the door on what had happened. Italians, mob guys, had very funny ways when it came to murder. Nothing was simple. There were all kinds of protocols and back-stabbing. He loaded a shotgun he had, put it on his desk and waited, tense . . . unsure. He trusted no one – certainly not Roy DeMeo.

Would DeMeo now look to kill him, he wondered, send people to take him out? Silence him. *Let 'em try*, he thought.

He called Barbara. She was making sandwiches for herself and the children, who were playing in the pool. He told her he'd be home in 'a few days'. Again, they talked about their planned trip to Disney World, hung up. Richard put on the TV and watched a news bulletin about the hit, wondering if an adult was keeping an eye on the kids as they played in the pool.

A news photographer somehow managed to get up on a roof overlooking the patio where Galante had been killed and took pictures of his corpse. Oddly, Galante still had the cigar he'd been smoking sticking out of his mouth; it had wedged itself into his mouth, which hung open now as if his jaw had come undone. His glasses were askew. Blood pooled around him in a glistening red puddle that drew flies. The stink of a dead body in the July heat filled the air; mixed with the lovely smell of freshly baked bread, it was an odd odour. When detectives at the scene saw the photographer, they yelled at him to get lost. 'Get the hell outta there!' one called.

The following day, however, one of those pictures appeared, not surprisingly, on the front page of all the New York papers – indeed on papers across the country. There was the terrible badass Carmine Galante dead as a doorstop with this ridiculous cigar sticking out of his slick mouth. Mafia families everywhere celebrated. A barbed thorn in their collective side had been removed, a cancer had been cut away; he was history – good riddance.

Carmine Galante hadn't shown anyone the proper respect, indeed any respect, and he not only got what he deserved, but the whole world got to see him in that compromising, embarrassing position, as if he were dog shit left on the sidewalk.

Toasts were made all over Mafiadom. Made men shook hands, congratulated one another, patted one another on the back as if there had been a marriage, as if one of their children had just graduated college with high honours.

'The prick got what the fuck he deserved,' Paul Castellano decreed in his Veterans and Friends Club on Eighty-sixth Street. When Richard saw the extraordinary photograph of Galante with the cigar sticking out of his mouth, he smiled, thinking: *The bigger they are, the harder they fall.* Several days later, Richard went to see DeMeo, and Roy was again all hugs and kisses and smiles. Richard had enhanced his rep in the world of organised crime. Because of Richard, DeMeo had gained new-found respect. He was finally being recognised for his unusual talent. He was sure he'd be promoted soon. Paul

Castellano would certainly reward him generously. How could he not? As they often did, they went out for a meal – to Rao's in Manhattan – and Richard again told DeMeo all the intricate details of how flawlessly the hit had gone down. Richard had never seen DeMeo so pleased. It looked as if he were going to jump on the table and do a jig any moment.

'Big Guy,' DeMeo said, 'we owe you! I'm going to make sure you earn seriously!'

Now another Gambino captain walked in: Sammy Gravano out of Bensonhurst, known as 'Sammy the Bull'. He was with an attractive blonde and another couple. DeMeo and he nodded to each other. Gravano took a table in the back of the small place. Richard knew who Gravano was and wondered if his being there was only coincidence. In fact, Gravano was there just to eat and have a good time. He would, however, play a large part in Richard's life in years to come. He too would play a large part in the murder of a capo di tutti.

DeMeo discreetly slid a sealed envelope filled with money over to Richard. 'For a job well done,' DeMeo said.

'Roy,' Richard said, 'I don't want anything. This one is a favour. Tell the big guy [Castellano] and the others that . . . truth is, it was my pleasure,' Richard said, quite the diplomat – a very smart move, this.

'You're the best! You're the fuckin' best,' DeMeo said in little more than a whisper.

After a delicious feast (this place served excellent home-made Neapolitan Italian food), coffee and after-dinner drinks, DeMeo offered to take Richard to a special cathouse and have four women do him at one time.

'All beautiful babes – like model beautiful, I swear!' DeMeo promised.

Richard declined. 'The only woman I sleep with is my wife,' he said. And soon he was on his way back home. Richard felt at the top of his game, as if he had the world by the balls. He knew he should be earning big now.

As usual, Richard did not drive straight home; he doubled

back, took turns, pulled off the freeway and waited, making sure he wasn't being followed. He still wasn't certain how all this would play out in the end. He figured he was still in danger if there was some kind of Italian double-cross in the wind. He still suspected DeMeo might have him killed; he didn't trust DeMeo, didn't consider him a friend. The only friends he had, Richard figured, were Barbara and his weapons. They never lied. They never cheated. They were always there when he wanted them, ready to do his bidding.

Little did Richard know how much Barbara had grown to resent him. She did her best to act as though it was all over when a tirade stopped, but it wasn't. When Richard arrived home, he took Barbara in his powerful arms and made love to her.

The next day, the Kuklinski family left for Florida. As always, they stopped for a nice lunch on the drive down. The man who had just blown away Carmine Galante was in the car with his family on the way to Florida singing a Beatles song – 'I Want to Hold Your Hand' – with his children, not a care in the world.

They stopped in a good hotel, the kids played in the pool, they had a nice leisurely dinner, and in the morning they drove straight on to Florida. They bought fireworks at a shack along the way, some Roman candles, rockets and firecrackers to amuse the children. Richard seemed to be in a good mood, and Barbara was pleased, as were Chris and Merrick.

Neither Richard nor Barbara had found out anything about what Chris had done with the man in the van. For a while after it happened, Chris had felt bad . . . dirty, was troubled by it. But all that had changed. Now she felt stronger because of it; she had asserted her individuality in the strongest way she could and was glad she'd done it.

When the family arrived in Florida, they went straight to Al Pedrici's home. As always, Al was very pleased to see Barbara and his grandchildren.

THE ICE MAN

The kids, of course, wanted to go out fishing on Al's boat, and he was happy to accommodate them. He had the boat ready to go already, with bait and soft drinks on board. As usual, Barbara declined to go, but Richard and the kids hopped on board, and off they went. Al made a comment to Richard about the picture of Galante on the front page of all the Florida papers. Richard acted as though he were as surprised by it as everyone else.

As per Barbara's instructions, Richard made sure he put sunblock on himself, Chris and Merrick. Dwayne didn't need any sunblock. He had the dark skin of a Mediterranean boy and didn't sunburn like his dad and sisters. They started catching snappers and blowfish right away. They also hooked a small sand shark, which Al let go. Seeing the shark fleetingly reminded Richard of the rapist he had tortured and killed in Miami. Richard rarely thought of the people he murdered. It was almost as if someone else had done those things. In a very real sense, there were two Richards. Even many years later, towards the end of his life, when Richard talked about things he did he often said 'we', referred to himself in the plural. Rarely did he say 'I'.

After staying at Al's home for a few days, going out to the best restaurants each evening, Richard dropping hundred-dollar bills as if they were used tissues, the family went on to Disney World, and the kids had a ball. Funny how Richard enjoyed Disney World so much. When he was there, he was more like a big kid. It seemed he was making up for the childhood he'd never had. He'd go on all the fun rides and had a bigger smile than the children. The family stayed at Disney World for six days, then headed back up to New Jersey, stopping in hotels as they went. It was a good vacation. Richard didn't lose his temper once. Everyone had a great time. Still, it was good to be back home. Home sweet home.

The following day was a Sunday, and the family went to church. Barbara made sure of that. Richard was an usher at the church, dutifully helping with the collections. He didn't believe in the Catholic Church or its teachings at all. He came and was an usher to please Barbara. He explained, *The church was all full of shit. A bunch of lying, money-hungry, hypocritical bastards. I used to see priests I knew in peep shows over on Eighth Avenue, in the shops I sold porn to.*

As the summer was coming to a close and autumn was approaching, Richard spent more and more time with Robert Pronge. He was fascinated by the unique methods Pronge had invented, developed and perfected to kill people. But the more Richard grew to know Pronge, the more he began to think that he was *a sick motherfucker*, as he put it – certainly an interesting characterisation coming from him.

Pronge had a piece of work to do in Queens. He used his Mister Softee van to scope out the mark's house. Intrigued, Richard went along with him to observe. Pronge pulled up right in front of the mark's house and actually sold ice cream to the man's children. Later that night, Pronge – with Richard still tagging along – went back to the mark's home, opened his car with a master key he had and planted a fragmentation grenade right under the front seat.

In the morning, now in Pronge's car, Pronge and Richard watched the mark get into his car and pull away. They followed him. Pronge had the triggering device in his hand. He had many good opportunities to set it off, but he waited, clearly enjoying toying with the mark's life, which troubled Richard. He seemed to enjoy too much having control over when and where the man died. Richard kept asking him to do it; he wanted to see how the grenade worked and to get this over with, but Pronge kept drawing it out, as if it were good sex he didn't want to end. Richard began to wonder about Pronge's sanity.

Finally, after two hours of following the mark around, Pronge set off the grenade, and, boy, did it work well. It not only killed the mark but blew the lower half of his body apart. Richard was impressed. He bought four of the radio-activated grenades from Pronge.

The police had no idea who had blown up the man or why. There was, of course, no connection between Pronge and the victim.

Richard, in turn, took Pronge on a job. Together, they abducted the mark from a parking lot using Richard's animal-tranquilliser dart. This was a situation where the order was for the mark to suffer, to be tortured. Richard took him to the caves in Bucks County, and Pronge watched him prepare the mark for the rats, set up the camera, the lights, the motion detector.

Pronge thought all this was just great, the best idea since the wheel. 'Fucking excellent!' he exclaimed.

When Pronge and Richard returned the next day, Pronge's eyes got all wide and he couldn't get over Richard's 'great fuckin' idea', as he called it: the rats had eaten the man alive, and Richard had it on tape. Wide-eyed, Pronge watched the tape and kept congratulating Richard on his 'great idea'.

On another job Pronge had, the mark never left his apartment. Pronge asked Richard what he'd do. Richard told him to go knock on the guy's door and shoot him with a .357 when he saw the mark approach through the peephole. Pronge tried it and it worked like a well-oiled clock.

For one of the few times in his life, other than Phil Solimene, Richard had a friend . . . someone he had much in common with; but that wouldn't last long.

Richard's daughter Chris was troubled. After witnessing her father's temper tantrums and sudden violence against Barbara and their home, she had lost part of her individuality, who she was; and to get that back, to feel whole again, like a complete person in charge of her own life, her destiny, she let boys take advantage of her. Actually, she says, she was using them. She came to think that if she did what she wanted that way, sexually, she was asserting her individuality, taking charge of her life, controlling her destiny. She became very popular in school, was voted most popular girl in class two years running, and it was, she explained, amused by the memories, laughing about it now, because she was having relations with nearly every boy in school.

Interestingly, it would seem that Merrick would be doing such things, not Chris. Merrick dressed wildly. Merrick had friends her mom and dad didn't approve of. Merrick had a very giving nature, was all about peace and love. But Merrick was a prude about sex. She wouldn't let a boy so much as touch her that way. It became, for Chris, like a dangerous game she played with herself. She'd let boys come over to the house and would 'fool around' with them in her lower-level bedroom – while Richard was home!

If Richard had known what she was doing, he would have gone absolutely bananas. He was very conservative about sex – even though he was now thought of as the porn king of New York – and if he had known his young daughter was having relations right there in the house, he would've exploded.

Chris was not enjoying any of these liaisons. She was doing these things to get back at her father in the only way she knew how – with her body. As time went by and Chris started hanging out with boys who could drive, she'd actually have relations in cars and vans parked right in front of the house.

Richard, of course, didn't realise what was going on because he simply would never in a million years suspect his daughter Chris, Little Miss Goody Two-Shoes, of all this flagrante delicto right in front of and even in the house. Ironically, Richard thought Merrick might be fooling around, and he actually followed her, went to parties and dances she attended.

Merrick recently explained: *My dad would suddenly just show up. I'd be, you know, at a party and he suddenly would be there, looking at me. He used to hide behind trees and bushes and watch me. I only saw him if he wanted me to. He had this . . . this kind of amazing ability to blend, to not be seen if he didn't want to. He was like a ghost. I never did anything I shouldn't because I never knew where my father was.*

Of course, Merrick had no way of knowing that her father

stalked people all the time, that he was a professional stalker. Considering Richard's huge size, he did have an amazing ability to not be seen if he didn't want to be.

Yet he never knew his daughter Chris was voted most popular girl in school because most of the boys had relations with her.

39

OFF THE RECORD

This was a very delicate, dangerous business for a whole host of reasons.

Nino Gaggi and Roy DeMeo found a great cocaine connection: two Brazilian brothers who were processing coca leaves from Bolivia into pure, high-grade cocaine. The brothers had apparently found a German scientist to refine the coca leaves expertly into a highly desirable product, called 'mother-of-pearl' because of its unique luminous, bluish-pink tint.

The problem was that drug dealing was a no-no for made men, forbidden by the Mafia commission. Carmine Galante had been killed because of it. Yet most captains were involved with it in one way or another – 'off the record', as they referred to it. There was just too much money to be made, so the rank and file of all the families across the country had their greedy, gluttonous fingers in this highly profitable business.

The '70s were coming to a close and cocaine was the in drug, the most popular drug of all time. It was served up at swank parties from Bel Air to Park Avenue. Everyone everywhere was doing it. And the Mafia could not resist the temptation and profit it readily presented to them.

So DeMeo contacted Richard to come for a meeting with Gaggi. They again met at the Villa on Twenty-sixth Avenue and had a nice meal, and when it was finished, Gaggi got to the point. 'We know,' he said, in his low, formal tone, 'you can be trusted. You've proven that many times. We have this situation we'd like to involve you in. If you don't want to get involved, no problem. But if you say you want in, you must be in all the way . . . you understand?'

'I understand.'

'We have two brothers, the Mediros. They live in Rio de Janeiro. They are processing babagna [cocaine] there in Brazil and bringing it over in ships, in those containers. They have, Roy tells me, the best stuff on the market. We want you to go there, meet them, see the operation and make the deal if you think it's right. They will deliver it to us here, to a warehouse we have in South Brooklyn. You will receive it and watch it until it's picked up by our people. Basically, that's it. You will get 15 per cent of all the profit. You want in?'

'Yeah, sure, definitely,' Richard said, pleased he was being asked. This, he thought, was pay-off for killing Galante.

'So be it,' Gaggi said, shaking Richard's enormous hand, and it was done.

Several days later, Richard was on a plane to Rio de Janeiro. It was a long, arduous trip, but he had a first-class seat and managed to sleep for most of the 11-hour flight. He'd never been to South America before. Always curious, Richard enjoyed seeing new places, peoples, cultures. He was met by a man who worked for the Mediro brothers after he went through customs. He was taken to a hotel in the centre of Rio called the Copacabana Palace, right across the street from the famous Copacabana Beach on Avenida Atlantica. He looked in awe at the beautiful stretch of white beach – Leme, Copacabana and Ipanema elegantly stretched out before him in a gentle horseshoe shape from one end of this glimmering city on the Atlantic to the other.

Arrangements were made for Richard to be picked up in a few hours. He freshened up in his room and went for a walk along Avenida Atlantica, marvelling at the beauty of

Rio, the coastline, Sugarloaf Mountain, the huge statue of Christ standing guard, it seemed, over the entire city. As is the custom, Brazilian women walked about the streets in tongas – the skimpiest of bikinis, their posteriors completely exposed – and Richard was taken aback by their outrageously beautiful curves and mocha-coloured suntans. He'd never seen such beautiful women before. *I can't stay here too long*, he thought, *or I'll get in trouble.*

As planned, he was picked up and taken to the Mediro home, a sprawling white house surrounded by a gorgeous, sweet-smelling garden. It was in the area where the Christ was, on a mountain overlooking the city.

The Mediro brothers were two intense, very polite Brazilians. Richard first met Eduardo, a handsome dark-haired man with flashing white teeth, dark predatory eyes and jet-black hair, slicked back. Richard and Eduardo went out onto a veranda, had cold drinks and talked. As they talked, Eduardo's brother, John Carlo, showed up. John Carlo was very dark, seemed, Richard thought, a Negro. He sat down, and they discussed the deal, price, delivery. Richard was on his best behaviour. When he wanted, he could be amazingly polite – the perfect gentleman. The brothers seemed to take to him. Eduardo had a gorgeous little girl, two or three years old, and she came running out onto the veranda, completely fascinated by Richard, taken by his huge size and white skin. Her name was Yada. Richard loved children, and he immediately began playing with Yada, picked her up and tickled her as she squealed with delight. A maid came and got her and took her for a nap.

'She is so very fascinated by people,' Eduardo explained, very much liking how Richard responded to his daughter. Now that the particulars of the business were out of the way, Eduardo said he'd like to show Richard their processing lab; then they'd go to eat.

'Fine,' said Richard. They piled into a yellow Mercedes sedan the brothers had and went for a two-hour drive, over a very long bridge, up into thick green hills. The lab was in a huge concrete warehouse. Armed guards sat in chairs in front of it. They jumped to attention when they saw the brothers' yellow car.

Inside, Richard was stunned by all the cocaine. There were large squares of it, tightly wrapped in thick plastic, neatly piled up from floor to ceiling. In the back, off to the left, was the lab. Huge vats of coca leaves were being turned into a nearly pure white powder. Eduardo offered Richard 'a taste'. He declined, said he never did drugs. Eduardo liked that too.

Impressed, Richard saw the whole operation, thinking he would surely make a fortune. He was, he knew, taking a big risk getting involved with so much cocaine, but he didn't think he'd get caught; the risks seemed *worth it*, as he put it.

From the warehouse, they went back to Rio, to an upscale barbecue restaurant in Ipanema, where they cooked all kinds of meat on metal spits over a wood fire in the centre of the restaurant, and Richard had the biggest, best steak of his life, he would later say. After this wonderful dinner, the brothers offered to take Richard sightseeing and horseback riding the next day, but Richard politely declined, said he needed to get back home. He missed his family.

'As you wish,' Eduardo said, and they took him back to his hotel. Richard called DeMeo and let him know all was good, the flight he'd be returning on. DeMeo said he'd come and pick him up. Later that evening, Richard was taken out to the airport and managed to catch a flight out of Rio to New York, with a brief stopover in Lima, Peru.

Richard was startled to see Gaggi with Roy at the airport. As they drove to a restaurant in nearby Bensonhurst, Richard told them about all that he'd seen. Gaggi said he had already spoken with the Mediro brothers, and they really liked Richard . . . even said how nice he was to the little girl, Yada.

'You did a good job,' Gaggi said. Then they had dinner and finalised plans to receive the first shipment of cocaine the following month.

* * *

George Malliband was a large, boisterous man, a two-bit hustler, a degenerate gambler, who happened to weigh 300 lb. Richard first met Malliband at Phil Solimene's store; they did a little business together, developed a relationship of sorts. George lived on a farm in Pennsylvania, and Richard went hunting there with him once in a while. When Malliband overextended himself and borrowed money from loan sharks because of gambling debts, he painted himself into a corner – a particularly dangerous corner. Like many other people, Malliband had heard stories about how dangerous Richard could be, and he turned to Richard for help. Richard, in his own way, had taken a shine to Malliband, or 'Georgie-Boy', as he called him, and he reluctantly came to his assistance: he arranged for the loan sharks to wait a few days for their money, and introduced Malliband to DeMeo, who wound up loaning Malliband thirty-five thousand dollars, at 'a friend's rate'.

Malliband paid off the Jersey sharks and people in Vegas whom he owed money. He had promised till he was blue in the face he'd pay DeMeo back in a timely fashion, sworn on his mother and father and everyone else, but he soon stopped making payments, and Roy put the squeeze on him. Malliband again ran to Richard for help.

'Look,' Richard said, 'I can't help you. You swore on your word of honour, on all your relatives, you'd do the right thing here, and now you're obligated. DeMeo . . . you can't fuck around with this guy, see. He's fuckin' dangerous.'

'Yeah, well, you can fix it for me, Rich. I know you can,' Malliband said. 'I just need a little more time here, that's all.'

'How much more?'

'A week, let's say a week.'

Again, Richard extended himself, went to see DeMeo and got Malliband a week.

Again, though, George Malliband had a song and dance instead of the money, and, again, Richard had a heart-to-heart talk with him, explained that DeMeo was hot, that DeMeo was talking about hurting him. They were now in Richard's van, driving along.

Malliband said, 'Big Guy . . . I know too much about what you do. I don't think you'd ever let DeMeo hurt me. Fact is, I know you won't. Remember, Big Guy, I know where you live, where your family lives. You won't let anything happen to me,' he said, thinking himself sly.

This incensed Richard. His face paled. His lips twisted off to the left. That soft clicking came from him. A threat to his family, by Jesus Christ himself, was something he could not tolerate. He was nearly blind with red-hot rage.

'You know, Georgie-Boy, you're wrong,' Richard said, pulling over to the kerb, and without another word he whipped out a .38 and shot Malliband five times, killing him.

I could see, he'd later say, *the bullets tearing into his clothes*.

Richard proceeded to take Malliband to the large North Bergen garage he used as a warehouse and a place to kill people, near where Pronge kept his Mister Softee van. Richard stuffed Malliband's huge body into a 55-gallon drum. But Malliband was too big for Richard to fit him properly into the drum, no matter how hard he pushed and squeezed, all the while talking to Malliband, saying: 'See, Georgie, see what you made me do? I didn't want to do this. See what you made me do?'

In the end, Richard had to get a saw and cut one of Malliband's legs so that he could bend it into the black metal drum, which he sealed and put into his van. It was over 300 lb, yet Richard picked it up easily. He now drove to Jersey City, his old stomping ground. There was a big chemical plant on Hope Street called Chemtex. Out the back there was a kind of dumping ground. It was February now, a bitterly cold day, snowing lightly. Everything was frozen and brittle. Frigid winds ripped off the Atlantic. Richard backed his van into this impromptu dumping area, pulled the drum out of the van, rolled it down a steep embankment that abutted an old railroad yard, got back in the van and left. For years, people had been using this area as a convenient dumping site, and Richard believed Malliband wouldn't be found for a long time, maybe never.

He was wrong. When the barrel hit a rock at the bottom of the ravine, the top popped off.

The man who owned the plant opened the rear door of the place and was standing there having a smoke when he noticed something odd – what looked like a man's leg sticking out of a big drum. He investigated and nearly fell down when he saw what was in the barrel: a very large dead man, his leg all cut up, his femur bone visible. The man ran to call the police.

The identity of the dead man was soon established. His family were contacted. Malliband's brother said George had been going to meet Richard Kuklinski of Dumont the day he disappeared. The police questioned Richard. He, of course, said he knew nothing about the murder. This was the first time he'd ever been connected to a homicide he'd done, though it didn't go any further. It stopped, for the time being, right there.

Richard was mad at himself. He should have buried Malliband, dumped him down one of the bottomless holes in the caves, fed him to the rats. *I must*, he told himself, *be more careful.*

As much as Richard loved his home life, being a 'family man', he came to believe that being married, having children, was making him . . . *soft*, he explained, taking away the razor-sharp edge a professional killer must have. He vowed to be more careful. He would get his razor edge back. In a bad mood now, he had a temper tantrum in the house and began breaking things.

The cocaine from Brazil arrived and was delivered to a warehouse Gaggi and DeMeo had found in South Brooklyn, down by the waterfront, near the old armoury.

Richard, seriously armed, was there to receive it. It was a

lot more than he'd thought it would be. The cocaine was on wooden pallets, two of them, all neatly wrapped in plastic. Richard set up a campbed for himself, put broken glass all over the floor, even installed two electronically activated beams at the entrance so no one could sneak in. He had to stay with the coke until it was picked up. Those were his orders. That night, a few of DeMeo's guys showed up and took the load away. Richard's job was done. He soon received a big bag of money from DeMeo, minus what Malliband had owed, of course. But DeMeo didn't charge any interest at all.

For months, this went on flawlessly. The loads came in; Richard received and guarded them until they were picked up; a short while later, he was given a bag filled with hundred-dollar bills. Richard was pleased. It was all working out well. Everyone was making money. There were no problems.

That soon changed.

DeMeo paged Richard; they met near the Tappan Zee Bridge.

'We've got problems,' DeMeo said, 'with the Brazilians.'

'What happened?' Richard asked, concerned.

DeMeo explained that he and Gaggi had found a better coke contact, Colombians out of Medellín, who sold coke for far less than the Mediro brothers, and DeMeo had not paid the Brazilians for the last load; furthermore, he wasn't going to pay them, he said.

'How much is involved?' Richard asked, thinking this was a stupid thing for DeMeo and Gaggi to be doing. Why, he wondered, were these Italians always so greedy?

'A little more than half a million. And they . . . well, they threatened us.'

'Of course. Roy, these are serious guys. I wouldn't fuck with them. Give them –'

'We ain't,' he interrupted.

'And what do you want me to do?'

'Go there with a few of the guys and kill the cocksuckers,' DeMeo said.

'In Brazil?'

'Yeah.'

'Roy, Rio is a big place. I don't know my way around.'

'I'll send you with three of the guys.'

Richard thought about this. It was a risky proposition, he knew . . . but he liked the challenge, even the danger, of it. 'If I go, I want to do this by myself,' he said.

'Any way you think is best. There's sixty large in it for you.'

'OK,' Richard said, intrigued by the challenge, the way the odds were stacked against him; his death wish was again coming into play.

'When can you go? The sooner the better,' DeMeo said.

'I'll leave tomorrow,' Richard said. 'That soon enough?'

'Good man,' DeMeo said, and hugged and kissed Richard. They both got back into their cars and went in opposite directions, Richard's mind playing over, as if he were studying a giant life-and-death chess match, what he would do, how he would do it.

By now, you know, he explained, *what I liked most was the hunt, the challenge of what the thing was. The killing for me was secondary. I got no rise as such out of it at all . . . for the most part. But the figuring it out, the challenge – the stalking and doing it right, successfully – that excited me a lot. The greater the odds against me, the more juice I got out of it.*

Gambling, it was all about gambling, I guess, you know, and I was betting my life, all I had; that was the bet. Me, alone, against them . . . I don't mean these guys necessarily, the Brazilian brothers – anyone I was going up against. This involved me, only me – it didn't put my family in danger at all. That I'd never do. Gamble with them. Their lives. Their well-being.

Richard didn't seem to realise that he was, in fact, putting his family in jeopardy. Serious jeopardy. South Americans, as a matter of course, regularly struck at enemies' families. For them, it was the norm. For Richard, it was anathema. As far as South Americans were concerned, the first, logical place to strike was to kill a man's family, and it was, they knew, much more painful and lasting than doing in the intended target.

Moreover, Richard didn't seem to connect what he was doing to the full spectrum of calamities that could and would befall his family if he was found out. Such a thing was so painful for him, he didn't think about it. Perhaps he couldn't think about it. He pushed it away somewhere in a dark corner of his mind and left it there.

Getting weapons to Rio, Richard knew, would be the first order of business. That night, he took apart two Italian automatics with silencers, put them in a wooden box, lined it with pieces of styrofoam. In the morning, he posted it and a box of nine-millimetre bullets to himself at the Copacabana Palace. (He was using a bogus name.)

As usual, he didn't say one word to Barbara about where he was going or what he was doing. He kissed her so long, drove himself to Kennedy Airport, left his car in the parking lot and boldly caught a Pan Am flight – first-class, of course – directly to Rio de Janeiro.

The plane ran into a fierce thunderstorm, and Richard was tossed about in his seat. He was a superstitious man, and he hoped the storm wasn't some kind of bad omen. As much as Richard could like anyone, he liked the Mediro brothers; he very much liked Eduardo's little girl, Yada. That weighed on him for a while, but he soon forgot about her. Richard was very good at compartmentalising his feelings, and he focused his thoughts, his energy, on murdering the brothers and getting away with it unscathed. That was all that mattered. That was the job at hand.

He took a cab from the airport directly to the lovely Copacabana Palace, checked in under his false name and went up to the luxurious room. It had a sweeping view of the beach, and Richard stood at the window admiring the tawny-coloured beach and the beautiful, nearly naked females all over the place.

The guns were supposed to arrive that day, but they never came. They were no doubt stolen by a customs agent, and now Richard was in Rio with no weapons, feeling as if he were in band practice with no instrument to play.

This was, of course, a dilemma. Richard knew no one here, didn't speak a word of Portuguese, didn't even know how to get to the Mediros' home. He walked onto Copacabana Beach, down to the water's edge, turned and faced the bustling, steaming city. Using the giant Christ as a point of reference, Richard had an idea where the house was, but he had no car.

Perplexed, concerned, he walked all the way to the Ipanema district and back. He sat at a shaded outdoor café, ordered an iced tea and watched the Brazilian people go about their fast-paced, hot-blooded lives. Here it was like summer, and the temperature was in the low 90s. The sun, so close to the equator, was much stronger than back in the States. Richard could see its searing heat rising from the black-and-white mosaic-tiled sidewalk in sensuous undulating waves. He just sat there watching people, the gorgeous women, thinking this thing out.

It didn't take long for Richard to spot street urchins dealing drugs along the sidewalk on the beach side of the wide avenue, on the other side of the street. They were tough little tykes, and as the sun began to set behind Sugarloaf Mountain, Richard approached a tall, skinny cappuccino-coloured kid. The kid saw him coming from across the street, thinking Richard was a gringo who wanted to suck his dick. Many such men approached him, for he was a handsome boy, maybe 15. He smiled at Richard, willing to let anyone who paid him suck his dick to his heart's content.

Using mime, his street savvy, Richard quickly managed to let the boy know he wanted to buy a gun, a pistol, a .38. The street kid, an outlaw, immediately understood exactly what Richard wanted and, using his fingers, let him know how much such a gun would be. More or less a hundred bucks. Richard said OK. They agreed to meet in this same spot at twelve the following afternoon. The boy asked for the money now; Richard said no – he'd get paid when he brought the *pistola*.

Not sure if the kid would deliver, Richard went back to the café and watched the busy thoroughfare some more. When darkness engulfed the city, he returned to his room and called Barbara. They talked about the kids. He said nothing about where he was. She didn't ask. He went back downstairs, had dinner, went for another long walk and retired early.

At noon the following day, Richard crossed the street, and the boy was there, holding a brown paper bag. Richard looked inside. Sure enough it was a .38 Smith & Wesson. Richard paid him. They shook hands and parted. Back in his room, Richard took the gun apart. It was old and somewhat beaten-up, but all the components worked. He cleaned and oiled it.

Now carrying the gun, Richard went back out and walked away from the beach, into Rio Central. He located a hardware store, bought a hammer, pliers and screwdriver, walked on. He found a quiet street and quickly managed to steal a van, using the tools he'd just bought. Now with wheels, he headed straight for the hills overlooking Rio, and, using the giant Christ as a point of direction, he actually managed to locate the Mediros' home within several hours. He smiled, parked down the street and waited, not sure what to do or how to do it. He hadn't been there an hour when the electronic gate suddenly opened and out came the yellow Mercedes. Both brothers and two other men were in it. Richard followed them back down to the beach area along Avenida Atlantica. They parked and went into a secluded restaurant on a quiet Ipanema street. Richard had six bullets. He knew every shot had to count, that surely they were armed and he had to move quickly. He managed to park near the Mercedes. He let the air out of the front left tyre, went back to the van and waited, tense like a coiled spring, a giant cat about to strike, but calm inside – ice-cold inside . . . an Ice Man. Richard was in his element. This is what Richard did. Stalk to kill. After two hours, they came out. They had obviously been drinking, were now laughing, relaxed. As they approached the Mercedes, Eduardo first noticed the flat. After appropriate curses, one of the other guys opened the boot of the Mercedes and pulled its spare tyre out. The others waited. They lit cigarettes. Richard stepped out of the van and calmly walked right towards them, staying in shadows as he went. John Carlo spotted him first – but he couldn't quite conceive that it was truly Richard. Richard pulled out the pistol and in a matter of several seconds fired four times, dropped all of them. However, he had to fire a second shot to finish off Eduardo.

The job done, Richard got into the van and pulled away. Shocked diners and waiters poured from the restaurant. Richard drove to the other side of the city, to Leme, and left the van there after carefully wiping all his prints off it. He threw the gun into the ocean and returned to the hotel. The following day, Richard left Rio on the first flight out.

Richard was very proud of this piece of work. It was the kind of accomplishment he wanted to tell people about, brag about, but of course he couldn't.

He got into his car and drove back to New Jersey, checking his rear-view mirror and making U-turns as he went. Near his home, he paged DeMeo from a phone booth. Roy called him within minutes. Richard let him know the brothers weren't a concern any more.

'Big Guy, you're the fuckin' best – the fuckin' best, you hear!' DeMeo said.

Richard thanked him, hung up and went home, pleased and proud of himself, but thinking DeMeo and Gaggi were greedy bastards.

Several days later, Richard met DeMeo at the diner near the Tappan Zee Bridge, and DeMeo gave him, as promised, a paper bag with sixty thousand dollars in it, in hundred-dollar bills. They hugged and kissed each other on the cheek and went their separate ways.

40

SAMMY 'THE BULL' GRAVANO

Sammy Gravano was born and raised in the heart of Mafia country, Bensonhurst, Brooklyn.

As a youth, Gravano was a tough kid, a member of the notorious street gang called the Rambers. It was headed by Gerald Pappa, a vicious, extremely tough street fighter with jet-black hair and light-blue eyes, one of the roughest guys in all of Brooklyn – no easy task. Gerald Pappa was known as 'Pappa Bear' because of his unusual strength. He, like Gravano, would eventually be inducted into one of the five New York crime families, the Gigante branch of the Genovese family, while Sammy would be made by the Gambinos. Sammy Gravano and Pappa were very close as teenagers. Gravano would eventually name his only son Gerald, in honour of Pappa.

Gravano had a bad habit of killing his friends and business partners; he murdered one of his own relatives, Eddie Garofalo. He was known as a greedy, black-hearted back-stabber. If Gravano called you up and invited you for dinner, a friendly drink, an espresso, it was a good idea to leave town in a hurry.

John Gotti would later take a shine to Gravano and promote him to underboss of the Gambino family – a fatal mistake

– after the two of them successfully conspired to kill Paul Castellano on 16 December 1985, in front of Sparks Steak House. Now it was early March 1980. Richard Kuklinski knew Gravano; they had met at restaurants and Roy's place over the years.

According to Richard, when Gravano had a 'special piece of work to do' – the killing of a cop – he contacted DeMeo, and DeMeo referred him to Richard and strongly vouched for him. DeMeo wanted nothing to do with killing a cop, even a crooked cop. No matter how you looked at that, it spelled trouble, and DeMeo knew it. The cop in question was Peter Calabro.

DeMeo let Richard know Gravano would be calling, and a meeting was set up at a diner on the Jersey side of the George Washington Bridge. They met in the parking lot, shook hands. Gravano came with a driver. As Richard and Gravano walked and talked, Gravano's car slowly followed. Gravano wasted no time. 'I've been hearing good things about you for a long time, Rich. I have a special piece of work I'd like you to do. It's gotta be done pretty quickly.'

'I'm available,' Richard said.

'The guy lives in Jersey. I've got his address and photo for you, even the weapon – a shotgun. You OK with that?' Gravano said, not mentioning that the mark was a cop.

'Sure. They're messy but they work.'

'OK. There's twenty-five large in it for you.'

'Sounds good.'

'Where's your car?'

'Just down the ramp here.'

'I'll give you everything right now, all right?'

'Sure.'

Richard led them to his parked car. Gravano had his driver open the boot of his car. In it was a green canvas bag, like a small army duffel bag. Gravano opened it. Inside was the shotgun, a walkie-talkie and a photo of the mark, a nice-looking, dark-haired man with an oval-shaped face. Gravano still said nothing about him being a detective out of the Brooklyn hot-car division. He had been working with the Gambino family for years now, providing a laundry list of services, some of which had caused people to be murdered. It was Calabro's wife, Carmella, that DeMeo had murdered. Calabro had got himself in trouble, and both Gravano and DeMeo were concerned he would turn on them. He had to go. Richard took the canvas bag and put it in the boot of his car.

'I'll pay you when it's done, OK?' Gravano asked.

'Sure. I know you, you know me, no problem,' Richard said, and it was done.

Peter Calabro lived with his young daughter, Melissa, and another detective, John Dougherty – also a widower – in a simple ranch-style house in Saddle River, New Jersey, a secluded wooded area. Richard checked out the house but decided not to do the murder there. He saw Calabro's young daughter with some other young girls and opted to do the hit on the road to the house, a narrow, little-used road with few houses on it.

The plan was for Calabro to be followed from work, and Richard would be informed via the walkie-talkie when he was approaching the house. Calabro knew he was marked – there had been threats against his life – and as he made his way from Brooklyn back home that evening, he took a secondary route, travelled on back roads, not Route 17. But still he was followed, and Richard knew when and from which direction he was coming. It was 14 March 1980, a cold night, snowing heavily.

Richard parked his van on the snow-covered road, put on his emergency lights, grabbed the shotgun, crouched in front of the van and waited for just the right moment. He was able to see the approaching car, its headlights reflecting off the snow as it came. He had parked his van so that Calabro was forced to go slowly. Richard raised the shotgun and, at exactly the right moment, when Calabro was abreast of him, let loose with both barrels of the blue-black 12-gauge, shooting Calabro in the side of the head with the .33 buckshot rounds. He was killed instantly. His brown Honda meandered for a short distance, then careened down a 30-foot embankment and crashed into a stand of trees.

Calmly, Richard got back into his van and left, still not knowing he had just killed a cop.

As he made his way back to Dumont, he dumped the shotgun into a stream near his home and went into the house. It was a Friday night. His daughters, Chris and Merrick, were in the living-room with some friends. Barbara was sleeping. Richard made himself a peanut-butter-and-jelly sandwich and retired.

At 2.15 a.m. on Saturday morning a snowplough crew clearing the road found Calabro's car. In the morning, Richard first learned that the man he had killed was a decorated NYPD detective. It didn't make any difference to Richard that he had killed a cop, but it would have been nice, the right thing to do, if Gravano had told him. Be that as it may, Gravano called Richard a few days later and made arrangements to give him the twenty-five thousand.

It was over and done with . . . for now.

In years to come, though, this murder would take on a life of its own and come back to haunt not only Sammy Gravano, but the United States Justice Department as well.

The accident occurred on 18 March of that same year. John Gotti's youngest son, Frank, borrowed a friend's motorised mini-bike, shot out onto the street where the Gottis lived and was struck and killed by a car driven by one John Favara.

Surely, Favara should immediately have left town, but what he did do was continue driving the car about the neighbourhood, infuriating Mrs Gotti and her husband. He should also certainly have gone to the Gotti home and told the family how genuinely sorry he was. He did neither. His days were numbered. It was by now well known that Richard did 'special work', and Gravano asked him that July if he'd be interested in applying his special talent to the man who had killed John Gotti's son. Richard knew all about what had happened.

'Sure, be happy to,' he said.

On 28 July, Richard met with a few other men, one of whom was Gene Gotti. They drove in a van to Favara's workplace and grabbed him as he made his way to his car – the same car with which he'd run over the young Frank Gotti. They drove to a junkyard in East New York. There, Gene Gotti and the others beat Favara to a bloody pulp, broke his bones, knocked out his teeth, knocked out an eye. Richard then went to work on him, bound him and tore off his clothes and used emergency flares to torture him, to burn off his genitals. He then stuffed the burning flare up Favara's anus. They all stood about and watched what was left of him suffer terribly, though not die. Gene Gotti then used a pipe to mercilessly beat Favara and finally kill him. Favara was then stuffed into a 55-gallon drum.

PART IV

THE MANHATTAN PROJECT

41

THE GANG THAT COULDN'T SHOOT STRAIGHT

Apart from the many other criminal enterprises Richard had become involved with, he also ran a breaking-and-entering crew. It consisted of Al Rinke, Gary Smith, Danny Deppner and Percy House. Richard had met each of them, over a period of years, at Phil Solimene's store. They broke into homes all over New Jersey and stole anything of value they could carry, much of which Phil Solimene sold, splitting the proceeds with the gang. They even stole cars from people's garages. Richard was both the muscle and the brains behind the operation; he was also the discipline: he made sure none of them talked or did anything that would compromise the gang and, more importantly, compromise him.

Percy House was the foreman. He was a short, squat, gruff man who always looked dirty and in need of a shave – a nasty piece of work indeed. Gary Smith was tall and lanky and wore thick black plastic glasses and an Abe Lincoln-type beard, had a harelip. Danny Deppner was also tall and thin, broad-shouldered and strong, had a mop of unruly black hair that always looked windblown. Al Rinke was small and frail and looked like a mouse. None of them had so much as a high-school education, and they were none too bright, but they took orders relatively well and, for the most part, did what Richard told them. They were all deathly afraid of Richard.

By now, he had garnered a very well-deserved reputation as a dangerous man, a stone-cold killer, and was the indisputable alpha predator in the criminal food chain. What he said went. He was the boss. The final arbiter. God.

In this world, might was always right.

Richard had always wanted his own gang, styled after a Mafia family. He too pined to be inducted into a Mafia clan. But he knew that could never happen, because he was not Italian, so he was, in his own way, developing his own crime empire. The problem was, these guys were all undisciplined and dumb. They would ultimately become the chink in Richard's armour of invisibility, breaking his incredible run of luck.

Louis Masgay had a variety store in Forty Fort, Pennsylvania. He bought a lot of swag from Phil Solimene, which he sold out of his shop. He also played cards in the weekend games in Solimene's store. Masgay had bought hijacked blank videos from Solimene and Richard. He wanted more of them and kept badgering Richard: 'When will you have more? I'll take all you can get, I got cash, no questions asked.'

This went on for months. Masgay was beginning to annoy Richard, and Richard began ducking him. Still, Masgay kept showing up at Solimene's store, looking for a big load of blank tapes, saying he had cash.

Finally, on 1 July 1981, Masgay came into Solimene's store late in the day. Solimene told him a new load of hijacked tapes had come in. Masgay was excited. Solimene asked if he had the money. Trusting Solimene, Louis Masgay told him he did, that it was hidden inside the door panel of his van. At that, Solimene picked up the phone, called Richard (he was one of the few people who had Richard's home phone number) and told him what was up. Richard said he'd be there in one hour. Masgay was excited.

Richard walked into the store an hour later. He had a .22 pistol with a silencer in his pocket. By now, the store was closed.

'Where is he?' Richard asked.

'In the john,' Solimene said.

Richard calmly walked to the bathroom, taking out the .22 as he went. Without a word, he quickly opened the bathroom door. A surprised Masgay was sitting on the toilet. Richard raised the .22 and shot him in the forehead, above his left eye, then shot him a second time square in the centre of his head, instantly killing him.

'Hope you don't mind I did it here,' Richard said.

'If I did it wouldn't matter now,' Solimene said. Richard trusted Phil Solimene; they had done many illegal things together over the years and there had never been a problem. Richard considered Solimene a friend . . . perhaps the only friend he'd ever had.

They put Louis Masgay into a large black plastic bag, went out to Masgay's van, pried open the door panel and found a neat stack of money held together with two rubber bands. Back in the store, they counted the money; there was ninety thousand dollars. Richard and Solimene split it down the middle. Richard proceeded to put Masgay in his van and took the body over to his warehouse in North Bergen. Out the back of the place, there was a hole in the ground, an old well, and ice-cold spring water ran into it.

Robert Pronge and Richard had frozen a man Pronge had killed, storing the body in a meat freezer. The man's wife had gone to Pronge and asked him to kill her husband so she could collect the insurance money. To pull this off successfully, it had to seem that the man had died later than the actual murder, to give her time to get the policy in place. Richard watched Pronge kill the man with his cyanide spray, and then they deep-froze him for several months before putting him where he'd be found. The wife did, in fact, collect the insurance money, which she ultimately split with Richard and Pronge.

Now Richard was wondering if the icy water in the well would slow the decomposition of a body. Solimene had told him that Masgay's family knew he was coming to meet the two of them, and Richard was thinking he'd freeze Masgay, then months later put him out somewhere he could be found. Richard carried Masgay to the well and dumped him inside, put a tyre on top of him, then a piece of plywood, then poured some cement on top of the wood, mostly covering the hole up. Now he went back to Solimene's place, and Solimene followed Richard as he drove Masgay's van onto the turnpike and left it on the side of the road right there out in the open. Then Richard got into Solimene's car, and they returned to the store.

Another job well done, it seemed. Solimene and Richard hugged and shook hands, and Richard went back to Dumont forty-five thousand dollars richer, carefully making sure he wasn't being followed as he went, listening to country music.

But Phil Solimene had a big mouth. Several weeks after the Masgay murder, he told Percy House what they'd done to Masgay and how Richard had killed George Malliband too. House was giving Solimene a hard time about money he owed him, and Solimene offhandedly threatened him with Richard.

Percy House wound up telling other members of the gang what he'd heard, they in turn told people – wives and friends – and soon a dozen individuals knew about Malliband's and Masgay's murders.

Thus, for the first time, the cat was let out of the proverbial bag.

42

THE LONE RANGER

Pat Kane, the young air force veteran whose brother Ed had convinced him to become a state trooper, was now a detective, the youngest in the Newton, New Jersey, outpost where he was stationed.

Pat was a religious man who went to church every Sunday and loved his job. He thought he was the luckiest guy in the world, getting paid for doing what he wanted to do more than anything: putting bad guys behind bars where they belonged. He often worked outdoors and had a chance to make the world a better place. What could be sweeter? For Pat, being a cop was not just a job, it was a calling, his passion in life. He was, in a very real sense, on a mission, and that mission was protecting women and children from the fang-toothed predators that so readily moved about in a free society. Pat did everything by the book. He was a genuinely honest man, would never take a free meal or drink from anyone, not even a cup of coffee. He had come to believe that the police were the last and final line of defence society had against chaos. Though he was highly religious, Pat Kane wouldn't have a second thought about killing a bad guy if it came to that. Detective Kane was a diligent, proactive investigator – the type of man who will not let go of something once he gets his teeth into it. Stubborn and tenacious, he was like a bulldog.

Pat Kane's boss was Lieutenant John Leck, a tall, well-built individual with a bald head, who looked like Telly Savalas. Towards the end of 1981, Leck called Detective Kane into his office. There had been an inordinate number of burglaries all over northern New Jersey, and Lieutenant Leck was concerned. A band of professional burglars, he explained, was breaking into homes with arrogant impunity and stealing everything that wasn't nailed down. They mostly chose nice houses in secluded areas and robbed them at will, as though they had a licence from the powers above to steal whatever the hell they pleased. A man representing himself as one of the gang had been caught robbing a house by the owner, and he was now in Lieutenant Leck's office, trying to make a deal. The lieutenant didn't know at this point whether the guy was for real or pulling his chain. On a map on the lieutenant's desk were dozens of red-pen marks where, Lieutenant Leck said, there had been unsolved burglaries. The lieutenant told Kane to take this burglar out and see if he, Kane, could match up what the burglar said with actual burglaries. Kane knew that Lieutenant Leck wasn't sure if this rodent-faced guy was for real or if he was bogus, another cornered rat trying to weasel out of a tight situation. *What else is new?* he thought.

Outside, as they approached Kane's unmarked police car, the rodent said, 'I'm going to help you and all, you know, show you all the jobs . . . but if *they* get wind a what I'm doing here, I'm dead. These are badass people. You understand that there?'

'Yes, I understand,' Kane said, thinking he was surely being melodramatic. Little did Kane know how truly dangerous this gang was; he himself would end up a target of them, tracked and stalked and set up for murder.

Kane proceeded to follow the informant's directions, and they slowly made their way across three rural counties of northern New Jersey, going up and down back roads filled with potholes, raising dust, bumping along, and as they went, the informant indicated houses the gang had robbed. Kane copied down all the addresses – some of the houses didn't even have addresses, they were so secluded. He would have to check every single one against Leck's map to see if there had been a burglary. The informant did seem to know the insides of these homes, even what had been stolen.

Over a two-day period, the informant pointed out forty-three houses. This wound up presenting a monumental task for the young detective. Now, working alone, he had to verify all these burglaries and compare them with what the informant had said. Meanwhile, the informant also named his accomplices: Danny Deppner, Gary Smith, Percy House and the leader of the gang – a guy known only as 'Big Rich'.

Who, Kane wondered, is Big Rich?

Kane rolled up his sleeves and went to work, carefully investigating each of these robberies. It ended up taking him months to verify all the burglaries and present what he found to a New Jersey prosecutor, who in turn presented the case to a grand jury. By October of 1982, Detective Kane had single-handedly secured a 153-count indictment against the gang members. He managed to locate and arrest Percy House, but the others were nowhere to be found. It seemed they had vanished into thin air. Intent upon locating the rest of the gang, Kane searched high and low for them. He staked out both Gary Smith's and Danny Deppner's apartments. Nothing. The Christmas holidays arrived. Terry Kane wanted Pat home with the family, their two children. This new case was obsessing her husband, she knew, and she didn't like it. He assured her he'd be home for Christmas – Lieutenant Leck had promised he'd give him time off. But it didn't work out that way. On Christmas Eve and Christmas Day, Pat was on stakeouts, looking for Deppner and Smith. True, they had the gang foreman, Percy House, in jail, but he refused to say one word about anything. He wouldn't even give them his name. He hated cops and had no qualms about expressing his animus.

Wondering where the hell Deppner and Smith had disappeared to, Kane continued to hunt for them, sensing something bigger was involved here but not knowing what.

One of the larger questions that loomed before him was where all the stolen goods had gone – televisions and VCRs, phone machines, all kinds of jewellery, guns, cars and stereos. When Kane pressed the informant about this, he said all he knew was that Big Rich was in charge of that, that Big Rich sometimes hung around a shop in Paterson called 'the store'.

'What store? What's the name?' Kane asked.

'I don't know,' the rodent-faced informant said. 'Just "the store".'

During the months in which Pat Kane was trying to piece together the work of the B&E gang, Richard was particularly busy killing people. During those months alone, he filled 15 murder contracts, all Mafia-sanctioned hits. Richard took all these victims to his garage/warehouse in North Bergen. It was an absolutely desolate area at night, perfect for Richard's requirements, and he beat to death the 15 men. He could have shot them or cut their throats, but he opted to kill them with his hands, beat them with a crowbar, a long screwdriver, hammers and pipes. He also used the screwdriver, 15 inches long and quite thick, to stab them and destroy their spines so they were paralysed but still alive, and he beat them further still while they couldn't move.

I was on a tear, he explained. *I was beating them to death and enjoying it. It was . . . more personal, you know, intimate, and I . . . I needed the exercise. I was also doing it, I mean beating them to death, to get out my frustrations, my anger – my hatred, I guess you could say, at the world.*

Richard taped the mouths of most of these victims so they couldn't scream while he smashed and beat and destroyed their bodies. He had bought a truckload of 55-gallon metal drums, which he stored in the garage. This space was wide enough to hold three cars. There was a hosepipe connected to a water supply, and Richard used it to wash away the blood on the floor, though there were bloodstains all over the walls and on the ceiling too.

THE ICE MAN

Richard got rid of these fifteen victims in two ways: inspired by DeMeo, he was now bleeding the bodies dry, then dismembering them, severing arms and legs at the joints so he didn't have to cut through bones. *It's easier that way.* Some of these victims he wrapped up in black plastic bags before depositing different pieces in various dumpsters he came upon. Most of them, however, he placed in the 55-gallon drums in several pieces; then he cut grapefruit-sized round holes in the drums and sealed them tight by welding the metal top on. He had learned to do this because George Malliband had been discovered behind the factory in Jersey City when the top of the drum had popped off; that would not happen again. Richard then placed the drum into his van, drove through the Lincoln Tunnel and returned to his old hunting ground, Manhattan's West Side. Here there were miles of rotting piers where he could reverse right up to the water, open the rear of the van and throw the barrels directly into the Hudson River. Because of the holes in the drums, they sank right away, and in no time crabs – exceedingly efficient scavengers – began to feast on the flesh of the bodies inside the drums, easily able to get in and out, ultimately taking every bit of flesh. Because the barrels were metal, Richard knew, the salt water quickly corroded them, and the bones would be taken away by the currents of the river. Richard got this idea from watching people going crabbing along the river and from a pirate movie in which people were fed to crabs. Thus Richard developed another unique way of disposing of bodies. He chose to come to Manhattan's West Side because there was so much traffic, he explained, so many vans and trucks; here, he knew, he could blend in. The piers and docks along Jersey City and Hoboken were abandoned at night, but he was more likely to get stopped by a nosy cop. On the West Side, he became one with the constant hurly-burly of the city.

Interesting how Richard kept returning to the West Side, his original killing field, as though it were his alma mater, the place where he'd gone to homicide school and graduated with honours, with a doctorate in murder.

That Christmas was a joyous time in the Kuklinski home. This was Barbara's favourite holiday. She went all out to decorate a beautiful tree and surround it with a lot of expensive gifts, all carefully wrapped, adorned with bows and fancy paper. Barbara painted Christmas scenes on the front windows, a waving Santa, reindeer, snowy hills with smiling children. Barbara and the children put up lights outside the house. Richard didn't help with any of this. He gladly bought whatever Barbara wanted, but he didn't pitch in. He seemed to both love and loathe Christmas. When it was time to pick out the tree, Barbara and Richard went to a tree farm, and he held up different ones so she could decide which was best. About this, Barbara was the boss. About all things relevant to the holidays, she was the boss. She chose a huge tree, as usual, and Richard dutifully carried it to the car, then into the house, where he put it into an oversized stand. Barbara and the kids had carefully, lovingly, decorated the tree, as Richard watched, seeming to enjoy it but not participating. Barbara would have preferred it if he weren't there, because with him present, there was tension. One never knew, she says, when he could go off. Barbara had Christmas carols playing on the stereo, Johnny Mathis and Barbra Streisand singing the Christmas classics.

Daughter Merrick now had a steady boyfriend, Richie Peterson, and he too helped decorate the tree. Richie was 6 ft 6 in., had blond hair and blue eyes. Richard seemed to like him, though in the near future Peterson would finger Richard and talk up a storm.

That Christmas Eve, Barbara had prepared her customary feast of all kinds of fish. Richard acted . . . strange; he had extreme highs and lows. Christmas reminded him of his childhood, of Stanley – the abuse, Florian's loss – and he inevitably became depressed. On the other hand, he very much enjoyed buying gifts for the children, watching the decorating. Nothing was too good for his children. He gave Barbara whatever money she said she needed. No problem. No questions. Take it.

THE ICE MAN

Barbara knew well how Richard could become quiet and gloomy during the holidays, just sit in his big easy chair and stare at the floor; stare as if he were seeing things from a long time ago; stare as if he were seeing something – someone – he wanted to hurt. Barbara did her best to keep the mood happy, but with Richard it was an uphill battle.

On Christmas morning, Barbara's mother and her boyfriend, Primo, came over early, to be there when they opened their gifts. Richard put on a red Santa hat and a red Santa jacket and happily gave out the gifts. This he seemed to enjoy immensely. He'd pick up a gift, read out the name on it and, smiling, hand the present out. This, for Richard, was a joyous time, what he had pined for as a child and never had. This was the best life could offer: to be surrounded by a loving family, everyone happy and smiling and filled with good cheer.

After the opening of the gifts, Richard took the whole family for breakfast at the Seville Diner in Westwood. Merrick's boyfriend, Richie Peterson, was there too. Barbara had given him a blue cashmere sweater for Christmas, which he proudly wore now. Merrick was a full 6 ft tall, and she and Richie were an attractive, though imposing, couple, wherever they went.

Later, they sat down to Christmas dinner, a six-course feast that consisted of antipasti, shrimp cocktails, salad, ham and roast beef, rosemary potatoes, stuffed artichokes and mushrooms, followed by pastries, fruit, coffee and nuts, as was the Italian custom. They then played bingo.

Life for the Kuklinskis that Christmas was good, filled with a lot of nice presents, warm feelings, much love.

That Christmas evening, Pat Kane dipped a somewhat stale cinnamon doughnut into a plastic container of lukewarm coffee. He was in his car, watching Danny Deppner's apartment, hoping he'd show up.

Pat missed his wife and children dearly – it was the first Christmas away from them – but he was a man with a mission.

He was sure he was onto something big here yet still wasn't sure what the hell it was. The chill late-December wind blew hard. The bare arthritic branches of trees shook violently. Deppner didn't show up the whole night. Over the next several days, Kane looked for him in all his haunts but couldn't find even a trace of him.

On 3 January, at 9.00 a.m., Pat Kane was in his office going over a burglary report when the phone rang. Kane had let all surrounding police jurisdictions know that he was looking for Smith and Deppner. A cop from nearby Franklin was calling.

'Pat,' he said, 'I got Danny Deppner's wife sitting here, and she's all bent out of shape – kind of hysterical.'

'Why?'

'Pat, I think we got a homicide here. Can you come over?'

'Homicide . . . sure, I'm on my way,' Kane said, and got in his car and sped over to the police station in Franklin, one town away. Not anticipating the violent storm he was walking into, Kane entered the barracks-like structure.

Barbara Deppner was a small, frail woman with dirty blond hair. She might have been attractive once, but now she looked worn out, beaten up, haggard – as if she hadn't slept for a long time, hadn't eaten well for longer. All of life's cruelties, it seemed, had manifested themselves on her face. She had deep lines around her narrow lips, dark circles under puffy eyes, bad teeth; she seemed dirty. She had had eight children with a series of different men, one of whom was Danny Deppner. Pat soon learned she was the girlfriend of Percy House, who was still in jail, still refusing to talk. Barbara was, in fact, pregnant with House's child.

Kane, as was his way, politely introduced himself and sat down, and Barbara Deppner began to pull open the curtain on one of the most horrific, sensational crime stories Pat Kane, indeed anyone in law enforcement, had ever heard. This was only the beginning, the first act in a violent Shakespearean tragedy that would span 47 years – since the murder of Florian Kuklinski, the murder of Charley Lane.

Barbara Deppner said, 'I heard from Danny. He's hiding from the police. After Percy was arrested, they took off. They had to. They are deathly afraid of him. He's the devil!'

'Who?' Kane asked, curiosity creasing his wide brow.

'Richard Kuklinski. He's a killer. I mean, that's what he does – he kills people!' she said.

'Is he a big man? Do they call him Big Rich?' Kane asked.

'Yeah, that's him. First, Kuklinski helped them, I mean hid them. He didn't want the police, you know, you guys to find them. He put them in this hotel and told them to stay put. But Gary disobeyed! Gary went to see his little daughter, hitch-hiked. Kuklinski found out, and he killed him. He murdered Gary for seeing his kid.'

'Killed him . . . I don't understand. Why?'

''Cause he disobeyed Kuklinski. I'm telling you, he's a real killer, he's the devil,' she said.

Kane noticed that her hands were trembling as she spoke. He didn't know if she was telling him the truth or not, but she certainly seemed to believe it was the truth. She was, it was obvious, *scared stiff*, Kane would later explain.

It was this fear that prompted Barbara to flee her home and go to stay with her sister, which ultimately brought her to the attention of the police. When Barbara's sister heard why Barbara was scared, she demanded that Barbara leave, fearing she would get killed too. They argued. A neighbour called the police. Barbara told her story to them, and she was brought in for further questioning. Barbara continued: 'So Kuklinski found out. He came to the room that night. He had three hamburgers with him. Two of them had pickles, one didn't. Gary ate this one. In minutes, he began choking, got all blue, and fell on the floor.'

'Danny told you this?' Kane asked, incredulous.

'Yeah. Kuklinski poisoned the hamburger, see. That's

what I'm sayin'. He's a killer. A professional killer . . . do you understand?'

'Yes,' Kane said, though he was having trouble wrapping his mind around all this. Why would someone kill because of a series of burglaries? What was that about? How could it be?

'But Gary was still alive, and Kuklinski made Danny choke Gary to death with a wire, a wire from a lamp there in the room. He told me, Danny told me.'

'What hotel?'

'The York Motel just outside the Lincoln Tunnel. Room 31,' she said with certainty. 'So Danny did it, did what Kuklinski said. He choked Gary to death with the wire.'

'Really?' Kane said, beginning to believe her, sensing she was telling the truth but still wary.

'Yeah, really,' she said.

This was a hard pill to swallow. Why, Kane wondered, would this Kuklinski guy kill Gary Smith, risk a murder charge, when all that was going on here was burglary? It didn't make sense. Though one look at Barbara, her trembling hands, her worried face, told Kane what she said was true.

'Where . . . where's Gary Smith now?' he asked.

'They left him there, in room 31, under the freaking bed. He was found there, by the police. Check if you don't believe me. Go ahead,' she said. 'Check.'

Kane immediately took her up on this, picked up the phone and called the North Bergen police.

When Percy House was first arrested and Danny and Gary were indicted, Richard knew he had to take fast, decisive action. Already, he regretted ever getting involved with Percy House and this motley crew, but House was Phil Solimene's brother-in-law, Phil had vouched for him seven ways from Sunday, and, little by little, over a period of several years, Richard had become more and more involved with them – and now it was all coming back to haunt him.

THE ICE MAN

At first, Richard tried to help Gary and Danny, to hide them from the police. He did in fact put them up in the York Motel, paid for them to stay there, warned them in no uncertain terms to stay put. But Gary went to see his five-year-old daughter. Richard knew he could have been spotted by the police and picked up, so Gary had to go. As far as Richard was concerned, Gary killed himself by disobeying him. Richard went to a diner near the hotel, bought three hamburgers, sprinkled cyanide on Gary's, went to the hotel, acting all warm and friendly, served up the burgers and sat down to eat with Danny and Gary as if he were a good friend, when in truth he was the grim reaper. Richard had become quite the actor. He could fool the stripes off a zebra if he put his mind to it. Almost immediately, Gary succumbed to the poison, fell over, had spasms, turned blue but didn't die, and Richard had Danny strangle him, so Danny would, by extension, be guilty of the murder, part of it, and keep quiet about it.

Then, after the deed was done, Richard made another mistake, as he had with George Malliband: he didn't permanently dispose of Gary's body. He foolishly had Danny stash it under the bed. Though he carefully wiped the place clear of prints, they left Gary there like that, dead, as blue as a rotting violet. When asked why he didn't dispose of Gary's corpse he said, *There was a security guy at the hotel and people about.* But Richard could have dumped Gary in a trunk and got him out of the room rather than just leaving him there to be found.

The room had been rented 12 times, couples had lustful hotel sex on the bed with Gary there, rotting away, and it was ultimately the stink of his corpse that caused him to be found and the cops summoned. Also, had he not been stashed under the bed, the incident might have been written up as a heart attack.

Meanwhile, Richard had Danny stay in Richie Peterson's apartment while Kuklinski let Richie stay in the spare room in his house. At first, he didn't want to kill Danny; but that would change soon enough.

* * *

362

Detective Pat Kane quickly found out that a body had in fact been discovered in room 31. That didn't necessarily prove that what Barbara had said was true, he was thinking, but it sure as hell pointed in that direction. He asked the North Bergen police if they'd return to the room and see if a cord had been taken from the lamp there. Within half an hour, they called Kane back. The cord was missing from the lamp.

Now, sure that Barbara Deppner had told the truth, knew the inside story, Kane was confronted with a diabolical homicide – and the possibility of another one. If this Richard Kuklinski had killed Gary for just going to see his kid, surely he'd kill Danny Deppner, and God knew who else. Kane first made sure to find a safe place for Barbara and her eight children. He then focused his energy on locating Danny Deppner, getting to the bottom of what had happened and finding this Richard Kuklinski. Kane couldn't quite get out of his head how Barbara kept saying Kuklinski was the devil, how terrified she was. It was *disconcerting*, he would later say.

Kane now directed his attention to finding Kuklinski. It didn't take him long. He soon learned that his quarry actually lived close to him, only two towns away, and that he was married and had three children. He found out too that Kuklinski was a film distributor. Kane phoned up the Dumont police, spoke to a detective and learned that Kuklinski apparently had a very bad temper: on two occasions he had broken the car windows of people whose driving had somehow offended him. First, he punched a hole with his bare fist in the windscreen of a car filled with teenaged boys, and in the second incident, a woman at a red light annoyed him, and he got out of his car and punched a hole in the passenger window. This was no easy task, Kane knew, punching holes in car windows, but this Kuklinski guy had done it twice. He was, Kane learned, 6 ft 5 in., 280 lb, and he was obviously endowed with great physical strength.

His curiosity piqued – the hunt on – Kane took a drive

over to Dumont. He cruised past the Kuklinski residence. There were two cars in the driveway. He copied down their licence-plate numbers and made his way over to the Dumont police station. There, he met a detective he knew and found out that, the year before, Kuklinski had been brought in on a bad-cheque incident, but the case never went anywhere because Kuklinski made the cheque good.

'But we took his mug shot.'

'Mug shot?' beamed Kane.

'Sure,' the detective said, and he rummaged through his desk and handed the mug shot to Kane. He was looking at a balding man with severe eyes, who sported a well-trimmed goatee. The Dumont detective made a copy for Kane, who soon returned to his office, pulled out a yellow manila file, wrote the name Richard Kuklinski on it and put it in his top right drawer. Thus began an exhausting investigation that would take four and a half years, strain Kane's marriage, cause him to be ridiculed by his colleagues; an investigation that would, ultimately, expose one of the most prolific killers in modern times; an investigation that would put Pat Kane in the crosshairs of Richard Kuklinski's .22 Ruger rifle.

Now, Kane knew, he had to find Danny Deppner, which proved to be a difficult thing to do. But he kept digging and soon found out that Richard Kuklinski was a large distributor of porno movies and had possible links to organised crime. He added this to the Kuklinski file on his desk.

For Richard, the killing of Gary Smith was nothing more than swatting a nuisance fly. Richard knew that Gary could and probably would implicate him in the burglaries, and he wanted to be safe, not sorry. As always, Richard's way of dealing with potential problems was murder, and thus he killed Gary. Now he had to deal with Danny Deppner. At first, he tried to help Danny, hid him from police scrutiny, but it didn't take long for Richard to learn that Danny had told his former wife (Barbara) all about Gary's murder, and, for Richard, that was reason enough to kill Danny, which he did two weeks after killing Gary Smith.

Danny had been staying in Richie Peterson's apartment, where Richard had been bringing him meals. When Richard made up his mind to kill Deppner, he decided to do so with cyanide. Deppner happily ate a roast-beef sandwich Richard bought him, and soon he was near death. Richard then shot him in the head with a .22 equipped with a silencer. The problem was that Richard had hurt his back and wasn't able to carry Deppner's body to get rid of it. Because of that, he said, he asked Richie Peterson, his daughter's boyfriend, to help him get rid of the corpse, and Peterson obliged. Richard told Peterson that Deppner had died of a drug overdose, and he believed him. Peterson erected fence posts for a living and was particularly strong; after Richard had wrapped the large, 200-lb body in black plastic bags, Peterson carried it to Richard's car. They drove to Clinton Road in West Milford and dumped the now stiff body in a desolate spot, near a reservoir, and there it became a feast for all manner of creatures that feed on the dead.

Paul Hoffman, the larcenous pharmacist who had been selling Richard lethal poisons for several years, wanted to buy hijacked Tagamet, a popular drug used to treat the pain caused by ulcers. It was easy to sell, and he kept badgering both Richard and Phil Solimene to find him a stolen load.

'I have cash,' he kept telling Phil, who of course reported this directly to Richard. Paul Hoffman was writing his own death warrant by telling the likes of Richard Kuklinski and Phil Solimene that he had all this cash he was so anxious to spend. Richard had never liked Hoffman. He thought of him as a greedy scumbag who would sell his own mother to turn a buck. If it wasn't for the poisons Hoffman had been providing him with, Richard might well have killed him long ago.

On 21 April 1982, Paul Hoffman showed up at Solimene's store, saying he had twenty-five thousand dollars with him and he wanted Tagamet. The going rate was thirty-six dollars for one hundred tablets. Hoffman believed he'd be paying nine. Richard had offhandedly mentioned to Hoffman several times that he might be getting a load, but it hadn't come to pass yet. He was, in a very real sense, setting out the bait. Phil now called Richard and told him that Hoffman was in the store claiming to have all this money with him.

'I'll be right there,' Richard said, and left his house and drove over to Paterson.

Richard knew a state police detective had been asking questions about him, driving past his house, but with both Deppner and Smith dead he figured, incorrectly, he had nothing to worry about. Percy House was still in jail, couldn't make bail, but Phil had assured Richard a dozen times that Percy was stand-up, that he'd keep his mouth shut. Richard had even given Phil money for Percy's lawyer. He was, he explained, *trying to do the right thing*. Richard was thinking that this state detective *smelled the smoke but had no idea where the fire was*, as he put it, and wasn't overly concerned now that Smith and Deppner were dead. He drove over to Paterson without concern that day. As always, he was armed, had two handguns on him and a hunting knife strapped to his massive calf. As always, he made sure he wasn't being tailed, made sudden U-turns, pulled onto the side of the road, sat there, waited, moved on. It was a nice spring day, a comfortable 71 degrees.

Richard met Hoffman at the store; they talked; Hoffman assured him he had the money, and Richard said the load of Tagamet had come in and that it was at his garage in North Bergen, where Louis Masgay was still stashed in the well with the ice-cold water. The garage was perfect for what Richard had in mind – sudden murder. Richard now drove over to North Bergen and Hoffman followed him.

There were some empty boxes against the back wall of the garage. Richard said they held the Tagamet. Hoffman pulled his car into the garage, thinking he was finally getting his hands on the much sought-after drug. The moment was right. Richard pulled out a .25 auto and shot Hoffman in the neck without a moment's hesitation. Richard pulled the trigger again, but the auto jammed and wouldn't fire.

Like a man possessed, Hoffman leaped from his car and attacked Richard with a lionlike ferocity. Hoffman was fighting for his very life. He was not a big or particularly strong man, but his adrenalin gave him nearly superhuman strength, and he fought Richard so hard he almost took control of the situation, even with a bullet in his neck, bleeding profusely. Richard finally managed to grab a tyre iron and with it beat Hoffman over the head, finally subduing him, destroying him, killing him there in the garage.

Richard was covered with Hoffman's blood. It was everywhere. Even inside his shoes. As usual, Richard had a change of clothes in his boot. After he washed up and changed, he put what was left of Paul Hoffman in one of the 55-gallon black metal drums, sealed it well and put it in his van. He next drove over to Solimene's store and offered to split the money with him, but Solimene told him to keep it all when he heard what had happened. Richard kept the twenty-five thousand.

Richard wanted to get rid of Hoffman's body, so he drove over to Harry's Luncheonette on Route 46 in Hackensack. He had a roast-beef sandwich and a Diet Pepsi and decided to put the barrel with Hoffman in it right behind Harry's Luncheonette. He discarded it there as though it were a used tyre that had outlived its purpose. For a long time, the barrel was there; a few times Richard actually had his lunch, a nice Harry's sandwich, right on the barrel. Then, one day, it just disappeared, and no one said anything about finding a body. Richard was amused by the whole thing. To his dying day, he had no idea where the barrel with Paul Hoffman in it disappeared to.

43

THE DISASSEMBLING
OF ROY DEMEO

Roy DeMeo had got himself into a heap of trouble. His egotistical, nothing-can-touch-me attitude had finally caught up with him and now had a stranglehold around his bull-like neck.

First, the senseless murder of Vinnie Governara had come back to haunt him. Nino Gaggi's nephew Dominick Montiglio had got himself into trouble because of drugs and wound up making a deal with the feds to get himself out of trouble if he gave up his uncle Nino – and Roy DeMeo – which is exactly what he did. Additionally, DeMeo was arrested for dealing in stolen cars, and he was responsible for Nino Gaggi getting arrested for killing Jimmy Esposito and his son Jimmy junior. There had been bad blood between DeMeo and Jimmy junior, stemming from a coke deal in which Jimmy junior believed he was cheated of several thousand dollars. The senior Esposito, an old-time Sicilian made by Carlo Gambino himself, complained to Paul Castellano that Nino and Roy were selling coke. In the old days, under Carlo's reign, this might have been a death sentence for Nino and Roy; Esposito was, in fact, trying to get them killed. But times had changed. Castellano himself had been taking a lot of money 'made off the record', and he ultimately gave Nino the proverbial nod to take out both Jimmy senior and Jimmy junior.

This, however, was not an easy task. The senior Esposito was a wily Sicilian. He didn't trust Gaggi, definitely didn't trust DeMeo. Nino finally managed to lure Jimmy senior to 'a friendly sit-down' at Roy's place. On the way there, in a lay-by along the Belt Parkway, Nino and DeMeo shot both Espositos to death, which proved to be a stupid, ill-conceived crime, for people driving on the Belt Parkway actually saw it happen, the police were summoned, and after a brief chase Nino Gaggi was arrested. DeMeo managed to get away, but this had all essentially been his plan, and he was now in deep shit: he had indirectly caused his boss – a Mafia captain – to be arrested and charged with a double homicide. A potential death sentence.

Roy believed his days were numbered now. The strain was taking an obvious toll on him. He didn't look or act in charge any more. He seemed like a beaten man, dishevelled, confused, drinking too much, a man about to crack; a man who might very well go to the police and try to make a deal for himself, for his family, to keep his money, for a new identity. The underworld knew DeMeo had a cousin who was a noted, highly respected law professor, Paul DeMeo, and rumours began to circulate that DeMeo couldn't be trusted, that his cousin was advising him to make a deal with the government. This numbered the days DeMeo had left. Men in all the crime families began sitting down and talking about the danger DeMeo posed, how much he knew; they talked about taking Roy DeMeo out.

Richard, of course, heard these drumbeats resonating loudly through the underworld jungle.

Detective Pat Kane's investigation was going nowhere fast. He couldn't find Danny Deppner anywhere. Barbara Deppner hadn't heard a word from him, and she kept telling Kane that he was surely dead, that Richard Kuklinski had killed him. But there was no proof of that, no body – nothing.

Still, Detective Kane believed that Richard was a stone-cold contract killer, a master criminal getting away with murder.

This was having a bad effect on the young Kane. His belief in what was right and just and proper was being turned upside down. He was beginning to drink more than he should. His relationship with his wife, Terry, was becoming strained. Even his colleagues thought he was 'seeing more in this than there really is'.

But Kane wasn't about to give up. He kept tirelessly working the case, kept looking into what he believed was the bold, insidious lie that was Richard Kuklinski's life. Kane knew Richard was liked by his neighbours, was thought of as a devoted family man. He knew also that Richard went to church every Sunday, was even a church usher. Nonetheless, he was sure that Richard was a monster, an agent of the devil himself disguised as a family man. Kane was a religious individual – he fervently believed in the Catholic Church and all its teachings and mandates. He was sure he was on a God-given mission to put an end to Richard Kuklinski's bloody career, a mission he could not fail.

Kane couldn't get out of his mind the fact that Kuklinski had killed Gary Smith with a poisoned hamburger because he'd gone to see his little girl. What the hell kind of man was capable of such a thing? He thought too about how Richard had smashed his fist through the windscreens of a teenager's and a woman's car over everyday driving incidents.

With nowhere else to turn, Kane began back at the beginning and went to see Percy House. House was still in jail, still couldn't make bail.

Percy House was a brutal outlaw, a sneering, mean-faced bully who abused anyone weaker than he. He beat up both Gary Smith and Danny for not following his orders; he beat up Barbara Deppner; he even beat up her children.

Richard didn't like anything about Percy House. One time he had seen Gary after Percy had given him a beating, and he looked like he'd run into a truck. Richard would surely have killed Percy House if it weren't for the fact that his sister was married to Phil Solimene. House had been stewing in jail for many months now, and his nasty disposition had soured even more, if such a thing was possible. Right off, Kane came to the point: 'I want Kuklinski. I know who he is and what he does. You help me nail him, I'll see to it that you make a plea bargain. Something you can live with. You help me, I'll help you. My word of honour. If you don't, I'll make sure you rot in jail! I mean rot!' he added.

Percy House was afraid of Richard. He knew how dangerous Richard was, that he'd kill as readily as he'd scratch an itch. But he hated being in jail; he wanted to be free, and he knew the only way he'd ever get out of jail was to talk, to tell what he knew, to cut a deal. Yet the prospect of crossing Richard was a daunting, unsettling thing. He took a long, deep breath and finally said: 'Look . . . I can give you some names. I'm not sayin' Big Rich killed 'em . . . but some people say he did kill 'em.' And House went on to tell Kane about the murders of three people: Louis Masgay, George Malliband and Paul Hoffman. He knew about these killings because his brother-in-law, Phil Solimene, had told him, and thus the investigation into Richard Kuklinski suddenly took on new life.

Armed with this information, Kane began to investigate these three killings. He did not like or trust Percy House, but he sensed he was telling the truth, though he needed concrete proof that could be used in a court of law. It didn't take Kane long to find out that in both the Hoffman and Masgay killings, Richard Kuklinski had briefly been questioned and had denied knowing either man. It had ended right there. Kane quickly realised that the fact that the crimes had happened in different police jurisdictions was hampering any kind of solid investigation from moving forward. Kane mentioned what he had to state prosecutor Ed Denning.

'Wait a second. Kuklinski . . . I know that name,' Denning said. 'But not connected to these murders. There was a grisly murder a while back, a guy named George Malliband. That was one of the names Percy House mentioned. He was found sticking out of a barrel in Jersey City. He'd been shot five times, dismembered, his leg cut off so it could fit in the barrel. A big man. He told his brother on the day he was murdered that he was going to meet this guy . . . this Richard Kuklinski.'

'You're kidding,' Kane said, stunned.

Denning continued: 'But no one ever saw Kuklinski with Malliband, and the investigation never went anywhere.'

It will now, Kane thought, and silently vowed that he would not rest, no matter what, until he got to the bottom of this. All things in his life would become secondary – his children, his wife, any other cases he'd been working on.

Back at his desk, Pat Kane wrote a meticulous report outlining everything he had learned. The file on Richard Kuklinski was growing. For the first time, someone in law enforcement was looking at the pieces, carefully scrutinising them, making sense of where they fitted.

However, when Kane told his superiors and colleagues what he had, what he thought, they flat out didn't believe him; in fact they mocked him, sniggered behind his back, made jokes at his expense. They sarcastically dubbed Kane's file on Kuklinski 'the Manhattan Project', after the atom bomb project, because the file had become so big, now containing crime-scene and morgue photos, maps and police reports from numerous jurisdictions.

Kane was right on target. Yet they treated him like a fool.

'Pat,' one of his bosses condescendingly said, 'you're saying you've got a guy here that poisons, shoots and strangles victims, cuts legs off too. There's no consistency here. Come on, open your eyes, Pat.'

Still, Pat Kane believed with all his heart and soul that Richard Kuklinski was a diabolical serial killer hiding in plain sight – a master criminal – and he was intent upon proving it. But how? Where to start?

Kane knew too that if he was right about Kuklinski, he and his own family might very well be in danger. He was sure Percy House was capable of telling Kuklinski about him. He knew Percy House might try to use Kuklinski to take him, Kane, out of the picture. With Kane gone, House would have a better shot at getting out of trouble. It was Pat Kane who had built the case against House, who had dotted all the i's and crossed the t's.

Kane's boss, John Leck, was worried about the young detective. He believed he was suffering from some kind of delusional fantasy. Resources were scarce. Leck could not afford to tie up one of his investigators in murders that had taken place in other jurisdictions, let alone murders whose victims were thieves and degenerate gamblers, the very dregs of society. Who cared? Leck put Kane's ineptness down to his youth, and he warned him to focus on other cases, to get over 'this obsession you have here'.

'Yes, sir,' Kane said, clenching his teeth.

Late that February, Roy DeMeo contacted Richard, and a meeting was set up for the following day. Richard left for Brooklyn a little after noon. He had a short-barrelled .38 stuck in his trousers, a pistol and a knife strapped to his calf.

Richard met Roy as planned at the Gemini. Roy didn't look good at all. Richard hadn't seen him in a month or so, but Roy looked as if he had aged ten years. He was gaunt, his hair was uncombed and there were aubergine-coloured circles under his eyes. They got into Roy's Cadillac, and as Roy drove, he told Richard about his concerns, about the cases against him, about how federal prosecutor Walter Mack was going to charge him with the murder of both Espositos.

Roy, Richard thought, seemed like a beaten man, a man at his wits' end. They parked in a desolate spot in Sheepshead Bay, and Roy went on and on about his troubles, how everything had turned against him. Richard had always viewed Roy as a tough, stand-up guy. But the man sitting next to him now was a mere shell of the man he knew.

Richard was concerned . . . indeed very concerned: after all, DeMeo knew the intimate details of numerous murders

Richard had committed. Sitting there listening to DeMeo whine, Richard remembered how DeMeo had pistol-whipped him, pointed the cocked Uzi at him, embarrassed him in front of everybody.

Rage soon began to replace any empathy Richard might have felt for DeMeo, and he made up his mind there and then finally to get even. Before DeMeo knew it, Richard pulled out his .38 and let loose, shooting him five times, twice in the head, killing him. Richard then struck DeMeo numerous times with the butt of the .38, just as Roy had struck him, cursing him as he did so. Richard opened the boot of DeMeo's car, threw him in it. There was, Richard noticed, a lamp on the back seat of the car. Richard knew it belonged to Roy's wife, Gladys, and he removed the lamp from the back seat and gingerly put it on top of Roy's body. He didn't want, he explained, anyone to steal it. He closed the boot and left DeMeo there like that, the lamp resting on his body.

As Richard began to walk in the direction of Flatbush, he had mixed feelings about what he'd just done. On the one hand, he was elated: he finally had his long-awaited revenge. On the other hand, he was sad: a part of him had taken a liking to Roy. They were, he knew, in many ways alike. Be that as it may, Richard walked on, glad DeMeo was dead, for dead men tell no tales.

It was a large, dark brown, mean-eyed turkey buzzard, and it was intently picking at something wrapped up in black plastic, violently tearing away pieces of flesh. By pure chance, a man on a mountain bike came riding down the lonely stretch of road near the West Milford reservoir, spotted the bird, slowed to see what it was eating. Through a hole in the bag, no doubt made by the sharp beak of the buzzard, the cyclist discerned a human arm, definitely a skeletonised human arm sticking out of the bag, seeming to wave for attention, for help. Disturbed, the buzzard took flight. Not sure if the arm was real or not, the cyclist moved closer and now saw a human head sticking out of the bag. It had a Fu Manchu moustache and missing front teeth. The bicyclist immediately went to summon the police, pedalling so hard he nearly fell twice as he went.

The police removed the bag with the remains to the medical examiner's office. As the ME peeled away the plastic, which has a tendency to preserve a body, a huge cloud of flies left the corpse, and then came hundreds of fast-moving carrion beetles out of every orifice. The ME found a wallet in the dead man's pocket filled with photographs of children. She laid these photos out in the hall of the medical examiner's office, hoping maybe someone would recognise the children.

Again by pure chance, a detective who knew Pat Kane and the case he'd been working on did recognise the children: they were Barbara Deppner's kids. Danny Deppner had been found. Pat Kane was soon notified. He hurried over to the medical examiner's office and quickly confirmed that the children in the photos were the Deppners'. Barbara Deppner was brought over, and she verified that the wallet and the photos were Danny's.

'I told you! I told you!' she kept saying.

The cause of death, Kane was first told, was strangulation, though there were no signs of a struggle, and a little-digested sandwich was still in Deppner's stomach, indicating, in Kane's mind, that he, like Gary Smith, had been poisoned and strangled. Then, however, Kane was informed that Danny had been shot in the head.

For Pat Kane, this verified what he'd been saying and thinking all along, but his superiors still – incredibly – weren't persuaded, and a very frustrated Pat Kane was just about ready to bang his head against a wall.

Who could blame him? To work off his frustrations, Kane beat a heavy bag he had set up in his basement. He went for long, arduous runs. What would have to happen, he wondered, asked out loud, for his bosses to see the light, to understand that there was a cunning, remorseless serial killer roaming free, murdering at will, when and where and how the hell he pleased?

Richard was concerned about Robert Pronge. He was beginning to think Pronge was truly crazy, completely out of touch with reality. The beginning of the end of their relationship came when Pronge asked Richard to murder his wife and eight-year-old son. As remorseless a killer as Richard surely was, he would not kill a woman or a child. For him, that was anathema, an unspeakable infamy, and he told Pronge just that. This created a chasm of sorts between the two men, and Richard was concerned. He had come to know Pronge as a raging psychopath, and he was thinking Pronge might very well kill him for refusing to murder his wife and child – for *judging* him.

The second issue that drove a stake between the two men was Pronge's plan to poison with ricin a small reservoir that acted as drinking water for an upstate community. Pronge said a man would pay him several hundred thousand dollars to do the job, which was to kill a particular family that used the water from this reservoir. The problem was that many other households used the water, and Pronge's plan would kill hundreds of innocents, women and children. This truly incensed Richard, who made up his mind to stop Pronge.

In mid-August, Richard walked in rubber-soled shoes to the garage where Pronge kept his Mister Softee van. Pronge had actually laid gravel on the ground so it would be difficult for someone to walk on it without making noise, but Richard used his catlike abilities and silently made his way right up to the truck. Pronge was inside cleaning it up. Without a word, Richard shot him five times with a .22 pistol equipped with a silencer, killing him, and left him there like that, dead, in his ice-cream van. It seemed appropriate, Richard thought. Pronge never knew what hit him, who killed him, or why.

After Pronge was discovered, Richard decided to get rid

of the warehouse, to finally get rid of Masgay's body. He now broke open the cement on top of the well head, retrieved Masgay's body, took it to a little-used area in upstate New York and left it there, wrapped in black plastic bags.

Again by pure chance, the body was found within several days, and the police were summoned. Interestingly, the frigid well water had completely preserved the corpse. Masgay had now been dead for two years, but he looked as if he had died – been murdered – only the day before. The clothes he was wearing were matched with his missing-persons report, and thus the authorities realised it was Louis Masgay, reported missing so long ago.

On the day Masgay disappeared, the police knew, he'd gone to see Richard Kuklinski with ninety thousand dollars cash on him. When word of this discovery reached Detective Kane, he hurried to tell Lieutenant Leck. The lieutenant said, 'Pat . . . Pat, you've made a believer out of me,' and he shook Kane's hand. This murder *finally* vindicated Kane, and he felt ten feet tall.

Now with Leck's permission and encouragement, Kane dug deeper and quickly learned that Louis Masgay was last seen on his way to have dinner with Kuklinski the day he vanished. He also learned that Masgay had been buying porn and blank tapes from Kuklinski. Kane now turned his attention back to the murder of George Malliband, spoke to his brother Gene and heard how Malliband was a heavy gambler, deep in debt to loan sharks and 'Mafia characters'.

Kane went for a long jog, thinking this out, trying to fit the jagged pieces of this bloody puzzle together. He had many good ideas while running, managed to see things in a new light – *from different angles*, as he says. While jogging, he had the idea of contacting the NYPD organised-crime unit to see if he could learn something more about Richard Kuklinski from them. He needed help, he knew. He was only a lowly detective in the small state police station at Newton, New Jersey, which had an absolute minimum of resources – a serious disadvantage, and Pat Kane had the good sense to know it. Kane's query to the NYPD proved to be fruitful. He not only asked about Kuklinski, but he provided the OC unit with Kuklinski's mug shot; it was shown to a Mafia informant – Freddy DiNome – and Kane soon learned that the photo was of 'the Polack', a proficient hit man who had worked with Roy DeMeo, who himself had recently been killed. 'He is supposed to be,' an NYPD detective told Kane, 'a specialist at getting rid of bodies.'

This confirmed what Kane had suspected all along, but to hear it from the NYPD OC unit was very sobering. It sent shivers up his spine.

How many people has he killed? Kane wondered, and his mind played over the long list of Mafia hits that had occurred all over New Jersey. With this new information, Kane became even more concerned for both his and his family's safety. If Kuklinski was a contract killer, what was to prevent him from coming after Kane, or his wife, or for that matter his children? Kane made sure to find out the licence-plate numbers not only of all Richard's cars but of his family's cars as well. With the information, he took Terry aside and explained that he was on the trail of a dangerous killer, a contract murderer, who lived near by, a ten-minute drive away, and he 'might', he said, come around looking to hurt him. This both troubled and confused Terry.

'Why,' she asked, 'would he come after you, Patrick, and not one of the other guys?'

'Because I've been pursuing him for a while, and I think . . . well, I think it's possible he found out about me.'

'You, I mean, just you?'

'Yes.'

'Why?'

'Terry, it's long and involved. Just suffice it to say that I'm . . . I'm concerned, and I want you to be . . .'

'To be what, Patrick?'

'On guard – alert,' he said. 'Keep your eyes open.'

'What about the children, Patrick? Would he . . . you know, hurt them?' she asked.

'Terry, I just want you to keep your eyes open, that's all. No. No, he won't hurt the children,' Kane said, but in truth he didn't know what Richard would do, what Richard was capable of.

Merrick Kuklinski's boyfriend, Richie Peterson, was becoming abusive. He first took to pushing Merrick around, then striking her and breaking things. As much as Merrick loved Peterson, she was not, she vowed, going to enter into an abusive relationship the way her mother had. So she unapologetically, irrevocably ended all romantic relations and ties with Peterson. He was heartbroken, crestfallen, pursued Merrick, begged her to reconsider, promised he'd change, but she didn't want to hear it.

If Merrick had told her father that Richie Peterson abused her, Richard would have killed him and fed him to the rats. But Merrick kept silent about the abuse, and Richard still treated Peterson well. It was out of character for Richard to trust Peterson – or anyone – so much. Peterson was young, not an outlaw and he had been involved with Merrick for a long time now. Richard thought of Peterson as a surrogate son. This familiarity, however, would come back to haunt Richard.

Chris Kuklinski was still asserting her individuality by having a lot of male friends. She would sometimes be fooling around in vans parked right outside the house with Richard at home; she would sometimes cavort with boys in her basement bedroom with Richard at home – just upstairs, watching TV.

Chris, of course, knew all about her father's bad temper, but she knew nothing about the second life he led; she had no idea what a truly thin, dangerous line she was crossing by doing these things. If Richard had caught her in these acts, he would have gone berserk and sent any male she was with to the hospital, or worse – a grave. This was a tragedy waiting to happen.

Several times, Pat Kane tried following Richard, but this proved to be very difficult. Richard's doubling back, making sudden turns, pulling over on the side of the road and just sitting there waiting made tailing him nearly impossible. Kane also thought about going into Phil Solimene's store in Paterson to see what he could find out, but Solimene knew Pat Kane through an odd quirk of circumstances and knew Kane was a cop, so he'd be sussed out the second he entered the store.

Kane came to view Solimene as a possible weak link, a way to get something on Richard, but the question was how. In truth, Solimene was a genuine black-hearted outlaw and knew very well just how dangerous Richard was, and he'd be loath to do anything to undermine Richard or help the cops in any way.

Though, with time, that would change.

Kane now turned his stubborn nature to Kuklinski's phone records and soon learned he had four different phone lines and ran up huge bills . . . several thousand dollars every month.

Upon closer scrutiny of Richard's phone calls, Kane realised that he had been making phone calls to Louis Masgay's number, which abruptly stopped the day Masgay disappeared.

'Interesting,' Lieutenant Leck observed when Kane brought this to his attention. 'Especially considering that Kuklinski denied even knowing Masgay.' As provocative as this was, it didn't in any way prove that Kuklinski had killed Louis Masgay, though it certainly pointed in that direction. Kane went back to checking the hundreds of numbers called from the Kuklinski home. This was gruelling, tedious work, comparing all these seemingly unrelated numbers, but, suddenly, one of the numbers seemed to jump off the page and slam Pat Kane right in the face. 'Bingo!' he shouted, and hurried into Lieutenant Leck's office. 'We got 'im,' he announced.

'What's up?' Leck asked.

* * *

Richard went about his business as usual. He accepted murder contracts across the country. He bought and sold hijacked merchandise, drugs and guns, distributed pornography from one end of America to the other. He rented an office in Emerson, Bergen County, now and started a new corporation he called Sunset Inc. He used the company to buy and sell lots of damaged goods and to sell counterfeit, knock-off items, jeans and sweaters, handbags, even perfume. Richard had bogus labels sewn into the clothing and sold it as the real McCoy. Wholesalers from flea markets across the country gobbled them up. Richard never brought home any of the pornography he dealt in. Barbara would never stand for such a thing. Once in a while, however, he kept loads of X-rated movies in the garage, wrapped in plastic, overnight. Richard's son, Dwayne, happened upon one such load and became all wide-eyed at the sight of the blatant porn all over the boxes – an exciting thing for any healthy teenage boy to see.

Dwayne had never been close to his father. Though Barbara and his sisters tried mightily to shield him from the truth, he knew Richard beat his mother, broke up furniture, tore things apart. Dwayne figured it would be just a matter of time before his father turned his wrath on him. He would gladly defend his mother with his life, and he often thought about just that – trying to stop his father from abusing his mother and suddenly becoming the target himself. Dwayne still made sure always to have weapons ready, so that when and if the time came to defend his mother from Richard, defend himself, he'd be prepared, ready for action.

But Dwayne had no idea just how dangerous, truly deadly, Richard was, and regardless of what preparations he made, he'd never be able to enter any kind of combat with his father and survive.

Richard did his best to please his son; he tried to be a good dad. He was buying Dwayne gifts all the time, mostly some sort of weapon: a sword, all kinds of knives, airguns, a crossbow. Not just any crossbow, but a super-deluxe one designed to bring down a bear, with razor-sharp arrows, made to kill, easily pierce flesh and muscle and break bones. Dwayne didn't take to any of these weapons, rarely used the crossbow – but he did think about using it against his father, indeed killing him with it to protect his mother. Dwayne was very close to Barbara, but he was by no means a mummy's boy. Dwayne loved sports and rough-and-tumble action, lifted weights and had a long, lean, muscular body. Dwayne's passion was wrestling, and he was very good at it, winning most of his matches. His whole family, including Richard, went to his wrestling matches and cheered him on wildly. Richard's attending Dwayne's matches was one of the few things Richard participated in that his son liked. Richard did not take him to baseball, soccer or football games, didn't go fishing with him, never did any of the things a father and son might do together. But Dwayne did enjoy it when his father came to his wrestling heats and cheered him on.

Richard seemed to thrive on family life. He very much enjoyed being home, with his family, cooking at barbecues, watching movies together, shopping for groceries, even going to church with the family on Sunday mornings. A healthy, loving family was what Richard had always wanted, coveted, and now he finally had it. Yet, his enjoyment, his obvious love of home life, could turn to explosive rage at the drop of a hat. He still struck Barbara, broke her nose, gave her black eyes. Though these incidents were certainly less frequent than in years past, they still happened. Both Merrick and Chris had grown into large, physically strong young women and would run to get between Richard and their mother when he had one of his outbursts.

Richard was bipolar and should have been taking medication to stabilise his behaviour, his sudden highs and lows, but going to see a psychiatrist was out of the question. He'd be admitting that something was wrong with him, and he'd never do that.

Conversely, family life was, he was beginning to think, making him soft, taking away his razor edge, and because of that he was becoming . . . *vulnerable*. But there was nothing he could do about it. The only thing in this world Richard Kuklinski ever cared about was his family, and he'd die, he often vowed, before he lost them.

He frequently fantasised now about making a lot of money and retiring from crime, going straight, buying a house near the ocean and enjoying the view every day, going for long walks with Barbara. Richard knew he'd been lucky for a very long time now, and somewhere in the back of his mind he knew that some day his luck would change, had to change – the law of averages dictated that.

Still, Richard did little to lessen his exposure, to step back and look at his life with a critical, rational eye. He plunged forward, intent upon one thing: making money, providing for his family and retiring one day. But he needed a lot of money for that, and the risks he was taking became secondary. They were a natural part of the landscape, and he accepted that. He vowed to be more careful, to plan and plot methodically and move only when the time was right.

Another potential problem for Richard was his explosive, homicidal temper. He was still getting into arguments with people about the way they drove, which could quickly escalate into sudden violence, even murder. Anyone who cut Richard up in traffic was taking his life in his hands.

One evening, Richard was returning to New Jersey and had just crossed the George Washington Bridge when he passed a tall, lanky hitch-hiker. The man tried to wave him down, but Richard kept moving, and the hitch-hiker gave him the finger. For some reason, this disrespectful gesture always outraged Richard; he couldn't let such a thing pass. He doubled back, taking a gun from the holster on his calf, rolled down the window, drove right up to the hitch-hiker and shot him in the chest, killing him. The hitch-hiker was found by a biker; the police were summoned. There were no witnesses, no motives, no weapons, no clues. Another unsolved killing for the homicide books.

Another time, Richard wanted to try out a new weapon – a small, black metal crossbow made in Italy. It seemed like a good assassin's weapon because it was so silent, so small, the size of a baseball glove, but would it really work, he wondered. To test it, Richard went out in his car looking for someone he could shoot with the crossbow. He wasn't angry, hadn't been drinking; it was just a test to see if the small crossbow would kill a human being, he explained. He spotted a man, his guinea pig, walking innocently on a secluded street, slowed, pulled up and asked for directions in his friendly way. The man approached Richard's car to answer, and in the next instant Richard shot him in the forehead with the six-inch steel-shafted arrow. The man went right down, the arrow in his brain, not knowing what had hit him or why . . . and was soon dead.

44

THE ELUSIVE MUSKIE

A man in Vineland, New Jersey, owed mob guys a lot of money – over $100,000. He was a hopelessly addicted gambler and a sexual degenerate and had got himself in deep with loan sharks of Italian persuasion. He paid his debt with a cheque that bounced – twice. Richard was asked to pay this man a visit. His name was John Spasudo, and he would wind up playing an important role in Richard's life.

Like Richard, Spasudo was a large man, but with long dark hair. He had refined the gift of the gab to a high art form, could talk the spots off a running cheetah if he had a mind to. Richard, however, had heard it all before, many times over, and did not fall for Spasudo's line of bull. Richard calmly explained the facts of life to Spasudo, and he did end up getting all the money due after a few days.

In the course of these days, Spasudo told Richard about this 'great opportunity' he had to make money buying and selling Nigerian currency and South African krugerrands, a coin made of pure gold. And he told Richard about an idea he was developing with Louis Arnold, a wealthy Pennsylvania businessman, to open a series of service stations specifically designed for trucks all along the interstate – a hotel, restaurant and garage where mechanical problems could be quickly addressed. It sounded like a reasonably good idea and piqued Richard's interest.

Richard, as always, was looking for new ways to make

money, and he listened to Spasudo with an open mind, heard more about how much could be made with gold coins and currency trading and was soon on his way to Zurich, Switzerland, with a whole new spectrum of opportunities before him, and a new list of victims to be sent to the grave.

Pat Kane hurried excitedly into Lieutenant Leck's office. He was sure he had found the rope they could use to hang Richard Kuklinski.

'Lieutenant,' he said, 'I have here clear, irrefutable proof that links Kuklinski to the York Motel. He called the place on 21 December, when Deppner and Smith were staying there. Let's see him try and deny this.'

'Good, very good work,' Leck said. While this was only circumstantial evidence and did not mean that Kuklinski had killed anyone, it did tie him directly to the place where Gary Smith had been found.

In Pat Kane's mind, it was further proof of what he'd been saying for years. This was not enough proof, however, to go out and handcuff Kuklinksi. More than anything he had ever wanted in his life, Kane wanted to arrest Richard Kuklinski and put him in a cell – cage him like the deranged animal Kane believed he was. This investigation had been very frustrating and disheartening for Kane. He knew Kuklinski was a mob contract killer, a distributor of pornography, had killed five people that he was aware of – Masgay, Hoffman, Malliband, Smith and Deppner – and he couldn't do anything about it, at least not yet. Kane was becoming quiet and morose. Terry could barely get him to talk, to acknowledge her or the children. He had always been a loving, extremely devoted and attentive husband, a doting father, but now he was like another man entirely: there, in the house, in the bed next to his wife, but not really present, not really a part of the family. *He was somewhere else most all the time*, Terry Kane would explain. Kane wasn't sleeping well, either. He'd lie in bed, toss and turn. Dark circles formed under his eyes. Sometimes at night, he'd hear a sound outside, get out of bed and go outside with a cocked gun in his hand. If Kuklinski came around looking to hurt him or his family, he'd kill him. End of story.

If Kane was going to get Kuklinski, stop his bloody one-man crime spree, he needed tangible, irrefutable evidence, he knew – the proverbial smoking gun, eyewitnesses, fingerprints, real evidence that would stand up in a court of law. Pat Kane went for gruelling runs, pounded his heavy bag, thinking only about this case, how to get Kuklinski off the streets. He fantasised often about getting into a shoot-out with Kuklinski and killing him. Kane was an excellent shot and wished he could face Kuklinski man to man. He believed that if anyone needed killing, it was surely Richard Kuklinski. But Kane knew such a thing was not possible. He had played it straight, within the rules and regulations of society, his whole life, and he wasn't about to change now, become a killer, because of Kuklinski. Still, he wished Kuklinski would give him cause to shoot him down like the rabid dog Kane was sure he was.

It was while fishing for muskellunge one Sunday – his favourite pastime – that an idea first came to Kane that could, he believed, move the investigation forward, perhaps even bring it to a successful conclusion. The muskellunge is a very clever, some say cunning, predator in the pike family. Known as 'muskies', these fish live in hard-to-reach spots in freshwater lakes. They are very hard to catch, cannot be fooled easily by lures and baits. They can grow to six feet in length, are fast and furious and have razor-like teeth. They are so vicious that they not only feed on other fish but actually attack and eat ducks, muskrats and other warm-blooded vertebrates. If there is a ruthless serial killer in the fresh waters of northern New Jersey, it is surely the muskie. As Kane was trying to catch the shadowy muskie that Sunday, with live bait, he first got the idea of using live bait to get Kuklinski.

Kuklinski was very much like a muskie, Kane was thinking – struck at will, was cunning, a hard-to-catch killer.

Yes, what Kane needed to get Kuklinski was live bait, a

beguiling decoy that could fool him and snare him. Pat Kane started asking around about a man who could get close to Kuklinski, an adept undercover cop who could draw him out into the open.

John Spasudo also had his fingers in many pies. His passport had been taken away because he was on bail in a forgery case, so he had asked Richard to go overseas to consummate this currency-exchange deal. Some crooked Nigerian government officials had stolen a lot of cash and managed to get it out of the country, to Zurich. The problem was that the money could not be turned into any other currency because no one wanted it. There was, however, another government official in Nigeria who would allow the currency back into the country for an under-the-table fee of ten cents on each dollar. This official would stamp the money as legitimate and cause a cheque to be issued to a second corporation that Richard would start, which would be paid in dollars.

Richard liked Zurich. It was clean and orderly, and the people were pleasant and accommodating. He checked into a hotel in the middle of town, the Hotel Zurich, met the man who had access to all this Nigerian currency, a Belgian named Remi, a short, heavy-set individual with thick eyebrows. Richard was wary, but Remi took him to an office just outside of town, and there was the Nigerian currency, packed in thick plastic squares – 150 lb of it. Richard would have to take the currency to Nigeria. He was not too excited about going to Africa, but he'd go anywhere to make money. It was now arranged for the money to be transported back to Nigeria. Richard would fly on the same plane, which left the following day. Richard had always had a kind of wanderlust, and he was curious to see Nigeria, one of the poorest, most violent countries in the world, where people were still bought and sold, where human sacrifice is still practised. As planned, Richard met the official – a dark-skinned, tall cadaver of a man – and the money was quickly approved for import back into the country. Richard had to stay overnight to catch a return flight to Zurich. He didn't like anything about Nigeria, its disorder, its overwhelming poverty, its dusty roads, withered palm trees, harried street dogs that seemed concerned that they could become someone's dinner at any moment. To say that Richard Kuklinski, with his fair Polish-Irish complexion, stood out was an understatement. He was glad to leave the next day and hoped he wouldn't have to come back.

Zurich was just the opposite, neat and tidy and prosperous. Richard, as was his way, took long walks, curiously watching the Swiss go about their fastidious, ordered lives. The one thing that struck Richard the most, that still stuck in his mind many years later, was how clean the place was – not even a piece of litter on the ground. Richard found a park that was open all night and people strolling about without a care, no fear of muggers or being robbed. While waiting for the cheque from Nigeria, Richard had glorious meals, mostly by himself, but a few with his new friend Remi.

Remi told Richard about a second scheme he'd been working on: a man who worked in a Swiss bank would provide him with the numbers of Swiss bank accounts, even cheques drawn on these accounts. 'I am talking here about huge accounts of giant corporations and people who have much money to hide, people who could never go to the police – understand?' Remi said, his lips barely moving as he talked, like a ventriloquist.

'I understand.'

'We need an account in the States where we can clear the cheques. Would you be interested in such an enterprise?'

'What's our end?'

'Half must go directly to the banker; we will split the other half.'

'And all I have to do is open an account and deposit these cheques, you say?'

'Exactly.'

'How much are we talking about here?'

'No more than $750,000. Once the amount goes above that, the transaction will automatically be looked at more closely.'

'You're kidding.'

'I don't kid about money.'

'Sure, I'm in,' Richard said, and agreed to open yet another corporate account back in the States to facilitate this scam. This all seemed too good to be true, but Richard had heard of far more bizarre things, and he knew well the black-hearted larceny that lived in men's hearts and readily accepted the deal Remi had laid out.

The cheque soon arrived from Nigeria. It was for $455,000. Richard's end would be 25 per cent. Richard took it and went back to the States in the first-class section of a Pan Am flight, with plans for returning soon to Zurich.

Pat Kane walked into Lieutenant Leck's office and said, 'The only way we are ever going to get Kuklinski is if we get someone close to him. We are going to need a really good undercover guy. Someone who could fool him. Draw him out into the open.'

'You have anyone in mind?' Leck asked.

'I was talking to the chief of homicide in Bergen County, Ed Denning. He says he knows a top-notch undercover guy – he's with Alcohol, Tobacco and Firearms. What do you think?'

'Sure, give it a try. Why not?' he said, knowing Kane was right – that he'd been right all along.

In early April, Pat Kane drove to Trenton, New Jersey, to meet this super undercover guy.

45

HOW THE
FUCK YOU DOIN'?

Dominick Polifrone was 39 years old, had hardened, dark street eyes, full cheeks, a Fu Manchu moustache, wore an ill-fitting black wig. He was nearly 6 ft tall, a strapping, powerful man with broad shoulders, a second generation Italian American with dark olive skin. Polifrone was happily married with three young children. He had successfully infiltrated mob circles numerous times, had gathered credible evidence that had been used in federal courts to get convictions, and no one he helped put away knew he was responsible. Polifrone knew the walk and the talk, how to dress, what to say and how to say it. He had taken on the persona, the rough exterior, swagger, speech and mannerisms of mob guys. Often, every other word out of his mouth was 'fuck'. Pat Kane was immediately impressed by Polifrone. When they first met, he not only thought he could do the job, but do it very well; he was, Pat would later say, perfect, *right out of a Mafia movie*. He was indeed *almost too good to be true*, Kane said.

The two men, as different as night and day, one brash and bold, the other polite and introspective, sat down, and Pat Kane slowly ran down everything he had. As he talked, Polifrone's high, wide brow creased with curiosity, the furrows deepening as Kane spoke. Curiosity soon turned to dismay, then outright anger. After Kane had laid out what he had, Polifrone said,

'You mean to tell me this fuckin' guy killed all these people and is still out there fuckin' walking around?'

'That's exactly what I'm saying,' Kane said, his boyish face rock hard, his gaze sure and steady, filled with resolute, steely resolve.

'That's fuckin' unbelievable!' he said.

'Tell me about it. Will you help?'

'The question isn't will I help, of course I will. It's how do I get my bosses to OK it?'

Polifrone worked for the Federal Bureau of Alcohol, Tobacco and Firearms (ATF), and they did not investigate murders; homicides were not their jurisdiction, which of course Pat Kane already well knew, and he had a ready answer:

'I'll tell you how,' he said. 'Firearms – he deals in firearms,' Kane said.

'Straight up?'

'Yes.'

'That'll fuckin' do it.' Polifrone went and made a few phone calls, ran down for his superiors what Kane had told him, and within an hour he was given the green light. He and Kane shook hands.

'Let's get this fuckin' guy!' Dominick said, and thus a rare coupling between the New Jersey State Police and the federal government came about. This pairing would grow to be one of the largest state–federal law enforcement efforts ever, a task force unequalled in New Jersey's history.

But 'Let's get this fuckin' guy' was a lot easier said than done.

Richard Kuklinski was a very untrusting, dangerous man. He could smell a cop a mile away. It was a talent he had developed, indeed honed, from a lifetime of crime, stalking and killing at will, a lifetime of being an alpha predator in a very dangerous jungle, as he perceived his world. How, they wondered, could they get Dominick Polifrone near Kuklinski, let alone get his faith and confidence? This was the million-dollar question, a giant mountain to climb.

All excited, very pleased, Pat Kane arrived home that

evening a man reborn. For one of the first times in far too long, he was smiling, not quiet and morose. For the first time since this ever expanding case fell into his lap, Kane could see light at the end of a dark, treacherous tunnel strewn with the many rotting corpses of Richard Leonard Kuklinski's victims.

When Richard arrived home from Zurich that weekend, he was in a good mood. He was always in a good mood when he made money. The following day, he went to see John Spasudo and told him about the trip, how well it had gone.

'I told you, I told you, Rich!' Spasudo said, shaking Richard's enormous hand.

'That you did, my friend – that you did,' Richard said, and the two of them split the profit from the Nigerian currency exchange; it was a good amount, and there was the prospect of making even more money. A lot more money. Richard hadn't believed it would be that easy, but now he was a true believer, and John Spasudo was – for now – his new best friend.

Why didn't Richard just kill Spasudo, take his share of the money and be done with him? When asked that question he said, *'Cause I had a use for him. If he could pull this off, there was no telling what he could do, I was thinking.*

But Richard didn't like John Spasudo, and the more he got to know him, the less he liked him. For instance, when Richard met Spasudo's wife, Spasudo told Richard, in a winking, conspiratorial tone, 'If you like, you can fuck her,' which stunned Richard, who was still very much a prude. What kind of man, Richard wondered, offered his wife like she was a favourite golf club? Spasudo also had a girlfriend, Sherry, and when Richard met her, Spasudo told him he could fuck her too.

'No thanks,' Richard said, thinking Spasudo surely had loose screws and nuts in his head. Then, something occurred that completely turned Richard off John Spasudo, indeed, numbered the days Spasudo had left on this planet. Richard was asked if he could get a few hundred pounds of pot. As usual, Richard would sell anything to turn a buck. He turned to Spasudo and asked him if he knew someone.

'Sure,' Spasudo said, only too happy to show Richard that he had contacts for anything, that he was a man of many talents and resources; and Spasudo took Richard to see 'a friend'.

This friend lived in a nice house in an exclusive area of North Jersey. He was a *bookish, nerd type*, as Richard referred to him. He had a secret panel in the living-room, behind which he had neatly stacked bales of marijuana wrapped in rough burlap. Richard got 200 lb, paid the guy a fair price and put the grass in his van. Back in the house, the dealer asked Richard if he'd like to 'see his toys'.

'What toys would that be?' asked Richard, and the dealer led Richard and Spasudo to a narrow stairwell, hidden in a panel under the main stairs to the second landing. They followed him down a narrow set of wooden steps into a secret converted basement. When Richard reached the bottom of the stairs, he was shocked to see children, ranging in ages from seven to fourteen, boys and girls, black and white, about a dozen of them. They were all quiet and wide-eyed, forlorn and frightened.

'Would you like one of them?' the dealer asked, as if they were tasty, fresh desserts on a tray in a busy restaurant.

'No, no thanks,' Richard growled as white-hot anger slowly welled up inside of him. The soft clicking sound immediately issued from his lips. John Spasudo had a big grin on his face. It was all Richard could do not to take out his gun and kill both of them on the spot. He quietly turned and went back up the stairs, his wide shoulders filling the space, making a silent promise that he'd return – for one reason only.

Seeing the children like that had an unusually bad effect on Richard. If there was one thing he hated, it was seeing children abused in any way. It caused a flood of repressed memories to come to the surface. No longer smiling, no longer friendly, Richard stared at the dealer with icy disdain. Richard explained: *I couldn't get the sight of those little kids out of my*

*head . . . It was eating at me. I had to do something. I couldn't
stop thinking about them. I'm getting mad even now, so many
years later, at the thought of it – the memory, you know.*

Outside, Richard told Spasudo that he didn't approve of
such things, in fact he deplored them. Spasudo thought it was
a big joke. For Richard, there was nothing funny about it.

The following day, Richard left for Georgia to open a
current account to facilitate the cashing of the stolen bank
cheques. He wasn't sure if this was for real, if it would work,
but Remi had come through once, with the Nigerian money.
It had gone as smoothly as a Swiss clock, and Richard was
optimistic. But as he drove down to Georgia, he kept thinking
of the children, what was being done to them. He thought too
about their parents and families – how he'd feel if one of his
three children was in such a position. He put on the radio and
listened to country music, trying to get his mind away from
those children, what was in their eyes, the sadness on their
small faces, his own childhood, but not having much luck.

Richard was opening the new corporate account in Georgia
because he had sold a lot of porn in Georgia over the years and
was familiar with the place, liked its live-and-let-live attitude.
He had no difficulty opening the account, under the name of
the Mercantile Corporation.

As Richard drove back to New Jersey, his mind returned to
the children. He resolved to go back to that house the following
day, but John Spasudo called and told Richard that Remi had
contacted him and that he had to go back to Zurich as soon
as possible.

'Tell him I'm on my way,' Richard said, and the next day
Richard was on his way back to Zurich. Barbara was used to
these sudden trips and didn't think twice about his abrupt
departure. She says she preferred it when he was gone. *There
was peace in the house*, she explained.

46

'THE STORE'

The key to getting close to Richard Kuklinski, Pat Kane had long believed, was Phil Solimene, the owner of 'the store' in Paterson, and Richard's only friend.

Solimene was perhaps the only person in the world – aside from Barbara – whom Richard trusted, whom Richard considered . . . a friend. Richard had known him for well over 20 years, had committed every imaginable crime with him, including murder. Solimene even knew where Richard and his family lived, had been to the Kuklinski home for drinks and coffee several times, with his wife, Percy House's sister.

Because of Kane's constant pressure, Percy House finally agreed to be a snitch to get out of jail; he wore a wire and went to 'the store,' where he managed to get Solimene's son, Phil junior, to admit his involvement in a burglary gone sour in which an elderly man had been murdered, beaten to death. House also tried to get Richard to incriminate himself on a secreted tape, but Richard didn't trust him, indeed flat-out threatened to kill him, and Percy House hurried from the store as though his ass were on fire and never went back.

Phil Solimene senior also got himself in trouble with the law, and when Pat Kane approached him and told him that he wanted him to set up Richard, Solimene reluctantly listened. Also, Solimene's son was now doing time in a Jersey state prison, and Kane thought he might be able to use that as leverage to turn the father. 'You help us nail Kuklinski,' Kane said, 'and your life will take a turn for the better. You don't help us, and your life will take a serious turn for the worse. It'll become a train wreck. I promise you.' Because Kane had an innocent, cherubic baby face, a threat coming from him was unsettling. 'Plus,' Kane continued, 'I'll make sure your son does easy time closer to you, in Rahway instead of Trenton State.'

As much as Solimene dreaded Richard – and he truly did – he dreaded losing his freedom even more; and after several meetings with Kane and federal agents from both the ATF (including Polifrone) and the FBI, Phil Solimene, the one person in the world Richard trusted, agreed to help the authorities. The rope to hang Richard Kuklinski suddenly became a little longer . . . stronger; a tangible reality slowly swinging, as if in a soft breeze, above Richard's head.

Richard arrived in Zurich and checked into his hotel. He hadn't been there ten minutes when Remi showed up. They had an early lunch together in a four-star restaurant near the hotel. Remi said, 'All is good. We will have the first cheque tomorrow.'

'Really?'

'Yes, really.'

'How much?'

'Five hundred thousand,' Remi said with a straight face as he shovelled buttery escargots into his mouth with practised efficiency.

'I'll believe it when I see it,' Richard said.

'You'll see it tomorrow,' Remi said with absolute certainty. That would leave Richard and Spasudo – if it was true – nearly sixty-three thousand each, after the banker got his half and Remi his end.

'When? Where? What time?' Richard asked, not quite believing this; it really did seem too good to be true.

'I'll bring it to your hotel,' Remi said.

And sure enough, the following day Remi showed up at the appointed time with a cheque made out to the Mercantile Corporation for $500,000. Richard could barely believe his eyes, but there it was in his huge hand. All smiles, Richard said, 'I didn't think you could pull it off, but you did. You're a good man, Remi – good man!' He shook Remi's pudgy hand. Richard noticed Remi didn't seem that happy for a guy who had just made so much money.

'Is there something wrong?' asked Richard.

'There is . . . a slight problem,' Remi said. 'A complication, you could say.'

'What is it?'

'Our friend, the banker, was apparently working with another group of people, and they, well, they screwed him and then demanded more money . . . a bigger share.'

Greedy bastards, Richard thought.

'And they have threatened to expose him.'

'Really?' Richard said, thinking, *Ain't it the way?*

'Yes.'

Richard took another look at the cheque in his hand. 'Well,' he said, 'why don't you take care of them?'

'How? They're dangerous people. I think . . . I think they're gangsters,' Remi added, whispering the word.

'Oh, gangsters, you say?' Richard said, amused.

'Yes! This is the problem, you see.'

'This isn't a problem,' Richard said confidently.

'It is . . . You don't understand – they're *dangerous*. They've threatened not only him, you know, but his family too. His wife and children.'

'Really?'

'Yes.'

'Listen, my friend, you show me who these dangerous gangsters are and I'll take care of them.'

'You? How? Do you, you know, know some people who – ?'

'I'll take care of it,' Richard repeated with such certainty that Remi believed him.

'I can show you the man,' he said.

'Good,' Richard said.

The following day, Remi took Richard to the bank and showed him the official. He was sitting behind an ornate cherrywood desk adorned with brass lamps. To Richard's surprise, he was Asian. The fellow trying to extort him was supposed to be coming to talk with him at noon, and he showed up on time. He was an Arab, sported a well-cut Italian suit, silk shirt, fancy tie. He carried a Vuitton attaché case. He had a short salt-and-pepper beard. He reminded Richard of the actor Omar Sharif. Richard smiled to himself, but his face was as cold and white as a marble statue in a cemetery on a winter night.

The plan was for Phil Solimene to act as if he'd known Dominick Polifrone for a long time. Polifrone would take on the name and persona of Dominick Provanzano. He had a driving licence in that name, and there were bogus warrants for Provanzano if anyone checked. It was no secret that crooked cops were checking out police files and computers and gleefully selling information to the bad guys. Everyone in law enforcement knew this. If Richard had a bent cop check out Dominick Provanzano, he'd pass the scrutiny with flying colours.

The plan was for Dominick to start hanging out at the store, play cards, become 'a regular', as it were. He would, they hoped, be accepted by the criminals who made the store their second home. Phil Solimene would go out of his way to make sure everyone knew that Dominick was one of them – a slick, well-connected hood he'd known for many years, a guy with connections in New York's Little Italy, trusted and confided in by 'important people'.

It was now early 1985. Pat Kane drove Dominick to the store in Paterson in an unmarked van, wished him luck and watched Dominick swagger across the street and enter the store. This was, he was hoping, the first step in finally nailing

Kuklinski. Kane had no idea about Richard's trips to Europe at this juncture; he had no idea he was even out of town.

When, that fateful day, Dominick Polifrone opened the door and entered the store, he metamorphosised into Dominick Provanzano. Phil Solimene looked up, saw him and called out, 'Hey, Dom, come on in!' a big smile on his chiselled face, hugged and kissed him, and proudly introduced him to the regulars. Here, Polifrone was in his element. He was, in fact, a born actor, a smooth, seamless, natural bullshit artist, and he quickly made himself at home, played cards with the guys, a rogues' gallery of thieves and thugs – men who lived on the outside of the law, made their own rules, would steal anything that wasn't bolted down and hurt anyone who got in their way, outlaws all. With Solimene's obvious blessing and endorsement, Polifrone was quickly and readily accepted as one of their own. Every other word out of Polifrone's mouth was 'fuck', and he quickly let it be known that he could get *any-fuckin-thing*, any kind of guns, drugs, silencers, hand grenades, assault rifles. People believed him. Why shouldn't they? After all, Phil Solimene – *Fagin himself* – said he was stand-up.

Dominick had the natural gift of the gab, was a wonderful teller of stories and jokes, and in no time he had everyone laughing and patting him on the back. He dressed, looked and sounded the part. He had a Cuban cigar in his mouth. Even Bobby De Niro couldn't've been more convincing. Dominick's bad, ill-fitting wig played well into his persona, though he hadn't planned that. He wore this wig all the time.

When, that first day, Dominick left the store, walked across the street and got into the unmarked van, Kane was relieved. If anything went wrong, if Dominick was hurt, it would surely be his fault, laid at his feet.

'How'd it go?' Kane asked.

'A fuckin' piece a cake,' Dominick said, 'Solimene's good. He even got *me* believing we go back a lotta years.'

'Great,' Kane said, finally seeing a golden glimmer of light at the end of that foul-smelling tunnel.

* * *

Back in Zurich, through the crooked Asian bank official, Remi found out where the Arab they'd seen lived, in a two-storey brick house on a quiet street in town. Richard and Remi checked it out. Richard immediately decided against a gun or overt violence. He wanted this to appear like a natural death. He didn't want any kind of police scrutiny. He decided that poison would be the best way to go. He said nothing of his plans to Remi. The less he knew the better. The first order of business, Richard knew, was to make sure the cheque cleared. He promised Remi that as soon as the money was in the account, he'd take care of the Arab.

'I believe you, I believe you will,' Remi said.

Richard soon left for the States, went to Georgia and warily deposited the $500,000 cheque. He was uncomfortable doing this. He was expecting lawmen to jump out with badges and guns. But no such thing happened, and, to his delight and amazement, the cheque cleared.

Richard began asking questions of mob guys he had met over the years about the best way to move money. He also spoke to a tax lawyer he knew in Hoboken who did a lot of work for people in the underworld. With the new information, Richard devised a plan to move the money through a series of banks, one in Luxembourg, one in the Cayman Islands and another in New Jersey, to disperse the money so that it wasn't traceable. This was all before the banking laws were changed to make such transactions much more difficult.

Phil Solimene called a few times and asked Richard to come by the store, said he had some 'good action', but Richard was very busy now with his new schemes, his mind preoccupied, and he wasn't as comfortable in the store as he used to be. He knew Percy House had become a rat and was concerned he'd somehow be tied to the murders of Danny Deppner and Gary Smith.

Richard now thought long and hard about killing his daughter Merrick's former boyfriend, Richie Peterson. He was a weak link in the chain, knew too much; but Richard ultimately decided against it. He was fond of Peterson, as was Barbara. He'd wait. But he knew he had made a mistake by allowing Peterson into his confidence.

Richard had to get back to Zurich and attend to the Arab. He carefully prepared the cyanide spray, put it in a special sprayer, wrapped it up well and placed it in his toiletries case. He had to leave for Zurich the following evening. But first there was this unfinished business of the dealer with the children in the basement. Richard had not forgotten about them; he kept seeing their faces, and he could not rest until he *fixed this problem*, as he put it.

He loaded a .38 revolver with hollow-point rounds, fitted it with a silencer and drove to the dealer's home. He had a hard time finding the place but finally did locate it. It was near midnight. Richard slowly moved past the house. Lights were on on the ground floor. He drove down the road, parked his car, put on plastic gloves, then walked back with his long, fast gait. Without hesitation, he moved straight onto the driveway and towards the house.

Suddenly, a motion detector triggered and lights went on. Richard froze. The lights went off. No one seemed to notice. He quickly moved right up against the house and along it, avoiding the radius of the motion detector. There were deer in the area, and Richard figured the dealer had got used to them triggering the motion detector and had become complacent.

Quickly, catlike, Richard moved to the back of the house. He approached a ground-floor window. It wasn't locked. He ever so slowly slid it up and in two movements was suddenly inside, big and foreboding and deadly serious. He heard men talking and moved forward, towards the voices, on silent feet. Three men – the dealer and two others Richard had never seen – were sitting at a dining-room table. He raised the .38, took aim, quickly shot the first two, pop-pop, in rapid succession. The third was shocked, looking around to see what the hell had happened, when he too was shot and crumpled to the floor. Richard made sure they were all dead. He then moved straight to the door that led to the basement, unlocked and opened it.

'Can any of you count to 20?' he called out.

No answer.

'I say can any one of you count to 20?' he repeated.

'I can,' a young girl said.

'OK, good. When I tell you, start counting. Then when you are finished all of you can come up here. There is a phone right in the kitchen. Those men can't hurt none of you no more. Don't be afraid. It's over now! Call the police – dial 911. Then all of you go outside. The police'll get you back to your people . . . OK, start counting,' Richard said, and made for the front door, unlocked it and left, leaving the door wide open. He quickly made his way across the driveway, back to the street and into his car and returned home to Dumont. He felt better now. He was sure those children would soon be in good hands. That night he slept well.

In the morning, after he took Barbara for a nice breakfast, they went to feed the ducks in Demarest – coincidentally, the town where Pat Kane had grown up. Richard was in an unusually good mood. Barbara was pleased. He said nothing about his recent business ventures. She didn't ask. They sat by the calm lake on a green wooden bench and fed the ducks. They were always happy to see Richard. He had given many of them names. They knew him, and he knew them. Richard then dropped Barbara off, went to see John Spasudo, brought him up to speed, saying nothing about killing the dealer and his friends or about the Arab he planned to kill. After seeing Spasudo, Richard drove over to Paterson. By now, Phil Solimene had called half a dozen times and Richard wanted to see what was up. The usual line-up of suspects was there. As always, everyone was happy to see Big Rich, the king of the jungle himself. Dominick wasn't there. Solimene and Richard walked out the back.

'Where ya been, Big Guy?' Solimene asked.

'Been busy,' Richard said, not mentioning anything about

Zurich. He still trusted Solimene; he was just tight-lipped by both nature and habit.

'An old buddy of mine came around the other day,' Solimene said. 'He's got a shitload of weapons, anything you want – including fucking rocket launchers.'

'Really, where from?'

'The city, downtown. I know him 20 years. He was away for a while. You need anything, I'll hook it up – anything.'

'Naw, I'm good right now. Can he get grenades?'

'Abso-fuckin-lutely. He's got some kinda in with the army, I think.'

'What's his name?'

'Dom Provanzano.'

'Related to Tony Pro?'

'Maybe, I'm not sure.'

'OK, good to know,' Richard said, and ended it there. He had other things on his mind, bigger fish to fry.

Solimene asked him why he hadn't been coming around. 'Something wrong, Big Guy?'

'No, just been tied up.'

'Why don't you come in for the game Saturday?'

'If I can,' Richard said, and soon left. He did not suspect Solimene in any way. As Richard drove back to Dumont, he wondered if this Dom guy could get his hands on some cyanide. Richard had killed both Paul Hoffman and Robert Pronge, his two sources for poisons, and would soon need a new contact.

Richard caught an early-evening flight back to Zurich, checked into the same hotel the following morning. Not wanting to waste any time, he showered, ate and made his way to the house where the Arab lived, the convenient cyanide spray in his jacket pocket. There was a café across the street and down the block. Richard sat down facing the building, ordered a tea. He had a newspaper with him, and he began to read it, keeping the paper high so he could watch the building. He sat there for three hours drinking tea. Nothing. He got up to leave, slowly walked past the house, reached the corner, turned and walked back, returning to the café and now ordering some food, watching, waiting – intent upon murder. Richard was a relentless, patient hunter when he had a job to do. It was as though he separated himself from reality; he could sit for hours on end just waiting.

As it grew dark, the Arab did show up, driving a grey car, and hurried inside. Richard was pleased; now he knew he was still in town. Richard finished eating, paid the bill and made his way back to the Arab's apartment. He was planning to knock on the door and spray him in the face when he opened it. As he walked, he slipped on plastic gloves. However, when Richard was some 30 steps from the house, the Arab came hurrying down the stairs, an unlit Cohiba cigar in his mouth. There was no wind. The time seemed right. Much of successful contract killing was about timing, moving swiftly and decisively. Richard took the little spray bottle out of his pocket. The mark got into his car, and as he was bringing a lighter to the tip of his cigar, holding the flame there, puffing away, Richard was suddenly next to him – *psst*, a quick spray directly into the man's face. Richard walked on as if nothing had happened; he didn't even look back. He knew he had a bullseye. It was amazing how quick and agile Richard was for such a big man. He was there, he was gone, like a puff of smoke.

The Arab did die. When he was found and the authorities were summoned, his death was written up as a normal passing – a heart attack – just as Richard had planned.

When, later, Richard met Remi and told him that the Arab wasn't a concern any more, Remi was very pleased, and bewildered.

'How,' he kept asking, 'did you manage this?' his brow all creased with curiosity.

'I arranged for him to have a heart attack,' Richard modestly said, and no more, a slight smile on his face.

The following day, Richard opened a numbered account in

Zurich, took a train to Luxembourg, opened a second account and returned to Zurich. Now all he had to do was open a fourth account in the Cayman Islands and it would be done.

Remi gave Richard a second cheque, this one for $675,000, made out to the Mercantile Corporation. Richard soon returned to the States, drove down to Georgia and deposited this cheque. He went to the Cayman Islands and opened yet another corporate account. Then he arranged for the funds from the second cheque to be transferred to the Cayman Islands account, then to the Zurich account and finally to the Luxembourg account, creating a trail of money nearly impossible to follow. Richard next arranged for Remi and the Asian bank official to get their ends from the Luxembourg account. He then gave Spasudo his end.

If, Richard decided, Spasudo kept coming up with viable schemes, without trouble, he'd play straight with him. Spasudo told Richard how the dealer and two of his friends had been shot to death. 'It's a dangerous world,' Richard said. Nothing more.

Phil Solimene again called and invited Richard to the store. Richard said he'd come by 'when I can'. Solimene knew he had to be very careful with Richard. If Richard sensed any kind of set-up, a double cross, he'd kill Solimene in a heartbeat, he knew, and so did everyone else – the state police and the ATF.

Unbeknownst to Kane and the authorities, Richard again left for Zurich. This time, he had to stay and wait for a cheque for nearly two weeks. He didn't like being away from home so long, but he had no alternative. He phoned Barbara several times a day, spent a fortune on phone calls, but that didn't matter. It got so that he missed Barbara to such a degree, wanted to make love to her so much, that he flew in, made love numerous times to his wife and left the very next day, went back to Zurich. There were many opportunities for Richard to bed women in Zurich, Remi offered him various females, but Richard declined. 'I look but don't touch,' he told Remi.

Richard did not cheat on Barbara. He thought that low-down and immoral and wouldn't do it. He had, though, no morality when it came to killing men, feeding live human beings to rats; such things, in truth, didn't even faze him. But, infidelity? Forget it. He wouldn't do it. Perhaps that was why he could be so brutal to Barbara: he viewed her not so much as a human being with feelings, but as an object that belonged to him, and because she was an object, he could do as he wished with her. Barbara says, *When he was away, the house was . . . peaceful. The pressure, the tension he brought weren't there. Truthfully, I preferred it when he was away. The kids and I had more fun. We didn't have to worry about him tossing over the dinner table.*

Dominick Polifrone showed up at the store just about every day now. He had been readily accepted by the regulars. Sometimes he had suitcases with him filled with exotic guns and silencers, and people wanted to buy what he had, but he'd always say these things were 'already promised', though he assured them that more would be forthcoming. Weeks quickly turned into months, and they all came to realise that Richard was staying away from the store. Much of this had to do with what he was doing in Zurich. He did, however, just show up unexpectedly at the store several times – which he had always done. He'd walk in, shoot the breeze, maybe play some cards and leave, always when Polifrone wasn't there. The investigation was going nowhere fast. Pat Kane became despondent and began to think that Kuklinski was just too clever for them; he seemed to have a kind of sixth sense that kept him out of trouble, out of their reach, out of harm's way. Kane knew Richard was a stone-cold killer, yet he and the others could do nothing to stop him. In frustration, he came home every night wearing his 'work face', as Terry called it . . . sad and forlorn, the light at the end of the tunnel diminishing, indeed disappearing.

47

SPARKS STEAK HOUSE

Much change was afoot in the Gambino crime family. Paul Castellano was in serious trouble not only with the law but with his own soldiers, lieutenants and captains. It was now common knowledge that the feds had bugged his home, and he had been taped talking endlessly about mob business and making ridiculous romantic ramblings to the housekeeper.

Violent, sudden change was in the wind, blowing strongly from the Bergin Hunt and Fish Club – John Gotti's home base.

With the help of Sammy Gravano, Gotti hatched an audacious plan to kill Castellano and take over the family. This was, they both knew, a very dangerous enterprise on numerous levels. Paul was the head of a family, and this hit was not sanctioned by the commission (a must), as it had been with Carmine Galante. But, brash to the point of recklessness, Gotti was resolved to take Paul out and take charge of the family. Most of the captains couldn't stand Paul, it was no secret, and Gotti was sure that once Paul was dead, his transition to boss would be a relatively smooth one, that all the captains would quickly fall into line behind him, which is exactly what happened.

The year 1985 was coming to an end. The holidays were rapidly approaching. Richard Kuklinski had just returned from one of the many trips he'd been making to Europe when Sammy Gravano phoned him and a meeting was arranged at the same diner on the Jersey side of the George Washington Bridge. Gravano knew that Richard could be trusted. He had proven that over and over again. He knew, too, that he had no allegiance to anyone and that he was an extremely efficient killer who always got the job done: Richard never took a contract he didn't fill, a fact he was still proud of until the day he died. Gravano came straight to the point and told Richard he had a 'special piece of work' that would involve 'a boss'. 'You have a problem in any way with that?'

'I'll go see anyone,' Richard said, which was exactly what Gravano wanted to hear. Richard had, in fact, heard rumours about this very thing. Many men in the underworld were talking about Paul Castellano being capped: for his greed; for insisting that everyone report to him every week, giving the feds a chance to take photos of all the skippers; for not keeping his home from being bugged; for his scandalous affair with his Colombian housekeeper while his wife – Carlo Gambino's sister – was actually in the house.

A fuckin' infamy was the collective opinion throughout Mafiadom.

'It's Paul,' Gravano said.

'Figured that,' Richard said.

'So you're down?' Gravano said.

'Absolutely,' Richard said.

'OK, good. John'll be pleased. We'll never forget this, you know, Rich.'

'Good to hear that.'

'There will be a meeting – a dinner meeting in New York. It'll go down there, in front of the place. On the street. You OK with that?'

'I aim to please. When?'

'Soon . . . within a week. Your job will be the bodyguard, Tommy Bilotti. He'll be driving. He's been with Paul over 20 years. Paul will be in the back seat. Don't concern yourself with him – just Bilotti, that's your target. Other guys'll take care of Paul.'

'Fine.'

'You'll be part of a team. I'm going to give you a hat. You'll all be wearing this same hat. Anyone near Paul's car don't have on this hat, cap 'im!'

'Got it,' Richard said.

Gravano went to his car, opened the boot, took out a bag. He handed it to Richard. Inside was a walkie-talkie and a fur hat, the Russian kind. Richard tried the hat on. It fitted. It also made him look seven feet tall.

'Use something large – a .38, .357, OK? And wear a trench coat; everyone will have one on. Bilotti is big, but he's fast – take care.'

'He won't even see me,' Richard said, and Gravano believed him. By now, Richard's reputation as an efficient killer was legendary.

'Keep the walkie-talkie with you. If something goes wrong, I'll let you know, all right?'

'OK.'

'Thirty large for you, OK?' Gravano asked.

'OK,' Richard said, and it was done.

The few times law enforcement tried to follow Richard, it proved impossible, so they gave up on the idea. Thus, he was able to move around at will, unobserved. Had the state police and the ATF tracked Richard that night, they would surely have seen him meet with Gravano.

Phil Solimene was still trying to entice Richard to the store, but he wasn't coming. He'd say he'd be there but wouldn't show up. At this point, it was a foregone conclusion that Richard was not coming to the store because he knew something was in the wind.

Richard needed to go back to Europe, but he now had this business to attend to. In a strange way, he looked forward to doing this job; the challenge of it, even the obvious danger, appealed to him. He personally didn't like Paul Castellano – for his greed, for cheating on his wife with a housekeeper.

He regretted only that his job was to kill the bodyguard, not Paul. He knew that he could very well be killed because he knew so much, but that only heightened the stakes; he was, in a very real sense, gambling. Gambling with his very life. *The ultimate high*, he said.

Richard was now making more money than he ever had, yet he didn't save any of it or buy property, stocks or bonds. What he did with much of the money was gamble it away. The old gambling addiction had returned with a vengeance, and Richard was losing small fortunes at various Atlantic City casinos and in high-stakes card games run by the mob in Hoboken. He figured he took chances and earned it, and he didn't feel guilty. He was giving Barbara all the money she needed, and he felt he had the right to do whatever the hell he pleased, regardless of how irresponsible it was. Richard had never grasped how to manage money. You would think with age he'd know better, but he pissed away money as if there were no tomorrow – no consequences, no piper to pay.

That weekend, Richard and Barbara went to Archer's in Cliffside Park for a fabulous dinner, expensive wine. By coincidence, they ran into Phil Solimene with his wife, and they had coffee and dessert together. Barbara, with Richard's approval, invited them for drinks back at the house, and they agreed to come. In the Kuklinski living-room, as Barbara and Phil's wife were in the kitchen, Phil again asked Richard why he wasn't coming around the store: 'There a problem, Big Guy?'

'No, just been busy.'

'You need anything, this guy Dom I told you about can get whatever you want – amazing stuff, even fuckin' bazookas.'

'I'll keep that in mind,' Richard said, still not suspicious. He had, after all, known Phil for a lifetime, had done dozens of crimes with him. Why should he suspect him of anything? Richard later said, *Most all my life I had no friends. Phil was probably the only guy I considered a friend. I liked him. Barbara liked him too. I had no idea about what a low-life back-stabber he was.*

True, Phil Solimene was working on behalf of the police to set Richard up, but he had seen Richard kill Louis Masgay, and that crime alone could have nailed him. Yet, Solimene never told Kane or Polifrone about that, fearful that the police would lock him up as an accessory. The evening ended with handshakes, hugs and kisses, and Solimene and his wife left.

'I like them,' Barbara said.

'Yeah, me too. Nice couple,' Richard said, having no idea about the law-enforcement firestorm Solimene was bringing to his door, rumbling and gathering just over the horizon.

It was 16 December 1985, a day that would become a milestone in Mafia folklore. Paul Castellano was going to a long-planned meeting with Armand Dellacroce to offer his condolences on the recent death of Aniello Dellacroce, Armand's father. If Paul had had his eyes open, his ear to the ground, his finger in the wind, he would surely have taken precautions. It was no secret that John Gotti hated Paul, that Gotti was extremely ambitious. The writing was on the wall, but Paul Castellano didn't see it, indeed was blind to it. He'd been running the Gambino family now for some nine years – far too long, just about everyone in the family felt.

Sparks Steak House was on East Forty-sixth Street, between Second and Third avenues, a busy street. It was an upscale, expensive place, a favourite of Paul's. There were Christmas decorations in most shop windows. On the bustling corner of Second Avenue, a Salvation Army Santa Claus rang a bell and ho-ho-hoed. Christmas was in the air. The streets were filled with shoppers, people on their way home from work, on the way to meet friends. Paul Castellano was supposed to arrive at 5.30. He was a stickler about punctuality. He was expected on time.

Richard left home at two o'clock that afternoon. He was wearing a trench coat over two warm sweaters. He had the hat Gravano gave him in his left pocket, a .38 in his right pocket, two more guns in his waistband. He also had a knife strapped to his calf and the walkie-talkie Gravano gave him in his left pocket. Rather than drive to Manhattan, he took the bus. He didn't want to worry about anyone seeing him getting in or out of his car, or a record of his car ever being in New York. He had a peaked cap on. He was excited by the prospect of this job, its danger, its sheer audacity. This was what Richard loved to do – tempt fate, walk on the wild side, cross the thin, dangerous line. He felt no fear or tension, just exhilaration. He was a hunter going after big game.

Richard exited the Port Authority building and walked uptown on Eighth, passing numerous shops that sold porno he had helped to supply. He took a right on Forty-sixth Street and headed east, directly towards Sparks. The streets were crowded with people, shoppers, holiday tourists – busy people in the busiest city in the world. There was much traffic, the constant honking of horns, the metallic ringing of bells in the white-gloved hands of Santa Clauses on just about every corner.

Richard was, as planned, a little early, and he killed time by casually window-shopping, going in and out of shops, slowly moving east, timing carefully when he would be in final position. He had scoped out the block the day before and knew exactly where he'd position himself. Because Forty-sixth was one-way east, he'd be on the north side of the street, so he could move directly to his intended target from the rear. As Richard reached Third Avenue, he put on the Russian fur hat. The walkie-talkie came to life. Richard learned that Paul would be there on time. He positioned himself just across the street from Sparks and waited. No one noticed him, no one cared. Standing there, he had no idea who the other killers on the team were. That was no accident. That was the way Gravano and Gotti wanted it.

If anyone had a gun, it would be Tommy Bilotti, Paul's bodyguard. Richard would make sure he never had time even to reach for it, let alone use it. That was his job. He would do it well or die trying.

THE ICE MAN

For Richard everything seemed to be in slow motion now. Sights and sounds became sharper, more precise, defined. He waited. At 5.30 sharp, Paul's dark town car pulled up in front of the restaurant. Paul was in the back seat. The car stopped. Men in trench coats and those fur hats quickly approached, seemingly out of nowhere. Richard made his move. He began towards the car, crossing the street rapidly. As Castellano stepped from the car, two men in trench coats wearing Russian hats were there, rapidly firing handguns into him. He didn't even know what hit him. Tommy Bilotti had no time to react. Shocked, stunned, he was watching Paul get shot through the driver's window, not reaching for a gun, both his large hands on the roof of the car. He didn't even see Richard as he drew near and shot him dead, turned and quickly made his way to Second Avenue, disappearing into the confused crowd. Richard turned to make sure he wasn't being followed, the gun still in his hand, ready to kill anyone stupid enough to dog him. He was not being followed.

On Second, Richard hailed a cab and had it take him uptown, got out of the cab at One-hundredth Street, hailed a second cab and had it take him directly to Port Authority. He took off the overcoat and fur hat, paid the fare and calmly went into Port Authority and caught the bus back to New Jersey, innocently blending with hurried commuters and shoppers with packages. He stepped off the bus in Bergenfield and dumped the coat and hat and walkie-talkie in a dumpster, making sure to push them down into the corner so they would not be found. Now he calmly walked home, enjoying the crisp December air, glad it had all gone well, like clockwork. Gravano and Gotti had planned it flawlessly, he thought.

When he arrived home, Barbara and Chris were wrapping Christmas gifts. Richard had the dinner Barbara had kept warm for him. He then watched news bulletins telling how Paul Castellano and his driver had been gunned down and were dead, and that all the killers had got away clean.

* * *

When Pat Kane heard about the Castellano hit, he immediately thought Richard might have had something to do with it – the Gambinos were the family Richard had been involved with, Kane knew, and it stood to reason that he might have been involved. He called the NYPD organised-crime unit and ran this by them and was told that it had happened with such lightning-like efficiency that they couldn't find a witness who could give them a viable, comprehensive description.

'Just guys in trench coats, wearing all the same fur hats, you know, the Russian kind, that's all we have at this point,' he was told by NYPD detective Kenny McGabe.

'Was any one of them particularly large?' Kane asked.

'Can't say just now,' McGabe replied.

Still, something told Kane that Richard was involved. It seemed the kind of thing that was right up his alley. (He was right again.) He ran this by some of his state police colleagues, Lieutenant Leck and Detective Ernest Volkman, but both of them thought Kane was off base, clutching at straws – an amazing thing considering how Kane had been so on the mark for so long.

Richard didn't want to be away for the holidays, so he put off his next trip to Europe until after New Year. As usual, Barbara went all out for Christmas. She gleefully spent a fortune on gifts, cooked up a storm for days. As usual, Richard became quiet and solemn, but dutifully went through the motions of enjoying himself. He did, however, truly enjoy giving out all the gifts Christmas morning, as he wore a red Santa jacket and a Santa hat.

Shortly after New Year, Richard returned to Zurich. Again, he checked into the Hotel Zurich. He had become more and more friendly with Remi. Remi had delivered everything he said, was a man of his word. Richard had, to the extent that he could, taken a liking to Remi. Richard was still involved with the Nigerian currency exchange, but it wasn't as lucrative as the bogus cheques. And Remi had yet another scheme which he shared with Richard. He didn't know how Richard had caused the Arab to have a heart attack, but he was impressed, believed Richard could pull off anything. This new scheme involved stealing a huge load of diamonds from a Belgian diamond dealer. Richard took a train to see Remi in his home town, Antwerp, and Remi explained that he had an in with a security guard of a huge diamond wholesale exchange. Richard went with Remi to check it out. The place was in the centre of the famous Antwerp diamond district. Richard was amazed by all the gorgeous diamonds on display, had never seen anything like this, but he didn't like the set-up at all. *The security was as tight as a nun's ass*, he explained, and he didn't want anything to do with trying to rob anyone in this place. There were serious-faced armed guards everywhere, strategically placed cameras pointing every which way, and there was one main street in and out, a natural trap for anyone trying to make a quick getaway.

'This isn't for me,' he told Remi. Though Richard really enjoyed seeing all the diamonds, he wanted absolutely nothing to do with robbing this place.

Back in Zurich, Richard received yet another cheque; then he returned to the States, went down to Georgia and deposited it. He didn't know how long this cash cow could be milked, so he worked diligently.

When Richard returned to Dumont, there were still more messages from Phil Solimene. Richard called him back. Solimene again invited him to the store. Richard said he'd meet him at a nearby Dunkin' Donuts, got into his car and went to see Solimene. They hugged and kissed hello as was their custom. They discussed the killing of Castellano, how adroitly John Gotti had taken over the family. 'He's got balls and he's got smarts,' Solimene said, fishing for information at Kane's request. But Richard said nothing about his part in the killing.

Yes, he still trusted Solimene, but this was none of his business. Nor did Richard tell him about his trips to Europe; that too was none of Solimene's business. Richard said, 'Phil,

I'm telling you this as a friend – get rid of the fuckin' store. It's served its purpose. It's over now. It's time to move on.'

'You know something, Big Guy?'

'I know it can't go on forever. The cops are onto it. Fucking Percy House made sure of that.'

This was a bone of contention between the two men. Solimene had vouched for House numerous times and been proven very wrong.

'Look,' Richard said, 'I know people make mistakes ... that he's family, and I'm not holding anything against you. Just get rid of the store. That's my advice, take it or leave it.'

'You think?'

'I do.'

'I will, soon.'

'Good.'

'I've got this Dom guy I told you about. He's getting people some amazing stuff.'

'You think he could get his hands on some cyanide?' Richard asked offhandedly.

'Sure, abso-fuckin-lutely. Why don't you meet him?'

'I'm just so busy right now, and the truth is I already know enough people.'

As much as Solimene wanted to campaign more for Polifrone, he kept his mouth shut now, was very wary about tipping Richard off. To do that – he knew – was certain death. 'I'll ask 'im,' he said, and nothing more.

Still, Richard very much wanted to kill Percy House. With him loose, cooperating with the authorities, Richard was vulnerable. Richard asked Solimene if he knew where Percy was, if his wife had heard from him.

'No, not at all, Rich. I have no idea where he is,' Solimene said.

'What about Barbara Deppner?'

'I heard she was staying with a sister, but I don't know where,' Solimene said.

Richard figured correctly that if the cops truly had anything they would already have arrested him, and he soon left for Zurich again and received another cheque, but not before killing a second man involved with the Arab he had murdered with the cyanide spray. This man had an office in a new building in central Zurich. Richard heard from Remi that he was now threatening to expose the Asian bank official.

'How many fucking people know about this guy?' Richard asked.

'Too many,' Remi said.

This second fellow was a currency trader, a nasty individual with a chip on his shoulder, Remi told Richard. Richard contacted the man, made believe that he was interested in doing business with him, went to his office late in the day, and, just at the right moment, he pulled out a knife he'd bought near the Central Station and stabbed the man in the back of the neck. To cut the throat and carotid arteries was far too messy. Richard left the currency trader dead right there on his desk.

Considering the police scrutiny and interest in Richard, it's amazing that he could travel so freely, leave the country and return at will with no one even knowing about it. This was because the police had given up on trying to trail Richard.

Pat Kane walked into his house with a long face. By now, it was already late spring, and they hadn't made any headway.

'I think we lost him,' he told Terry. 'Everyone . . . everyone is right. He's just too savvy for me, for us, for what we're trying to do.'

'Patrick, you'll get him. Just don't give up. That's not like you,' Terry said, and he knew she was right. This wasn't like him at all.

48

WOULD YOU LIKE
SOME TEA?

By this time, Richard had grown to despise John Spasudo.
If he hadn't needed him, if Spasudo hadn't come up with
these profitable scams, Richard would already have killed him
several times over. Their relationship came to a head, in a
manner of speaking, when Richard went to see Spasudo to
give him money, his share of the last cheque. When Spasudo
opened the door, he didn't invite Richard inside. *Strange*,
Richard thought.

'What's the matter, do I smell?' Richard asked, offended.

'No, I just have my girl inside.'

'And so? I've seen her naked a half dozen times,' Richard
said, and walked right past Spasudo, sensing something. 'You
playing me, John?'

'No, nothing like that.'

Richard could see in the bedroom the form of someone
under the sheets on the bed, but the figure, he knew, was too
small to be Spasudo's girlfriend.

'Hi,' Richard said.

No answer.

He repeated, 'Hi there, it's me, Rich.'

Nothing.

Richard walked right into the bedroom and pulled the
sheets off the bed, revealing a naked young girl with frightened

419

eyes. She was, Richard realised with a start, very young, prepubescent. He could feel the anger moving up his body to the top of his head. His lips twisted, and he made that soft clicking sound.

'John, are you fucking kidding me here? What's wrong with you?'

'Just fooling around. I didn't hurt her. Tell him I didn't hurt you, honey,' he told the girl. She didn't answer.

Richard wanted to kill him on the spot, but he didn't want to traumatise the child. He turned and stormed out of the bedroom. Spasudo sheepishly followed.

'John, you're fucked up. Get her back to where you found her,' he said, and left, planning to do in Spasudo. The problem was that too many people knew of his involvement with Spasudo and that if something happened to Spasudo he'd be the first suspect, he was sure. For now, he had to be judicious, he knew. He'd wait for the right time: when their business was done, when he had no further use for Spasudo, he'd poison him and make his death look like a heart attack. But he had no more poison. *Hmm – what to do?*

Sammy Gravano paged Richard. Richard phoned him. A meeting was set up at the diner. Richard was on edge about this particular meeting. He knew Gravano was a killer; he knew, too, that he might be the next target. Richard was a direct, tangible link between Gravano and the Castellano hit, a link Gravano might very well make disappear. Richard armed himself heavily, for war, and went to see Gravano. He had a Ruger .22 Magnum sawn-off rifle with a thirty-round clip under the front seat of his van, three handguns on his body. He arrived at the diner an hour early, parked the van so he could easily see who came and who went – in case there was any kind of set-up in the wind. Gravano arrived on time in a black Mercedes. Just him and a driver. All seemed OK. Richard was still very on guard, ready for action, as he stepped from the van. They hugged and kissed hello.

Gravano congratulated Richard on his good work and gave him a paper bag with the agreed-upon thirty grand, 'plus a little bonus', he said.

'I appreciate that,' Richard said, and he did.

'I hear,' Gravano said, 'you do special kinky work too.'

'Like I said, I aim to please,' Richard said.

'I've got a good friend. His daughter was knocked up by this coke-sniffing asshole and the father wants him to suffer. To suffer bad!'

'No problem,' Richard said. 'My pleasure.'

Gravano told Richard he'd have the mark in a bar in Brooklyn on Friday night.

'You want me to grab him then?' Richard asked.

'Sure, sooner the better. John asked me to tell you that you did good. We plan to use you a lot,' Gravano said.

'Sounds good, I'm available,' Richard said.

Gravano told him where to be Friday night, and they shook hands, kissed, hugged and parted.

On Friday night, Richard showed up at the bar, wary and on guard, heavily armed, a fragmentation grenade in his pocket. This, he knew, could be a set-up, though his instincts told him Gravano's request was on the level. The bar was called Tali's. It was on Eighteenth Avenue. Richard had the camera with him, as well as the dart gun. Gravano was already there. He introduced the mark to Richard. The mark was about 25, had greasy black hair, *another guido wannabe whose dick got him into trouble*, Richard thought. The two started talking, had a drink. Sammy drifted away. Richard offhandedly told the mark that he had some 'good coke' he needed to get rid of, quickly putting out the bait, as Richard thought of it.

'Sammy know about this?' the mark asked.

'No. This is off the record.'

'Sure, I can move it. Got a taste?'

'Out in the van,' Richard said, thinking this was going to be easier than he'd thought. They both walked outside.

Inside Richard's van, parked just off Eighteenth Avenue

on a quiet side street, Richard knocked the mark unconscious with a jawbreaker, taped him up, covered him with a plaid blanket and headed for Pennsylvania . . . rat country. He didn't particularly like to drive so far with the mark in the back of the van, but if he was stopped by cops or state troopers, he'd shoot them dead in a heartbeat. He had a .38 right under the seat for easy, quick access. He did, however, stick to the speed limit and drove carefully, listening to country music as he went. A few times, the mark acted up, but Richard told him to be quiet or he'd beat him with a hammer.

Richard hadn't intended to do this any more – feed people to rats. But if Gravano wanted the guy to really suffer, so be it. It was convenient, easy to do and very effective. Richard was curious, still, to see his own reaction to this barbarity he had created.

By the time Richard reached the caves where the rats dwelled, it was nearly 3.00 a.m. He made the mark walk to his own grisly end. There was a nearly full moon out and it was easy to see. Richard knew the rats had acquired a taste for human flesh, that they'd be on the mark *like white on rice*, as he puts it. The mark tried to run but Richard knocked him down, made him get up and marched him into the cave. The stink of the rats was strong – a foul, pungent, fetid odour. Richard made him lie down, used duct tape and bound his legs together. He set up the camera. He could hear the rats towards the back of the cave, even saw a few of them, skulking about the shadows. The mark was moaning and begging. Richard turned and left.

The following day, Richard returned to the cave. There was no sign of the mark, not a bone, not even a piece of cloth. Richard retrieved the camera, set up a meeting with Gravano, went to Brooklyn, and showed both Gravano and the girl's father the tape. Neither of them could bear looking at it. Pleased, the father paid Richard twenty thousand dollars. Richard went back to New Jersey. A few days later, he left for Zurich.

* * *

WOULD YOU LIKE SOME TEA?

Pat Kane had to do something. The investigation was going nowhere fast. Richard had completely stopped coming to the store. Dominick Polifrone was in the store just about every day, playing cards, shooting the breeze, brilliantly telling dirty jokes, waiting on Richard to no avail. Kane went and spoke to Lieutenant Leck.

'I have an idea, Lieutenant,' he said.

'Shoot.'

'We need to shake up Kuklinski. We've got to stir up the pot.'

'What do you have in mind?'

'I'd like to go talk to him . . . ask him a few questions – see what kind of response we get . . . I'm thinking it's time we rattle his cage, Lieutenant.'

'Have you run this by Dominick?'

'I did. He thinks it's a good idea. Right now nothing at all is happening, Lieutenant. We've got to be more proactive.'

'Give it a go. Take Volkman with you.'

'OK,' Kane said, though in truth he didn't want to take Ernest Volkman with him. Volkman had been one of the most disbelieving of Kane's colleagues, had made wisecracks about Kane's theory that Kuklinski was a serial contract killer hiding in plain sight, had laughed the loudest.

Nevertheless, Kane went and found him. He readily agreed to go and confront Richard with him, and together they set out to 'rattle Richard's cage'.

By now, it was late August of 1986. Richard had just returned from Zurich. He was planning to drive down to Georgia come nightfall. It was very hot and humid when New Jersey state detectives Pat Kane and Ernest Volkman pulled up in front of the Kuklinski residence. Richard's car was in the driveway. Although it was nearly 90 degrees, both Kane and Volkman had to wear jackets and ties. This was mandated by the state police dress code. Kane was looking forward to this. For years now, Richard Kuklinski had played a big part in his life, had taken on a larger-than-life omnipotence, and for the

first time he was about to confront him – up close and personal.
Not knowing what to expect, the two detectives stepped out of
the air-conditioned black Plymouth, walked to the Kuklinskis'
front door and rang the bell. The family dog, Shaba, started
to bark. It was a loud, bellowing bark. The inside door slowly
opened. Suddenly, Richard was before them, his huge size
completely filling the doorway.

'What do you want?' asked Richard, looming in front of
them. Kane was taken aback by how big he was. At 6 ft 5 in.,
nearly 300 lb, Richard towered over them.

The detectives showed their gold badges and introduced
themselves.

'OK, what do you want?' Richard repeated, annoyed by
their presence and the fact that they had the temerity to come
knocking on his door unannounced. Nothing riled Richard
more than uninvited people coming to the house . . . especially
two grave-faced cops with obvious bad intentions. Richard was
wearing tinted prescription sunglasses, so they couldn't see his
eyes, but they could feel the quiet animus coming from them
like the August heat issuing from the sidewalks.

'We are investigating several murders,' Kane said. 'We'd
like to talk with you about that.'

'Yeah, well talk,' said Richard.

'Did you know either Louis Masgay, George Malliband,
Paul Hoffman, Danny Deppner or Gary Smith?' Kane
asked.

'Can't say that I do,' Richard said, realising now that this
was the cop who had been investigating him all along, the
cop who smelled the smoke but didn't yet know where the
fire was.

'So you say you don't know them?' Kane repeated, knowing
Richard was lying.

'Nope.'

'How about Robert Pronge or Roy DeMeo. Did you know
them?' Kane asked.

Richard stared at them, taken aback to hear Kane mention

DeMeo's name. Richard had borrowed DeMeo's car when he was using Richard's van, and Richard figured – incorrectly – that the police had copied down the plate number of Roy's car when it had been in front of the house. Richard had no idea until near the end of his life that Freddy DiNome, one of DeMeo's serial killers, had tied him to DeMeo.

'I know you guys saw his car in front of my home. You know I know him,' Richard said.

'You know anything about his murder?' Volkman asked.

'It's hot out here. Come on in,' Richard said, breaking the cardinal rule of the street: you never talk to cops.

The Kuklinski house was nice and cool, clean and well appointed, neat and tidy. Barbara was out shopping. The kids were off with friends. Richard offered the detectives iced tea. They both declined. They'd never accept anything from Kuklinski out of fear of poison, no matter how thirsty they were. Richard sat in his easy chair as the detectives sat stiffly on the couch facing him. He kept his sunglasses on. Kane looked at an oil portrait of a loving Richard and Barbara on the wall above his head.

'I know nothing about the murder of Roy DeMeo,' Kuklinski said.

'But you knew him?' Volkman asked.

'Sure, I knew him. You guys know I knew him. Why don't you like me, Mr Kane?' Richard asked.

'Who says I don't like you?' Kane asked, surprised by the question. The truth was Kane hated Richard. Kane truly believed Richard was evil, an agent of Satan himself.

'I can see that . . . it's in your eyes,' Richard said matter-of-factly.

'I don't take any of my work personally,' Kane said. 'For me, you're just work product. So you say you didn't know Deppner, Masgay or Smith?'

'That's right,' Richard said, daring Kane to prove he knew them. Kane, of course, had documentation that a call from Kuklinski's home had been placed to the York Motel, where

Gary had been found under the bed, and he now reminded Richard of that phone call.

'Really? I don't know anything about that,' Richard said, caught off guard that Kane had so carefully scrutinised his phone calls. He didn't like that. Now Richard knew for sure that this cop Pat Kane had been the thorn in his side for the last few years. A thorn he wanted removed. Richard stared at Kane with malice, though Kane could not see the disdain because Richard kept his shades on. They asked him a few more questions, to which they got evasive answers. Richard remained a gentleman, but he let them know he didn't want to talk any more. He stood up. They followed suit. He led them to the door. Kane couldn't get over how big he was.

'Thanks for talking to us,' Kane said as he stepped back into the stifling, white August heat.

'Any time,' Richard said, closing the door.

This really pissed Richard off. How dare these motherfuckers come around his house? How dare they knock on his door unannounced? Who the hell did they think they were?!

Richard believed that if he got rid of Kane this whole thing would more than likely go away. The murders he was asking about were years old – yesterday's news. If Kane was taken out of the equation, they'd stay old news.

He would, he resolved, kill Kane. That was the answer. Of course. You have a problem, kill it. The solve-all remedy.

It didn't take Richard long to find out that Kane worked out of the Newton station. He borrowed a van from John Spasudo, went and staked out the station. He spotted Kane leaving the squat brick building after his shift and followed him. He had the sawn-off Ruger rifle with him; he'd use it to do the job if the situation presented itself.

When Kane left Richard's house that day, he figured they'd done what they'd set out to do. Even now, he didn't truly comprehend how dangerous Richard was. He never thought

WOULD YOU LIKE SOME TEA?

Richard would really stalk him, kill him. Pat Kane was part of a culture in which police were not murdered. To kill a cop was, he knew, like sticking a pointed stick into a hornet's nest. It just wasn't worth the risk. But Richard was intent upon killing Kane. The question wasn't if but how he should do it – make it overt, make it look like an accident or maybe just make him disappear. He decided on the latter.

Richard followed Kane to a nearby bar called the Wander Inn, a crowded blue-collar place. Kane began putting away drinks while standing at the bar. Richard actually walked in and watched Kane from a darkened corner. *This*, Richard thought, *will be easy. The guy's a lush.* But it didn't take long for Richard to figure out that Kane was drinking with cops; the place was filled with cops, and he slunk out the door unnoticed, like a giant, silent snake.

When Kane left the bar, he got into his car, not realising he was being watched – stalked – and drove straight home. By force of habit, he checked his rear-view mirror (most cops do), but Richard was exceedingly adept at trailing people unnoticed and soon learned where Pat Kane lived with his wife and two children.

The thing Kane had dreaded from the very beginning had just happened.

Now, Richard thought, it was just a matter of figuring out how best to do this – dispose of Pat Kane once and for all and for it not to come back to him. To amuse himself, Richard took a bead on Kane with the rifle as he stepped from his car. *Bang, you're dead*, he whispered, though he didn't pull the trigger.

49

I'VE GOT SOME RATS I HAVE TO GET RID OF

The more Richard thought about killing Kane, the more he realised he'd bring a law-enforcement firestorm down on his own head. The link between anything happening to Kane and him would be immediate, he knew. To do this job properly, he decided, he had to make Kane's murder look like an accident; that was the key, and he was sure he could do it, but he needed poison. He needed the cyanide spray to pull it off, but he didn't have any. He began asking people he knew in the underworld in Jersey City, Hoboken and New York if anyone could get his hands on some cyanide. No luck. Richard's plan was to spray Kane in the face as he was leaving the bar after a few drinks; he'd keel over dead right there. Everyone would believe it was a heart attack. *Perfect.* Applied in the right dosage, cyanide was very difficult to detect.

He'd first give Kane a flat, then, as he was changing the tyre, he'd get him. It'd be a piece of cake. He smiled at the thought, knowing it would work. However, he was having a hard time finding high-grade, lab-quality cyanide. He had only one shot at this, he knew, and it had to work. There would be no second chance. Kane was armed and dangerous.

Richard was supposed to go to Zurich that Friday, but he put off the trip until the following week. He'd plot and plan Pat Kane's murder.

* * *

I'VE GOT SOME RATS I HAVE TO GET RID OF

Now, for the second time in less than a week, strange men came knocking on Richard's door, and this second incident upset Richard to the point of absolute distraction. It was, for him, a Waterloo of sorts – in a sense, the beginning of the end. It all had to do with John Spasudo.

So far, with Richard, John Spasudo had made a small fortune, but he was a degenerate gambler and not only pissed the money away but also indebted himself to drug dealers, to cocaine wholesalers. He was apparently taking drugs on consignment, selling them and losing the money gambling, and he had got himself into hot water with some Colombians. Spasudo had never been to Richard's home. However, by using a trace on Richard's licence-plate number, he was able to find out his address.

When the Colombians put a squeeze on Spasudo, he got it into his head to tell them Richard had their money, which wasn't at all true, and Spasudo actually took two of them to Richard's home. Spasudo believed Richard wasn't in town, that he'd gone to Zurich, but he was actually in the house when they knocked on the door. Richard saw them through the curtain – Spasudo sitting in the car – and was angry beyond words that street people, thugs, had come to his home.

This was not supposed to happen.

Richard had always been scrupulously careful about keeping the street, his nefarious dealings, far away from his home, his family. Now the street was actually knocking on his door, ringing his bell. He explained: *I realised that day that I'd made mistakes. I'd allowed what I was doing to touch my family. It was what I'd always dreaded, and yet it happened. For me . . . for me, it was like getting hit by a speeding train. I would fix it. I had to fix it. My plan was to kill them all. To kill everyone close to me – I mean everyone!*

As the Colombians stood there, Dwayne innocently pulled into the drive. The two of them approached Dwayne and asked where his dad was. They were friendly, but there was an undercurrent of danger, of threat.

'He's out of town,' Dwayne said.

That seemed to placate them for now. They told Dwayne to tell his dad they'd been there and would be back. One of them touched Dwayne's arm as he spoke. Richard saw this from the window and nearly exploded with rage. His lips twisted into a snarl. He wanted to run outside and kill them with his bare hands, but that would have to wait. He controlled himself, gritting his teeth, as the soft clicking sound came from his lips. They got back into their car and left. As they pulled away, Richard stared at Spasudo there in the back seat. Rage made his head spin. He actually had to sit down.

Early that evening, Richard went and found Spasudo. He was shocked to see Richard.

Richard bellowed, 'How fucking dare you bring those spics to my house!'

'Rich, I thought you were out of town. I was just trying to stall them. I'm sorry. I'm sorry, Rich!'

If, Richard later explained, he hadn't been doing things with Spasudo, he'd have killed him right then and there, got rid of his body – fed him to the rats. But that luxury, for now, wasn't his; Spasudo's days, however, were now numbered. Richard pulled out a pistol and stuck it right in Spasudo's mouth, pulled the hammer back.

'You ever bring someone near my home again, I'll kill you, John. You understand?'

'I do, I swear, I understand!' he mumbled.

Richard then went to kill the two Colombians. By doing this, he was getting Spasudo out of debt, but that certainly was not his intention. He just wanted to kill the men who had dared to come to his door.

Next would be Pat Kane.

Now, out of irrational desperation, Richard did what Pat Kane and Dominick Polifrone had been hoping and praying for all along: he used a payphone and called Phil Solimene.

Polifrone was, by pure chance, sitting in the store playing cards.

'Hey, Big Guy,' Solimene greeted Richard.

'That friend you have, this Dom, he around?' Richard asked.

'Yeah, he's sitting right here.'

'Put him on.'

'Hey, Dom,' Solimene called out. 'It's for you: Big Rich.' He smiled and winked as he handed the phone to Dominick.

'How ya doin'?' Dominick said, very pleased that finally, after all these months, he was actually making contact with the elusive Richard Kuklinski. The devil himself was calling.

'I'm good. I hear you have some good contacts.'

'Fuckin' A.'

'Let's talk. I need something special. I don't want to come there. Can you meet me at the Dunkin' Donuts down the street?'

'Sure, Rich, no problem,' the agent said.

'Five minutes?'

'OK,' Polifrone said, and hung up.

Solimene was smiling. 'I told you he'd call.'

'That you did,' Dom said. 'He wants to meet me at the Dunkin' Donuts.'

'I'll be here,' Phil said, and Dominick left.

Dominick walked outside. There was no time to contact Kane or even his own ATF people. He was truly on his own, and he had to move fast. He slid into his black Lincoln sedan and drove over to the Dunkin' Donuts. He knew he should have been wearing a wire, but there was no time for that. It was 10.45 a.m. The sky was filled with sombre greys. Dominick was nervous, excited, concerned, all at the same time. He had been planning this for so long, had begun to think it would never happen. But it was. He'd just spoken to the devil himself. Dom was armed. He had a Walther PPK in his pocket. He was an excellent shot. He didn't think Kuklinski would try to pull something in broad daylight, at a Dunkin' Donuts, but he had no real idea what was up, what Kuklinski wanted – what was in the wind. As he pulled into the parking lot, he spotted Richard. He was in Dwayne's silver Camaro. Polifrone parked and walked over, swaggering as he went, now seriously in his wiseguy mode.

'Hey, how ya doin'?' he greeted Richard.

'OK, good,' Richard said, getting out of the car and shaking Polifrone's outstretched hand. The agent was taken aback by Richard's size.

'Let's grab some coffee,' Richard said, and they headed inside the Dunkin' Donuts. It was just about empty. Richard moved to a quiet corner on the left, thinking this Dominick guy might have great contacts in the underworld and all, but he was wearing the worst wig he'd ever seen. *It looked like a raccoon went and died on his head*, he'd later say.

The bad wig aside, Richard had taken his 'friend' Phil Solimene at his word: that Dominick was 'good people', that they went back a lot of years. They both ordered coffees. Dominick was concerned about poison, that somehow Richard knew he was a plant and that he'd somehow manage to slip poison into his coffee. He purposely didn't order anything to eat and made sure to keep his coffee close, actually in his hand.

'I'm glad we're finally fuckin' meeting, Rich. I hear all kinds of good fuckin' things about you.'

'And me you. So you know Phil a long time?'

'Yeah, we go back. You too, I hear.'

'I know Phil . . . what, now, over 20 years.'

'He's a great guy. Stand-up.'

'Yeah . . . So let me tell you what I need, OK?'

'Sure, please.'

'I want to get some cyanide.'

'Cyanide, you mean like the fuckin' poison?'

'Yeah.'

'Hey, Rich, go to, you know, go to a fuckin' gardening store.'

'No, I mean high-grade stuff – laboratory quality. I got some rats I need to get rid of,' he said, amused.

'Yeah, well sure, I'm certain I could get ya that,' Dominick said, all serious. He wanted to, had to, draw Richard further out: cyanide, after all, was not illegal, nor was asking for it illegal. He had to get Richard involved in something that was overtly illegal. Dominick knew the game, knew what to say. The question was, would Richard take the bait?

'Rich,' he said, 'I hear you got good contacts for serious weapons, I'm talking heavy steel here. My guy had to take off recently. I've got a good customer, a broad who's hooked up with the IRA, and they got serious bucks and are looking for heavy steel. Can you help me there? You know, one hand washes the other?'

'Sure. Let me make a few calls,' Richard said.

There was something about Polifrone that Richard wasn't comfortable with, that put him off. Yet they exchanged pager and telephone numbers and planned to do business. The meeting soon ended. They walked outside together. The sky was lower and darker.

'I'm thinking of stopping and saying hello to Phil,' Richard said.

'Sure, good idea. I'll follow you over,' Dominick said, and made his way back to his Lincoln and followed Richard to the store. They walked inside together. What a pair. As different as night and day.

'Hey, Rich!' Phil called out, acting overjoyed to see him. 'Glad you two finally hooked up.'

Richard hugged Solimene and kissed him on the cheek, said hello to some of the other guys. During all the months Polifrone had been hanging around the store, he'd been clocking the action – he knew who was involved in counterfeit money, hijacking, robberies; but he couldn't make any kind of move, yet. However, at the right time, he'd make sure all these criminals, the regular thugs that hung out at the store, were picked up.

'So you and Dom here go back,' Richard said offhandedly.

'Abso-fuckin-lutely,' Phil said. 'You can treat him like me, Rich. He's 1,000 per cent!'

'OK,' Richard said, 'good enough for me,' readily accepting what Solimene was saying. This was out of character for Richard. He was usually a particularly untrusting, suspicious individual. But he believed Phil and had no real reservations about Polifrone, other than regarding his terrible hairpiece. He felt whoever had sold it to him should be arrested.

Phil, Richard and Polifrone did a three-way handshake.

'Salud,' Phil said, wishing them luck on whatever enterprise they did together.

Richard had apparently taken the bait. He said he had to get going and soon disappeared.

'I told you, I told you I'd deliver him,' Solimene told Dominick.

'And you did. Good work,' Dominick said. He was anxious to let his superiors know he had finally hooked Kuklinski. He had been getting flak about a lack of results, but now he had something concrete to show for all the months he'd been working this case, the endless card games, cursing, cigar smoking, bullshit. When he left the store, he drove a few blocks, making sure he wasn't tailed, used a payphone and told his people what had happened, what was said. 'Our man has taken the bait,' he told headquarters.

Polifrone next called Kane. When Kane heard what had happened, he let out a loud whoop. He hurried into Lieutenant Leck's office and told him the good news. They shook hands, high-fived each other.

'So we got him on the hook,' Kane said. 'Now all we have to do is get him in the boat.'

As it happened, this was easier said than done.

What Kane and Polifrone needed now to pull this off successfully was a larger, more sophisticated operation. They had not only to get Kuklinski to incriminate himself but to record it and make it all admissible and viable in a court of law. They needed help – more resources, wiretaps, electronic surveillance, manpower, helicopters, money – and they would get most of it in the form of New Jersey Deputy Attorney General Bob Carroll.

It was time to take off the gloves.

Two days after their first meeting, Richard paged Polifrone. The agent called him back. Richard wanted to know if he had secured the cyanide. He was anxious to get rid of Kane, and to do it properly, he needed the cyanide.

'I'm working on it, Rich. How about you – you find what I need?'

'Got feelers out,' Richard said.

'OK, I'll get back to you on that ASAP, all right?'

'Yeah, good, OK,' Richard said.

Richard wanted to go back to Zurich, but he was hesitant to leave with this up in the air; now the first order of business was getting rid of Kane. He believed once that was done he'd be in the clear. But he knew it had to be done right, made to look like a heart attack. He imagined spraying Kane in his surprised face, saw it happen in his mind.

Pssst, you're dead, fuck you.

Since the two Colombians had come to the house, Richard was, Barbara noticed, quiet and withdrawn . . . introspective. He barely talked. She explained, *I never saw him like this. He was just moping around the house, sitting in his chair and staring into space. He didn't want to talk; he didn't even want to go feed the ducks. I knew something was wrong, but I had no idea what.*

50

OPERATION ICE MAN

Bob Carroll was a diligent, hard-working prosecutor. He had a full, baby face, was stocky and square, appeared somewhat like the Pillsbury Doughboy. That cherubic baby face, however, belied a tenacious prosecutor who won most trials he took before a jury. Bob Carroll was a supervisor of the New Jersey Organized Crime and Racketeering Bureau task force, a relatively new unit put together to cross jurisdictions and build up and prosecute cases across the state of New Jersey, focusing on organised crime. Carroll worked out of a secretive, unmarked two-storey red-brick building in Fairfield. The entrance to the building was round the back, away from prying eyes. There were strategically placed surveillance cameras everywhere. If New Jersey had a Pentagon, a place from which to fight wars, this was surely it. When Carroll heard about the Kuklinski case, he contacted Kane and asked to see 'the file'.

By now Kane's one folder had grown to many carefully put-together files, all contained in a large brown cardboard box. For two days, Bob Carroll pored over Kane's files, more and more amazed – stunned, actually – at what the young detective had single-handedly put together. *It was*, he would later say, *one of the most significant, incredible files I'd ever seen*.

Thus the New Jersey attorney general's office lined up behind the investigation that Detective Pat Kane had started.

OPERATION ICE MAN

On the evening of 6 September 1986 – four days after Dominick Polifrone had his first meeting with Kuklinski – Pat Kane sat down in a windowless war room in the New Jersey attorney general's Fairfield building. He was surrounded by law-enforcement heavies, including Bob Carroll, Deputy State Police Chief Bob Buccino, Lieutenant John Leck and New Jersey Organized Crime and Racketeering Bureau investigators Paul Smith and Ron Donahue, all interested, all there because of Kane's diligence. No one doubted any longer what he'd been saying. Here Operation Ice Man – named thus because they believed Richard had frozen Masgay – was formed, and the rope to hang Richard Kuklinski became longer still.

Over takeaway Chinese, Pat Kane and Bob Carroll carefully laid out all the information Kane had gathered over the many months he'd been working the case: how it all began as a series of unsolved burglaries; the murders of Masgay, Smith and Deppner, and the disappearance of Hoffman; Kuklinski's connections to Roy DeMeo and organised crime. All that Kane had found out, put together, was tremendously helpful. But the attorney general's office needed tangible evidence that would hold up under the withering scrutiny of a crack defence attorney.

Dominick Polifrone was the answer. They would use him to get Kuklinski to incriminate himself. If Kuklinski had asked Polifrone for cyanide at their very first meeting at the Dunkin' Donuts, it stood to reason that Polifrone was 'in', that Kuklinski would hang himself.

Cyanide was the key – that would be the beam from which to hang the rope.

With permission from his superiors, Polifrone soon attended a second meeting of the Operation Ice Man task force, and Bob Carroll ran down for Polifrone what he wanted. Again present were Pat Kane and the heavies – investigators Paul Smith and Ron Donahue, Deputy Chief Bob Buccino and John Leck. Ron Donahue was a seasoned, hardened investigator, notorious for his toughness on the streets. He was actually booed by mob guys when he showed up in court or walked into mob hangouts. He looked very much like the boxer Jack Dempsey and was tough like him. Paul Smith was in his early 30s, had a Beatle haircut, hooded, dark eyes. He was an adept undercover guy. Only Leck wore a uniform. Bob Buccino had a thick head of silver hair, was a patient, intelligent man, a good administrator, adept at getting people to work well together. They all sat down. Now there was an eight-by-ten glossy of Kuklinski taped to the wall, a bullseye drawn on it.

Bob Carroll began: 'Dom, at this point, the key is the cyanide. See if you can get him to talk more about it – how it works, how long it takes, could it really be used to fool a medical examiner. Details. Get him to talk about details, other victims.'

'I know exactly what you want, and I'll get it,' Polifrone said.

They all knew that Polifrone was the man for the job. It was obvious to everyone there that Polifrone knew the walk and knew the talk.

'The problem is,' Polifrone said, 'he already paged me, and I called him back, and he *really* wants the cyanide.'

'Yeah, well under no circumstances can we give him cyanide,' John Leck said. 'Just think about the ramifications if he uses it to kill someone.'

'I'm only going to be able to stall him so long. I mean, if he doesn't get it from me, he'll get it somewhere else, and I might very well lose him. Right now, the cyanide is the hook, line and sinker.'

'You've got a point,' Carroll said, and they discussed the pros and cons of providing real cyanide to Richard, but in the end that idea was shot down. There was no way that they could give Richard Kuklinski cyanide.

Bob Carroll said, 'Stall him, just keep stalling him, all the while getting him to talk. I think he believes he's above the law at this point, that he'll never get caught, and we'll use that against him.'

They now discussed the fact that someone (not Richard) had spiked a packet soup in a grocery store in Camden, New Jersey, with cyanide, and a local man had bought the soup, eaten it and died. It was a big news item, and Polifrone said he could use this as an excuse to stall Richard. As they were talking, Polifrone's pager sounded; amazingly, it was actually Richard. Leck wanted Polifrone to call him right back.

'Let 'im stew a little bit,' Polifrone said. 'I don't want to, you know, seem too anxious.'

'Agent Polifrone, your target called, call him back!' Leck insisted.

Polifrone repeated what he'd said. Of course, he was right. It seemed, however, that Leck wanted to get into a pissing contest with the ATF agent. Finally, Carroll had to step in and tell Leck that Polifrone would decide how to work this.

'Who's running this investigation, us or the ATF?!' Leck demanded.

'This,' Carroll said, 'is a joint operation, and I have every confidence in Dominick's expertise.' Leck had to accept that. He stared at Dominick as if he wanted to take a bite out of him.

This was, Dominick had known all along, one of the biggest problems with inter-agency cooperation, or actually the lack of it: everyone wanted to be the boss, everyone wanted the glory. No matter what this uniformed stiff said, though, Polifrone was going to work this case the way he saw fit. It was his ass on the line, not Leck's. It didn't seem like a good match, but he'd do whatever he could to make it work.

Now, based on Polifrone's initial contact with Kuklinski, Carroll planned to get warrants to tap all of Kuklinski's phones, and an elaborate plan was put in place that would allow the calls to be legally recorded in a safe house near the Kuklinski home. Conversations would be listened to and transmitted into text by a team of typists in a second location. They had to catch every word accurately if these tapes were to be used in court. By the time they'd agreed on the nuts and bolts of this aspect of the operation, it was nearly 9.00 p.m., and now Dominick returned Kuklinski's call. He had made him wait two hours.

Richard said he wanted to get together to discuss the arms deal, that he would bring his dealer and they could meet at the Vince Lombardi Service Area off the New Jersey Turnpike in Ridgefield. This caught Dominick off guard, first because Richard wanted to introduce him to his contact, and second because there wasn't enough time to properly set up a comprehensive surveillance operation. If what Polifrone had heard about Kuklinski was true, and he had no reason to believe it wasn't, Kuklinski was by far the most dangerous man he'd ever come up against, and he wanted to be sure all the ducks were lined up properly before he put himself on the line. What concerned Polifrone further was the fact that this was a joint, inter-agency operation. There was therefore no focal point of command – simply put, there were too many chefs in the kitchen. Polifrone had a wife he loved dearly, three children he was crazy about, and he wasn't about to give that up by getting caught up and hurt in an inter-agency pissing contest.

Plus, Polifrone had no idea if Phil Solimene was playing them off against each other or was on the level. For all he knew, Solimene had been feeding Kuklinski information and setting him up. He had heard of much stranger things than that. When it came to mob guys, he knew, there was no telling what they'd do. They were dangerous, unpredictable jungle creatures, not creatures of habit, rhyme or reason.

Richard did in fact have plans for this Dominick Provanzano, and those plans were to set up an arms sale, take what money he had, kill him and get rid of his body. He was going to have John Spasudo help him play Dominick, take the order for all the 'heavy steel' he said he wanted, but instead of delivering guns he was going to shoot Dominick in the head; and he was going to kill Spasudo at the same time. It was still eating away at Richard that Spasudo had brought people to his house, and he hadn't forgotten the young girl in Spasudo's bed. He would not just kill Spasudo, but he'd feed him to the rats. Yes, that was better. Spasudo would die *the death of a thousand bites*, as Richard had come to think of it, amused by his creativity. After he'd got the poison from Dominick, he'd get rid of both of them at the same time and keep all the money. All neat, all tidy.

Barbara was right. A very real change had come over Richard. The Colombians coming to his house had upset him to the point of perpetual distraction. He blamed himself. He was getting sloppy, losing his edge. Married life, family life, he was thinking, had taken a toll on him, had softened him, made him less diligent . . . aware. He actually began to think of retiring. Getting away from the life. He'd been reckless in many ways, but had always been lucky. His luck, he was thinking, was apparently running out. He resolved to start saving money, to start putting all the money he was earning in a safe place. He'd stop gambling, stop taking unnecessary chances. He knew that if he didn't become more cautious, he was destined for a bad end. Once this thorn in his side, this Pat Kane, was dead and buried, he'd be able to get on with his plans – save a lot of money and get the hell away from crime, from killing people for both profit and personal gratification.

What Richard dreaded more than anything, what haunted him now, was the thought of his being uncovered and the shame and embarrassment his family would surely have to suffer and endure. They had nothing to do with any of his many crimes, all the pain and suffering he wrought; they were truly innocent. Yet, he knew, they'd suffer greatly, perhaps irreversibly, if he was ever found out, discovered, exposed. Just the thought of that gave him a splitting headache, made him reel.

If it ever came down to the police trying to arrest him, he vowed he'd go out in a blaze of glory. He'd never let them take him alive. He'd shoot as many of them as he could. They'd have to kill him. With him dead, he figured, they could never conclusively prove anything. What he'd done would be buried with his body, and the incentive for them to prove something would be mitigated, he was sure, by his demise.

Suicide by cop, that was the way to go.

First and foremost, though, he needed cyanide to take care of Pat Kane properly.

Second, he needed a truckload of money to retire properly.

Third, he'd stop gambling; he'd control that urge. He had to. He felt trapped and cornered, and the only answer was money. A lot of it. Money was the passport to a better life.

On 11 September at 8.00 a.m., Pat Kane went to the location where Richard's phone calls were being tapped. Kane, Bob Carroll, Paul Smith and Ron Donahue would be manning the lines 24 hours a day. They were legally able to record all the calls, even the ones by Richard's family, his two daughters talking to their boyfriends, Dwayne talking to friends, Barbara ordering groceries – always the best of everything for her. However, legally, they were allowed to transcribe only the conversations of Richard's that were specifically relevant to . . . *crimes*.

Pat Kane was upbeat now. He was sure it was just a matter of time before they landed Richard in the boat. Kane still viewed Richard as the elusive, predatory muskie and was sure now that this new bait would do the trick. Pat returned to his old self now. He was much more attentive to his loving wife, had more time for his children. The old twinkle in his eyes was back. It was as if, Terry thought, the storm cloud hanging over her husband's head was abruptly gone.

Terry had, of course, no idea that the brooding storm cloud was actually following her husband around, stalking him – planning to swiftly and efficiently kill the only man she had ever kissed.

* * *

In his quest to earn money, Richard again left for Zurich. The task force was still intent upon not letting Richard know that they were onto him, and they were certain he'd spot a tail in a minute, so they just left him alone; they didn't even know he was out of the country.

Consequently, all they got from the phone taps was the family going about their lives. Dominick left messages for Richard, which went unreturned.

In Zurich, Richard was relaxed. He knew no one was watching him, and while waiting for more cheques, more receipts from the Nigerian government official, he sat in parks and cafés, looking like a man enjoying the tranquillity of the park, though he was plotting and planning Pat Kane's, Dominick Polifrone's and John Spasudo's murders. He actually drew strength from just the thought of these killings. All his life, since he'd beaten Charley Lane to death, Richard had solved his problems with murder. Murder was an anchor that kept him stable; murder would make everything right. Sitting in a Zurich café near the Central Station, Richard planned murder. All he needed was a little cyanide and he'd be free of Pat Kane, the man who was trying to take everything away from him.

As days passed, the phone taps proved fruitless, unless knowing that Barbara ordered a lot of filet mignon from the Dumont butcher meant something. Not knowing that Richard was actually out of the country, the task force became concerned. Not only were they not hearing anything that would be useful in court, but Richard wasn't even calling Polifrone back. What the hell was that about? They began to think Richard knew Polifrone was an agent, that Solimene had been playing both sides of the fence. Surely that was the problem.

Then, on 25 September, everything suddenly changed. Richard got back from Zurich, deposited yet another cheque in the Georgia account, contacted Spasudo and told him how he was planning to rip off Dominick and that he wanted to use him to impersonate an arms dealer. Though Spasudo was as ugly as sin, both a degenerate gambler and a sexual degenerate, he was not stupid. In fact, he had a mind as sharp as a tack. He readily agreed to go along with Richard's scheme; he would have enough knowledge about firearms because Richard would make him read up on all kinds of armaments. Spasudo had no idea that Richard was planning to kill him too, planning to feed him alive to rats. At 6 ft 5 in., he would be, Richard was thinking, a huge feast for the rats. Richard called Polifrone from a payphone in a shopping centre in south Jersey.

Now Dominick, in the ATF's Newark offices, was wired and ready for action. He returned Richard's call. The first thing Richard asked was if Dominick was at a payphone.

'Yeah, we can talk freely,' Dominick said, baiting the trap, smiling as he did so, and Richard walked right into it: he told Dominick he had his arms contact there and said he'd put Spasudo on the phone, telling Dominick his name was Tim. Spasudo took the phone and, with flourish and authority, told Dominick he could get him all the heavy armaments he wanted, rattling off different weapons as if he were selling fresh fruit at a busy market. Richard was proud of Spasudo. He was doing a good job. He sounded like the real McCoy. Polifrone then asked to speak to Richard, now ready to spring the trap.

'Hey, Rich, I told Tim what I needed. Now tell me the truth. Is this guy gonna deliver? I don't wanna hear a lotta promises, then get a lotta excuses down the line. You know what I'm saying?'

'You don't have to worry, Dom. If he says he can get you something, he'll get it. If he can't, he'll be straight with you.'

'All right. I don't wanna end up looking bad on this. My IRA girl, she looks like a schoolteacher, but she can be a real ballbuster. You disappoint her once, that's it, no second chances. She'll find somebody else. And I'm telling you, she's one customer I do not want to lose. You understand me?'

'I hear you, Dom.'

'Now I understand that Tim's got all his heavy stuff in the Mediterranean, so it's gonna take some time to get us some samples. But let's keep my girl happy, OK? Get me a few silencers so I can show her something. Just something I can show. I'll pay you – don't worry about that. But just get me something.'

'Did Tim tell you he had silencers available?'

'Yeah.'

'Here?'

'Yes.'

'Then don't worry about it. We'll get you something as soon as we can.'

'OK, but don't make me wait. I'm telling you, we can both make a lotta money off this broad. Let's not screw it up. OK?'

'I hear you. Don't worry.'

'OK, Rich, let's stay in touch.'

'Say, Dom, you didn't get any word on that stuff I was looking for? You know what I'm talking about?' Richard said, putting a noose around his own neck.

'Yeah, I know. I talked to my people, but they're all nervous about this Lipton soup thing.'

'Why? That was a couple of weeks ago.'

'They heard that there's a lot of federal people going around asking questions about all that shit. Now, I know they got a chemist who gets that stuff for them, but, like I said, they're all nervous. I got stuff like that from these people before for other customers of mine, so I'm pretty sure they can get it. They just wanna wait till this Lipton soup thing cools down before they'll give it to me. In the meantime, I'll get you the other stuff, the – you're on a payphone, right?' Dominick said, drawing Richard further in.

'Yeah, aren't you?'

'Yeah, of course. The cyanide, you gotta be careful because, you know, I don't know how you fucking want to use it. But that's your business, Rich. I'm not asking.'

'Well, it won't be a problem of exposure. I don't intend to resell it to anybody. I'm intending to use it myself.'

'Yeah? Well, don't *you* take it,' Dominick said, laughing.

'No, no, I don't intend to. I just have a few problems I want to dispose of. I have some rats I want to get rid of,' Richard said, chuckling.

'Yeah? Why not use a fucking piece of iron to get rid of these fucking people? Why fuck around with cyanide?' Dominick said, opening the door wider still.

'Why be messy, Dom? You do it nice and clean with cyanide.'

'Lemme ask you something then. You do the same thing I do once in a while. But I always use steel. You know what I'm saying?'

'Yeah, I understand what you're saying.'

'So what I'm asking is, would you be willing to do a – you know – a contract with me?'

'Dominick, if the price is right, I'll talk to anybody,' Richard said, drawing the noose a bit tighter.

'Yeah?'

'Sure.'

'And you mean to tell me your way is nice and clean, and nothing fuckin' shows up?'

'Well, it may show, my friend, but it's quiet, it's not messy. It's not as noisy.'

'Yeah, but how the fuck do you put it together, you know what I'm saying?'

'Well, there's always a way. There's a will, there's a way, my friend.'

Dominick laughed. 'All right, listen, we'll have to talk about this some time. It sounds interesting.'

'There're even spray mists around,' Richard volunteered.

'Yeah?'

'Sure. You put that stuff in a mist, you spray it in somebody's face, and they go to sleep,' he said.

'Fast? How long does it take?'

Kuklinski snapped his fingers. 'About that fast,' he said, bragging.

'No shit. I thought – you mean, you don't have to put it in the guy's drink, something like that?'

'Not necessary. That will work too, but it's very detectable that way.'

'Yeah?'

'You make it up as a mist. As soon as they inhale it, they've already had enough. Just one squirt. That's all it takes.'

'Well, shit, if it's that easy, Rich, there are definitely a couple of things we could get involved with, without any fucking problems. You know, as I said, contracts.'

'Can do it either way. If a guy wants it done with lead, then it could be lead. If the guy wants to prove a point and he wants steel, it could be done with steel. I'm not averse to guns, I'm not averse to knives, I'm not averse to, you know, whatever,' Richard said.

'As long as he's dead, that's the bottom line, Rich.'

'Well, that's the thing, isn't it? If that's what they want.'

'Your way sounds like a fucking James Bond movie, but if it works, then –'

'Dominick, I've done it all ways, whatever you've known or heard. There aren't too many things I haven't tried. I'll try whatever sounds workable. Some guys want it done messy, and they want it as proof of the pudding. They want it shown. So I'll do it that way.'

'But your way, what you were telling me, with the cyanide – there's no problem with that?'

'I don't have a problem. I'm not saying it's not detectable. I'm just saying it's quiet and fast.'

'In other words, you've done this before? You know there's no problem?'

'Well, nobody's going to give you proof of anything like that, my friend.'

'I'm not saying proof. I'm just asking if it's really been done.'

'It's been done.'

'This sounds interesting. We gotta fucking go for coffee, break bread over this thing. It sounds good.'

'Well, Dom, you know what they say. There's more than one way to skin something.'

'I hear ya, I hear ya.'

'It all depends on how determined you are to get it done.'

They both laughed.

'As long as it gets done. Right, Rich?'

'As long as the guy who's paying you gets it done the way he wants. It's the finished product that they're interested in. And I haven't had any complaints, because as you can see, I'm still around. If I had any complaints, I'm sure I wouldn't be here.'

'I hear you, brother. I hear you. But getting back to the other stuff with Tim, what should we do? You wanna page me or should I call you?'

'Why don't you call me this weekend? But just in case I'm not at that other number, lemme give you my new pager number.'

'You've got a pager now, Rich?'

'Yeah. This number is for me and Tim, we both use it. OK?'

'I understand.'

'OK, the number is 1-800-402 . . .' Richard said, gave him the number and soon hung up the phone and smiled, not having any idea that he had just hung himself.

Considering all the years Richard had spent on the street, how tight-lipped he'd always been, it was amazing that he talked so openly to Polifrone. He was figuring to rip off Polifrone and kill him. What difference did it make what he said? In his mind, he was just setting up Polifrone and these IRA people to rip them off. The first order of business, thought Richard, was to get Dominick the hit kit – a .22 with a silencer. No problem.

In reality, Richard had just handed the task force a golden opportunity to hang him high and watch him slowly swing.

51

HIT KIT

Dominick Polifrone couldn't believe that Richard had actually admitted to killing people. Not only that, but using a cyanide mist to do people in. He immediately called Bob Carroll and ran down what he had and was now hurrying over to the attorney general's fortress-like offices in Fairfield. Every word of the conversation had been taped, and Polifrone had a copy of the tape in his pocket. The agent had, he knew, hit pay dirt. As he made his way along Route 23 in his big-ass black Lincoln, his pager sounded. It was Kuklinski. Polifrone was reluctant to call him right back. But Kuklinski was on the hook now, and Dominick didn't want to give him any slack, a chance to get away, break the line. No, he'd call Kuklinski straight back. He spotted a payphone in front of a restaurant, pulled over and phoned Richard.

Again, Richard asked if he was at a payphone.

'Yeah, I'm cool,' the wily agent said, and Richard went on to explain that he had the hit kit.

Richard had had it all along; he had half a dozen of them, kept them in a suitcase at Barbara's mother's house. He told Polifrone he could let him have it for eleven hundred, but that was a special 'sample price'. Richard again suggested they meet at the Vince Lombardi service station. Dominick agreed. What the hell, it was out in the open, would be an easy place to set up surveillance and a back-up team. But he stalled the meeting; they needed time, he knew, to set everything up properly. Richard said he'd bring the hit kit. The meeting was set for the following week. Dominick got back into his black Lincoln and drove on to the attorney general's building in Fairfield. When he got there, Bob Carroll, Pat Kane, Ron Donahue and Paul Smith were all anxiously waiting to hear the tape. They sat around the same conference-room table, the eight-by-ten of Richard still on the wall and, astounded, listened to Kuklinski incriminate, indeed hang, himself. When it was over, they all shook hands, gave Dominick high fives.

'Dominick,' Bob Carroll said, 'you are the best! Smooth like melted butter. We have him – we have him by the nuts,' he said, a big smile lighting up his full face. Pat Kane hugged Dominick.

'Great job, Dom. Great job,' he said, feeling an elation he'd never known before.

Smiling and proud, Dominick knew he'd done a hell of a job. It had been a long, bumpy road, but the end, he was sure, was in sight. They now talked about setting up comprehensive surveillance of the meeting at the Lombardi service station.

Even Richard's daughters, Chris and Merrick, noticed the change that had come over their father. He barely talked. He walked around the house as if he were in a daze. Neither of them had ever seen him like this. Yes, he'd always been moody, had highs and lows, but he'd never been this quiet and introspective for days on end. Chris dismissed it as another of her father's quirks; he was full of them. But Merrick was concerned. She felt a true change had come over her father – not a good one – and she was worried. Merrick tried to talk to him, get him to go and feed the ducks with her, but he wasn't interested. That alone was reason for concern. Merrick had grown into a very attractive woman with dark hair and large almond-shaped eyes the colour of warmed honey. She had a good job at the Allstate Insurance Company, had been promoted and given a raise; she had a new boyfriend, Mark, and was in love with him, and marriage had been discussed though not yet formalised. She was happy, except for the fact that her dad was acting . . . *weird*, as she later put it.

Merrick, like everyone else in the house, heard the strange clicks on the phone, but didn't think anything of them. Barbara, on the other hand, suspected they were being tapped, but didn't give much thought to it. If, she believed, her husband was doing anything illegal, it had to do with knock-off copies of name brands. She still had no idea to whom she was married. Richard had told her about Kane and Volkman's visit but hadn't said anything about their questioning him regarding five murders they suspected him of committing.

The next meeting between Richard and Agent Polifrone happened on 2 October, the following week, at the Vince Lombardi service station. It was eight miles as the crow flies from the George Washington Bridge, had half a dozen fast-food restaurants, toilets, a petrol station; on the left was a grassy area with some tables and benches where people could gobble down fast food. This was a transient place. Those who stopped here did so for a little while and quickly moved on. Richard had suggested this place because it was open and easy to get to, easy to spot a trap. The Ice Man task force had ample time to set up proper surveillance and back-up. Ron Donahue, Paul Smith and Bob Carroll were all there, as were several other teams, made up of both men and women, sitting in various unmarked cars, heavily armed. Kuklinski was dangerous in the extreme, they knew – cunning and unpredictable.

Agent Polifrone arrived on time, 2.00 p.m. He was armed and wearing a tiny Kel transmitter and a small Nagra tape recorder secreted at the nape of his neck. He sported a baggy black leather jacket to conceal the tape recorder. It was essential that whatever was said was accurately recorded. With the help of an AID radio receiver, all the teams would hear – and be able to record – what was said. This was a momentous meeting, they all knew; if Polifrone did his job well, got Richard to talk openly, they would use his own words to nail him.

So far, most of what they had, other than the first tape, was circumstantial. Bob Carroll was hoping that would change today. Meanwhile, Richard was late.

After lunch that day, Richard was busy on the phones, talking to John Spasudo and Remi. More problems had come up because of the Zurich bank official's former associates, and Remi was concerned. All these 'business calls' Richard made from phone booths all over Dumont. The calls made him late for his meeting with Polifrone. He paged Polifrone half an hour after he was supposed to be there, and Dominick called him right back; Richard apologised, said he was on his way and hurried from his house, carrying a bag containing the hit kit. Richard was planning to use the .22 and silencer, clearly an assassin's weapon, to bait Polifrone further into a bigger sale of such guns. Instead of delivering the weapons, however, he was going to deliver death.

As Richard drove to the service station, he thought about feeding Spasudo to the rats. Oh, how he'd enjoy that! He was still intent upon killing Pat Kane, but he needed cyanide to pull that off properly, to make it appear like a heart attack; that was the key, and he still hoped Polifrone could get him the cyanide. If it looked like a hit, the police would, he was sure, be on him like white on rice.

Richard arrived at nearly 3.00 p.m., unaware of the law-enforcement encampment he was entering. This was very much unlike him. He normally came early to such meetings, hid in a van and made sure all was clear, using binoculars and his well-honed sixth sense. The fact that he planned to murder Polifrone, he would say, made him drop his guard; he was walking straight to the gallows steps of his own volition. It was a chilly, grey day. A cold wind blew across the flat french-fry-smelling expanse around the service station. The sounds of cars and trucks whizzing by was constant, punctuated by fleeting truck and car horns. The many planes landing and taking off from nearby Newark Airport passed low overhead, adding to the cacophony of fast-moving sounds. Polifrone was ready. He knew what he had to say and how to say it. After greetings, Richard again apologised about being late. He said he had the hit kit with him, opened the boot and showed it to Polifrone. 'This is,' he said, 'a .22 long barrel, military capacity with a screw-off front. You screw the suppressor on.' He handed it to Polifrone and told him he could let him have it for eleven hundred dollars, but the price would have to be fifteen hundred for a large load; this was, he said, only to get the deal moving. 'A sample price.'

Bob Carroll was pleased: they could now arrest Richard and charge him with the sale of this gun and silencer. The silencer was a major felony. But Carroll wanted more, had to have more. His intention was to make sure Richard got serious time, spent the rest of his life behind bars or, better yet, got a death sentence. Tensed, he waited to hear Polifrone draw Richard further into his carefully laid trap. As this was happening, Pat Kane was waiting back at the attorney general's bunker, nervously pacing like an expectant father. He couldn't be seen here. If Richard recognised him, all was instantly lost, everyone knew.

Now Kuklinski showed Dominick how to put on the silencer. He handled the gun with knowing familiarity. They were off near a bank of telephones. Richard used the open boot of his car to block anyone from seeing what he was doing. Polifrone gave him the eleven hundred dollars, which had been provided by the State of New Jersey. This is what was recorded:

'Listen, Rich. Remember you were telling me about how you use cyanide?'

'Yeah?'

'Well I got this fucking rich Jewish kid I been supplying with coke. He wants me to get him two kilos now, which I can do, but the kid's a real fucking pain in my balls, you know?

So what I'm asking is, you think it's possible we can dope up the coke with cyanide?'

'Definitely.'

'What I was figuring, we can make a quick score. Do the kid and go halfsies on the bread he brings for the two keys.'

'Does he always come alone?'

'Yeah, he always comes alone.'

'And he brings cash?'

'The kid's rich from his old man. He's rolling in it. Money's not the problem. He's the problem. I can't stand the little fuck any more.'

'All right. Just tell me when. Dom, you understand that the price of these pieces goes up after this one, right? It's eleven for this one, but it'll be fifteen apiece, even in quantity.'

'Without the nose?' (A 'nose' is a silencer.)

'No, with the nose. The same as you got here, except it'll be fifteen hundred, not eleven.'

'What calibre?'

'I didn't even ask. Probably .22.'

'Hey, what the fuck do I care? It's the Irish broad's money, not mine. I don't give a fuck. Personally I could give two shits about their cause over there. I'm gonna give you your price today. Whatever it is tomorrow is her problem.'

'Whatever, I'm just telling you, Dom. And as for that other guy, that sounds very interesting, fuck it, I'll hit a Jew in a minute. Who the fuck cares?'

'Yeah.'

'Not only that, you say we can make a nice buck off this.'

'That's what I'm telling you, Rich. You know what we can do? I don't know if you wanna do this, but I can bring the kid here some day. I'll meet him here for coffee, and you can come and take a look at him if you want.'

'No problem. Tell him you'll meet him over by the phones, and I'll park over there so I can see what he looks like.'

'Good, good. Only thing is, Rich, I don't want him whacked. His old man's got money up the ass. He'll hire private investigators and all kinds of shit. That's why it's gotta look like an OD. You know what I'm saying?'

'No problem. I can do it, but you gotta get me the cyanide. I'll make it up and hit him in the face with it. I can make the – you know, then just one hit, and that's it. He goes to sleep.'

'Or we put it in the coke. I don't give a shit really, just as long as he's gone and it looks like an overdose.'

'My friend, there's more than one way to do it. You don't want him shot, we can do it another way. There's millions of ways.'

'An OD, that's what I want.'

'Well, we can give him some pure shit and make him really OD.'

'Whatever. I gotta run now, but we'll talk about this some more later. All right, Big Guy?'

'You got it. See you later.'

Richard and Polifrone walked in different directions. Richard got back into his car and drove out of the service station. Carroll was overjoyed. They now clearly had Kuklinski for conspiracy to commit murder. The list of charges, as he was hoping, was lengthening, and because Kuklinski obviously trusted Polifrone, Bob Carroll was thinking they could take this even further, build and fortify the case against Kuklinski they already had. Carroll was thinking of using Paul Smith, sitting next to him now, as the rich Jewish kid looking to buy cocaine. Carroll could've had Richard arrested on the spot, but he wanted more. He wanted to be sure that when they arrested him, they had an airtight case against him, that he would die in jail, either of old age or by execution – preferably the latter.

As the Ice Man task force planned and plotted its next move, Richard left for Zurich again, and again they had no idea he'd gone anywhere. Had Richard known what was going on, how Solimene had set him up, who Polifrone truly was, he would have stayed in Zurich. He still believed Polifrone would buy a huge load of armaments and help set up this rich Jewish kid. He was not yet suspicious. Polifrone was a means to an end – more money, and cyanide. After that, he was dead.

Remi and Richard met in a glass-walled café in the centre of town, and yet again Richard heard how another man in this 'gang' was trying to shake down the Asian bank official.

Remi said, 'Now, you know, he's really scared. He's talking about quitting and going back to Japan, and then we are lost. We must stop that. You have to do your magic thing again. I know you know the right people.'

'I am the right people,' Richard said, his voice low and deadly serious, a slight smile on his high-cheekboned, Slavic face.

Remi blanched. 'You . . . I don't believe it.'

'Isn't any big deal,' Richard said.

Remi's eyes widened. He blinked rapidly. He didn't know how to handle this . . . revelation. 'My goodness,' he said.

'OK, listen. Tell the bank official to relax. Tell him we'll take care of everything. What I'm concerned with is more of this *gang* popping up. You have to find out how many people know about him – and who they are. The right thing to do would be to get rid of all of them at one time.'

'Yes, yes, of course . . . you . . . you can do such a thing?' Remi asked, incredulous.

Richard smiled. He was amused. 'Of course I can, no problem, my friend. Do you think you can get me a handgun?' Richard asked, and took a bite out of a sugar-powdered almond croissant.

'Yes,' Remi said.

'OK, you get me the gun, show me where this gang is, and I'll do the rest,' Richard said.

'Really?' Remi asked, looking at Richard now in a completely different way, with shocked awe. He knew now Richard had killed the first two members of the gang. 'You're, I think, a very rare man, you know.'

'There aren't too many people like me around,' Richard said.

'My goodness, no,' Remi said.

'Tell the bank guy to get all the members of the gang in one place. That we will take care of this.'

'You're sure?'

'Sure as shit.'

'I see,' Remi said. 'OK.'

Because Richard was in Zurich, the tap on his phone was temporarily useless; Polifrone paged Richard several times, left messages that went unanswered. Perplexed, the Ice Man task force scratched its collective head.

Remi secured a Walther P .38 for Richard, with a full clip and a box of bullets. This was a gun Richard knew well. Now, armed, Richard had Remi rent a van, and from it they watched the Asian bank official meet with two men in a café in town.

The bank official told the two men that he would work with them again, provide them with new cheques, but that it would take a week or so. He repeatedly assured them that he would continue doing business with them. After the meeting, Remi and Richard trailed the two men to the same house visited by the man Richard had killed with the cyanide spray. This was a quiet residential street, not good for what Richard had in mind – shooting them in the head. But he'd make it work. Richard now told Remi to leave; he would do this alone. Gladly, Remi got out of the van and hurried away, not looking back as he went. Richard pulled the van right up in front of the house, thinking about the best way to do this.

If he fired the gun, the cops would be summoned. He had with him a hunting knife, and he decided to use it. Richard stepped from the van and boldly walked right up to their door, knocked. One of the men opened it, and with lightning speed Richard stuck the automatic in his face, told him to be quiet and pushed his way in, quickly, like a tango dancer. He made both men lie on the floor. He cut the lamp cords and used the wire to bind their hands tightly behind their backs. He then stuck socks into their mouths and killed one, then the other, by pushing the knife, at an upward angle, into the backs of their heads. Concerned that the double murder might in some way be linked with the bank official, Richard decided to get rid of the bodies. To do this, he took the blankets off two beds in the apartment, rolled each of the bodies in a blanket, picked up one and placed it in the back of the van, made sure he wasn't being observed, returned, hoisted the second one over his massive shoulder, put him in the van and slowly pulled away. People who sped drew attention. When he was transporting bodies, Richard never hurried.

As Richard made his way out of town, he passed a hardware shop with ladders and colourful wheelbarrows out the front; he turned around, went back and bought a long-handled copper-headed spade, then continued on. He managed to get onto a highway, drove on it for half an hour, pulled off and went looking for a suitable place to get rid of the bodies, just as he had done when he was a boy back in Jersey City: déjà vu all over again. He hadn't counted on any of this and didn't like it, but it had to be done, so he was doing it. However, he would demand a larger share of the money now, and get it. It didn't take Richard long to find a secluded area in the woods, dig a hole, quickly dump the two men in it and cover it with earth, leaves and branches. He got back in the van and returned to Zurich, called Remi and told him all was 'taken care of'. He also told him to come and get the van and return it. That done, Richard took a shower, met Remi and returned the van – after making sure there was no blood inside it – and they went for dinner in a five-star French restaurant.

Remi was impressed. He couldn't believe any one man could be so . . . efficient at making people – problems – disappear. He looked at Richard now with a new-found respect. Richard told him he wanted 'a larger slice of the pie'.

'Of course, of course, you deserve it!' Remi said. 'Absolutely!'

Two days later, Richard returned to New Jersey, went back down to Georgia, deposited the latest cheque and returned to Dumont. The task force was pleased to hear him talking on the phone again. Polifrone called him, paged him, and Richard finally got back to Polifrone on 8 October. He called him from a diner. Richard was by now expecting Polifrone to have the cyanide, and he asked him about it right off the bat. Again, however, Polifrone stalled him. Richard asked him about the IRA woman; Polifrone said she was pleased, that he was waiting to hear from her.

'How about this Jewish kid?' Richard asked.

'He moves around a lot, travels a lot. I should be hearing from him soon. You'll be around?'

'I'll be around. He who hesitates is lost, my friend,' Richard said.

'You are right about that.'

'Gotta move while the iron is hot,' Richard said.

'I hear you,' Polifrone said. 'I'll let you know when the time is right.'

They hung up. Richard was beginning to think Polifrone was, in a word, *bullshit*. If he had what he said he had, what he said he could get, it would be on the table by now. Polifrone was, Richard decided, just another bigmouthed wannabe braggart. He'd met this kind of man all his life. Nothing new. People who said they had all these contacts, knew all these people, turned out to be as empty as a used paper bag.

Polifrone was thinking Richard was cold and distant, that maybe he had been stringing Kuklinski along for too long. He was right. He knew if he didn't deliver something soon, Kuklinski would just move on – stop returning his calls altogether.

Which, apparently, is exactly what happened.

Polifrone called, left messages, paged Richard, without any response. One time, 'Tim' (Spasudo) called him back, but that didn't accomplish anything one way or the other; the task force knew Spasudo was just a tool, a shill, for Richard. The situation was becoming untenable. Bob Carroll talked about bringing in Kuklinski on what they had so far, but in the end it was decided they needed more if they really wanted to put him away for good. One of the guys taped a mug shot of Richard onto a new bottle of Jack Daniel's, from which they drank sparingly during late-night brainstorming sessions. It became a ritual. When they truly nailed Kuklinski, Carroll promised, there would be bottles of good champagne.

Finally, towards the end of October, Richard did call Agent Polifrone back. He said he'd been busy, that he had misplaced Polifrone's number. He didn't seem interested any more. He was, Polifrone knew, ready to spit the hook. Polifrone told Richard the rich Jewish kid was back – asking for product, anxious for it – and the IRA broad wanted to place an order . . . a big one, he said.

Reluctantly, Richard agreed to meet Polifrone again, and a time was set for 26 October, again at the Vince Lombardi service station, this time inside the Roy Rogers fast-food restaurant there. There was, as before, enough time for the task force to set up proper surveillance and back-up for Polifrone. Jersey plain-clothes detectives stationed themselves in and around the Roy Rogers. Rough-and-ready Ron Donahue was sitting inside the Roy Rogers, nursing his second coffee. It was still lunchtime and crowded. The weather had grown much colder. The sky was low and grey and mean, as if a storm were about to strike. Polifrone was on edge. He well knew he'd lost the momentum he'd had with Richard. Too much time had gone by, and he hadn't delivered anything but promises. Not good. For all he knew, Richard was in fact onto him and was planning to kill him. Polifrone made sure he had quick and easy access to his heat. He was coiled like a rattlesnake about to strike, ready for action, whatever it was.

Polifrone took solace in the presence of Ron Donahue. If Kuklinski had to be subdued, put down, killed, Ron Donahue was the man to do it, Polifrone knew. His toughness was legendary in police circles. There was tension, palpable and real, in the chilly autumn air.

Richard showed up on time, at 2.00 p.m. sharp, driving a red Oldsmobile, Barbara's car. He had on sunglasses, which Polifrone didn't like because you couldn't see his eyes.

'Hey, Dom, what's new?' Richard greeted the agent, seemingly aloof, not at all friendly. Polifrone said he was hungry.

'Would you like something, Rich?' he offered, gesturing towards the restaurant.

'Nothing for me . . . just coffee,' Richard said. Polifrone bought two coffees, fries and a burger for himself. They took seats. As the agent ate, he asked Richard about more hit kits, how many could he get and when he could get them.

'You can,' Richard said, 'get all you want, but they are down in Delaware. I'm not bringing them across the state line.' So there it was – Richard was backing off, clearly not being as congenial as before.

'Sure, I'll get them, no problem. Just tell me where, OK? Can I get ten?'

'You can get all you want, my friend,' Richard said, using the signal word – 'friend' – indicating that Polifrone's days were numbered. All along, Polifrone had been talking about a big buy, lots of money; now just ten hit kits. *He's full of shit*, Richard thought. *Bullshit.*

Polifrone again pitched Richard the line about the rich Jewish kid, saying how he wanted two, maybe even three kilos of coke; and again he peppered Richard with questions about how the cyanide works, and again, Richard took the bait and went on to describe how once someone is sprayed in the face it's all over.

'I've used it,' he said. 'I sprayed guys and they were dead within minutes.'

'Really?' Polifrone said, wide-eyed. 'Wow.'

'Really.'

'OK, so when we take off the kid, you'll do him with this,

but the body, we gotta get rid of the body,' Polifrone further baited Richard.

'Why get rid of it?' Richard said, gobbling up the bait, his every word being immortalised. 'Just leave him there. It'll look like he's sleeping . . . that he died a natural death. All neat and tidy.'

'OK, sounds perfect. Let's do it,' Polifrone said, and explained that he'd get the rich Jewish kid to a meeting at the rest stop, and Richard should come and see him and check him out. Richard said he'd be available, to let him know when.

Richard, still oblivious of the fact that Polifrone might be a cop, planned to kill 'the Jewish kid' and Polifrone at the same time and take all the money. He had grown to really dislike Polifrone and looked forward to killing him – if there really was a Jewish kid with bucks looking to score. He had his doubts. They made plans to talk again soon, and Richard left.

On 30 October, Polifrone spoke to Richard and told him he'd be with the coke buyer at the service station at ten o'clock the following morning. Richard said he'd be there.

The next day, 31 October, was also a particularly cold, grey one. A frigid wind whipped across the service station. At 10.00 a.m., Polifrone and Detective Paul Smith, posing as the Jewish rich kid, were sitting at an outdoor table in the grassy area. It was so cold their breath fogged. Teams of detectives surrounded the service station. Polifrone feigned giving Detective Smith a bag of coke. The detective looked into the bag. They didn't know if Richard was there, watching from afar, or not.

This was, in fact, all kinds of ridiculous. Seeing this superficial ruse wouldn't sway Richard one way or the other. Still, Bob Carroll and Polifrone felt it was worth a try. According to all the surveillance teams, however, Richard was nowhere near them. Finally, after waiting out in the cold for half an hour, Polifrone and Smith went off in different directions, not knowing if Richard had seen them or not.

Richard wasn't even in Jersey that day. He had a murder contract to fill in South Carolina. Another gambler had borrowed money from the wrong people and refused to pay, threatening to call the police. Richard was dispatched and killed the man as he came home with groceries, shot him dead with a .22 equipped with a silencer as he stepped out of his car. He returned to Dumont and took Barbara shopping. Barbara was already talking about the Christmas holidays, the type of tree she wanted this year, gifts she'd buy, who would get what, even her plans for the window decorations. Silently, Richard listened; he had, she knew, never got excited about the holidays, but he was even more removed from what she was saying now. Richard had changed. What, she wondered, could it be? She asked him.

'Nothing,' he said.

'You feeling OK?'

'I'm fine, just thinking,' he said.

'What about?' she pressed.

'Business,' he said with finality, ending the conversation.

That evening the family had a nice dinner, veal Milanese and mashed potatoes, one of Richard's favourites, but he was silent and withdrawn, just chewed his food and stared at something only he saw. After dinner, Merrick asked if he'd like to go and feed the ducks.

'No, not now,' he said, and went and watched a game show, thinking about doing away with Pat Kane, thinking about money – making enough money to get out of the life, to go straight. Money was the key. It always had been. He was leaving the following day for Zurich, and he planned to press Remi to get cheques more frequently. He looked forward to being away. He didn't want to be around people, even his own family, now. He wanted to be alone.

The following day, Richard got into his Camaro, drove to the airport unobserved and boarded a plane for Zurich. One of the first things he asked Remi when he saw him was if he knew anyone who could get cyanide.

* * *

Again, the task force stopped hearing Richard on the phone. Days went by. They held a meeting on the evening of 13 November. By this time, Dominick hadn't heard from Richard for two weeks.

Polifrone wanted to wait, to not chase Richard. He said that Kuklinski was cunning, that he was staying away to get the mark off balance. Deputy Chief Buccino had concerns. What if Kuklinski killed again? What if he secured cyanide somewhere else? What if it became public knowledge that they could have arrested him but didn't and he killed someone? 'We cannot leave this guy on the street much longer!' he said.

He had a valid point. Ron Donahue, however, agreed with Polifrone: they had to be patient, he said, the first rule of a good hunter. 'This guy is big game, and that's how we have to work him, play him,' he said.

In this way, it went back and forth, as the task-force members took discreet shots from the Jack Daniel's bottle with Richard's picture on it.

They discussed sending Kane and Volkman to Kuklinski's house again 'to rattle his cage'. That had seemed to work before.

In the end, Bob Carroll decided to side with Polifrone and give it some more time. The last thing he wanted to do was move prematurely. The case had to be airtight, carefully orchestrated. They would have one shot, and it had to be a bullseye.

'Let's send Kane to go see him again, see what happens,' he said. 'It worked last time.'

Two days before Thanksgiving, 22 November 1986, Richard was still in Europe, waiting for the largest cheque he'd got to date. Barbara went shopping for all the makings of a Thanksgiving feast. Her car was filled with bags of groceries when she pulled into the drive of her Dumont home. Barbara's mother used to serve lasagna before the turkey, but everyone would fill up on the pasta and not eat the turkey, so Barbara had stopped making lasagna.

Daughter Chris was now seeing a guy named Matt. He was the only man she had loved, and being intimate with him was 'special', not any kind of rebellion, as in years past. Daughter Merrick was going to marry Mark, her new boyfriend. Barbara liked him and was pleased Merrick had found 'a nice boy', as she thought of him. When Barbara pulled up in front of the house that day, Matt came out to help bring the packages inside. He was a strapping, good-looking man, always polite. Barbara liked him, too, as did Richard. As Matt and Chris and Barbara were bringing all the bags of food into the house, seemingly out of nowhere, Detectives Pat Kane and Ernest Volkman appeared, walked up the driveway.

'Excuse me, Mrs Kuklinski,' Kane said, 'I'm Detective Kane and this is Detective Volkman.' Both of them showed their shiny gold badges.

'We are looking for your husband,' Volkman said. They knew Richard wasn't there. His car was gone. They were doing this for one reason: to rattle Richard, to cause him to react, to upset him, his family life. The task force knew Richard loved Barbara, was exceedingly protective of her and his family. That was obvious by the phone calls he had with her that they had eavesdropped on.

Startled, Barbara regarded them with surprise, which quickly turned to disdain. 'Is something the matter?' she asked, not pleased by this sudden, unexpected presence. Who the hell did they think they were?

'We need to talk with him,' Kane said.

'What about?' she asked.

'He home?' Volkman asked, curt and unfriendly . . . *rude*, she thought.

Barbara was still very much her own woman, still had a razor-sharp tongue, a somewhat supercilious attitude.

'You know where he is?' Kane asked.

'No,' she said.

'Can you get in touch with him?' Kane said.

'I just said I don't know where he is. What's this about?' she demanded, not asked.

'You have a number where you can reach him?' Volkman put in.

'I don't. I don't know where he is, don't you hear?' she asked.

Now Matt came out of the house. Chris, a worried look on her face, stood in the doorway holding the family dog, Shaba, by the collar. Shaba, a large Irish wolfhound, was barking at the two detectives.

'What's wrong, Mom?' Chris called.

The two detectives moved towards Matt. 'Are you Richard Kuklinski?' Volkman asked.

'No,' he said.

'What's your name? What are you doing here?' Volkman asked.

Really annoyed now, Barbara put herself between Matt and the two detectives. 'None of your business!' she said. 'Where do you two get off? What's this about?' she again demanded.

Kane said, 'We need to talk to your husband about a couple of murders.'

'What?' she said. 'Murders?'

'Murders we think he committed,' Kane added.

Barbara couldn't believe what she'd just heard. She felt as if she'd been slapped with a red-hot hand. 'You have a warrant to be here on my property?' she asked.

'No.'

'Then get the hell off it,' she said.

They stood there.

'Chris,' Barbara said, 'let the dog loose!'

Chris froze. She didn't know what to do, holding the huge dog, which was now trying hard to break away.

'I said,' Barbara repeated, venom in her voice now, 'let the dog loose!'

If Chris had let Shaba go, Kane would have shot him dead. He was ready to reach for his gun. That, he knew, would surely get Richard's goat. But Chris had the good sense to hold on to Shaba's massive collar. The detectives had done what they'd set out to do – upset the apple cart. Kane took out a business card and handed it to Barbara. He said, 'Mrs Kuklinski, when your husband comes home, please have him call me.'

The detectives turned and walked back to their car, got in it and slowly left, knowing they'd be hearing from Richard Kuklinski soon.

'Tough lady,' Volkman said.

'Gotta be tough to be married to Rich,' Kane said.

Barbara was fit to be tied. These detectives had, she thought, purposely ruined the family's Thanksgiving.

When Richard, still in the Hotel Zurich, heard how Kane and Volkman had harassed his wife, his precious Barbara, telling her he was suspected of killing people, murder, he was enraged. He punched holes in walls. He broke furniture. He got on the first flight back to the States. Now more than ever, he wanted to kill Kane, had to kill him. He had no right talking to Barbara like that, telling her these disgusting things.

This year, Thanksgiving in the Kuklinski home was quiet and sombre. Richard barely talked, barely ate. He had grown noticeably pale. He was there at the head of the table but seemed to be somewhere else. No one could cheer him up, not even Merrick. Gloom hung over the table. After the meal, he went up to his office, sat at his desk and stared at Kane's card. He had left Zurich in such a hurry, he hadn't even got the cheque. This one was supposed to be for seven hundred thousand dollars.

He sat there fantasising about killing Kane, cutting him up, shooting him, torturing him, hanging him, feeding him to rats. But those things were all luxuries he knew he didn't have. The only way to murder Kane and get away with it clean was with cyanide – a quick spray in his face as he was changing his tyre. *Hey, buddy, pssst* – all over. Case closed. It would look like a natural death; he could get away with it.

Once Kane was gone, he reasoned, the case would fold on itself. Whatever Barbara Deppner and Percy House had told the cops, it wasn't enough to arrest him, Richard believed (correctly), or he would already have been arrested.

Richard called Kane and told him to stop coming to his home, that he had no right to do that, that if he wanted to talk to him he should let him know and he'd come over to the station with his attorney. Richard made a point of being pleasant, not wanting to alarm Kane in any way. Kane said he understood and would do as Richard asked. He too was polite.

'Thank you,' Richard said, and hung up.

Kane . . .

Kane had to go! But Richard had to get cyanide to pull that off . . . His mind went back to Polifrone. As much as Richard believed Polifrone was a bunch of hot air, *full of shit*, maybe he really could get his hands on cyanide. If you knew the right person, it wasn't actually that hard. Richard picked up the phone and paged Polifrone.

Pleased, Polifrone called him back within the hour, and yet another meeting was arranged at the service station. Richard also contacted Solimene and asked him if he knew where he could get some poison, 'preferably cyanide', he said.

'I'll see what I can do,' Solimene said.

Saturday, 6 December was another cold, grey day. The meeting was scheduled for 10.00 a.m. Because it was a Saturday morning, the service station was more crowded than usual. Polifrone was waiting for Richard at the bank of telephones, a prearranged spot. On time, Richard pulled up in his gleaming white Cadillac and stepped from the car wearing a blue silk shirt, a suit and tie, and a wool overcoat with a high collar. He looked sharp. Polifrone greeted him warmly. Bob Carroll and other task-force members were watching from strategic locations. Carroll had carefully prepped Polifrone on what to say to get Richard to incriminate himself further. The first thing Polifrone did, as though he were Richard's friend, was tell him that Kane and Volkman had stopped him coming out of the store and asked him a whole bunch of questions about Richard Kuklinski.

'What did you say?' Richard asked.

'Nothing. I told him I don't know a fuckin' thing about any fuckin' body. A guy named Pat . . .'

'Kane.' Richard spat out the word. 'He's been up my ass since 1980. He don't know shit. He's got a couple of rats, but no one will believe their bullshit. If he had anything he'd have booked me already,' he said, and then he went on to describe how he'd got rid of Smith and Deppner and how Percy House was a 'pointer' (a rat).

Polifrone was both surprised and delighted, and wondered why Kuklinski was being so forthcoming. Either he had a really big mouth (not likely), or he was planning to kill him. He believed it was the latter. Polifrone explained that he had the cyanide and had called him half a dozen times to tell him.

'Great,' Richard said. 'I could really use it now.'

'Yeah, well,' Polifrone said, 'I brought it back to the guys I got it from. I didn't wanna fuckin' be driving around with that shit. But I can get it for ya.'

Richard was obviously pleased; he actually smiled. It was a chilling smile to see.

Now Polifrone again brought up the rich Jewish kid looking for coke. Richard said he was still interested; he'd bring his van, and they'd get the kid in the van, take his money and kill him. Simple. He talked about murder, Polifrone noted, as if he were discussing the weather.

Ice Man was the perfect nickname for him, Polifrone was thinking.

If, Richard said, they wanted to make the body 'disappear', they could throw the corpse down some abandoned mine shafts he knew about. 'They are so deep,' he said, 'you don't even hear them bounce.'

Ice-fuckin-Man indeed, Polifrone thought. 'Good, sounds

good. What about his car? Should we leave it or get rid of it?' the agent asked.

'Either or. We could sell it for parts. I know a place – bam, bam, they cut it up and sell it for parts the same day.'

Polifrone asked questions about being able to fool the coroner if, in fact, they poisoned the rich kid and left him in his car, and, incredibly, Richard said the medical examiner would be fooled and went on to tell Polifrone how he had once frozen a victim, which had confused the ME. Polifrone knew he was talking about Louis Masgay. Bingo. Polifrone prayed the tape was recording all this; it was far more than they had ever hoped for.

Richard went on to describe, again, the best ways to administer cyanide, said that putting it in food was much better, easier and safer. He talked too about retiring, getting out of 'this dirty business'. He even said he had set some money aside, 'out of the country', he volunteered.

Why Richard was telling Polifrone all this was strange indeed . . . perplexing. Even if he was planning to kill him eventually, it didn't make sense. He barely knew Polifrone, who now wanted to shake Richard's hand and thank him for being so helpful. After an hour of Richard digging his own grave, the meeting ended. The two men agreed to meet again soon. Polifrone promised Richard the cyanide and said that he'd call him when he had the rich Jewish kid set up and the kid had the money. They shook hands. Richard got back into his shiny white Caddy and took off. Polifrone soon checked the tape. It had been working.

We got him by the balls, he thought, and soon he handed the Nagra tape recorder to Detective Paul Smith.

PART V

HOMICIDE SUPERSTAR

52

THE QUIET BEFORE
THE STORM

Christmas was in the air. Barbara Kuklinski had her shopping
list prepared, was buying and wrapping gifts. Most homes on
the Kuklinskis' block had Christmas decorations up already.
Barbara was feeling a little under the weather, but the prospect
of Christmas cheered and motivated her.

Richard was talking to Remi several times a day. He was
most often using stolen phone cards to make these calls. He
believed, correctly, that his phones were tapped – thanks
to Kane – and was careful about what he said. Remi kept
saying that another cheque was 'forthcoming'. Richard said
he'd leave when Remi had it, that he didn't want to sit
around in Zurich waiting for it just right now. Richard made
several trips to Jersey City and Hoboken, his old stomping
grounds, trying to find someone who had access to cyanide;
he wasn't having much luck. He now thought seriously about
just making Kane disappear, but that, he decided, would be
worse than killing him and allowing the body to be found
because the cops wouldn't rest until they knew what had
happened to him. He thought, too, about giving Kane a flat,
killing him with a blow to the head, then putting his head
under the wheel and kicking the jack out of place, crushing
his head and making it impossible to discern that a blow to
the head had done him in. But he knew that to do such a

thing he would need more privacy than the bar parking lot could afford.

Barbara was concerned about her husband. He had become more and more distant. He was not the same man any more. He hadn't lost his temper or raised his voice once for many weeks. Strange.

It was, she decided, the quiet before the storm. Something was brewing; something was in the air; she just didn't know what it was. Rather than worry, she focused her energy on preparing for Christmas, shopping, buying gifts – spending money, one of her favourite pastimes.

Again, at Bob Carroll's insistence, Polifrone contacted Richard and told him he had the coke buyer all set up; everything was 'a go', and the cyanide was forthcoming. Another meeting at the Lombardi service station was set up.

Richard's reservations about Polifrone were outweighed by two considerations: getting his hands on cyanide to kill Pat Kane properly; and taking off this rich Jewish kid, keeping all the money and finally getting rid of Polifrone and his bad wig once and for all. It all fitted together perfectly. To some degree, the fact that Polifrone had been laid-back, hadn't chased Richard, made him believe Polifrone might very well get the cyanide, might have access to a rich kid looking to buy coke. After all, coke was the in drug. Almost everyone was doing it, even mob guys, and all the hip, fancy people.

This third meeting between Richard and Polifrone took place on 12 December. It had snowed a few days earlier, and the service station was pocked with mounds of dirty snow. Richard showed up on time, at 11.00 a.m.

Polifrone said: 'Listen to this. The Jewish kid asked me if I can get him three kilos. I said yeah, of course. Eighty-five thousand, cash. Wednesday morning he's coming. He'll be here around nine fuckin' thirty. Now here's the thing. I'll pick up the cyanide that morning from my guy.'

'Doesn't give me enough time. I need a couple of days to get it ready.' Richard went on to describe how he had to have a chemist mix a special liquid – the DMSO – with the cyanide. That would take a few days. Such a thing couldn't be rushed.

Polifrone, wanting to move this thing forward and finally have Richard arrested, suggested they instead give the coke buyer 'an egg sandwich' and kill him that way. He went on to say the Jewish kid loved egg sandwiches, was always ordering them.

'But will the kid eat?' Richard asked.

'Yeah, no problem.'

'Then that'll work.'

'Guaranteed. It'll be an egg sandwich. Every time I meet this kid, he orders an egg sandwich. We'll get him an egg sandwich.'

'We can do that. Do they sell egg sandwiches here? I don't even know if they do.'

Polifrone took care of this by saying *he'd* bring the egg sandwich, and the vial of cyanide.

This should have set off alarm bells in Richard's head – giving the coke buyer an egg sandwich Polifrone would *bring* – but it didn't. He seemed to accept what Polifrone was laying down. For him, none of this really mattered, though: in his mind both Polifrone and the coke buyer were going to die. Simple. He'd shoot them both in the head with a .22 equipped with a silencer, the same type of weapon he had sold to Polifrone weeks earlier.

That evening, there was yet another meeting in the war room at the attorney general's office. The task force sat around the large table listening to the most recent tape and debating how to bring the case to a close. The final act of this drama was about to unfold, they all knew, one way or another. The question was, what was the best way to finally arrest Richard? Bob Carroll suggested that they use an apartment and get

Kuklinski on film actually giving the coke buyer – Detective Paul Smith – the cyanide-laced egg sandwich.

Smith didn't like this idea at all. 'What if he just decides to pull out a gun and shoot me – and Dom?'

He had a point.

It was decided, therefore, that the final act would play out at the Lombardi service station.

Polifrone contacted Richard the following day. The deal would go down, it was agreed, on Wednesday, 17 December. He would bring the coke buyer to the meeting place. Richard said he'd get a van so they could get the kid in the van. Polifrone said he'd meet with Richard earlier and give him three egg sandwiches and a vial of cyanide (actually harmless white powder), which Richard would use to poison the coke buyer's sandwich as he saw fit.

For Richard, the sandwich had become irrelevant nonsense; as soon as the coke buyer and Polifrone were in the van, Richard was going to kill them. End of story. He planned to borrow a van from Jimmy DiVita, a small-time hustler from New London, Connecticut. He would take the bodies to Pennsylvania and dump them in an abandoned mine shaft.

To humour Polifrone and play out the sting, Richard agreed to meet him early on Wednesday morning, 17 December, to get the egg sandwiches and cyanide. The cyanide he'd use to kill Pat Kane. That was Richard's plan.

53

WITH A WIGGLE

It was 17 December 1986, a day that would live in infamy.

As usual, Richard was up early. He had coffee and toast and sat in the living-room staring at the floor, wondering if he should go and meet Polifrone or not. He had, he would later say, an uncomfortable feeling about the whole set-up; but he decided he'd see how it went. After all, he reasoned, he'd put so much time into this thing already, he might as well see how it played out. He stood up, put on a waist-length black jacket and headed out the door. Barbara wasn't feeling well and was still in bed.

At 8.45 a.m., ATF Agent Dominick Polifrone was standing at the usual spot in front of the bank of the phones at the service station. It was a bitterly cold day. Frigid winds tore across the area. People hurried to and from their cars to one of the six fast-food outlets. The sky was filled with churning, angry clouds that seemed at war with one another; traffic whizzed by; planes roared low overhead.

Polifrone had a white paper bag in his hand. It contained three egg sandwiches. In the pocket of his coat, he had a thumb-sized glass vial, the supposed cyanide, which would be used to 'poison' one of the sandwiches. Polifrone was armed to the teeth, wired up. Task-force detectives monitored his every move. Everyone was tense. This was it. This was D-day. This was the day it would go down. Everyone knew Richard was lethal – definitely armed, wouldn't hesitate to kill. Polifrone looked forward to getting this done once and for all. He'd been on this cursed case now for nearly 19 months. He was tired of it, tired of the bullshit, tired of the Ice Man task force, tired of walking on the edge. He stared at the access road and spotted Richard's Oldsmobile Calais with Richard's unmistakable, huge form behind the wheel.

'There he is,' he whispered, his words instantly transmitted to all the members of the task force. Pat Kane, Bob Carroll, Paul Smith and Ron Donahue were hidden in a dark Chevy van with tinted windows and had a clear view of Polifrone.

Pat Kane could barely sleep the night before. All his effort, all his sweat and tears and sleepless nights, was finally paying off. He had never believed this day would come, but it was here. Richard Kuklinski would soon be behind bars, or dead. Those were the only two options. Bob Carroll had promised him that when the time came to arrest Kuklinski, he, Pat Kane, could do it – tell him he was under arrest and actually put the cuffs on him. This would be the highlight of Kane's career, his life. As he lay in bed thinking about what would happen, he prayed – gave thanks for the help he was sure God had given him, given Polifrone and the task force, given Bob Carroll. Kane was sure God's hand had played an integral role in all this, in all that would happen. Surely God, he believed, had provided Dominick Polifrone. As far as he was concerned, Richard Kuklinski was an instrument of Satan himself, and now, finally, he would be getting his due.

'How you doin', Dom?' Richard asked as he approached.

'Good. I spoke to the kid last night. It's all set. Here's the sandwiches. I'll go get him and be back in 15 minutes.' Richard took the bag.

'You sure?' he asked.

'Yeah, yeah,' Polifrone assured. He didn't like the way Richard was acting; he seemed distant . . . wary. 'I'll go get the kid and be back in 15 minutes.'

'OK. I'll go get the van. It isn't far from here. Just down the next exit. It's just a ten-minute ride,' Richard said.

'What colour is it, so I'll know?'

'Blue.'

'Now, where are you gonna park it so I can bring him right there?'

'Right here. We might as well do it over here out of the way of everybody. I'll be sitting in the driver's seat. You can't miss it.'

'OK, I'm gonna bring him right into the back of the van to let him test the coke.'

'OK.'

Polifrone now took a small bag out of his jacket pocket. 'Here's the cyanide,' he said, amplifying the word 'cyanide' loud and clear so it would certainly be recorded. Polifrone said there was enough of the deadly poison to kill a lot of people. He asked where Richard was going to get rid of the coke buyer's body.

'I'm going to put it away for safekeeping,' he said, and laughed. It was an ice-cold laugh filled with malice, no mirth, his breath fogging in the cold. Richard now spotted the task-force black van with the tinted windows. Something wasn't right about it . . . it was *hinky*, suspicious, he would later explain.

'Let's walk,' Richard said, and started across the lot, right towards the van. They saw him coming; all quickly got down.

'Where you going?' Polifrone asked, concerned, his hand moving towards his piece.

'Just to walk a little,' Richard said. He got up to the van and actually looked inside. He couldn't see anything. Now he started back towards his car, Polifrone following him, trying to get Richard to use the word 'murder'. Richard opened his boot and put the sandwiches inside, got in his car and started the engine. He assured Polifrone he'd be back with the van, said it was two-toned, light and dark blue. Richard's plan was to come back in his car, and if the rich Jewish kid was there, he'd say the van wouldn't start, the coke was in his warehouse, and they should follow him there. Once inside the warehouse, Richard would kill both Polifrone and the coke buyer. Richard had, in fact, tried to borrow a van the day before from Jimmy DiVita, but his van had too many windows. Anyway, the warehouse would be a better place to do the double homicide. Richard said he'd be back in 20 minutes. Polifrone said he'd be back with the coke buyer in exactly 30 minutes. Richard pulled away. As he went, he passed the bank of phones. In one was Deputy Chief Bob Buccino, making believe he was talking. He'd been listening to every word said. He had a nine-millimetre wrapped in a newspaper, was ready to blow Richard away. The chief truly hated Richard and was looking for an excuse to end it all right there, no long, expensive trial.

They could have arrested Richard there and then, but Bob Carroll wanted Richard to put the white powder on the sandwich and actually give it to Detective Paul Smith; that, he felt, would strengthen the case, tie Kuklinski directly to the murder of Gary Smith. When Richard returned, they'd nail him red-handed. The parking lot was saturated with attorney general's people and ATF and FBI agents, all ready to pounce, to bring down this serial killer who poisoned, shot and stabbed people with impunity, as though he had some divine right.

Richard drove out of the service station. He went half a mile down the road, pulled over, put on plastic gloves and carefully opened the vial. It didn't look, he immediately thought, like cyanide. He ever so carefully sniffed the air – no distinct scent of almonds, the odour of cyanide.

This is fuckin' bullshit! he thought, and sat there wondering what was up, more perplexed than anything else. He put the car back in gear and drove a short distance, spotted a mangy dog sniffing around a group of rubbish bins. He pulled into a restaurant, bought a hamburger, took it to the car, carefully – just in case – put some of the white powder on the burger and walked over to the large rust-coloured mutt. The dog smelled the meat, and its ears perked right up. Richard offered it the burger. With trepidation, as though it'd been tricked before, the dog took the burger and quickly gobbled it down as Richard curiously watched to see what would happen, his head tilted to the left with curiosity.

Happy, the dog moved off down the road, wagging its scrawny tail as it went.

Fucking liar! Richard thought. He didn't yet know what the hell Polifrone was up to, but he wanted nothing more to do with it, whatever it was. He began thinking that Polifrone was maybe a contract killer who was, in fact, trying to set him up.

'Fuck 'im,' Richard said out loud, and drove to a phone booth and called Barbara to see how she felt. For the last two days, her arthritis had been acting up, and she had a slight headache and a low-grade fever.

'I'm OK. I'm lying down,' she said.

'Would you like to go for breakfast?' he asked.

'Sure, I guess . . . OK.'

'I'm going to stop and pick up some things at the store and then come home.'

'Fine,' she said, and hung up. Richard drove over to the Grand Union supermarket and bought some groceries. As always, he bought more than was actually needed; one of Richard's biggest pleasures in life was providing well for his family. He left the Grand Union with four big bags brimming with groceries, put them in the boot, slid into his car and slowly drove home, unaware of the gathering law-enforcement storm.

State detectives Tommy Trainer and Denny Cortez were watching the Kuklinski home that morning. That was their assignment. Every 20 minutes or so, they cruised past the split-level Kuklinski residence. It was a damp, very chilly day. The sky was a mass of angry clouds the colour of gunpowder.

The promise of snow hung in the air. Christmas was just around the corner, and all hell was about to break loose on this quiet Dumont street.

Close to ten that morning, Cortez and Trainer drove past the house, and there was Richard in the driveway, taking the four bags of groceries from the car's boot.

Shocked to see him just suddenly there like that, not at the service station where he was supposed to be, they called the task force, who were equally shocked to learn that Richard was in Dumont. He obviously wasn't planning on coming back to the service station. Richard saw the two detectives cruise by, giving him the hairy eyeball. He wondered why they were staring so intently at him. He did not connect these men to Polifrone – kind of strange, given his suspicious nature.

Deputy Chief Bob Buccino was running the show that morning. He now ordered the strike force to go to Richard's home and arrest him there, and they all started towards Dumont, over 15 unmarked vehicles, sirens screaming, red lights frantically spinning. More than anything, Buccino wanted to avoid a shoot-out on the residential street. He assumed Richard had all kinds of heavy-duty weapons in the house – assault rifles with armour-piercing rounds, hand grenades, dynamite, God knew what else. Fearing Richard had contacts in the Dumont police force, Buccino did not tell the Dumont police what was about to happen, a courtesy normally given to the local cops when a big bust is about to go down.

Richard put the groceries on the kitchen counter and began to unpack and put them away. Barbara, feeling weak, a bit pale, only hoped she wasn't sick for the holidays, the putting up of the tree, all the cooking, the joyful opening of presents. As she watched Richard unpacking the groceries, she thought about how kind and good he could be when he wanted to, how mean and sadistic he could be at other times. There were, she was thinking, more sure than ever, two Richards. She had married two men.

'Ready, Lady?' he asked.

'Ready,' she said.

By now, Richard had forgotten about Polifrone. He had washed his hands of him, would never have anything to do with him again. He planned to call Phil Solimene after breakfast and tell him how Polifrone was full of shit, ask why the fuck he would vouch for such a jive-ass blowhard. Richard used the bathroom. Barbara slowly slipped on a blue goose-down ski jacket Richard had recently bought her. It was nice and warm but had one of those zips that went diagonally across the front, from left to right. The zip often became stuck when she tried to close it, as it did now. She asked Richard to close it for her. She didn't want to get a chill. Using his pliers-like grip, he easily managed to zip the jacket closed. As mean and violent as Richard could be to Barbara, he loved her dearly. She was the only woman he'd ever loved, and he held her in high esteem, thought the world of her.

'After we eat, I'm taking you to the doctor,' he said.

'That's not necessary. I just need rest, Richard.'

'Yeah, well, let the doctor take a look at you,' he insisted.

She didn't answer. She was in no mood to argue. She just wanted a nice breakfast, scrambled eggs with bacon that had 'a little wiggle', as she put it, not too well done. They headed for the door. He opened it for her.

By now, the strike force had reached Dumont and had gathered at the south end of Sunset Street just down the block. Deputy Chief Buccino, the detectives and the agents were discussing what was the best way to take Richard down. As they spoke, one of the agents spotted Richard and Barbara leaving the house and getting in the car.

'He's coming!' he shouted. 'He's with his wife!' he added.

They all hurried back to their vehicles and got ready to pounce.

Detective Pat Kane was pumped up. Now, finally, Richard was going down. All his work had paid off. This was it. The moment he'd been hoping for, praying for, was finally here.

Polifrone wasn't there. He'd gone to the courthouse in Hackensack at Buccino's request.

After Richard helped Barbara into the car, he got behind the wheel, started the car and drove right towards the gathered strike force, completely unaware he was driving into the proverbial hornet's nest, and then some. Richard had a .25 automatic under the seat. The strike force was armed with machine guns and shotguns. As he slowly made his way south along the street where he had lived for 17 years, he spotted the strike-force vehicles haphazardly lined up.

'Something must've happened,' he said to Barbara

Suddenly, all the vehicles surged forward and came barrelling directly towards Richard and Barbara, no spinning red lights, no sirens.

'What the hell?!' Richard said.

'Watch out!' Barbara exclaimed.

At first, Richard thought it was a hit, that he was going to get killed, that all he had done – or something he'd recently done – had finally caught up with him. He veered to the right. The car hit the kerb. Agents and detectives burst from the vehicles and surrounded him. One jumped on the bonnet of the car and pointed a gun, in combat position. Richard thought about reaching for the .25, but he was afraid, knowing many shots would surely be fired at him, at the car, and Barbara might get hit.

There was a cocked nine-millimetre pointed at his head. 'Don't fuckin' move!' he was told. The car door was ripped open. Richard was roughly pulled from the car by Kane and men piled onto him, trying to push him to the ground, trying to pin his massive arms behind his back so he could be handcuffed. Barbara's door was torn open. Deputy Chief Buccino grabbed her and made her get on the ground, physically pushing her down. When Richard saw this, rage exploded inside his head.

'She has nothing to do with this, leave her. Leave her be!' he yelled.

'Fuck yourself,' Buccino said, his animus showing, and he roughly pushed Barbara to the ground and put his boot on her back while she was cuffed.

'What are you doing?!' she asked. 'Richard, help me!'

Richard went berserk. He got up and made for Buccino, intent on killing him, tearing him apart, not caring if he was shot dead trying.

Eight strike-force members were now fighting with him, struggling with him, wrestling with him, Pat Kane, Donahue and Volkman among them, all of them amazed by Richard's superhuman strength. Richard actually made it to the rear of the car, halfway to Buccino. Now the agents and cops lifted him up off the ground and slammed him to the bonnet of the car. It took four men to get his hands behind his back, but Kane couldn't get the handcuffs on his wrists, they were so thick. He finally had to use leg irons to shackle Richard's arms behind his back.

Richard was blind with rage at Barbara's being manhandled, and even shackled with thick leg irons, he resisted and tried to get to Buccino.

'Calm down, calm down,' Kane told him. 'It's over, Rich, it's over. You're under arrest.'

'There's no reason to involve her!' Richard bellowed. 'She's innocent. You know that!'

'It's out of my hands,' Kane said.

Barbara was helped up and led to a van. The cops and troopers were still struggling to keep Richard from getting to Deputy Chief Buccino, who was ready to shoot Richard dead. Stunned, people on the block had called the Dumont police, and now two squad cars showed up.

All his life, throughout his long, sordid career in crime, Richard had always imagined he'd go out in a fierce gun battle to the death. He had, in fact, specifically planned that. He would much rather have been killed in a shoot-out than face the music, see the embarrassment, humiliation and shame his family would surely suffer if who he really was were ever exposed. Of all things, Richard dreaded that – the humiliation of his cherished family. That was all he cared about.

Now a mob of strike-force members boldly picked Richard up and put him in the back of the black van. He was literally fit to be tied.

54

THE POLITICS
OF MURDER

Attorney General Al Smit, Bob Carroll's boss, viewed the arrest of Richard Kuklinski as the absolute pinnacle of his career, and he wanted to get as much mileage out of it as possible. Knowing the arrest would go down today, he had ordered his office to contact the media so they'd be there in full force to cover the bust. The tagline the media was given was that lawmen were arresting 'a serial killer who froze people, who killed with cyanide, guns, knives, and who also happened to be a mob hit man', which, needless to say, caused a media stampede.

Al Smit had political aspirations. He was hoping for a shot at the governor's office, and what better way to get there than this arrest, this media blitz? There is a long list of crime fighters turned politicians who rode well-publicised cases to higher office. The most obvious examples would be Rudy Giuliani using his prosecutions of Mafia bosses in the Southern District of New York to get himself elected mayor, and Thomas E. Dewey using his highly publicised prosecution of Lucky Luciano to become the governor of New York State.

When, that morning, Richard was on the way to the Hackensack courthouse to be arrested, booked, photographed and fingerprinted, a call came in that the press was lined up outside the courtroom and Kuklinski should look 'presentable for media consumption'. At that, the van pulled over, and five detectives helped Richard get out, made sure he didn't look too messed up and put him in the back of a black detective's car. He had calmed down somewhat but was still pissed off that Barbara had been roughed up. He didn't give a flying fuck what they did to him, but to abuse Barbara, throw her down and cuff her, was unthinkable, unspeakable, an infamy. Until he killed Buccino, he would not rest. If he died doing it, he didn't care; so be it.

'You know my wife is innocent. You know my wife didn't do anything,' he kept saying, almost more to himself than to any of the detectives in the car, one of whom was Pat Kane.

'Nobody hurt her. Calm down, Rich. Calm down,' Kane said.

'She's sick. There was no reason to treat her like that – no reason!'

Instead of driving the car directly up to the entrance, they parked a good 30 feet away so Richard would have to walk the distance, giving the mob of wide-eyed, stunned reporters, producers and cameramen a good look at this giant serial killer who murdered and froze human beings. Richard did not try to hide his anger; he huffed and puffed and grumbled, seeming as if he might explode into a homicidal rage at any moment.

'How many people did you kill?' a reporter asked.

'Did you really freeze people? How many?' another begged.

'These cops,' Richard growled, his face a twisted mask of barely contained fury, 'have seen too many movies.'

Inside, Richard was taken to a holding area, still bellowing about Barbara's treatment. That was all he cared about. On the way to a holding cell, he spotted a bewildered, frightened Barbara sitting in the homicide squad room. She was still cuffed, crying, upset. How could she not be?

'Get those fucking cuffs off her!' he demanded. 'She knows nothing, she's innocent!' He tried to snap the thick chains holding his massive hands behind his back.

'Get those fuckin' cuffs off her!' he roared, so loudly that the reporters heard him all the way outside, the walls reverberating with his angry words. It took half a dozen detectives to wrestle him into the holding cell. Normally, the cuffs are removed from a prisoner at this point, but no one was taking the cuffs off Richard. It was obvious he'd kill anyone he could get his hands on.

Now, like a crazed beast suddenly plucked from a dangerous jungle, Richard paced his cell, cursing every cop he saw, taunting them, daring them to take the shackles off of him.

'I will kill you motherfuckers – I'll kill you all, you motherfuckers!' he roared.

Back in Dumont, an army of police personnel armed with warrants flooded the Kuklinski home. They were sure they'd find a huge trove of weapons, the freezer Richard used to freeze his victims; but they found no arms, no freezer – nothing illegal at all.

That night, every six o'clock news show across America reported the arrest of Richard Kuklinski. He was big news. The hot lead-off story. Based on what the police had told the media, anchormen and anchorwomen in turn told America that Richard had killed five people – naming George Malliband, Louis Masgay, Paul Hoffman, Gary Smith and Danny Deppner – that he used cyanide to kill and that he froze some of his victims to confuse the police as to the time of death, hence the moniker: the Ice Man.

Aghast at the thought of such a thing, America watched him being led into the rear of the courthouse, his face twisted into a snarl – over and over again across the country.

The following day, the story was reported in sensational large print on the front pages of New York's three major newspapers – the *Post*, the *Daily News* and the venerable *New York Times*. The police had given Richard the perfect nickname. 'The Ice Man' was evil and sinister and simple all at the same time, ideal for headlines and taglines for opening news reports. From the East Coast to the West Coast and everywhere in between, America heard about the diabolical machinations of the Ice Man, a contract killer like no other. He killed for fun and he killed for the mob. When the media realised that the Ice Man was married with children, reporters and outside-broadcast units swarmed Sunset Street in Dumont, trying to get interviews with the Kuklinskis' shocked neighbours, with the Kuklinski children. Richard's worst fear had come true in bold, living colour.

Barbara was released on her own recognisance, but the police charged her with possession of the .25 auto they found under the seat of her car. The police, of course, knew the gun was not Barbara's, but they filed charges against her thinking they could use that as leverage against Richard down the road, which is exactly what they did. When Barbara arrived home, her hands were still trembling. A mob of reporters surrounded her. She had to fight her way through them to get inside.

When Richard was finally allowed to make his mandatory phone call, he phoned Phil Solimene.

'Hey, Philly, how you doin'?' Richard asked, his voice dripping with syrupy disdain.

'Rich?' Solimene said, shocked. 'What happened? Where are you?'

'I just got off Route 80. I'm coming to see you,' Richard said, and hung up.

Solimene ran from the store as if his ass were on fire, his face filled with fear and panic and dread.

Pat Kane was finally at peace. He had done what he'd set out to do. It had taken nearly six years, but he had prevailed. All his hard work and diligence had paid off. Richard Kuklinski was in a cage where he belonged. Though there was still much to do, that night Pat Kane slept like a baby, his wife in his arms.

Life was good.

Life held much promise.

Kane had caught the cunning, very dangerous muskie.

55

THE STATE OF NEW JERSEY V. RICHARD LEONARD KUKLINSKI

On 18 December, Richard appeared in New Jersey Superior Court, in front of Judge Peter Riolina, and was officially charged with 19 criminal offences. Here, for the first time, Richard saw his nemesis – Deputy Attorney General Bob Carroll – and he did not like what he saw. It was obvious that Carroll knew the facts and details backwards, that he had planned and orchestrated Richard's arrest and that he would be trying the state's case. Richard was now formally charged with the murders of Masgay, Malliband, Hoffman, Smith and Deppner.

After the brief proceeding, Richard was taken to a cell at the courthouse jail. It would be here that he would wait while the wheels of justice slowly, inexorably turned and the case was adjudicated.

When Barbara heard what the charges were against her husband, she was apalled; she didn't believe them. Daughter Chris wasn't surprised at all. She felt, in fact, that her father was absolutely capable of what the police were saying he'd done. Richard's son, Dwayne, now 18, also felt his father eminently capable of having done what the police alleged.

For a long time, Dwayne had felt that sooner or later he would have some kind of life-and-death struggle with his father, and now Dwayne realised that such a confrontation would surely have ended with his being killed.

More than anyone else, Dwayne felt the stigma of being Richard's son, a Kuklinski. By now, both Chris and Merrick were out of school, but Dwayne was still attending school, and he saw the strange, curious stares, the pointing, heard the whispering. Richard's favourite, Merrick, wasn't surprised either at what the police said her dad had done, but still she was hurt and deeply troubled that her dad was in jail. No matter what he'd done, what heinous crimes the police said he'd committed, he was innocent until proved guilty. Merrick would love him and support him and be there 10,000 per cent for him to the end.

When Richard learned that Dominick Polifrone was a plant, an ATF agent, and that he had taped most of their conversations, he knew he was dead in the water. Unless some kind of miracle happened, he'd never get out of jail, never see the light of day, would more than likely get a death sentence. He was so angry with himself, how stupid and gullible he'd been, that he couldn't even look at himself in a mirror without getting angry and calling himself names. *You idiot, you fool, what the fuck were you thinking?* he said over and over again.

He paced his cell. He silently cursed heaven and hell, the world and everyone in it.

Richard often thought about killing Deputy Chief Bob Buccino, how he would torture him and make him suffer. Oh, how he wanted to see Buccino suffer, see the rats feed on him. He believed that Kane and Polifrone were, for the most part, just doing their jobs, but Buccino was another story. The way he had treated Barbara was, he believed, totally uncalled for, was bully-like, and he hated the man with a fiery, burning passion. Even many years later, towards the end of his life, Richard got angry, his face paled, his lips twisted, when he thought of Deputy Chief Buccino. *I don't know*, he said, *if the prick is still alive or dead, but if he died, I hope it was a painful death. I hope he died of cancer of the asshole.*

Shortly after his arrest, Richard decided not even to try to mount any kind of viable defence. His was a hopeless case; once a jury heard him talking, burying himself, he'd get convicted. The only question was whether he would get the death sentence or life in jail. Either way, it didn't matter. He had fucked up big-time, and he knew it, accepted it, didn't try to blame anyone else. Yes, of course, his 'friend' Phil Solimene had set him up, but he should have sensed something was up, smelled it in the wind, seen the writing on the wall. Richard had never been trusting or easily fooled, yet he had walked into the carefully laid trap, he says, *like a wide-eyed schoolkid with no sense at all.*

Because of all the extraordinary media coverage of the case, the jury pool, he knew, was irreversibly tainted, and he had less chance than a snowball in hell. Also because of all the media attention he'd received, Richard was by far the most notorious prisoner in the county jail. One of his fellow prisoners began taunting him and teasing him every time he passed his cell. 'Ice Man, my ass,' he said. 'You ain't shit. You ain't so tough.' Richard just smiled, knowing sooner or later he'd get his hands on this guy. He was in a foul, homicidal mood, looking to kill someone, anyone. Murder would be like an aspirin for a headache.

Barbara was, in a sense, relieved that Richard was finally out of the house. For the first time since she'd married Richard, she knew a new kind of peace and tranquillity, she explained. For weeks after Richard's arrest, reporters hounded her and her children, but they were coming around less and less, thank God.

Pat Kane woke up every day with a smile on his face. He had done it. It had been a long, bumpy road, but he'd done it.

He was ten feet tall.

56

IT WAS DUE TO BUSINESS

Thirteen months after Richard's arrest, on 25 January 1988, his trial for the murders of Gary Smith and Danny Deppner began. The state had decided to have two trials; the second trial would be for the murders of Louis Masgay and George Malliband. Bob Carroll had decided not to try Richard for the murder of Paul Hoffman, because without Mr Hoffman's body, the case would be difficult to prove, so, for now, he dropped it.

A young lawyer with the public defender's office, Neal Frank, became Richard's attorney. Richard was claiming to be indigent, and the state was forced to provide him with counsel. Perhaps out of lack of experience or naivety, Neal Frank felt there was a fighting chance and told both Richard and Barbara that. But Richard knew better. He didn't feel he had any chance of walking.

Barbara, however, believed Frank, believed that Richard would beat the charges and come home. She was torn about his return. On the one hand, she was finally free of him, not subjected to his volatile mood swings, his duality, his sudden, extraordinary violence. On the other, she missed the good Richard.

Still, she quickly got used to sleeping alone and liked it, she says.

* * *

Neal Frank told Barbara that she and the family should show up in court, to let the jury see them. It was important for the jury to know that Richard had a loving, supportive family. They had to see that Richard wasn't the diabolical serial killer the press had consistently portrayed him as. This, the Ice Man story, had by now appeared on hundreds of front pages across New Jersey, indeed across the country.

The presiding judge was a stern, forbidding individual who wore granny glasses, slicked his sparse grey hair back and was known as 'the Time Machine' because he had a tendency to mete out the harshest sentences the law permitted. His name was Fred Kuchenmeister, and he regularly showed open disdain for defendants. In his court, defence lawyers claimed, you were guilty until you proved yourself innocent.

By the time jury selection was completed and the trial actually began, it was 17 February. Finding a fair-minded jury had been, for Neal Frank, a Herculean task, with all the media attention, but Frank felt he had managed to secure a reasonable jury that would listen to the case with 'an open mind'.

Bob Carroll first presented an extremely well put-together case, tight as a wet drum. Carroll, with co-counsel Charley Waldron, a tall, grey-haired man who knew his way around a courtroom well, put a series of witnesses on the stand, beginning with Barbara Deppner. Also up were Percy House, Richard Peterson, Pat Kane, two pathologists, Deputy Chief Bob Buccino, Jimmy DiVita and Gary Smith's wife. Carroll even put on the stand Darlene Pecorato, a stewardess who had rented Richie Peterson's apartment after he moved out. This was the place where Danny Deppner had been shot in the head by Richard, and Pecorato told about the bloodstained rug that had been there when she moved in. Paul Smith then told how he had discovered bloodstains in the wood floor under the rug. And finally, Dominick Polifrone took the stand. When Dominick walked in front of Richard, Richard said, 'Hey, Dom, how you doin'?' actually smiling. Dominick was still, to Richard's amazement, wearing that terrible wig.

IT WAS DUE TO BUSINESS

Now the jury heard Richard's own words, words that clearly opened the door wide, everyone knew, to convicting Richard. Neal Frank tried to make the jury believe Richard had only been bragging, but this was a hard sell, and everyone knew it.

All through the fast-moving proceedings, Barbara Kuklinski didn't believe what the state was contending until she heard her husband readily admitting to killing people with guns, knives and cyanide. Until she heard him say that he had frozen a man to confuse the police, she still thought that he had been framed. When she heard Richard tell Agent Polifrone what he had done and how he had done it, she was stunned to numb silence. She had always known Richard to be exceedingly tight-lipped. She hadn't been able to get anything out of his mouth with a crowbar since she met him 26 years before; yet here he was admitting to a cop all that he'd done, how he'd done it, even when and where.

Barbara wanted to run from the courtroom. She had no idea, she realised as if she'd been struck by lightning, to whom she'd really been married for so many years. She felt fooled and duped; she felt like an out-of-touch idiot. She wanted to stand up and yell at him, *How could you?! How could you?!* But she sat there still like stone, her mouth slightly agape, listening to her husband admit to murder as if he were talking about feeding the ducks or the colour of tie he should wear.

Numb, she left the courtroom, sure Richard would never get out of jail, never be free, shaking her head in dismay. *I was married*, she later explained, *to a monster and didn't know it. I mean, I knew he had a bad temper, could be violent, but I had no idea of who he really was and what he was really about. I felt . . . I felt like I'd been hit by a lightning bolt . . . was all burned and in shock.*

Now, for the first time, Barbara knew whom she had married, with whom she'd had three children. Her head spun with the incomprehensible reality of it all.

My God, she kept saying to herself. *My God*, suddenly feeling very old and all beaten up.

While Richard had been incarcerated, Merrick had wed her boyfriend, Mark (it disturbed Richard no end that he could not walk Merrick down the aisle). She had a baby, and Merrick religiously showed up in court carrying the child, a boy she named Sean. Neal Frank said it might make the jury 'more sympathetic', if such a thing was possible, but Barbara thought that a real long shot. No jury anywhere would show sympathy, she was sure, for her husband. She could clearly see in the jurors' eyes the absolute fear they had of Richard. After Barbara heard the tapes, she knew Richard would never get out of jail.

After four weeks of carefully orchestrated, damaging testimony, then the summations of Carroll and Frank, and the judge's charge, the jury began deliberations.

At Richard's request, Frank did not put up any defence at all. Richard refused to take the stand. He knew, he said, that testifying would only open a can of worms. *I got on that stand*, he said, *Carroll would have torn into me – given me a second asshole.*

Richard was sick and tired of it all. He knew the inevitable outcome and just wanted to get it over with. It took the jury a mere four hours to find Richard guilty on all counts. They did not, however, recommend a death sentence, to Richard's surprise. That is what he'd been expecting all along, was ready for. This was because there had been no eyewitnesses to the murders of Deppner and Smith.

Neal Frank had, he felt, achieved his goal – he had saved Richard's life. Now, Richard knew, he would spend the rest of his life behind bars, which for him was far worse than any death sentence. For the first time since he'd been a young boy back in Jersey City, he would have to do as he was told, abide by the strict rules and regulations set down by the state, like everyone else. For him, this was anathema.

* * *

IT WAS DUE TO BUSINESS

After the trial, Neal Frank, a tall, handsome man with his hair combed to the left, entered into extended negotiations with Bob Carroll and the attorney general's office. At issue were the charges of gun possession against Barbara and some marijuana possession charges lodged against Dwayne Kuklinski. Dwayne had been driving some friends home from a party, and a state trooper had pulled him over. When the trooper realised Dwayne was Richard Kuklinski's son, he made Dwayne and his three friends get out of the car, and the trooper found a small amount of marijuana on one of the boys and, incredibly, charged Dwayne with possession, not the boy who actually had it.

To get these charges against Barbara and his son dismissed, Richard readily agreed to plead guilty to the murders of George Malliband and Louis Masgay. He already knew that he'd spend the rest of his life in prison, and by this point he wanted to get it the hell over with, wanted his family to get on with their lives.

On 25 May 1988, Richard again appeared before Judge Kuchenmeister. As agreed, he pleaded guilty to the murders of George Malliband and Louis Masgay. When asked by the judge why he had killed Malliband, Richard said, 'It was – it was due to business.' Richard now had Frank read in open court a short statement in which Richard apologised to his family – no one else – for what he had put them through. The judge proceeded to give Richard two life sentences, one for the murders of Smith and Deppner, the second for the killings of Masgay and Malliband.

Unrepentant, his head high, his shoulders back, defiant, projecting an air of power and invincibility, of 'fuck you', Richard was led from the courtroom and taken to the place where he would spend the rest of his life, Trenton State Prison, in Trenton, New Jersey. Coincidentally, Richard's brother, Joseph, also serving a life sentence, for the murder of Pamela Dial, was still housed in the same facility. Stanley and Anna had produced two murderers, and both of them ended up in the same facility with life sentences.

THE ICE MAN

Every newspaper in New Jersey and New York had a front-page story about Richard's sentencing, with photos of him and grisly summaries of his crimes.

The sad, violent story of Richard Kuklinski was over and done with . . . it appeared.

But the story of Richard's life, what had been done to him, what he'd done, was only just beginning.

57

IT'S NOT TV,
IT'S HBO

An aspiring film producer named George Samuels learned about the extraordinary case of Richard Kuklinski from a friend in the New Jersey attorney general's office. Thinking he might be able to get cable TV network HBO interested in doing a documentary based on Richard's crimes, Samuels approached Richard's attorney, Neal Frank, who listened to what he said and ultimately put him in touch with Barbara.

Because Barbara had grown fond of Frank and trusted him, she agreed to meet Samuels and listen to him. Samuels, a short, balding, fast-talking individual, made all kinds of promises to her, and Barbara agreed to be interviewed on camera, talk about some of her life with the now infamous Ice Man.

The problem with Samuels was that he was duplicitous and was also working with the attorney general's office. The authorities believed that Richard had, in fact, committed many more crimes than those they'd nailed him for (how true!) and were hoping Samuels could get Richard to agree to talk about murders they knew nothing of. Richard had nothing to lose, they reasoned; maybe, they hoped, he'd open up and clear up some unsolved killings.

By now, Richard had already been in jail for four years. For the most part, he had learned to accept his fate. He minded his own business, adopted a live-and-let-live policy. In truth, both inside and out, Richard was as tough as rusted railroad spikes. He knew the only way the state could truly punish him was if he allowed his incarceration to bother him, so he wouldn't let that happen.

What did trouble him – deeply – was the loss of his beloved family . . . his Barbara. His Lady. For the most part, he didn't allow himself to think about them, but when he did, it got to him. He'd sit on his cell bunk and cry. He never did this in front of anyone. Knowing that he would die in jail, only be taken out dead, he suggested to Barbara that they get divorced. This was very hard for him, one of the most difficult things he'd ever done, but he wanted Barbara *to get on with her life*, he says, and, with the help of the Social Services Division at Trenton State Prison, Richard divorced Barbara. It was a terribly painful milestone for him, but he stoically signed the papers and didn't allow himself to think about it, to think of Barbara with another man. Richard had always had an amazing ability to compartmentalise his emotions, and he did that now. Still, he loved Barbara more than ever. He wrote her letters every single day. He poured out his heart to her. He told her how much he loved her; he told her how much he missed her; he told her over and over how sorry he was.

Barbara rarely wrote back to him. He was, she had come to believe, 'a monster'. A monster that had fooled her and duped her and used her.

Richard's cell at Trenton State's maximum-security facility was six by eight feet, far too small for a man his size, but he became *used to it*, he said. In it, there was a toilet bowl, a metal bunk bed, on which was a thin mattress, bolted to the steel wall, and a sink; that was it. He had a small television and could listen to the radio with earphones when he pleased. By this time, he didn't pace his cell any more, look at himself in the mirror and curse at what he saw. He had accepted his lot in life, his destiny.

Strangely, Richard seemed to thrive in prison. He never looked better. He grew a thick salt-and-pepper goatee, remained robust and strong, and moved about as if he owned the place, with a bounce in every step. Everyone knew who he was, prisoners and guards alike, and everyone gave him a wide berth. He secured a job in the prison law library, gave out books and checked books in. The routine in all state prisons across the country is always the same. That routine is an essential part of a successful prison – to teach the inmates that there is a preordained schedule, a mandated regimen which they have to adhere to. Breakfast is served at 6.30 a.m., lunch at 11.30, dinner at 4.30 p.m. Prisoners with jobs are allowed to leave their cells to go to work. In the beginning, Richard wanted nothing to do with a job, but he quickly came to realise he couldn't just sit in his cell, stew and rot, and so he decided to make the best of the situation.

Prisons are notoriously dangerous places, but hardly anyone wanted to tangle with the Ice Man. Richard grew to like his nickname; he felt it was quite appropriate, for he really was like ice, he knew. Since he was a teenager, he had been able to kill a human being or torture an animal and never think twice about it. He did not know if he was born that way or made that way, but he knew he was very different from other people, and he liked that. He was proud of it.

Richard still thought about his father, still regretted not killing him. If any one factor contributed to his becoming the Ice Man, Richard believed, it was surely Stanley Kuklinski: *I'm not blaming anyone for anything, but he made me a mean son of a bitch, I can tell you that.*

Richard's brother Joseph had slipped deeply into mental illness. By the time Richard arrived, he'd been in prison some 18 years. He constantly talked to himself, regularly told other inmates and even guards about the girl he killed. He was proud of it. Most of his teeth had fallen out. He had to be forced to bathe and shower. When he did shower, he kept his clothes on. Over the years, he had married several men in prison, and he'd had to have operations on his rectum because he'd been sodomised so often, so roughly.

Richard had absolutely nothing to do with his brother. He never forgot what Joseph had done and still held it against him. Once in a while, they passed each other, and Richard acted as if Joseph were invisible, looked right through him as if he were a glass of water. Joseph had to be kept in the Special Care Unit. He captured roaches, Trenton Prison guard Silverstein explained, dried them, crushed them up, mixed them with sawdust and pencil shavings and smoked them in rolled-up toilet paper. Joseph told Silverstein that he was married to the child he killed, that she had been his wife. When a parole officer came to see Joseph to talk about his release, he pulled down his trousers and mooned him. Joseph did not want to leave prison; he wanted to die in jail, and that came to pass in the winter of 2003. When Richard heard his brother was dead, he was glad. He still thought of his brother as a rapist, a killer of children, and had no use for him. *In life or in death*, he said.

Richard maintained his passionate hatred for rapists. The first time he had a problem at Trenton State, it was because a fellow inmate in his section was a convicted rapist, and Richard told the man to stay the hell away from him, that if he came near him, he'd 'break every bone in your miserable fucking body!'

To be threatened by Richard was a frightening, disconcerting experience. The rapist ran to a guard and told him what Richard had said, and Richard was punished – put in solitary for a while. He didn't mind. Nothing bothered him. He truly became an Ice Man. When he was returned to the section, the rapist was gone, moved to another section. Lucky for him.

Richard agreed to be interviewed on camera by Samuels. Because Samuels was working as an agent for the attorney general's office (unbeknownst to Richard), he was given unencumbered access to Richard at the prison.

Samuels had never interviewed a stone-cold killer like Kuklinski, and he was out of his element, in over his head. Richard didn't like him from the moment he set eyes on him. Richard felt he was condescending, supercilious and judgemental.

Samuels had the camera focus tightly on Richard's disconcerting face and began asking him questions about his crimes, about murder. Oddly, when one looks at this footage, Richard appears fit as a fiddle, healthy, with good colour, rested and relaxed. He looks better, in fact, than when he was sent away. He looks like he's been at a country club playing golf, certainly not in an austere maximum-security prison. When asked about this later, he said it was because of his attitude. *I am not*, he said, *going to let them beat me. Never.*

Reluctantly, over several days of interviews – all on camera – Richard talked about murder. However, it soon became obvious to him that New Jersey state detectives were in a nearby room, watching on a small monitor and listening to what was being said, even giving Samuels questions to ask (Richard saw a second cable running from the camera under a closed door), and this really pissed him off. He had known what he was saying was for public consumption; what angered him was that Samuels didn't tell him there were detectives eavesdropping and feeding him questions. Samuels was trying to hustle Richard, fool him, and Richard's anger was becoming more and more evident. His lips began twisting off to the left. His face became stony. He wanted to throttle Samuels, break his neck, kill him, but he forced himself to stay calm and gave Samuels, for the most part, what he wanted. Samuels had no idea how close he came to being killed by Richard. Richard talked about these new murders because he had nothing to lose, he said.

Samuels then interviewed Barbara. This was done at the pond in Demarest where she and Richard used to go to feed the ducks. She did not like being on camera, was uncomfortable talking about her relationship with Richard, but she did it. She told how kind, considerate and excessively romantic he had been, said that she'd had no idea about the violence he was committing. She said, 'What he'd done is against God and man, and I still have a real hard time reconciling it.'

Samuels managed to get Pat Kane, Dominick Polifrone and Bob Carroll to promise interviews. Then, using the many front-page stories about Richard and several *New York Times* articles, Samuels managed to secure an appointment with Sheila Nevins, the head of HBO's documentary division.

Nevins watched Richard's interviews and immediately saw how unique and promising he was, and she gave Samuels a development deal and attached HBO producer Gaby Monet to the project.

Gaby Monet was a professional documentary filmmaker with a list of acclaimed pieces to her credit. She sat down with Samuels and listened to what he had, and together they created the 'look' of the story and went out into the field and interviewed Bob Carroll, Dominick Polifrone, Pat Kane and medical examiner Michael Baden (who testified for the prosecution at Richard's trial). Using these interviews and a series of carefully put-together re-enactments, Gaby Monet took the footage into an editing room and worked day and night for weeks, putting together a gripping, compelling documentary called *The Iceman Tapes: Conversations with a Killer*.

When HBO big shots saw what Gaby Monet had done, they were thrilled. It was riveting and compelling and very original. It gave everyone who saw it chills. What made *Conversations with a Killer* so compelling was the matter-of-fact, truthful way Richard talked about the violence and murders he had committed. He didn't brag or boast; he wasn't proud of what he'd done. He just told it as it was – the way he saw it and felt it and what had happened – in a calm, detached voice, the camera tight on his face, cold like ice. However, at the end of the piece, when Richard talked about his family, emotion welled up and he struggled to hold back tears. 'I hurt the only people in the world that ever meant anything to me,' he said in a strained voice, tears in his leather-coloured eyes. This was a side of the Ice Man never seen before. HBO got behind the project and advertised it, and it was aired for the first time in November of 1999.

Overnight, Richard Kuklinski became a homicide superstar. He had told only a very small part of what he'd actually done, but that small part was enough to make Americans stand up and take notice. *Conversations with a Killer* was critically acclaimed and received overwhelming feedback. The *New York Times* praised it for 'its chilling originality'.

Suddenly, Richard Kuklinski of Jersey City had a distinguished place in the homicide hall of fame. Mail poured into HBO from the public, mostly praising *Conversations with a Killer*, though some people demanded to know why HBO was 'lionising a cold-blooded killer'.

Gaby Monet's answer was that Richard Kuklinski was so unique, spoke about violence and murder with such candid sincerity and authority, that it would be, in a sense, a public disservice *not* to let the world get a glimpse into his life.

Richard received thousands of letters at the prison, from murder groupies, criminologists and forensic doctors, reporters and news producers. Suddenly, everyone wanted to talk to the Ice Man. Television journalist Geraldo Rivera went to the prison to interview Richard; Richard refused to see him. Oprah Winfrey tried to get him to appear on her show; Richard refused. He also received, oddly enough (especially to him), many love letters from scores of women around the world who wanted to have relations with him. Many women even sent photographs of themselves to him. In some of these, the women were buck naked, boldly exposing all their charms. Richard was disgusted by these. He immediately threw them away. He explained: *Any woman that puts a naked photograph in a letter to a stranger is a pig.*

Richard didn't seem to realise that to these women he was no stranger, because he'd been so honest and candid in *Conversations with a Killer*. He was the ultimate 'bad boy', thus, to some, the ultimate aphrodisiac. Go figure.

One of them had her legs open so wide, you could see her tonsils, he said, making a face.

58

SECRETS OF A MAFIA HIT MAN

The Iceman Tapes: Conversations with a Killer was such an overwhelming success that Sheila Nevins and HBO decided to do a second 60-minute documentary featuring Richard. This time, George Samuels would have nothing to do with it. In fact, Richard refused even to be in the same room as him.

By now, Gaby Monet, an intense dark-haired woman with wise, contemplative eyes, had grown quite fond of Richard. They had had many phone conversations since the first piece aired, and Gaby had come to view Richard as an incredibly interesting man who had a lot to say about a subject few people knew as well as he did: murder. He was, in a sense, the Einstein of murder.

Thus the second set of interviews, now with Gaby Monet asking the questions, was done at Trenton State Prison. This time, without the assistance of the attorney general's office, it wasn't so easy to get a film crew into the prison, but HBO managed to pull some strings, and Gaby Monet sat down and, over a six-day period, did a second, much more revealing, candid series of interviews with Richard.

This second documentary was entitled *The Iceman: Secrets of a Mafia Hit Man*, and in it Richard was far more relaxed and forthcoming, and for the first time told the world about some of the mob-related murders he had committed. The stress and strain he had been under when Samuels was asking the questions were gone, and a calm, even demure, Richard described the shotgun murder of NYPD detective Peter Calabro. This was an earthshaking revelation. Richard said that at the time of the killing he didn't know Calabro was a cop (which was true). 'But,' he added, 'I would've done it anyway.'

Secrets of a Mafia Hit Man was aired in December 2001, and again was greeted with both scorn and praise. For the most part, it was received well, though some critics wondered if the public should really be subjected to the dark musings of a stone-cold killer; as one reviewer put it: 'Some things are better left unsaid.'

Be that as it may, *Secrets of a Mafia Hit Man*'s ratings went through the roof. It was one of the most-watched shows HBO had ever aired. Again, mail poured into HBO, praising the network's courage for bringing a person like Richard from the dark into the light. Hundreds of pieces of mail arrived at Richard's cell every week. Even more women wrote to him, sent him photographs, asked if they could meet him.

Secrets of a Mafia Hit Man was such an overwhelming success that the powers that be at HBO decided to do yet another documentary featuring Richard. This was unprecedented – no killer in the history of television had ever received this kind of attention – but HBO felt Richard was so unique, so colourful and three-dimensional, so scary, that a third documentary was warranted. This one would feature Richard talking to a forensic psychiatrist and would, logically enough, be called *The Iceman and the Psychiatrist*. HBO hired noted psychiatrist Park Dietz to do the interview with Richard.

Now, however, the New Jersey attorney general's office had suddenly become interested in Richard Kuklinski again. Detective Peter Calabro was, after all, murdered in New Jersey, and detectives from the attorney general's office were dispatched to Trenton State Prison to talk to Richard and see what they could find out.

* * *

Detective Robert Anzalotti was a nice-looking, baby-faced young man who, coincidentally, had gone to school with Richard's son, Dwayne. Anzalotti was a tenacious investigator, but he had a nice way about him, was easy to talk to, never took himself too seriously. Married with two young children, Robert Anzalotti was sent to the prison to see if he could get Richard to tell who had ordered the Calabro hit. Anzalotti's partner was Mark Bennul, a quiet, introspective Asian American who said little but missed nothing.

When the two detectives showed up at the prison, Richard refused to see them. At this point, he wanted nothing to do with cops, especially cops for the attorney general's office. He was surprised that the police hadn't come around asking questions sooner. He told the prison guard who came to get him to tell the two detectives to contact his lawyer, Neal Frank, which they promptly did. Detective Anzalotti told Frank that they wanted to discuss the murder of Peter Calabro; Frank relayed this request to Richard by phone.

'Should I talk to them?' Richard asked Frank.

'It's up to you, Rich. It's your call.'

Curious, Richard agreed to see them, and thus a whole new can of worms was opened, and that can of worms was one Sammy 'the Bull' Gravano.

By now, Richard was the most famous prisoner at Trenton State, indeed in any American prison. Everyone, including the guards, had taken to calling him Ice Man, which he liked. Richard also liked his new-found celebrity. He felt he was finally getting just recognition for the 'unusual' man he truly was.

In truth, Richard had become one of the most infamous killers of modern times, thanks to the HBO specials. HBO had aired the pieces they'd done on Richard several times every month, and more and more people were stunned, shocked and horrified – yet always intrigued – by Richard's chilling words and demeanour. Now many millions of people across America saw and heard and knew about Richard Kuklinski.

His crimes, what he said, were becoming legendary. People around the world were watching Richard, for HBO is aired all over Europe and in parts of Asia and South America.

Richard Kuklinski, in a sense, became the Mick Jagger of murder.

59

THE ICE MAN VERSUS
SAMMY THE BULL

When Richard first sat down with Anzalotti and Bennul,
he was quiet and stand-offish. But Rob Anzalotti had a very
likeable way about him. His boyish face and youth were
disarming, and when Anzalotti told Richard that he had been
a schoolmate of Dwayne's, that they had been in the same class,
Richard warmed to him. Richard explained, *I wasn't going to
tell them a fuckin' thing, but when I found out Anzalotti went to
school with my son, I kind of saw him like my son. I . . . I took
a shine to him, and I told him about the Calabro hit.*

Stunned, the two detectives sat and listened to how Peter
Calabro was murdered on that cold, snowy February night.
Anzalotti already had the file on the case, and it was immediately
obvious that Richard knew facts and details that only the killer
could have known. When Anzalotti asked Richard who ordered
the hit, Richard refused to tell him unless he was given some
kind of immunity. He knew he could get a death sentence
for killing a cop. As much as Richard hated prison, it was, he
reasoned, better than death. Anzalotti went back to his boss,
who agreed to let Richard plead guilty to the murder of Peter
Calabro, for which he would get only another life sentence. Neal
Frank became involved, a deal was agreed upon, and Richard
again sat down with Anzalotti and Bennul, and, for the first
time, told how Sammy Gravano had contracted the killing; how

Gravano and he had met in the parking lot and agreed upon a price, how Richard received the shotgun and photo of Calabro from Gravano. Richard felt no allegiance to Gravano. He knew that Gravano had cut a deal with the feds to testify against John Gotti and many other goodfellas. Richard viewed Gravano as a rat, a low-life scumbag, and had no qualms about telling the cops how Gravano had hired him, thus opening the door for Gravano to be tried for the killing of a cop.

'I realise now,' Richard told Anzalotti and Bennul, 'that the little fuck was using me. I mean, he never told me the guy was a cop. He came to me because he didn't want to kill a cop, because he didn't want any of his guys to kill a cop. I realise that now, but of course I didn't back then. Sure, use the dumb Polack to kill a cop. Dumb Polack, my ass . . .

'Truth is, I would've done it anyway – even if he did tell me he was a cop. I'm not going to lie. But he didn't and he should've.'

Armed with this information, the New Jersey attorney general's office contemplated bringing charges against Gravano for ordering the killing of Peter Calabro. Calabro might have been a crooked cop, had surely worked with the mob, but he was still a cop and still murdered in Saddle River, New Jersey.

When Sammy Gravano decided to become a witness against John Gotti, the federal prosecutors in the Southern District of New York were overjoyed, wanted to go and do a jig in Times Square. They wanted John Gotti so badly that they were willing to cut a deal with Gravano that would enable him not only to serve just a few years but also to keep all the money he had earned from a lifetime of crime. The only problem was that Gravano had admitted to personally killing 19 people. He was obviously a very dangerous man, a clear and present danger, a true menace to society, a remorseless cold-blooded killer; yet the feds were still willing – it seems anxious – to give him his freedom, let him loose in society, if he helped them nail John Gotti.

For Gravano, this was a sweetheart deal, to say the least. He should have had to spend the rest of his days in jail, or at the very least serve a minimum murder sentence – seven to ten years – but the federal government decided to give him his freedom, and all his ill-gotten gains, if he cooperated with them – an infamy. Surely, if any government anywhere ever made a pact with the devil, this was certainly it, in living colour, in broad daylight.

Gravano, dressed in a sharp dark-blue suit, dutifully took the stand at Gotti's trial and told the jury and the world in a strong, believable voice the crimes he had freely committed with Gotti – foremost of which was the carefully orchestrated killing of Paul Castellano and Tommy Bilotti in front of Sparks Steak House.

True, at this point Richard Kuklinski was already in prison, but somehow Gravano neglected to tell the government that Richard Kuklinski was part of the hit team, that Richard had killed Tommy Bilotti at the specific request of Gravano.

Gravano said nothing because he might be accused of direct complicity in the murder of a cop, Peter Calabro. Gravano knew that if he fingered Kuklinski for the Bilotti hit, Richard would tell the authorities that he had murdered Calabro for twenty-five thousand dollars with a shotgun that Gravano had given him.

Gravano knew that if it became public knowledge that he had ordered the murder of a cop – even a dirty cop – there was no way in hell the government could cut him a deal.

It was rumoured, however, that Gravano did in fact tell the feds about the Calabro hit, and they opted to keep it quiet, to sweep it under the rug, knowing they could never cut a deal with a cop killer. If they did such a thing, there would be hell to pay, a hue and cry that would shake the very foundations of the Justice Department, from both the public and law-enforcement professionals.

'The truth,' Detective Anzalotti recently told an enquiring journalist, 'will all soon come out in the wash.'

* * *

On 27 September 1998, Sammy 'the Bull' Gravano appeared in Brooklyn before federal judge Leo Glasser for sentencing. By this time, Gravano had testified in scores of trials, causing the convictions of 40 wiseguys, the most prominent of whom was, of course, John Gotti.

Judge Glasser, approvingly quoting law-enforcement officers, praised Gravano to high heaven, said, 'You have done the bravest thing I've ever seen,' and went on to pass a sentence that essentially amounted to time served – a mere five years all told. This for his admitted part in the killing of 19 human beings. Many people in law enforcement and the public felt this was an appalling travesty of justice. The families of Gravano's victims held an angry press conference and bitterly complained about what the government had done. The daughter of Eddie Garofalo said, 'This guy took my father away from me, from us. He is a vicious brutal killer, and yet the government is letting him walk. It's outrageous. It's heartbreaking. It's a sin. How could they do such a despicable thing? Sammy Gravano is a monster! An animal. He should be kept in a cage like the dangerous beast he is. I can't sleep at night thinking that Gravano will be free after killing my father and all those others. It's an outrage!'

Several months later, Sammy Gravano did, in fact, walk out of a federal prison after having served five years. He was never charged with ordering the hit of Peter Calabro. He quickly disappeared into the wide expanses of the federal witness-protection programme, where noted author Peter Maas found him and wrote a bestselling book about Gravano called *Underboss*. It should have been called, many said, *The Luckiest Guy in the World*.

Gaby Monet and forensic psychiatrist Park Dietz, with an HBO film crew in tow, showed up at Trenton State Prison to do the third documentary featuring Richard Kuklinski. By now, Richard had put on weight as a result of his sedentary lifestyle. He did no exercise, didn't go out in the yard; but he was still as strong as a bull and very dangerous. He'd been in jail for over ten years. He had become used to prison, had accepted it as his permanent home, the place where he'd die. He wouldn't let anyone in his family come to visit him any more. He didn't want his daughters and Barbara frisked by the female guards, so he put a stop to them visiting the prison.

A somewhat kinder, gentler Richard sat down with Dr Park Dietz, and, for the first time ever, Richard spoke to a forensic psychiatrist who had interviewed serial killers before. A tall, reserved man with piercing blue eyes, Dietz had worked with law-enforcement outfits across the country, including the FBI's Behavioural Science Unit, and had talked to Jeffrey Dahmer, John Wayne Gacy and other infamous serial murderers; he frequently appeared on news shows to discuss the little-understood phenomenon of serial murder.

A change had clearly come over Richard. He now joked often, was outgoing, friendly, introspective and even self-effacing. He was not morose and stony-faced as he had been in the first two HBO specials. Much of this 'new Richard' had to do with Gaby Monet's kind, gentle ways. Richard had grown fond of her. He trusted her and considered her a friend – perhaps the only real friend he'd ever had, he said. Gaby, too, had grown quite fond of Richard. Shortly before his death, she said of him: *Richard is one of a kind: he is smart, charming, funny and a mesmerising storyteller. He has a very likeable side, and thank goodness that's the only side of him I've ever known.*

When Richard was sent to prison, he weighed 290 lb. He was now about 315 lb, but still moved with catlike efficiency and agility. His face was noticeably fuller, his cheeks and jowls somewhat loose on his face. He also had lines and creases where before there'd been none. Prison had clearly taken its toll on Richard.

For thirteen hours, over a six-day period, Dietz asked Richard pointed, probing questions about his violence, which Richard answered with chilling honesty. He was now even more engaging because he was so open and readily shared his true feelings about the murders he'd committed, about his childhood, the animals he'd tortured, his cold lack of empathy for the people he'd killed, tortured, shot, stabbed and poisoned. He talked about murder like a chef discussing the various ingredients of different perfected dishes. He readily spoke about his father, the violence he'd suffered at his hands, the violence he'd suffered at his mother's hands. He wasn't, it was obvious to Dietz, looking for an excuse or someone to blame for the path he'd walked in life – he was just telling the truth about what he'd been through as a boy, what he saw, what he felt, the hatred that lived inside his head.

When Richard told Dietz about the three men he killed in South Carolina while coming back from Florida, Dietz said, 'Was that, you think, a capital offence, this guy cutting you off?'

Richard did not like the question or the way Dietz asked it. He was, Richard felt, judging him, speaking down to him, and, right there on camera, one can easily see the anger Richard felt colour his face like a ripe strawberry.

'Now,' Richard said, 'you've made me angry,' and he stared at Dietz with cold, detached, deadly eyes. If looks could kill, Dietz would have keeled over dead. After some tense seconds slowly passed, they discussed what had upset Richard about Dietz's question, and Richard acknowledged that it was because Dietz had 'spoke down to me' – judged him.

'Perhaps,' Dietz suggested, 'like your father had?'

'Just like my father,' Richard readily agreed, and went on to say how he still regretted not killing Stanley.

Many say this third documentary was the most compelling of all because in it Richard was at his most open and relaxed, and the world soon got another 60 minutes of Richard telling how he killed people and got rid of bodies, how he dismembered people with knives and saws and threw them down mine shafts, further horrifying and shocking people all over the globe. At the end of the piece, Dietz told Richard he had a lot of pent-up anger because of what his father had done to him – no shit, Sherlock.

Richard sat and listened politely, now the perfect gentleman, a far cry from the person he had been when he was sent to prison.

'Interesting,' Richard said contemplatively.

In the course of telling detectives Robert Anzalotti and Mark Bennul about the hit on Detective Peter Calabro, Richard had grown comfortable and at ease with the two men, especially Anzalotti, and he began telling them about more New Jersey murders he had committed that had never been attached to him. He remembered details, times and places with uncanny accuracy, the detectives realised.

Everything Richard said was checked and rechecked by Anzalotti and his partner, and all proved true. Soon, the two detectives had cleared up 12 unsolved murders thanks to Richard, including the killing of Robert Pronge, aka Mister Softee.

'For the most part,' Anzalotti recently said, 'everything he said was true; where he shot people, the calibre he used.'

In December of 2004, Richard appeared in Bergen County Superior Court and pleaded guilty to the murder of Detective Peter Calabro and the murder of Robert Pronge, and received yet another life sentence. That day, Peter Calabro's daughter was also in the courtroom. She had been four when her father was killed. She wanted to talk to Richard, wanted to know why he killed her father, but Anzalotti wouldn't let her. Richard, in fact, wanted to talk to her, wanted to tell her it was nothing personal, that if he hadn't done it, someone else would.

'Stupid is as stupid does,' were Forrest Gump's immortal words, and what Sammy Gravano – the crime-fighting hero of the federal government, a man who won glowing praise from scores of federal prosecutors – did with his freedom was stupid.

Very stupid!

Gravano ended up living in Arizona, where he started a removal business and began selling Ecstasy to schoolkids. He not only got involved in this sordid business, but he involved his family – his wife and son Gerald. They were all arrested; Gravano went to trial, was found guilty and sentenced to 20 years. Gravano had been the poster boy for the federal government's witness-protection programme, and he wound up using his ill-gotten freedom to sell drugs to kids.

'Stupid is as stupid does' indeed.

When the New Jersey attorney general's office felt it had an airtight case against Gravano for his complicity in the shotgun murder of Detective Calabro and had obtained an indictment against him for the murder, Detectives Robert Anzalotti and Mark Bennul flew to Arizona and placed Gravano under arrest for this killing.

Many in the New Jersey attorney general's office, and certainly Detectives Anzalotti and Bennul, believe that the federal government knew about Gravano's part in the Calabro killing but hid it, and they planned to prove it in open court. Richard would, of course, have been the state's star witness against Gravano. The trial was scheduled for the summer of 2006 and would have taken place in the Bergen County Superior Court – the same court where Richard was tried, convicted and sentenced.

In early April of 2005, Gravano's lawyer, Anthony Ricco, went to see Richard at Trenton State Prison. Richard claimed that Ricco offered him $200,000 not to testify against Gravano.

Conversely, Anthony Ricco claimed it was Richard who offered to throw the case for $200,000. Who, if anyone, solicited a bribe has not been established. Anthony Ricco, however, had to withdraw from representing Gravano because he was scheduled to appear as a witness on Gravano's behalf at Gravano's trial for the killing of Detective Peter Calabro.

60

NO SUNSET,
NO SUNRISE

For the rest of his life, Richard was housed in the maximum-security unit at Trenton State Prison. To control his mercurial temper, he was given daily doses of Ativan and Paxil, once in the morning, once at night. These drugs, for the most part, made him placid and easygoing.

At all meals, Richard shared a table with three mob guys, all skippers, all of them serving life sentences. They regularly shared war stories about the days when they were free, the women they knew, the great food they ate, the wonderful places they saw, their appeals, sport, the mistakes they made to wind up in prison.

For Richard, there were no sunrises, no sunsets. From his tiny cell at Trenton State Prison, he could not see outside, could not see the sky, the sunrise or the sunset. He never went outside. Life for him was a monotonous regimen that rarely, if ever, varied. When asked if he had any regrets, he said, *I wish I had taken another path in life, been a good husband and father; but that . . . that wasn't in the cards.*

Barbara Kuklinski lives with daughter Chris and Chris's son, John, in southern New Jersey. Barbara never remarried. She has severe arthritis of the spine and is in constant pain; her condition prevents her from working.

THE ICE MAN

When Barbara talks about her life with Richard, her hands still tremble and she gets angry. She regrets, she says, ever having met Richard. She explained: *When Richard was in a good mood, he was the best husband any woman could have had. When he was in a bad mood, he was cruel beyond description. I've gotten used to being alone. I have my children, my grandchildren – and they are the only ones in this world who mean anything to me. I'm . . . I'm very thankful for them.*

Chris Kuklinski still holds what her father did against him. She only wishes he'd been arrested sooner. In an interview shortly before his death, she said, *I always knew he could be mean, you know, I mean I saw it, I grew up with it, but I never imagined he was . . . he was a cold-blooded monster, a hit man for the Mafia.* Shaking her head sadly, she continued: *He is where he belongs. I think even he realises that.*

Richard's son, Dwayne, doesn't think much about his father. He is happy. He has a good job as an electrician and is marrying his long-time sweetheart, settling down and having a family of his own.

Merrick Kuklinski deeply misses her father, still loves him dearly. She is quick to defend him, readily points out the fact that life was stacked against him from the very beginning. *I'm not making excuses for him*, she said, *but the truth is my father didn't have a chance. When you look at what he went through, the childhood he had, it's not such a big surprise he turned out the way he did. I love him – I love him with all my heart and soul. He was, for me, a* wonderful *father. I will never ever forget how he was always there for me, how he helped sick children who had nothing in the hospitals where I often was as a child. He couldn't see a child suffer without wanting to help, running to help – doing something. I saw him bring children he didn't know food and toys and clothes without ever being asked. No other dad ever did that! He was no ice man. He was a caring, giving man with a heart as big and warm as the sun. For me, my father was the nicest, most giving man I ever knew. I will go to my grave believing that! I love him very much.*

61

A FLYING FUCK

When Richard was asked shortly before his death what he would like to say at the close of this, his story, he said: *I'd rather be known as a nice man, not the Ice Man.*

Upon reflection, Richard added: *I was made. I didn't create myself. I never chose to be this way, to be in this place. Yeah, I for sure wish my life took another turn, that I had an education and a good job, but none of that was in the cards for me.*

I am what I am, and the truth is I don't give a flying fuck what anyone thinks about me, said Richard 'the Ice Man' Kuklinski, formerly of Jersey City, New Jersey, the second born to Anna and Stanley Kuklinski.

EPILOGUE

THE MELTING OF
THE ICE MAN

Richard Kuklinski died at St Vincent's Hospital in Trenton, New Jersey, on Sunday, 5 March 2006 at 1.03 a.m. The exact cause of his death has not been definitively determined, although the timing of his passing was particularly suspect, for the day after he died, the charges against Sammy 'the Bull' Gravano – that he ordered the murder of NYPD detective Peter Calabro – were dropped by the Bergen County Prosecutor's Office. Those in the know believe that this was not a coincidence. The famed medical examiner Dr Michael Baden, on behalf of the Kuklinski family, requested toxicology tests to see if, in fact, Richard was poisoned or if he died of natural causes.

Richard's health began to deteriorate in late October 2005. Supposedly, two doctors at Trenton State Prison each ordered different blood-pressure medicines, which were administered to Richard simultaneously, causing his potassium and electrolyte counts to become 'dangerously low'. He began passing out and experiencing vertigo. He was removed from his cell and placed in the infirmary. His health continued to decline, and his blood pressure dropped. He was taken to St Vincent's Hospital for a period of 30 hours, then 'signed himself out', an official at the prison said, and he was returned to Trenton Prison's infirmary. Richard called me and told me that he believed he was being poisoned and that I should call the media. I assumed that he was delusional and told him I'd do what I could. What I did do was discuss this with Barbara Kuklinski, and we decided Richard was imagining things. His health, however, continued to decline, and he stopped eating. His speech, I noted when he called, was slurred. He was taken back to St Vincent's again, and doctors observed that his lungs were congested and that his kidneys were failing. He was tentatively diagnosed as having Wegener's disease, a rare, potentially lethal malady that, if treated with drugs, is not fatal.

Richard's health continued to get worse. He suddenly developed a form of dementia, experienced loss of memory and had a skin rash on his hands and legs; he also refused to eat. Dr Wong from the hospital called Barbara and told her he was doing all he could, and he first gave a diagnosis of Wegener's disease. He said that they were also going to do a CAT scan of Richard's brain to see if he had had a stroke . . . perhaps the cause of his dementia. At this point, Richard couldn't even remember Barbara's phone number. This was very odd considering that Richard had *a very good memory* when it came to numbers, as Barbara put it. Dr Wong also said they were performing a biopsy on Richard's kidney.

The CAT scan indicated no stroke. The biopsy indicated no cancer. Yet Richard's health continued to deteriorate. His blood pressure fluctuated abnormally: first it was high, then low.

The holidays – Thanksgiving, Christmas, New Year – all passed, and Richard didn't call his family, as he always had done. The family became very concerned. I now tried to visit Richard at the hospital but was told by a prison official that this was not possible, that only immediate family could visit. Barbara and Chris did go to see him and were shocked by his gaunt appearance, due to his loss of weight.

It looked, Barbara explained, *like he lost 100 lb. He spoke in little more than a whisper. He told us, 'They're trying to kill me,' that we should call the police; 'Call the media,' he said. At this point, I thought – perhaps incorrectly, I'm thinking now – that he was just delusional. The police were there, I mean guarding him, three guys in plain clothes and two uniform cops. He was in a nice room at the end of the hall. We sat there for 45 minutes. He was drifting in and out. He then said, 'If I don't leave the hospital it's because I was murdered.'*

'Why?' I said. 'Why are you saying that, Richard?' He did not answer me. Chris had not seen him in quite a few years, and she was shocked at how thin he'd become; for that matter, I was, too. I now asked him why he had signed himself out of the hospital. He said he did not sign himself out, which, of course, I thought was . . . strange.

Barbara explained that she absolutely did not love Richard, that any warm feelings she once had for him were *long gone*, but still he was the father of her children, and she wanted to make sure anything that could be done for him was done.

Richard's health continued to fail. Dr Wong told Barbara he didn't think Richard would survive. Barbara and Merrick visited him again on 9 February. He looked still worse. He could now barely speak. Though he did, again, tell Barbara and now Merrick that he was being killed . . . 'murdered', he said.

Merrick was very traumatised by her father's appearance due to his illness. She still very much loved her dad, indeed loved him more than ever, and she prayed for him and tried to tell him he'd be OK, that he should will himself to get better. Again, however, he just managed to say that he was being 'murdered'.

'By who, Dad? Who?' Merrick asked.

'Them,' he whispered. 'If I don't get out of here alive, it's because I was murdered,' he said yet again.

Distraught, Merrick held her father's hand, a once powerful killing tool, now weak and frail, pocked with black-and-blue marks from the IV needles. That day, there were four IVs feeding him different fluids and medications. Barbara was informed that he was also bleeding internally, that blood was in his urine and issuing from his rectum. Dr Wong said it was probably an ulcer, which Barbara found kind of odd, for Richard had no history of ulcers at all.

Merrick left her father that day crying, upset and traumatised, remembering how he had so diligently cared for her when she was a child, when she was in the hospital. She was heartbroken to see her father a mere shell of the powerful, omnipotent man he had once been.

Dr Wong called Barbara on the evening of 28 February and said Richard did not have long, and, in fact, he passed away on Sunday morning, 5 March. Barbara was relieved. *We finally have closure*, she said.

Richard was laid out at the Gaiga Funeral Home in Little Falls, New Jersey. The service was attended by only the immediate family, me, Gaby Monet and friends of Merrick, Chris and Dwayne. There was no priest.

Barbara said, *If we had a priest eulogise him, Richard would have sat up in his coffin and said, 'Get him the fuck out of here!'*

In all the time I spent with Richard, it was hard not to grow fond of him. I know people will be offended by my saying this, ask how I could feel warmly about such a cold-blooded killer. I did not know Richard in the outside world. By the time I met him, he'd been incarcerated for many years. I found Richard to be warm and considerate and very polite; in a word, a gentleman. He always asked after me and my family and was solicitous and thoughtful when I couldn't visit because I had the flu. The truth is, he was a hell of a nice guy, and certainly one of the funniest people I've ever known. He had a keen, deadpan (pun intended) sense of humour that was very rare indeed. One time, I remember, I told him, 'Richard you are the funniest guy I've ever known; you should have been a stand-up comedian.'

He said, 'Yeah, I'll come out on stage with my tacky prison garb, say, "Good evening, ladies and gents. I got a hundred jokes that'll kill you, and if they don't kill you, I will,"' laughing as he said this.

THE ICE MAN

Meeting and getting to know Richard Kuklinski so intimately was a unique, sobering experience – an education – and made me much more aware of the nuts and bolts, the wheels and pulleys that make a psychopath work. Regardless of my warm feelings for Richard, however, I have no doubt that he was a particularly cunning, highly motivated psychopath. In all my interaction with him, I never lost sight of the fact that he was a very dangerous man, a human predator the likes of which have not been seen in modern times. Personally, I came to view Richard's life as a classic case of a severely abused child, filled with seething rage, becoming an abuser, and turning into a remorseless killer. At the time of writing, the tests to determine if Richard had been poisoned have not been completed.

Rest in peace Richard Leonard Kuklinski.

POSTSCRIPT

- Detective Pat Kane was promoted to lieutenant before retiring from the New Jersey State Police. Today, he is working as a fire ranger and loves being outdoors.
- ATF Agent Dominick Polifrone is retired. He had been training younger agents in successful undercover work.
- Bob Carroll retired from the state attorney general's office and today is a practising attorney; his speciality is criminal law.
- Stanley Kuklinski died of a heart attack in 1979. Until the end of his life, Richard regretted not having killed him.
- Richard's sister, Roberta, moved to the West Coast, and he didn't hear from her in the 30 years leading up to his death.
- Barbara Kuklinski has severe arthritis, chain-smokes, loves to read, loves her grandchildren. *My whole life*, she says, *is my children and grandchildren*.
- Charges against Sammy Gravano for the murder of NYPD detective Peter Calabro were dropped the day after Richard Kuklinski died.
- Roy DeMeo's boss, Nino Gaggi, died in a federal prison of a heart attack.
- The police never discovered any of the videos Richard made of feeding people to rats.
- HBO's Gaby Monet had been planning to do yet another special on Richard Kuklinski, this one entitled *The Iceman*

Cold Case File, which would have explored more unsolved murders of Richard's.

- Detective Robert Anzalotti was promoted to sergeant because he was able to get Richard to talk about murders he'd committed that the police knew nothing about.
- Richard's three children, Merrick, Chris and Dwayne, are doing very well; all of them live in New Jersey.
- You may contact Philip Carlo at: PCarlo1847@aol.com. www.philipcarlo.com